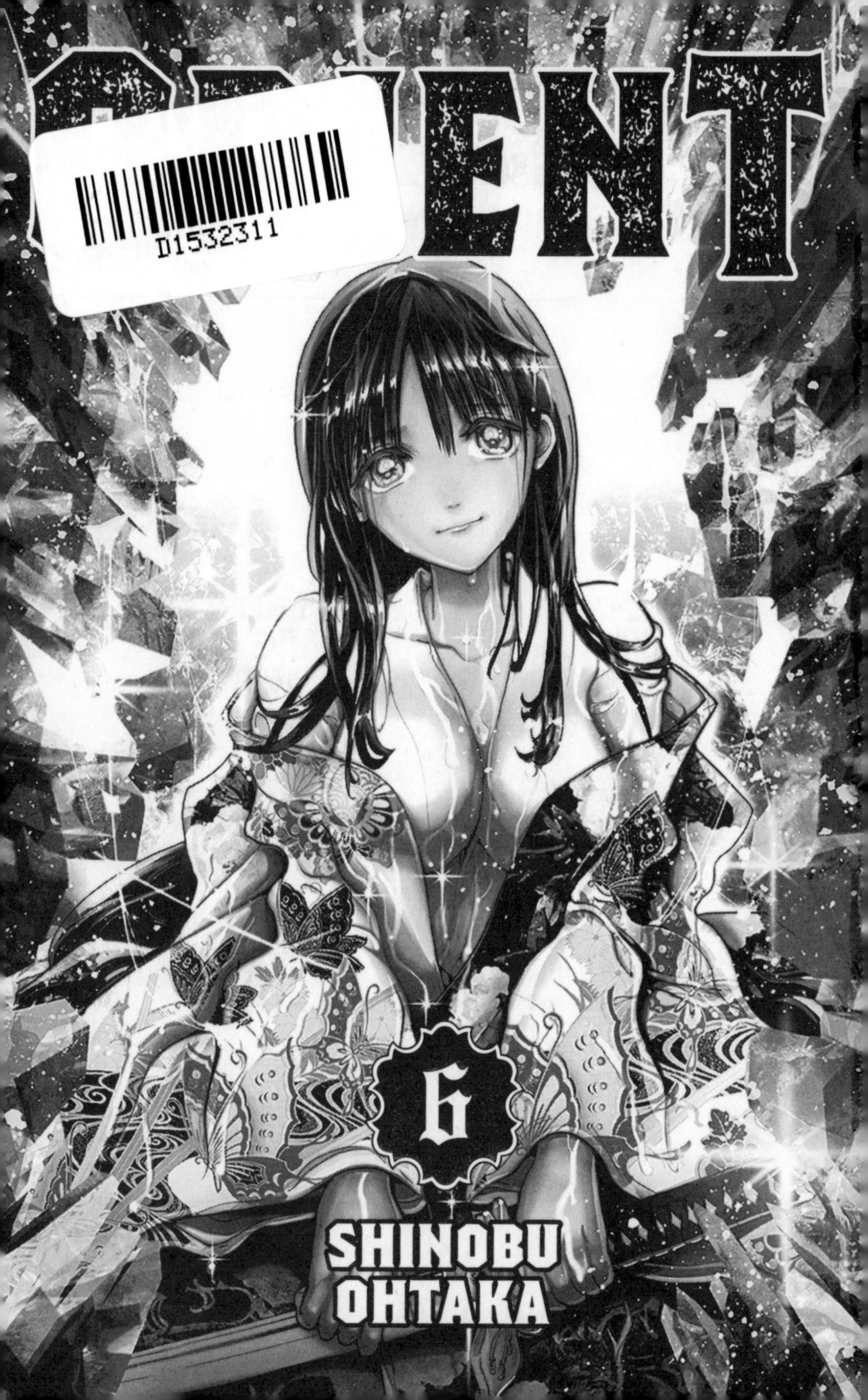
ENT
6
SHINOBU
OHTAKA

ORIENT

6

SHINOBU OHTAKA

CONTENTS

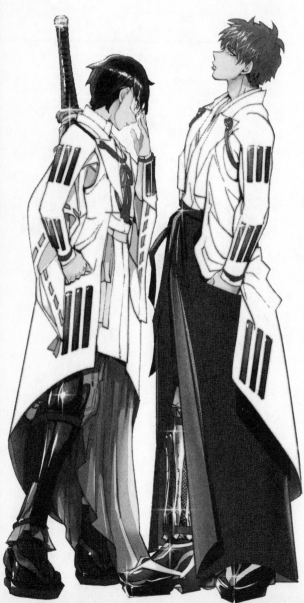

ORIENT

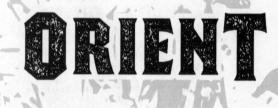

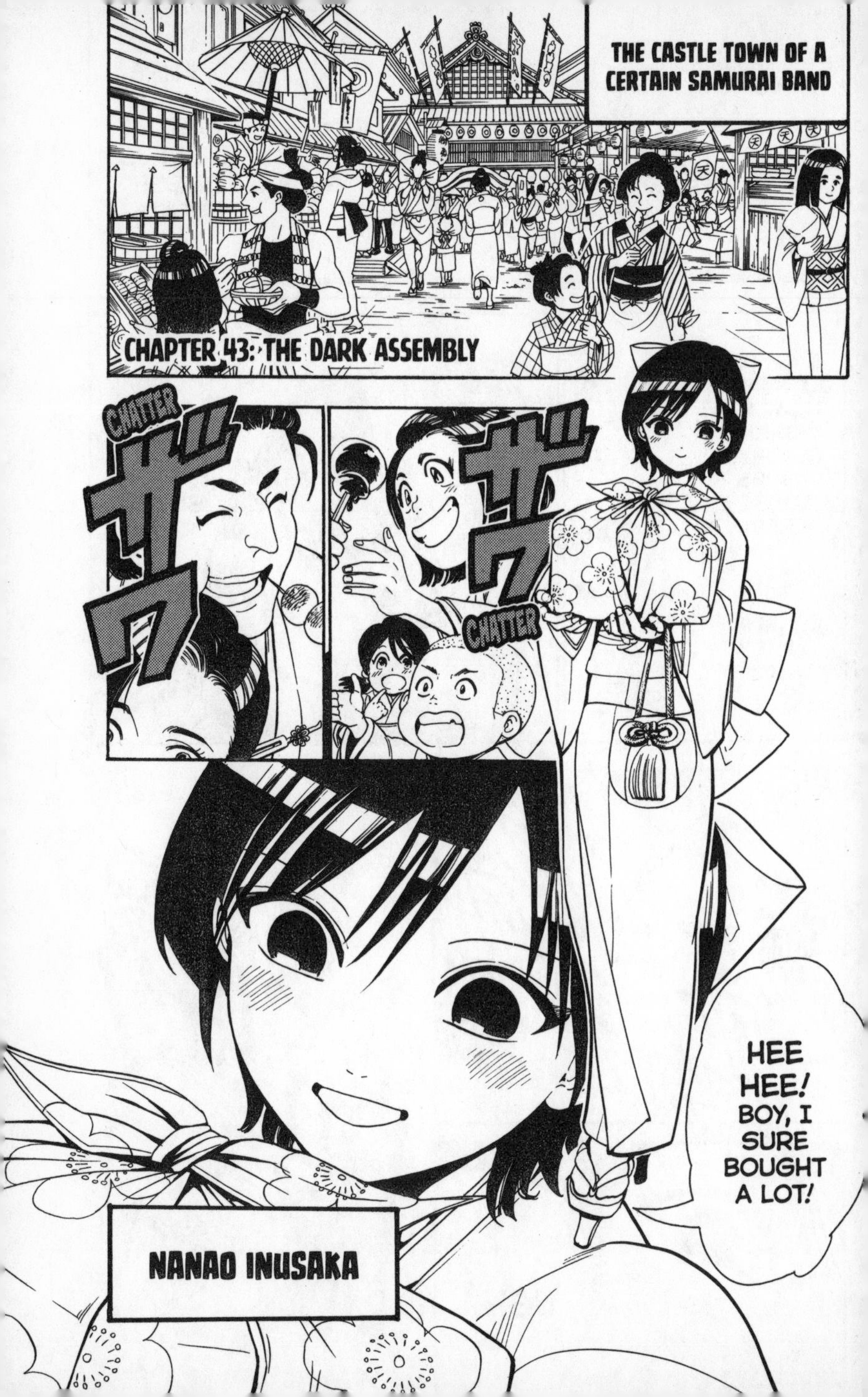
THE CASTLE TOWN OF A CERTAIN SAMURAI BAND
CHAPTER 43: THE DARK ASSEMBLY
ザワ
CHATTER
ザワ
CHATTER
HEE HEE! BOY, I SURE BOUGHT A LOT!
NANAO INUSAKA

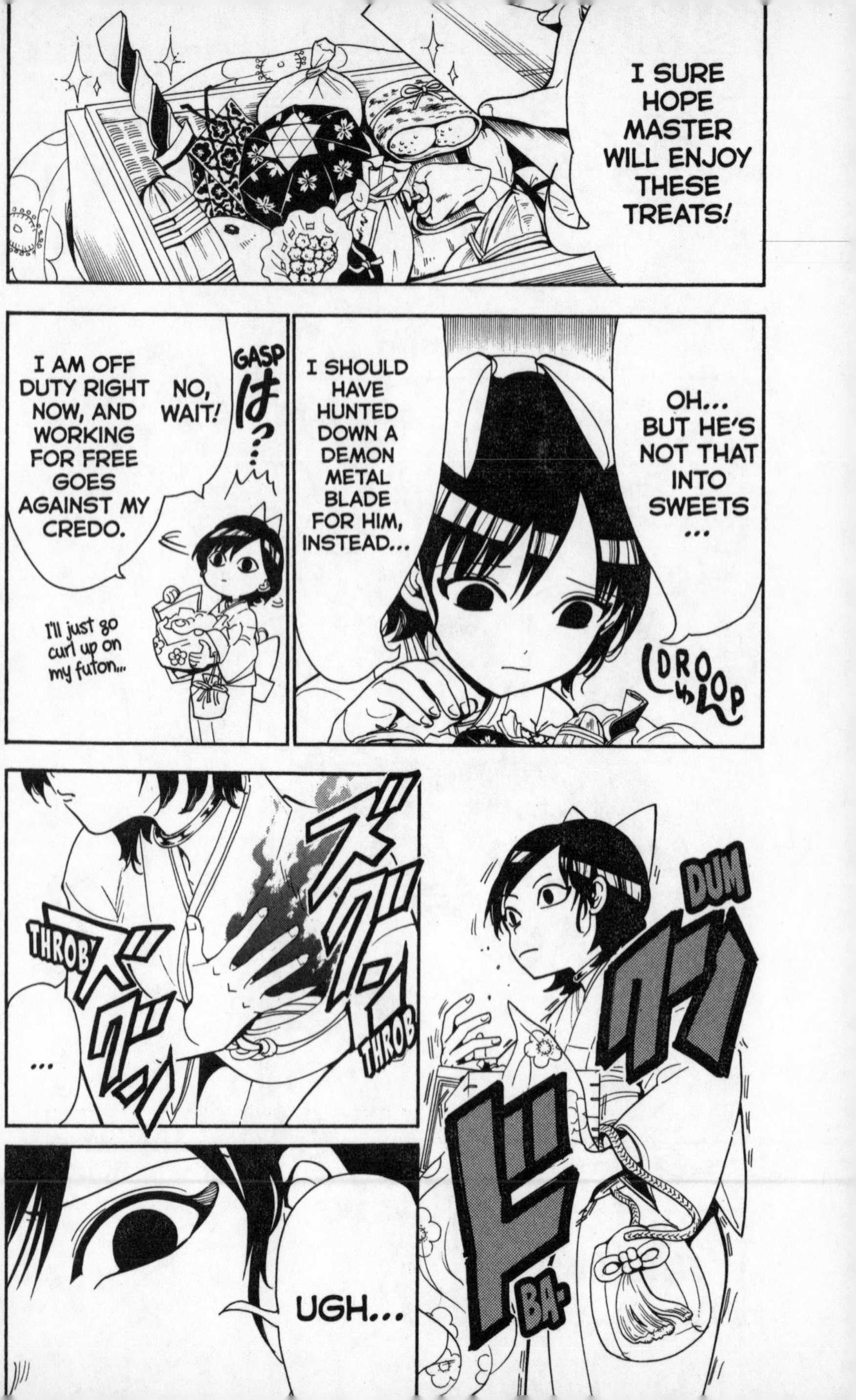
I SURE HOPE MASTER WILL ENJOY THESE TREATS!
OH... BUT HE'S NOT THAT INTO SWEETS ...
DROOOP
しゅん
I SHOULD HAVE HUNTED DOWN A DEMON METAL BLADE FOR HIM, INSTEAD...
GASP
はっ
NO, WAIT!
I AM OFF DUTY RIGHT NOW, AND WORKING FOR FREE GOES AGAINST MY CREDO.
I'll just go curl up on my futon...
BA-
DUM
THROB
THROB
...
UGH...

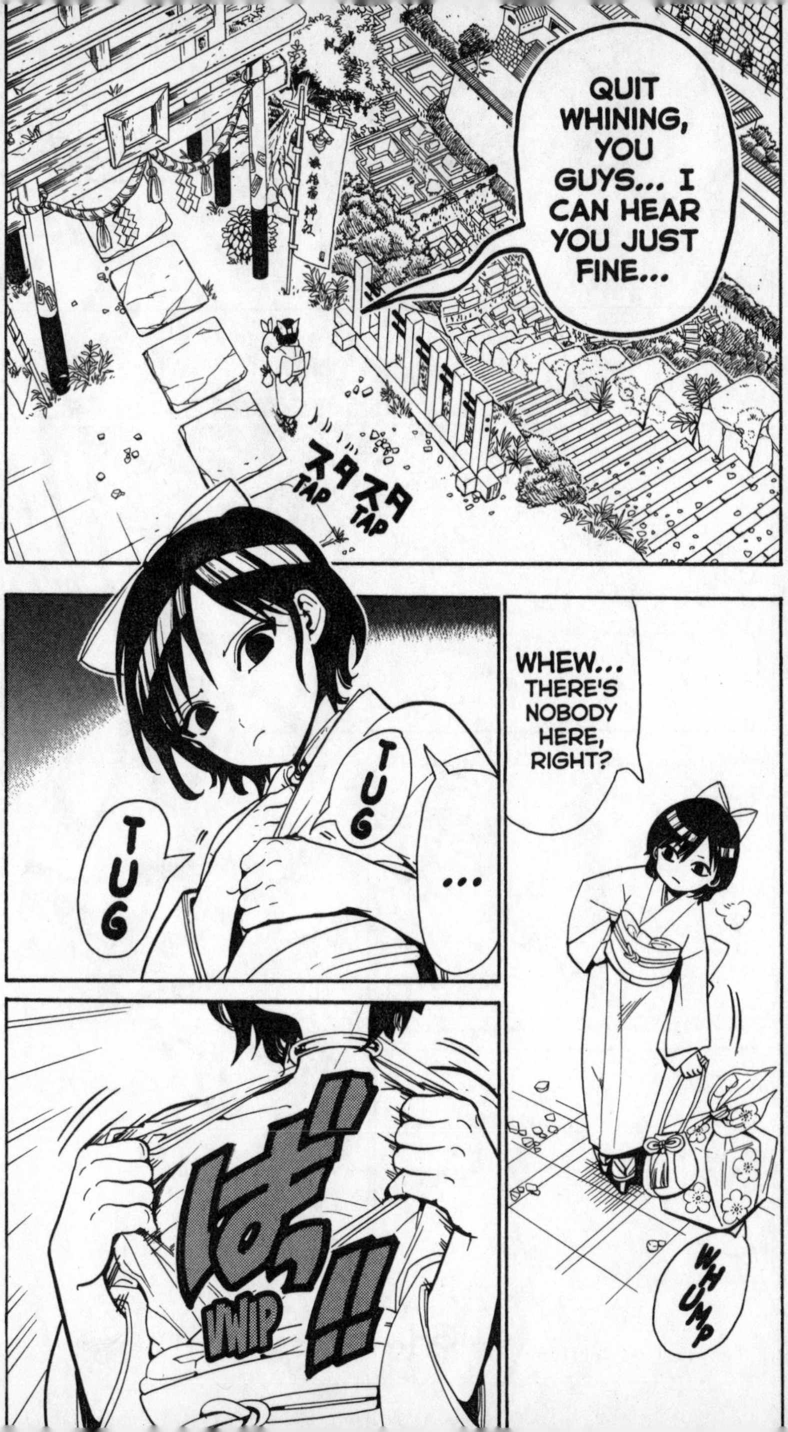
QUIT WHINING, YOU GUYS... I CAN HEAR YOU JUST FINE...
スタスタ
TAP TAP
WHEW... THERE'S NOBODY HERE, RIGHT?
WHUMP
TUG
...
TUG
WHIP

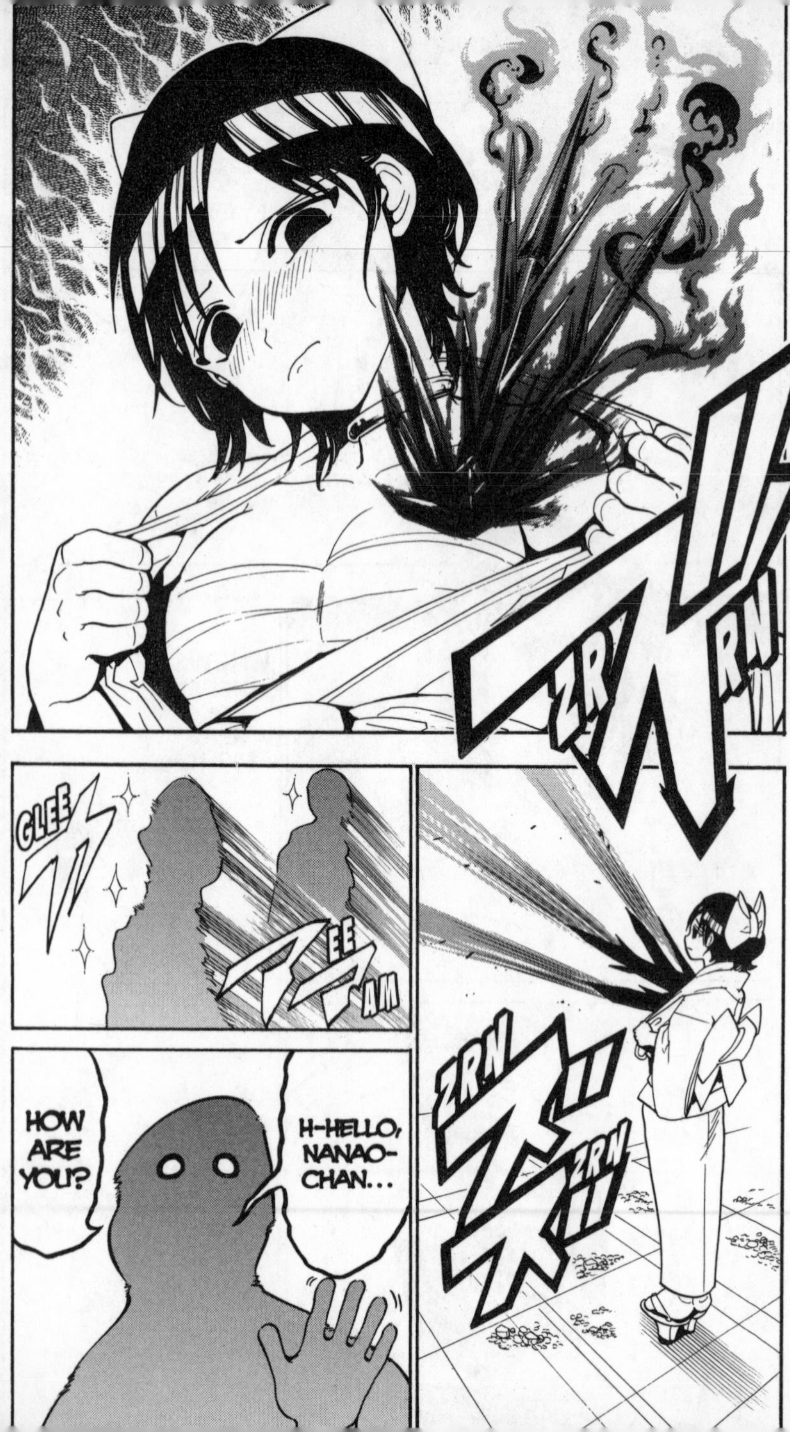
ZR
RN
ZRN
ZRN
GLEE
EE
AM
H-HELLO, NANAO-CHAN...
HOW ARE YOU?

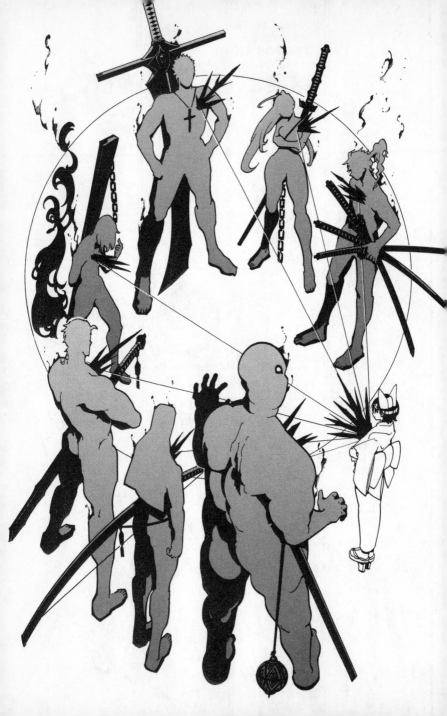

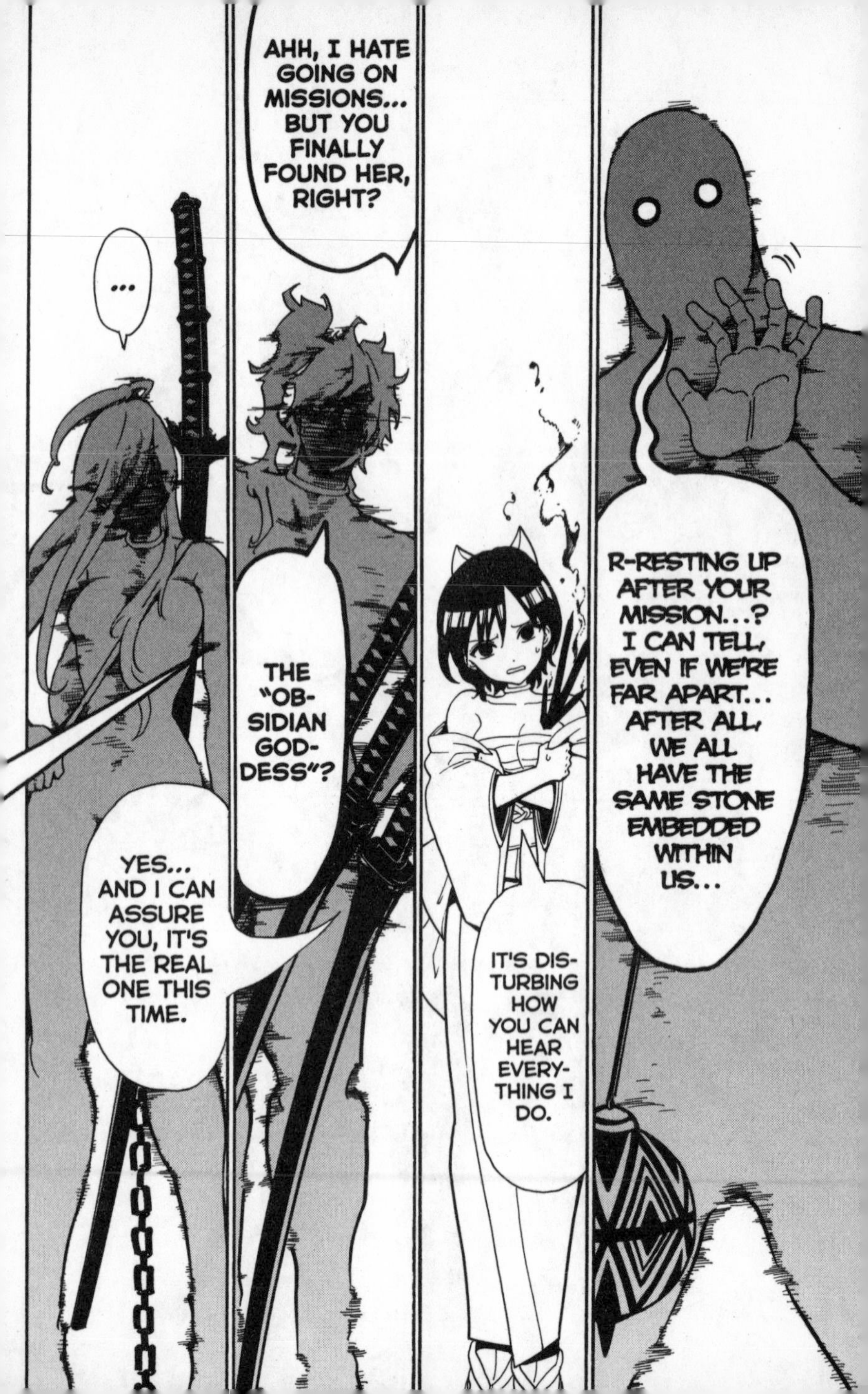
R-RESTING UP AFTER YOUR MISSION...? I CAN TELL, EVEN IF WE'RE FAR APART... AFTER ALL, WE ALL HAVE THE SAME STONE EMBEDDED WITHIN US...
IT'S DIS-TURBING HOW YOU CAN HEAR EVERY-THING I DO.
AHH, I HATE GOING ON MISSIONS... BUT YOU FINALLY FOUND HER, RIGHT?
THE "OB-SIDIAN GOD-DESS"?
...
YES... AND I CAN ASSURE YOU, IT'S THE REAL ONE THIS TIME.

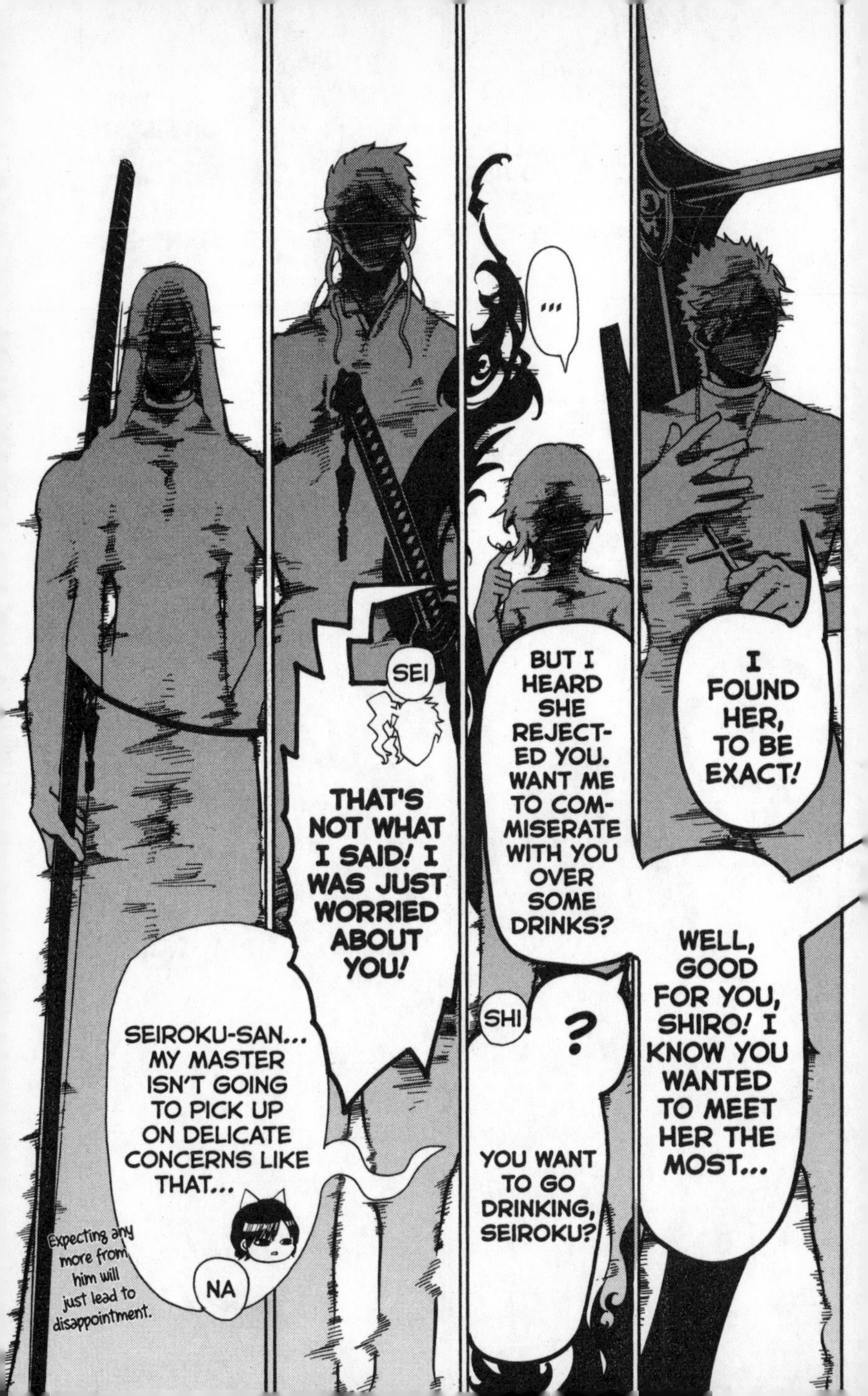
WELL, GOOD FOR YOU, SHIRO! I KNOW YOU WANTED TO MEET HER THE MOST...
I FOUND HER, TO BE EXACT!
...
BUT I HEARD SHE REJECTED YOU. WANT ME TO COMMISERATE WITH YOU OVER SOME DRINKS?
SHI
?
YOU WANT TO GO DRINKING, SEIROKU?
SEI
THAT'S NOT WHAT I SAID! I WAS JUST WORRIED ABOUT YOU!
SEIROKU-SAN... MY MASTER ISN'T GOING TO PICK UP ON DELICATE CONCERNS LIKE THAT...
NA
Expecting any more from him will just lead to disappointment.

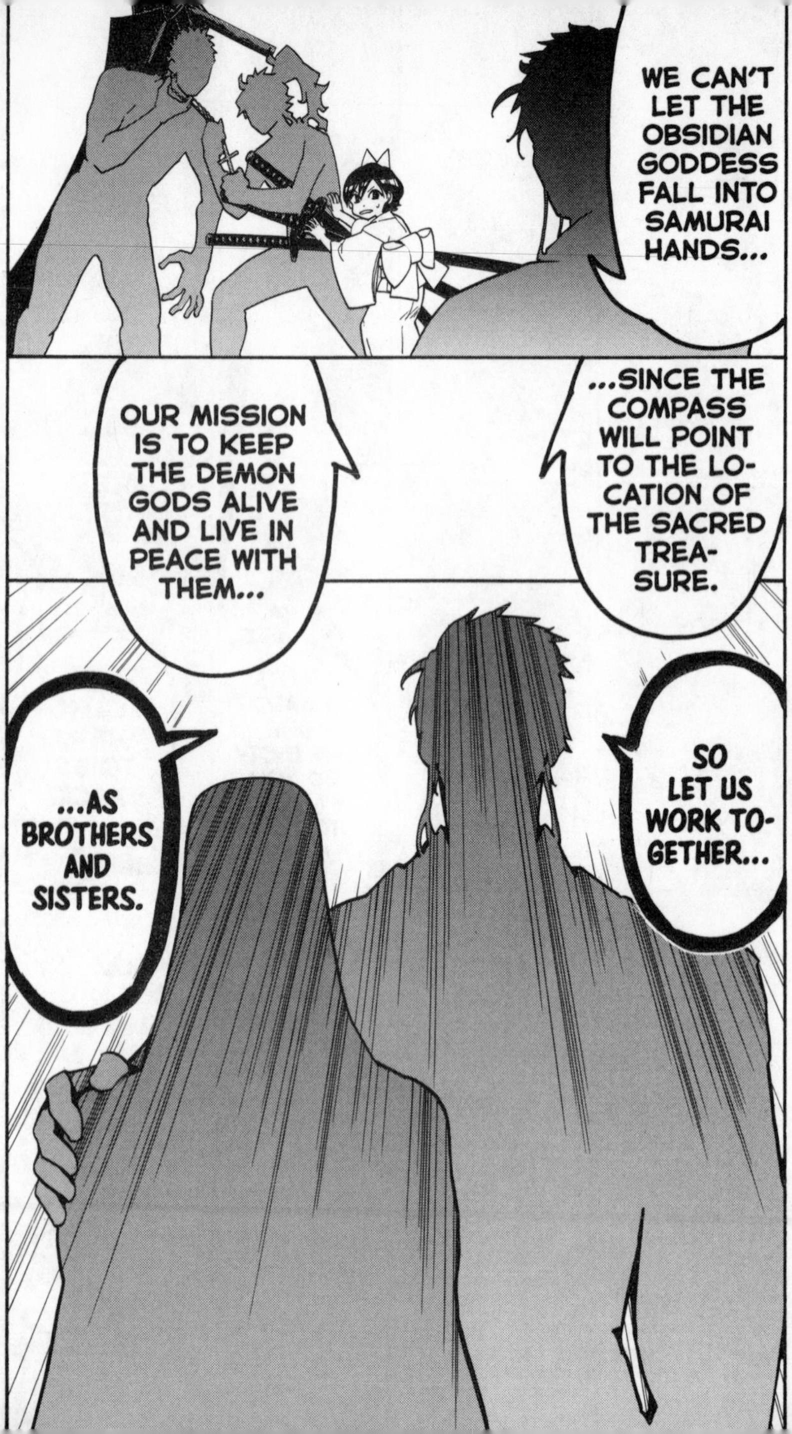
WE CAN'T LET THE OBSIDIAN GODDESS FALL INTO SAMURAI HANDS...
...SINCE THE COMPASS WILL POINT TO THE LOCATION OF THE SACRED TREASURE.
OUR MISSION IS TO KEEP THE DEMON GODS ALIVE AND LIVE IN PEACE WITH THEM...
SO LET US WORK TOGETHER...
...AS BROTHERS AND SISTERS.

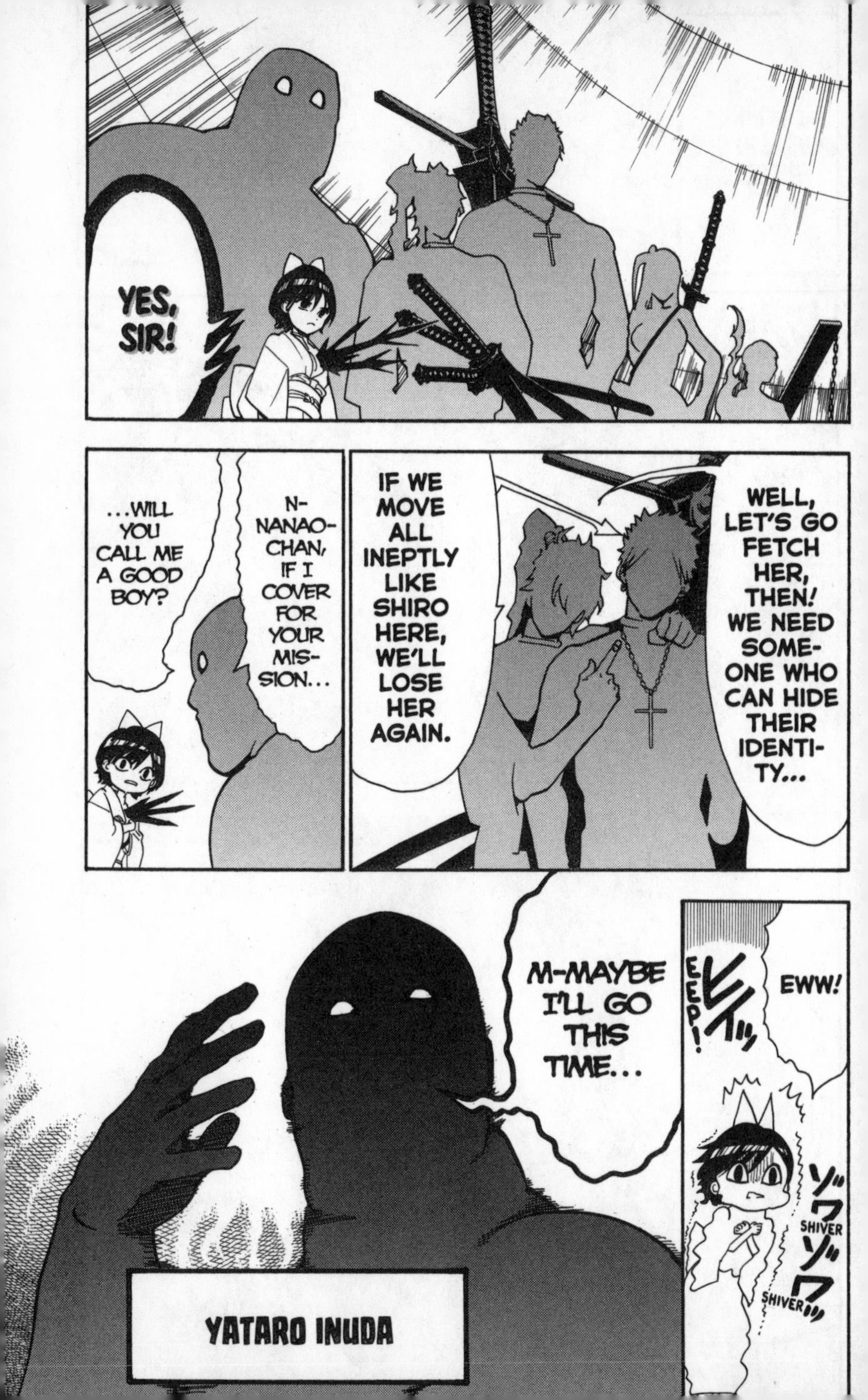
YES, SIR!
WELL, LET'S GO FETCH HER, THEN! WE NEED SOMEONE WHO CAN HIDE THEIR IDENTITY...
IF WE MOVE ALL INEPTLY LIKE SHIRO HERE, WE'LL LOSE HER AGAIN.
N-NANAO-CHAN, IF I COVER FOR YOUR MISSION...
...WILL YOU CALL ME A GOOD BOY?
EWW!
EEP!
SHIVER
SHIVER
M-MAYBE I'LL GO THIS TIME...
YATARO INUDA

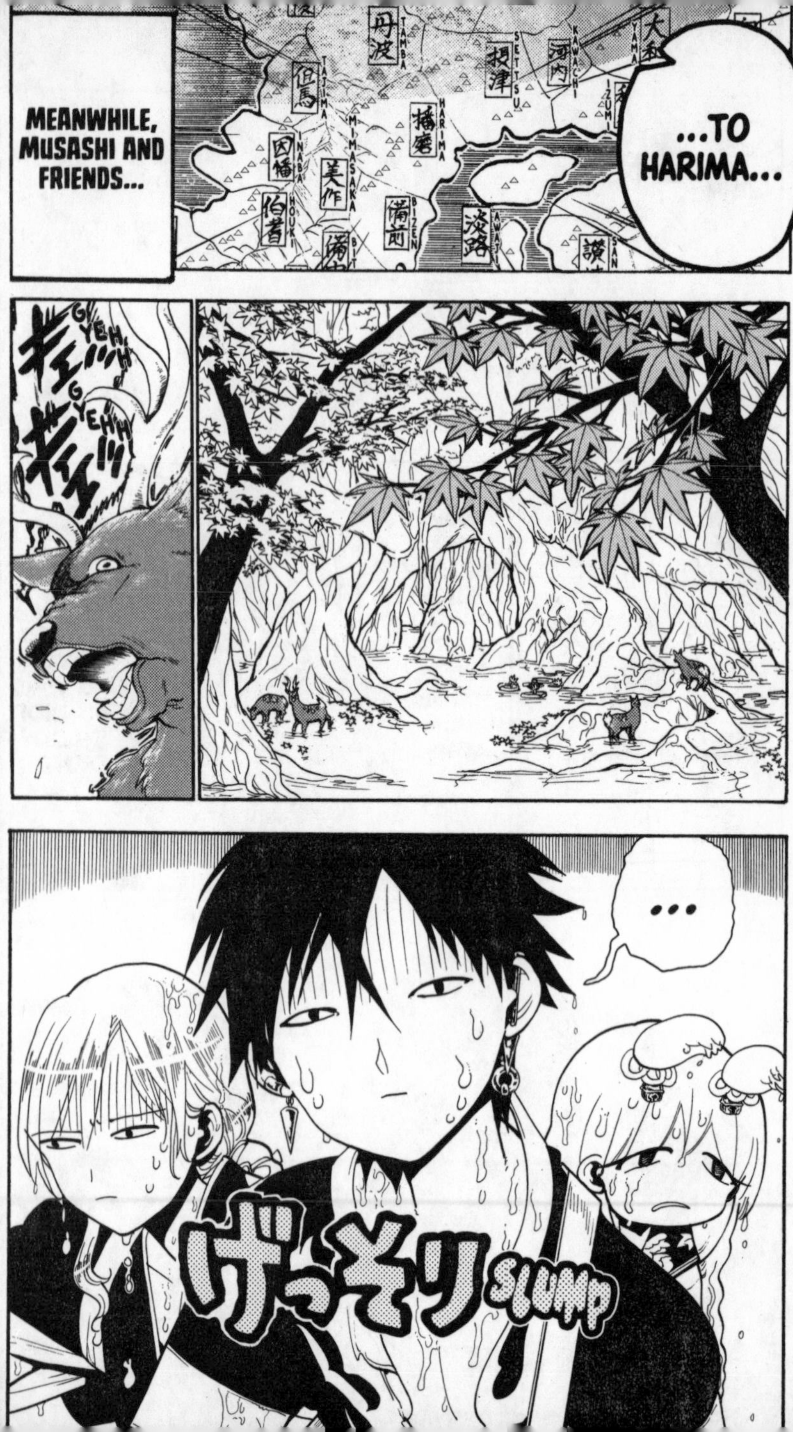
MEANWHILE, MUSASHI AND FRIENDS...
...TO HARIMA...
大和 YAMA
河内 KAWACHI
IZUMI
摂津 SETTSU
丹波 TAMBA
播磨 HARIMA
但馬 TAJIMA
美作 MIMASAKA
因幡 INABA
伯耆 HOUKI
備前 BIZEN
淡路 AWAJI
キェ GYEHH
キィエッ GYEHH
...
げっそり SLUMP

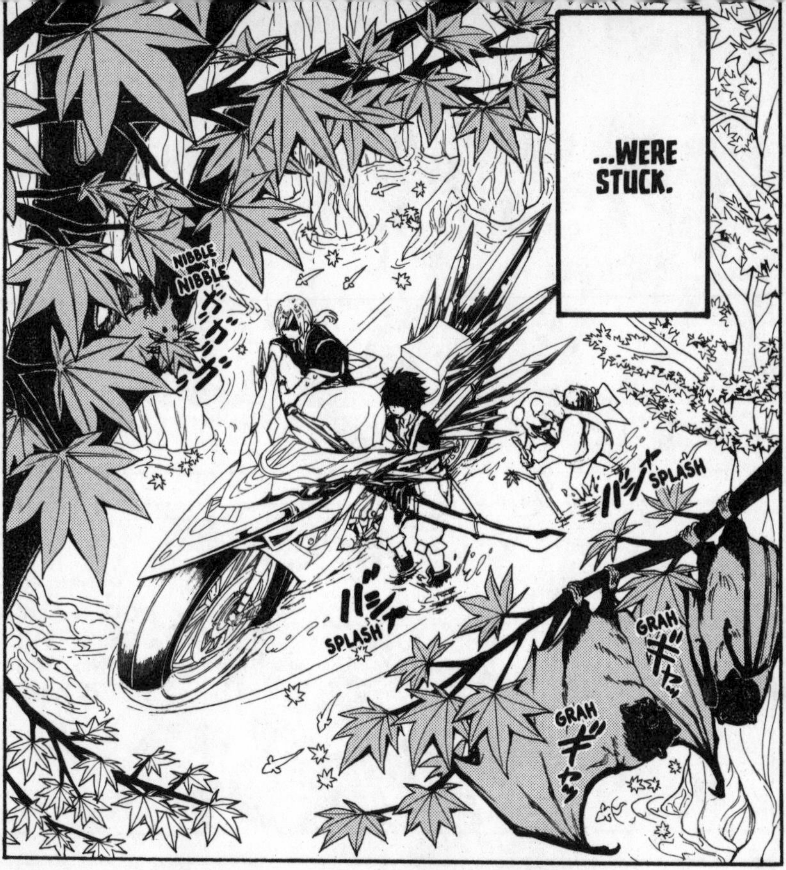
...WERE STUCK.
SPLASH
GRAH
GRAH
SPLASH
NIBBLE NIBBLE

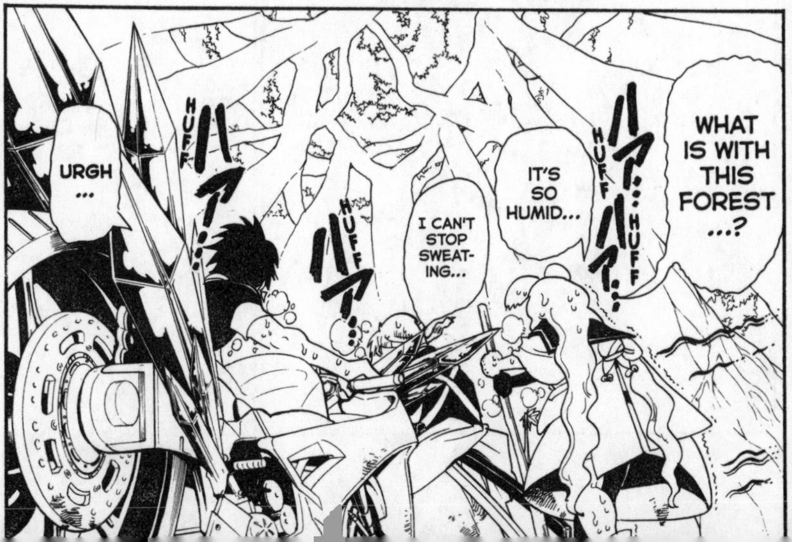
WHAT IS WITH THIS FOREST ...?
HUFF HUFF
IT'S SO HUMID...
I CAN'T STOP SWEAT-ING...
HUFF
HUFF
URGH ...

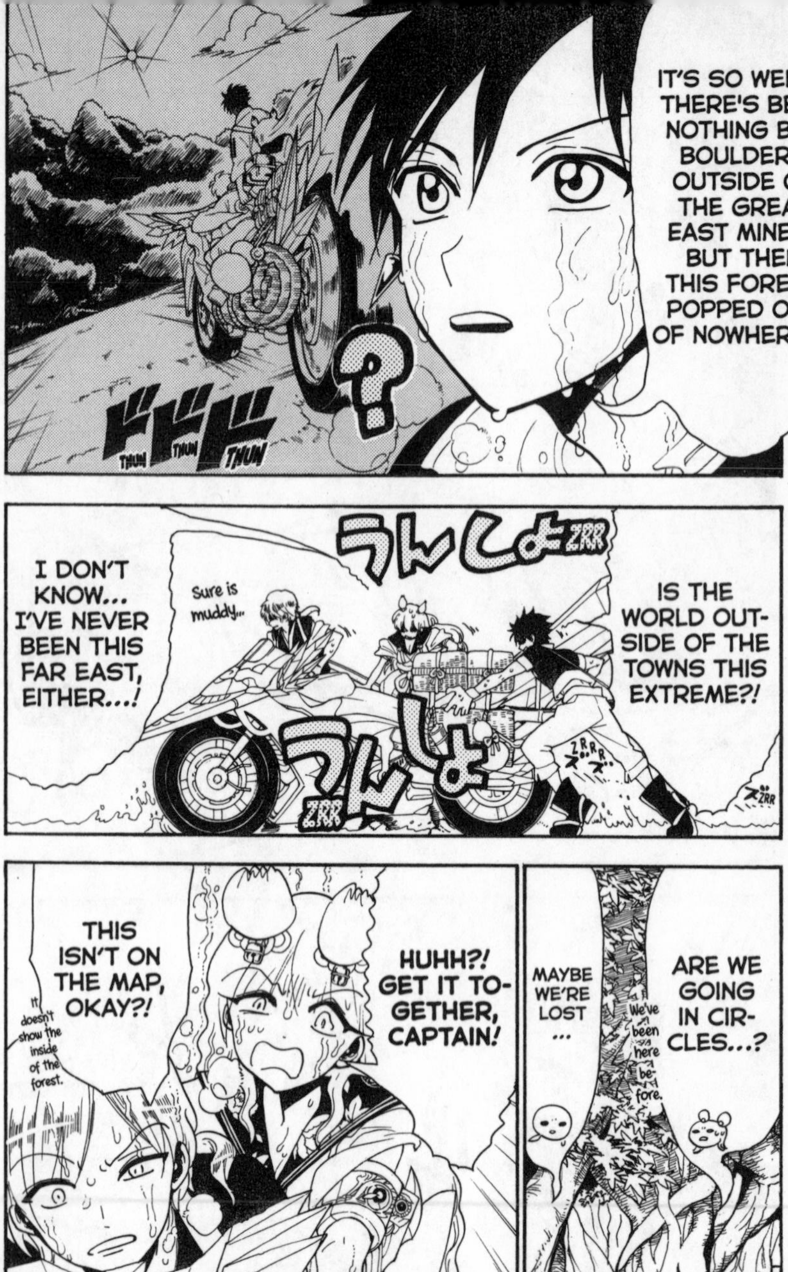

IT'S SO WEIRD. THERE'S BEEN NOTHING BUT BOULDERS OUTSIDE OF THE GREAT EAST MINE... BUT THEN THIS FOREST POPPED OUT OF NOWHERE...
?
ドドド
THUN THUN THUN
うんしょ ZRR
IS THE WORLD OUT-SIDE OF THE TOWNS THIS EXTREME?!
Sure is muddy...
I DON'T KNOW... I'VE NEVER BEEN THIS FAR EAST, EITHER...!
うんしょ ZRR
ZRR
ZRR
ARE WE GOING IN CIR-CLES...?
We've been here be-fore.
MAYBE WE'RE LOST ...
HUHH?! GET IT TO-GETHER, CAPTAIN!
THIS ISN'T ON THE MAP, OKAY?!
It doesn't show the inside of the forest.

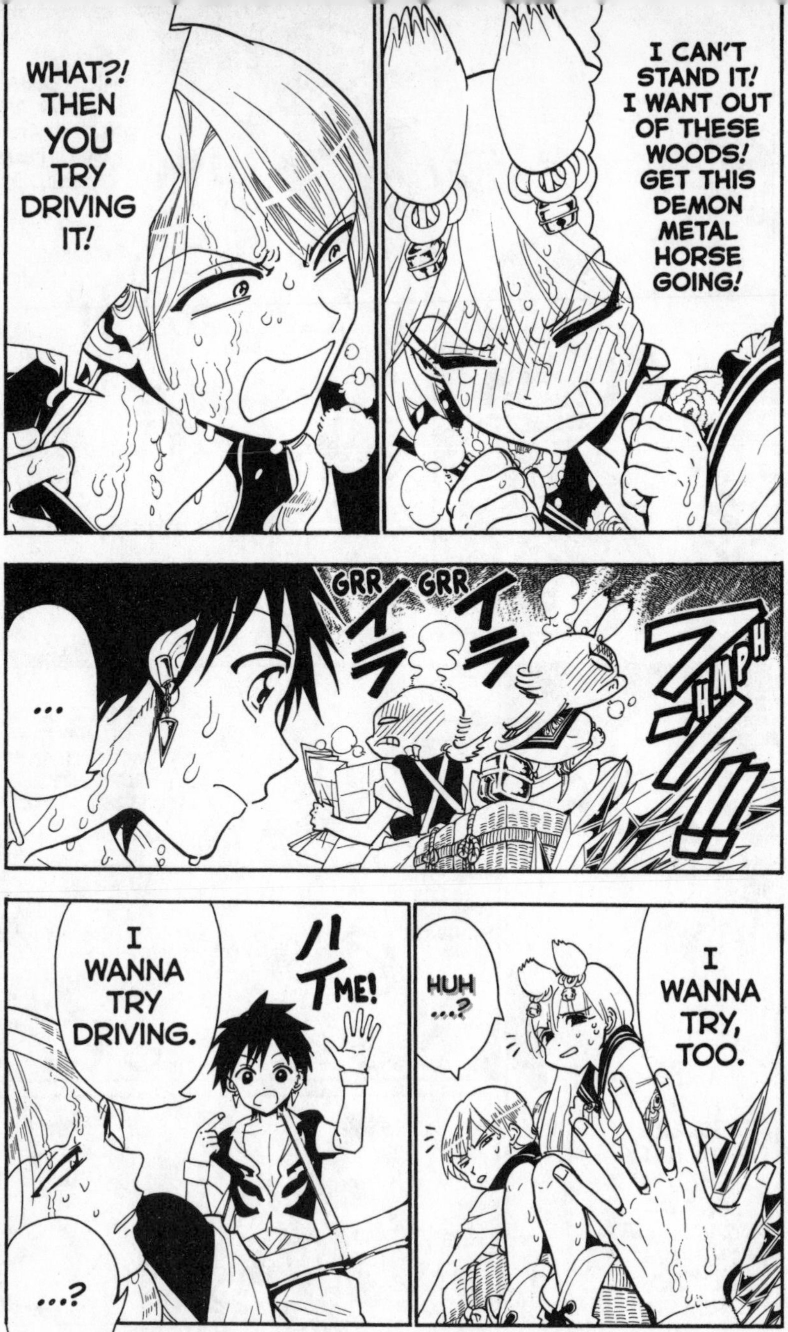
I CAN'T STAND IT! I WANT OUT OF THESE WOODS! GET THIS DEMON METAL HORSE GOING!
WHAT?! THEN YOU TRY DRIVING IT!
HMPH
フン!!
GRR
イラ
GRR
イラ
...
I WANNA TRY, TOO.
HUH ...?
ハイ
ME!
I WANNA TRY DRIVING.
...?

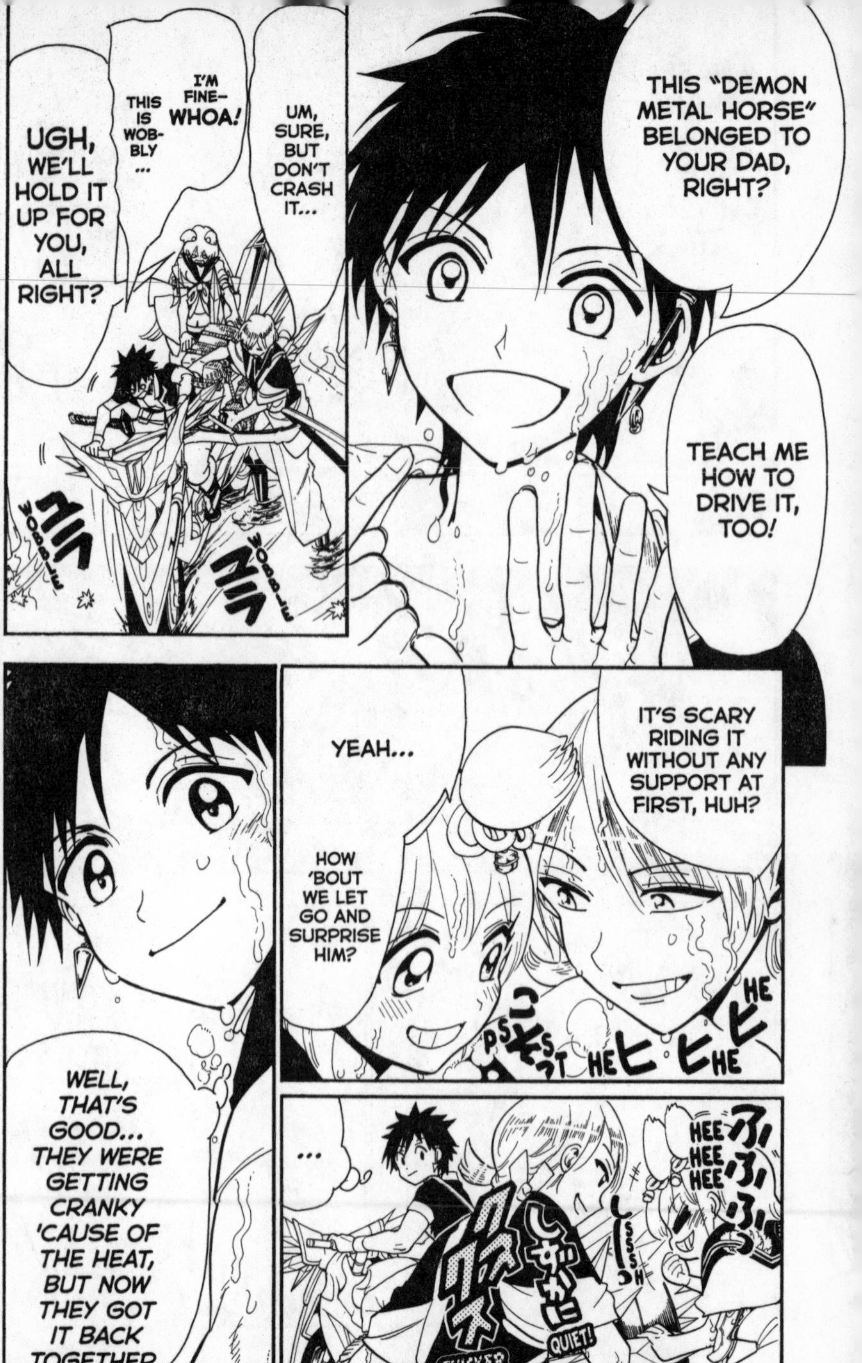
THIS "DEMON METAL HORSE" BELONGED TO YOUR DAD, RIGHT?
TEACH ME HOW TO DRIVE IT, TOO!
UM, SURE, BUT DON'T CRASH IT...
I'M FINE— WHOA!
THIS IS WOB-BLY ...
UGH, WE'LL HOLD IT UP FOR YOU, ALL RIGHT?
WOBBLE
WOBBLE
IT'S SCARY RIDING IT WITHOUT ANY SUPPORT AT FIRST, HUH?
YEAH...
HOW 'BOUT WE LET GO AND SURPRISE HIM?
PSST
HE HE HE HE
HEE HEE HEE
SSSSH
QUIET!
SNICKER SNICKER
...
WELL, THAT'S GOOD... THEY WERE GETTING CRANKY 'CAUSE OF THE HEAT, BUT NOW THEY GOT IT BACK TOGETHER.

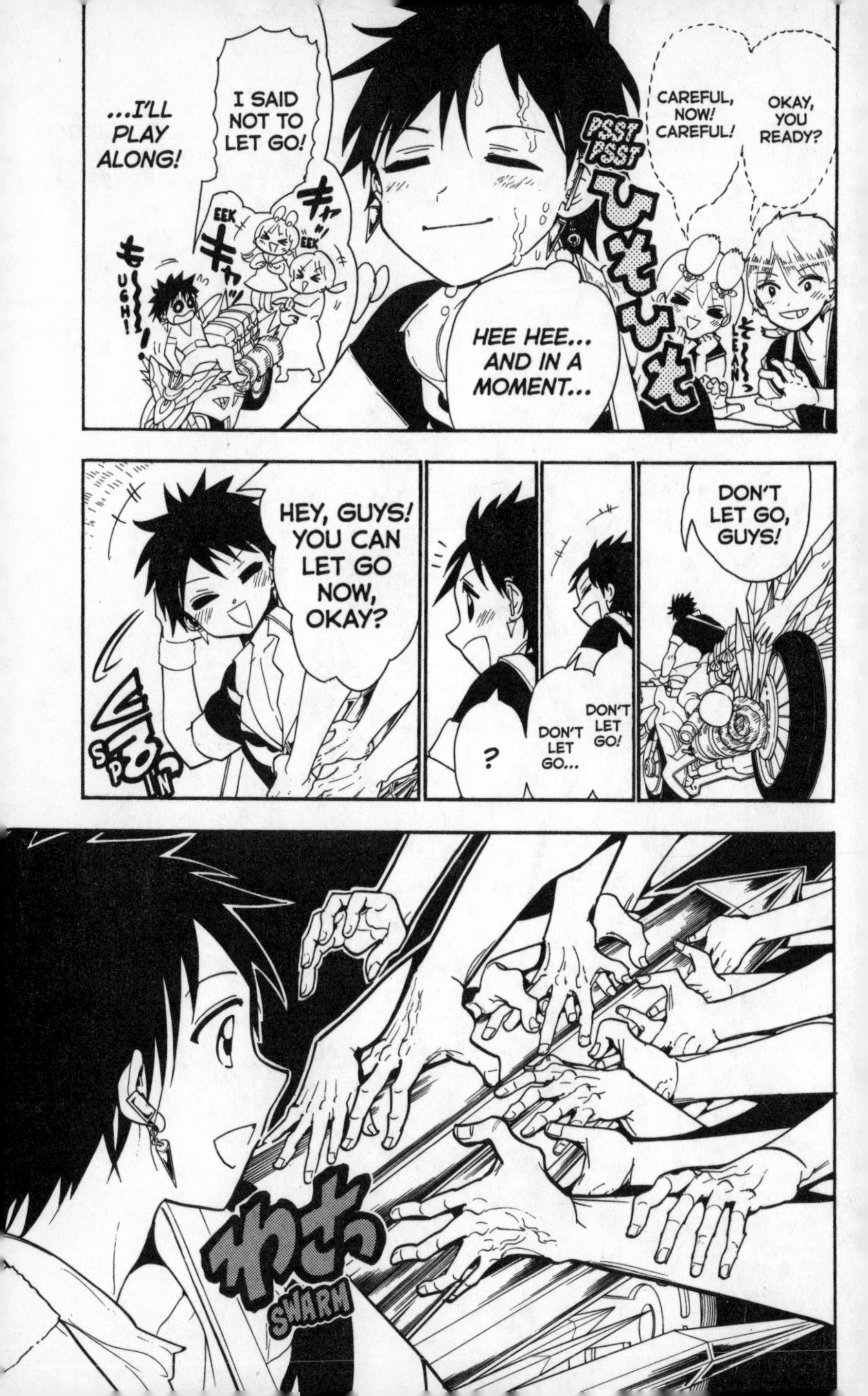
OKAY, YOU READY?
CAREFUL, NOW! CAREFUL!
PSST PSST
LEAN~
HEE HEE... AND IN A MOMENT...
I SAID NOT TO LET GO!
EEK
EEK
...I'LL PLAY ALONG!
UGH!
DON'T LET GO, GUYS!
DON'T LET GO!
DON'T LET GO...
?
HEY, GUYS! YOU CAN LET GO NOW, OKAY?
SPIN
SWARM

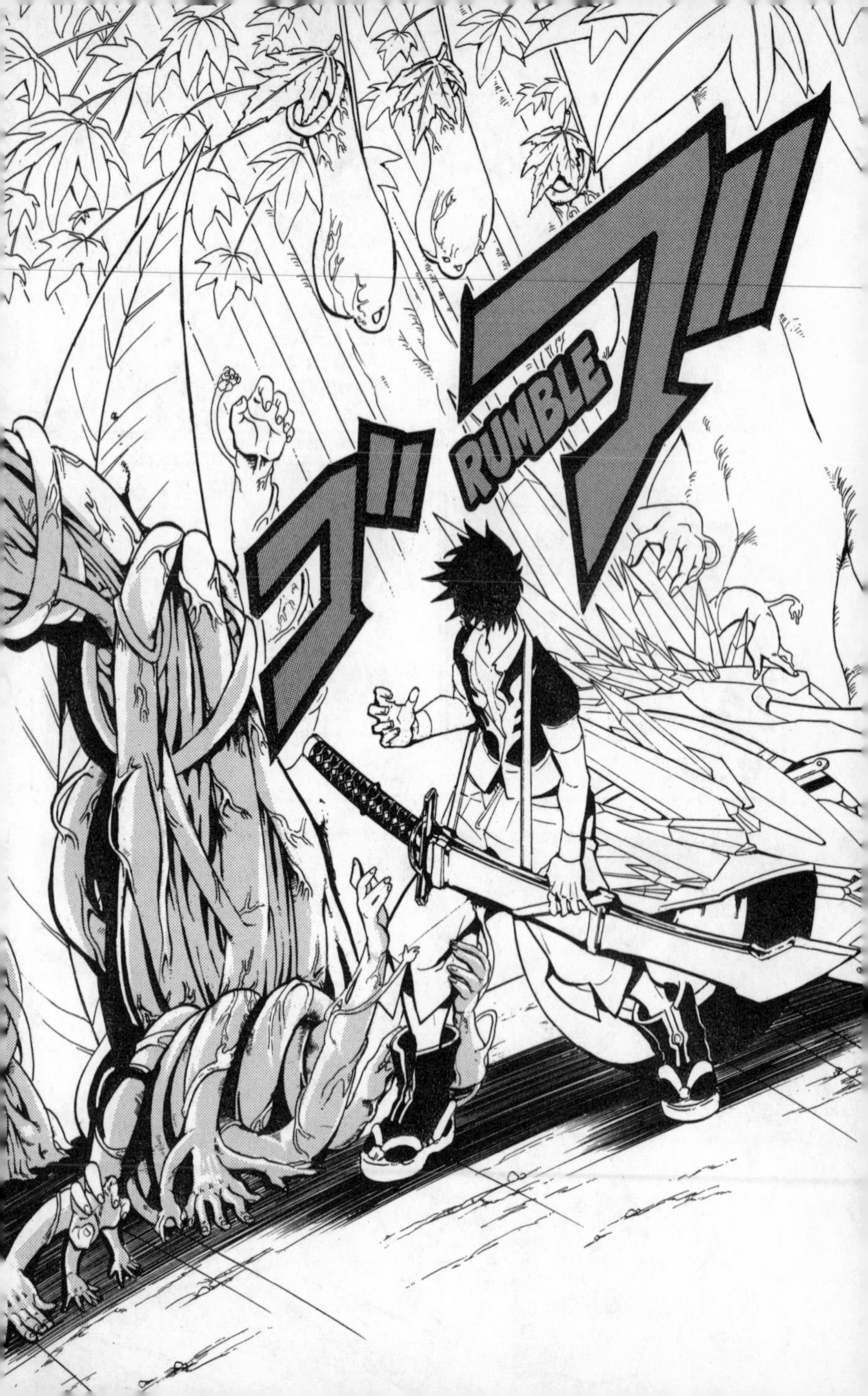
ゴゴ
RUMBLE

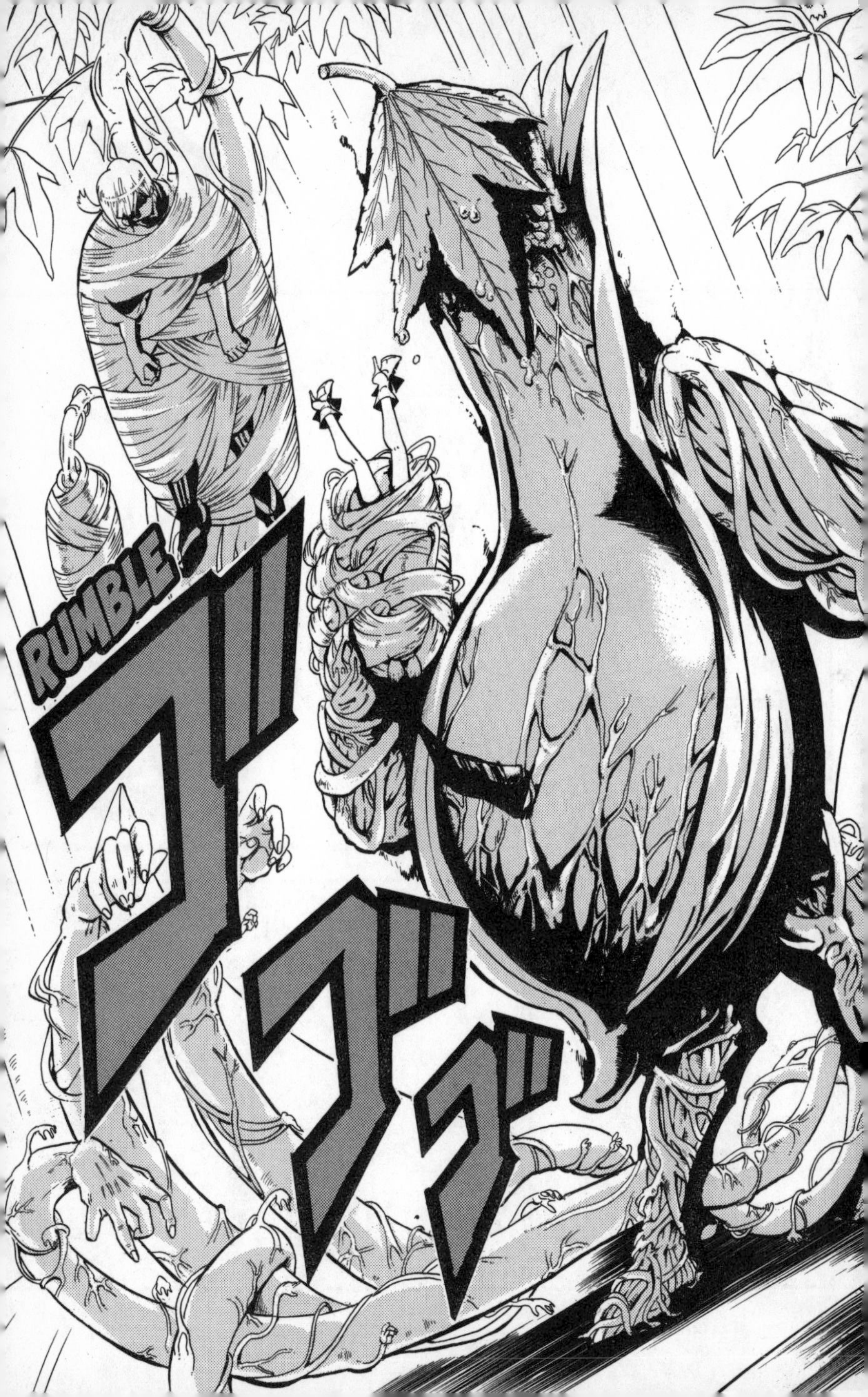
RUMBLE
ゴゴゴ

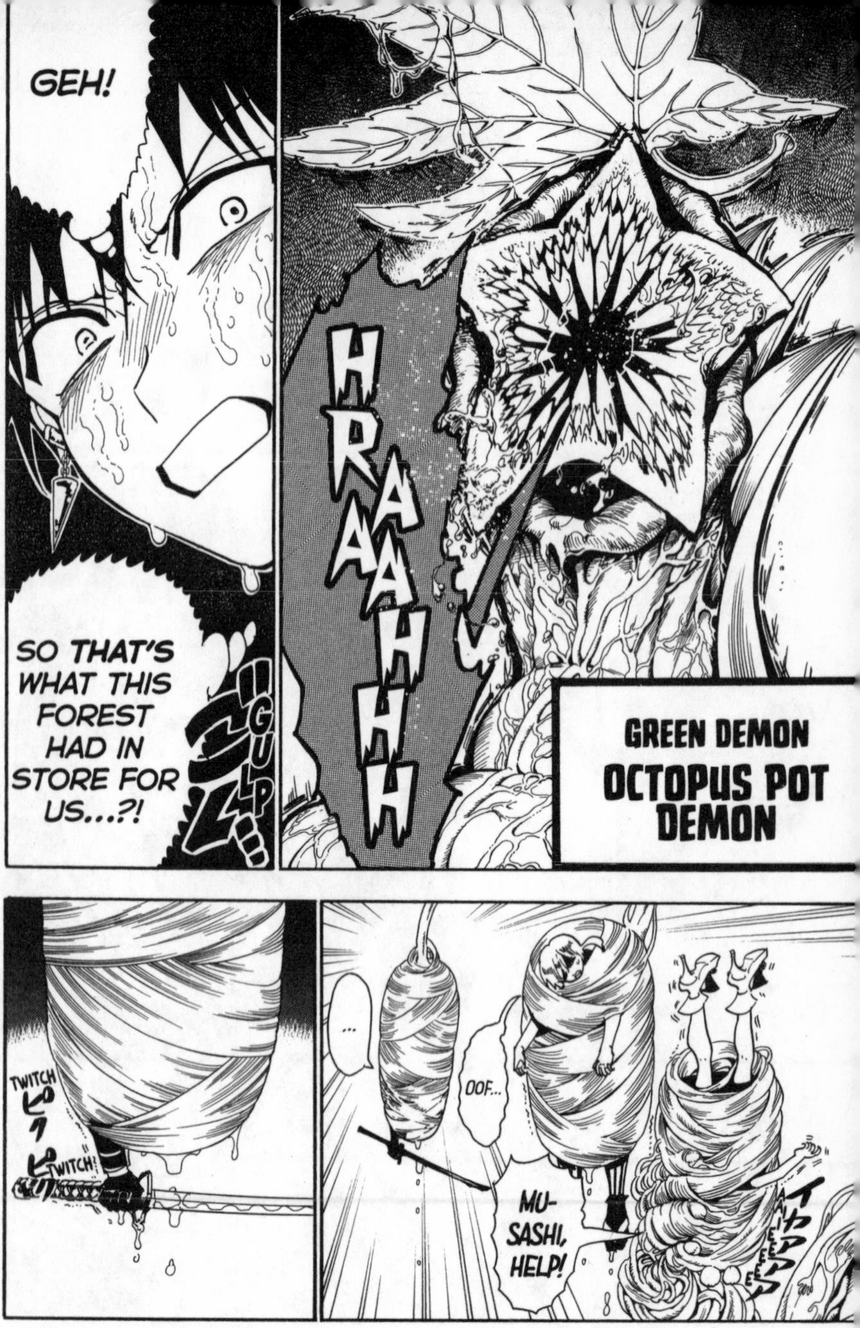
HRAAAHHH
GREEN DEMON
OCTOPUS POT DEMON
GEH!
SO THAT'S WHAT THIS FOREST HAD IN STORE FOR US...?!
GULP
...
OOF...
MU-SASHI, HELP!
TWITCH
ピク
ピ
TWITCH!

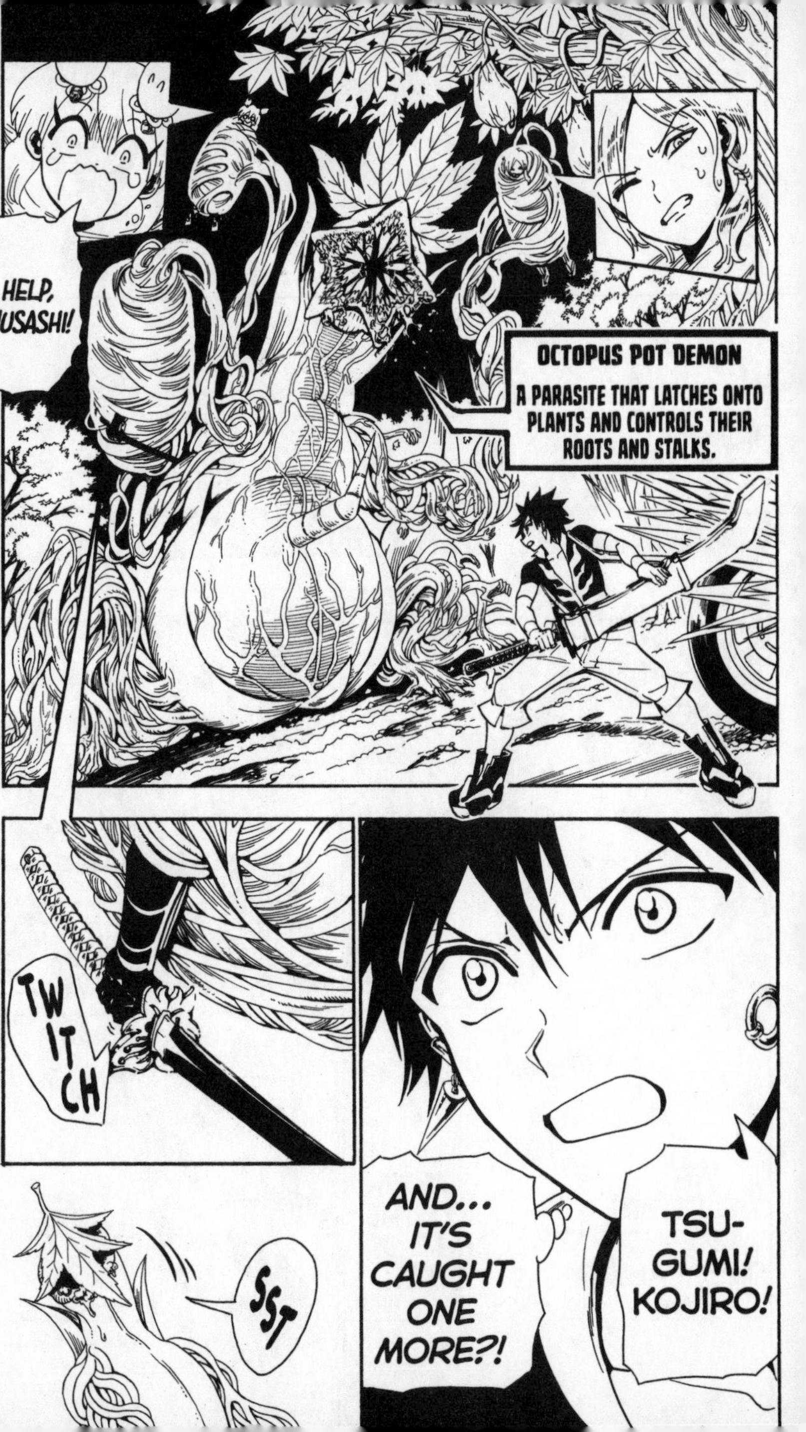
OCTOPUS POT DEMON
A PARASITE THAT LATCHES ONTO PLANTS AND CONTROLS THEIR ROOTS AND STALKS.
HELP, MUSASHI!
TSU-GUMI! KOJIRO!
AND... IT'S CAUGHT ONE MORE?!
TWITCH
SST

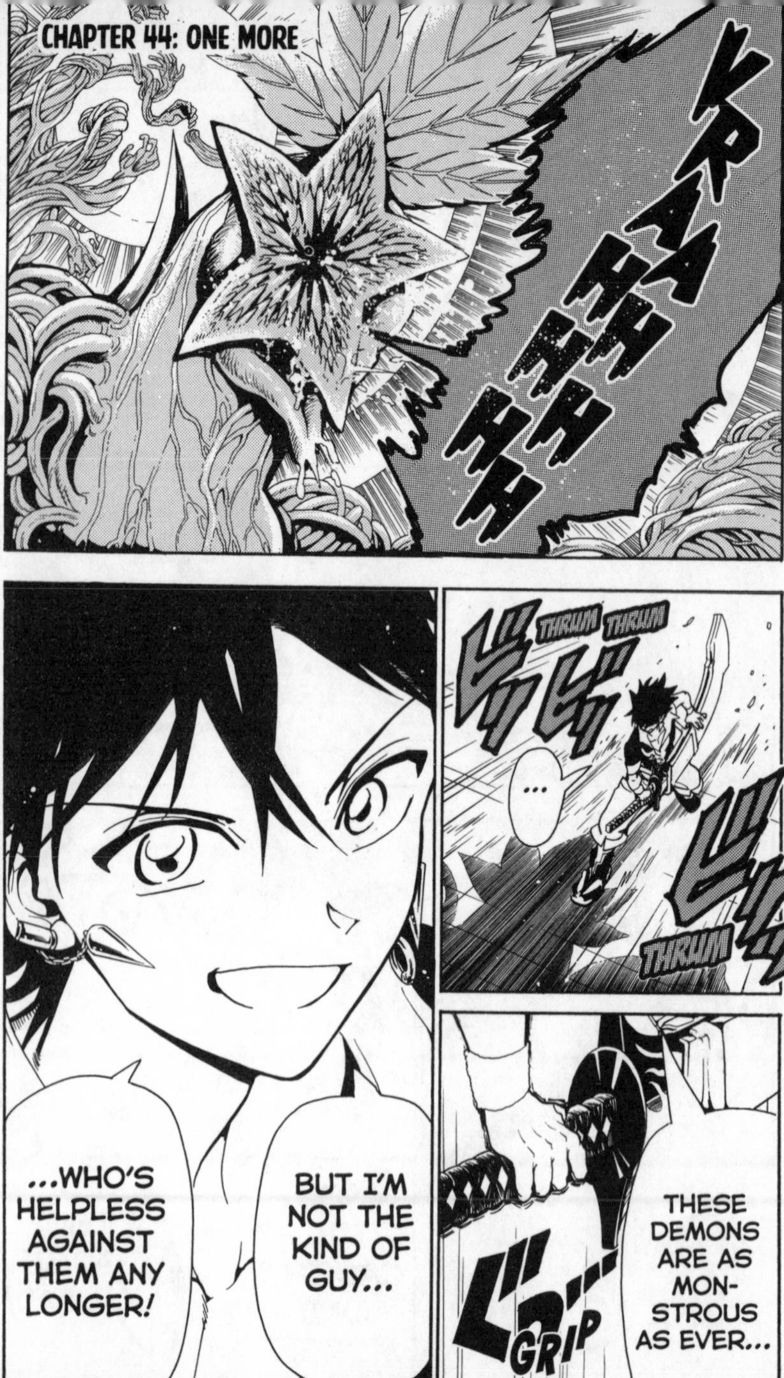
CHAPTER 44: ONE MORE
KRAAHHHHHH
THRUM THRUM
...
THRUM
THESE DEMONS ARE AS MON-STROUS AS EVER...
GRIP
BUT I'M NOT THE KIND OF GUY...
...WHO'S HELPLESS AGAINST THEM ANY LONGER!

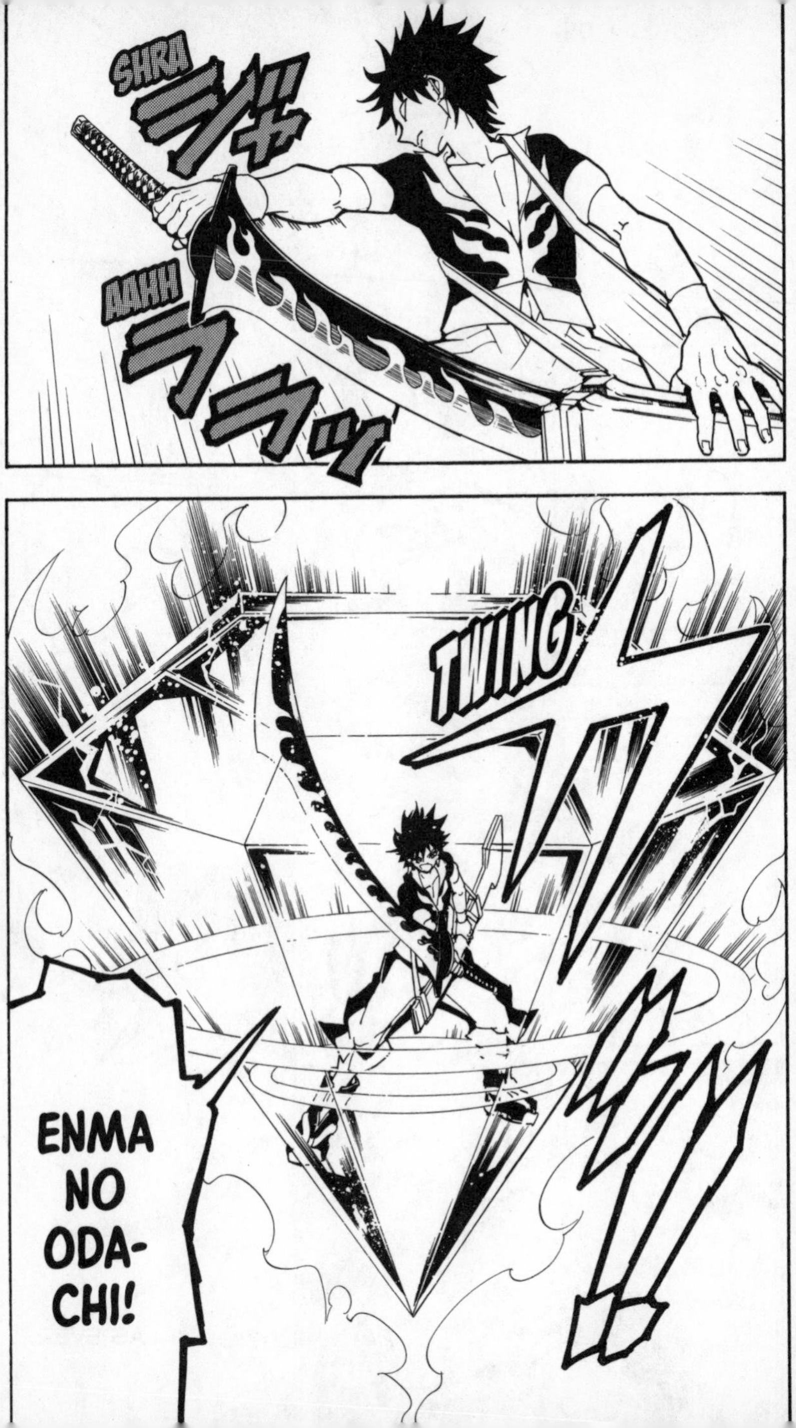
SHRA
AAHH
TWING
ENMA NO ODA-CHI!

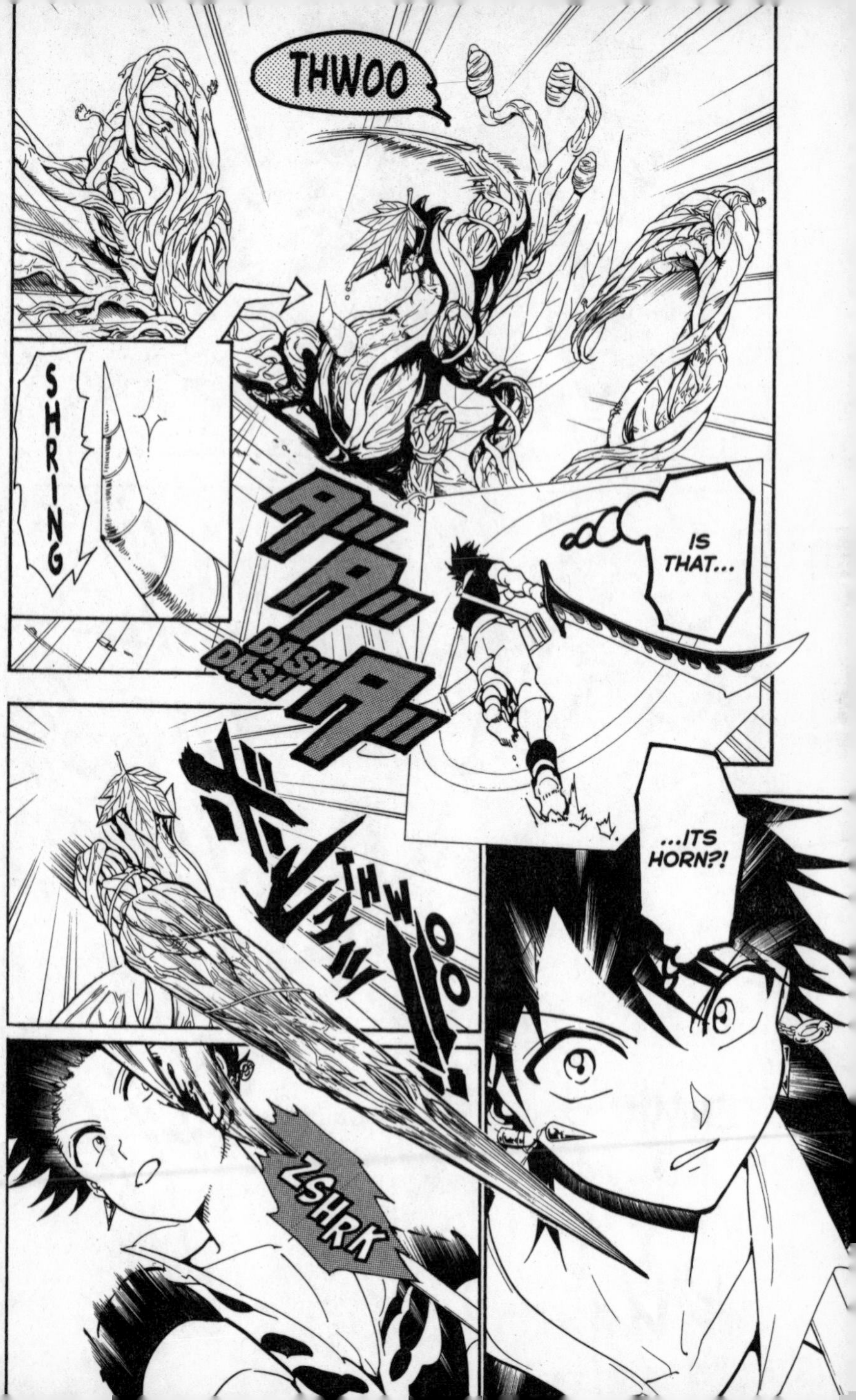
THWOO
SHRING
IS THAT...
DASH DASH
...ITS HORN?!
THWOO
ZSHRK

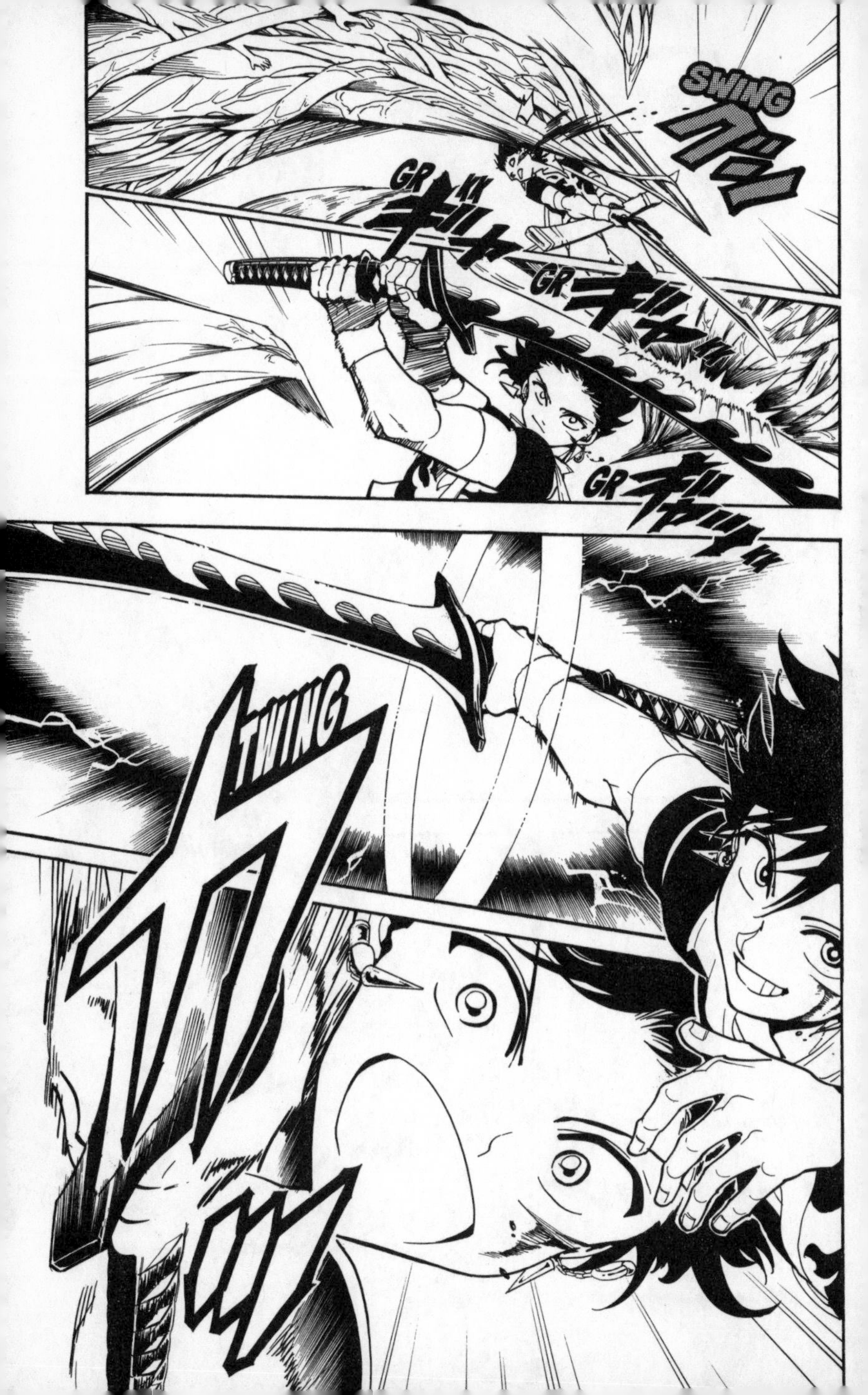
SWING
GR KK
GR
GR
TWING

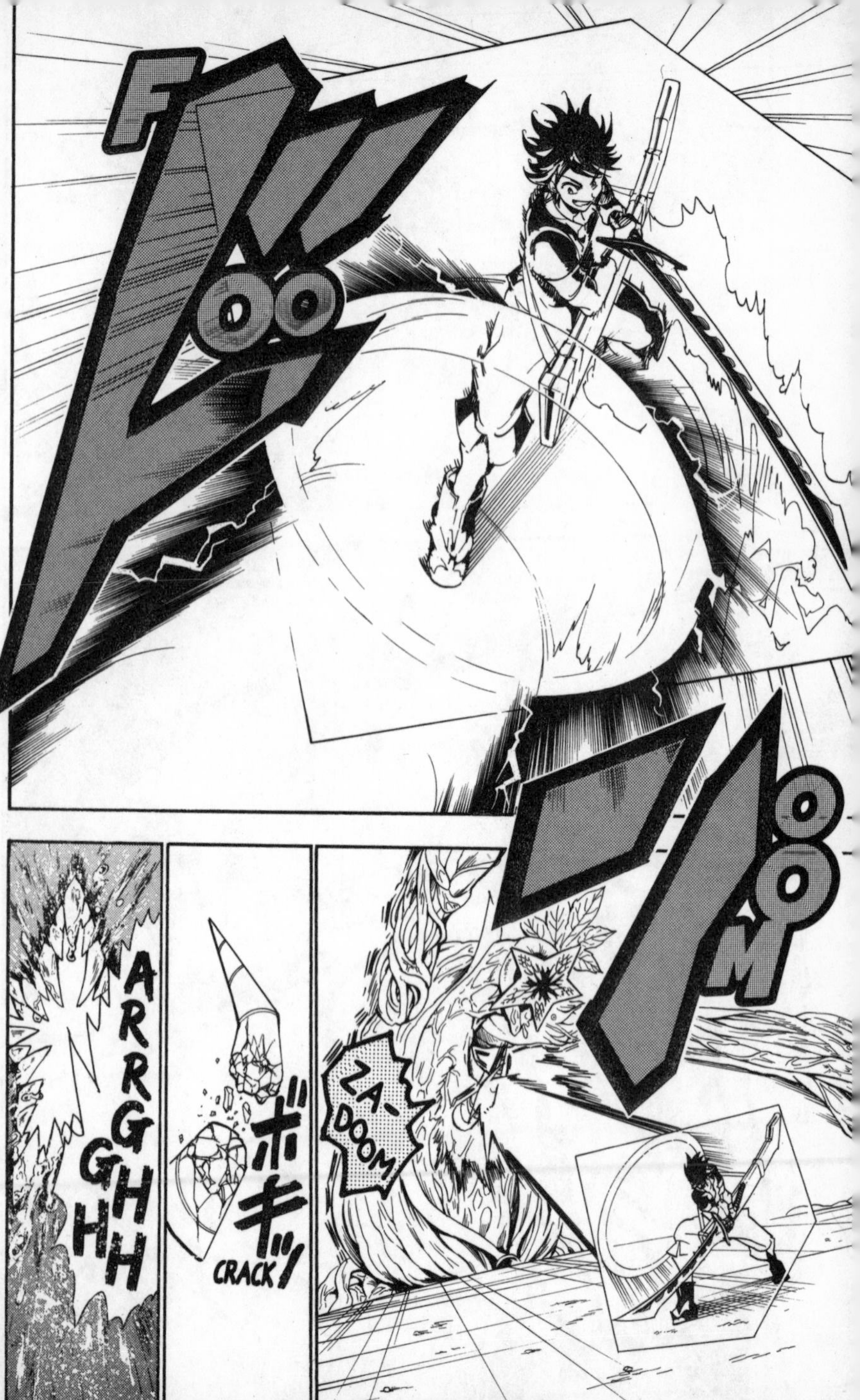
FWOO
OOM
ZA-DOOM
ボキッ
CRACK!
ARRGHH
GHH

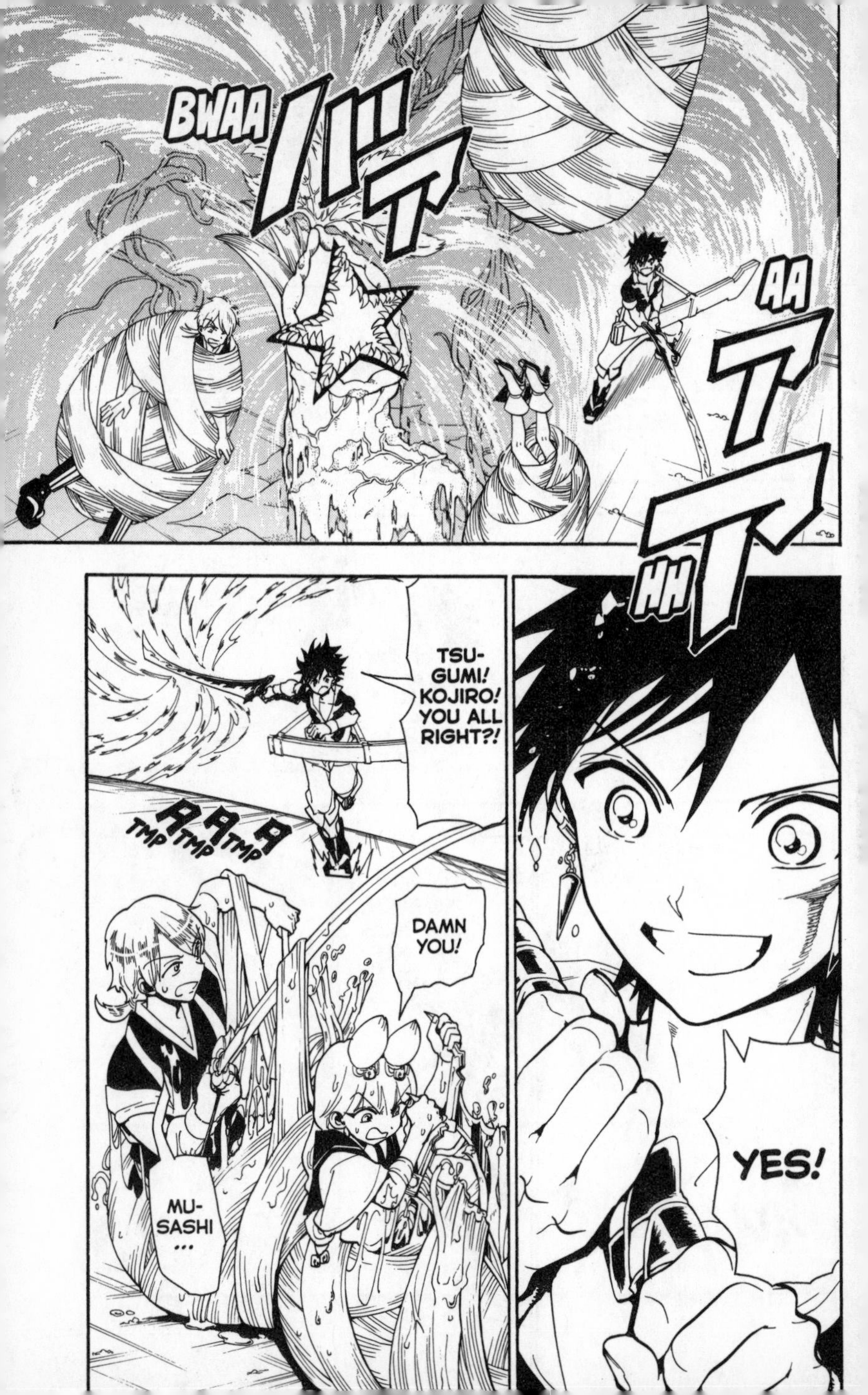
BWAA
AA
HH
YES!
TSU-GUMI! KOJIRO! YOU ALL RIGHT?!
TMP TMP TMP
DAMN YOU!
MU-SASHI...

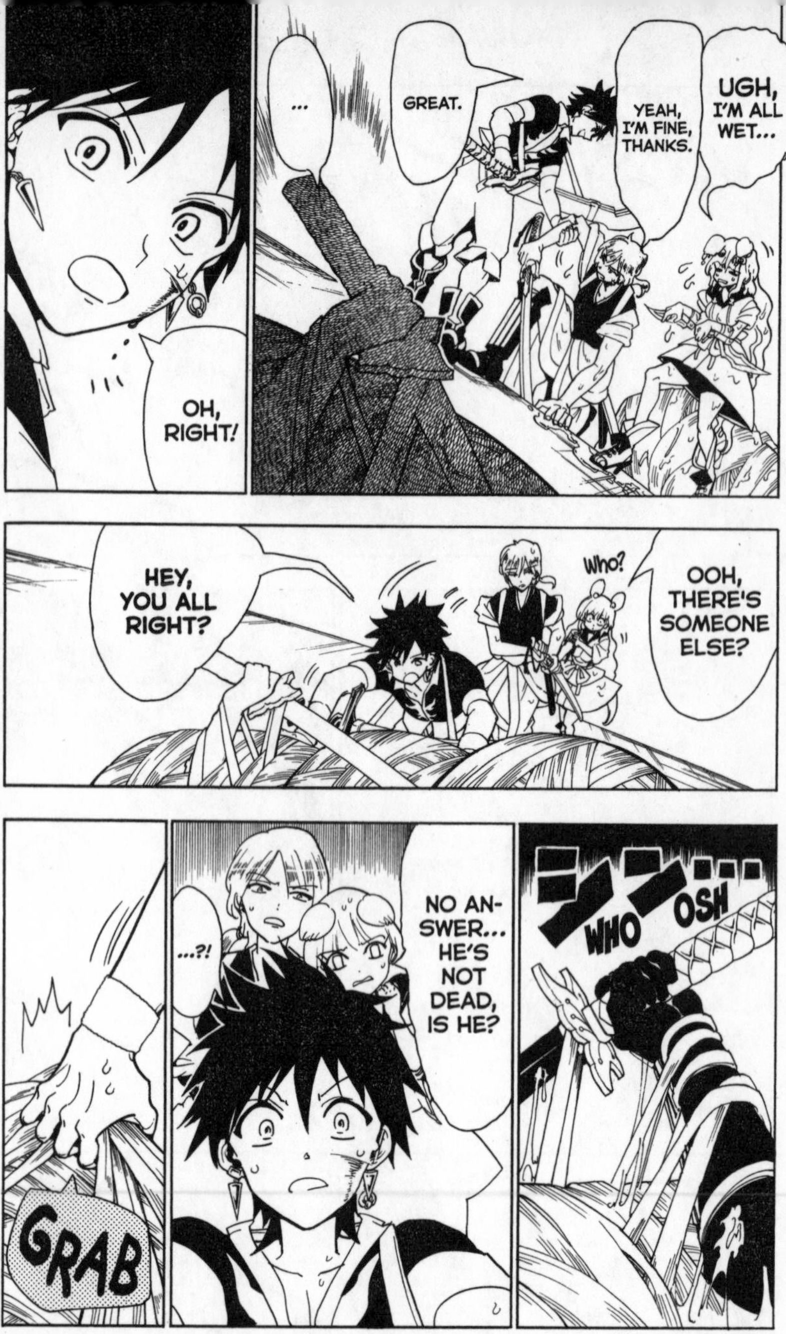
UGH, I'M ALL WET...
YEAH, I'M FINE, THANKS.
GREAT.
...
OH, RIGHT!
OOH, THERE'S SOMEONE ELSE?
Who?
HEY, YOU ALL RIGHT?
WHOOSH
NO AN-SWER... HE'S NOT DEAD, IS HE?
...?!
GRAB

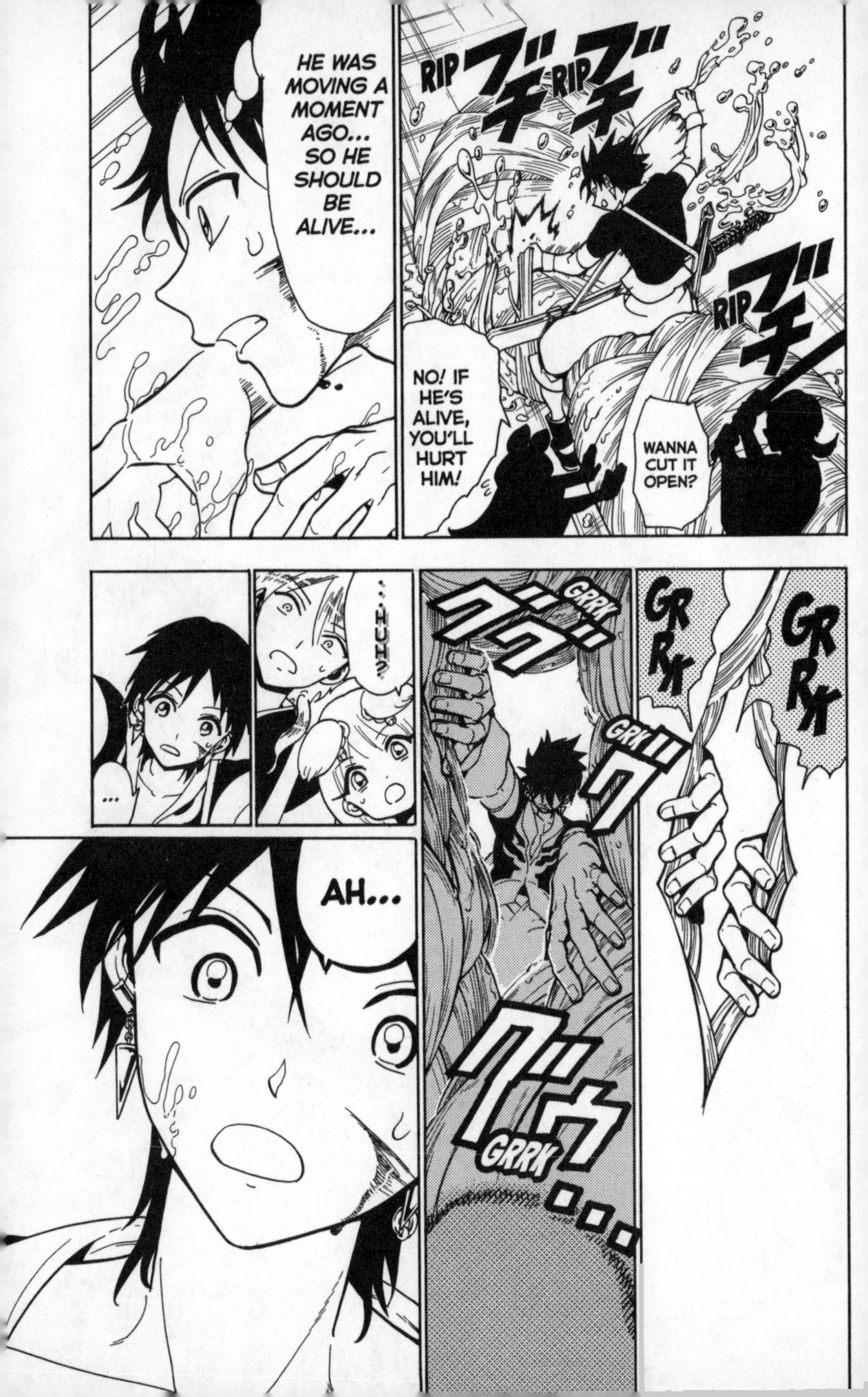
RIP
RIP
RIP
WANNA CUT IT OPEN?
NO! IF HE'S ALIVE, YOU'LL HURT HIM!
HE WAS MOVING A MOMENT AGO... SO HE SHOULD BE ALIVE...
GRRK
GRRK
GRRK
GRK
GRRK...
...HUH?
...
AH...

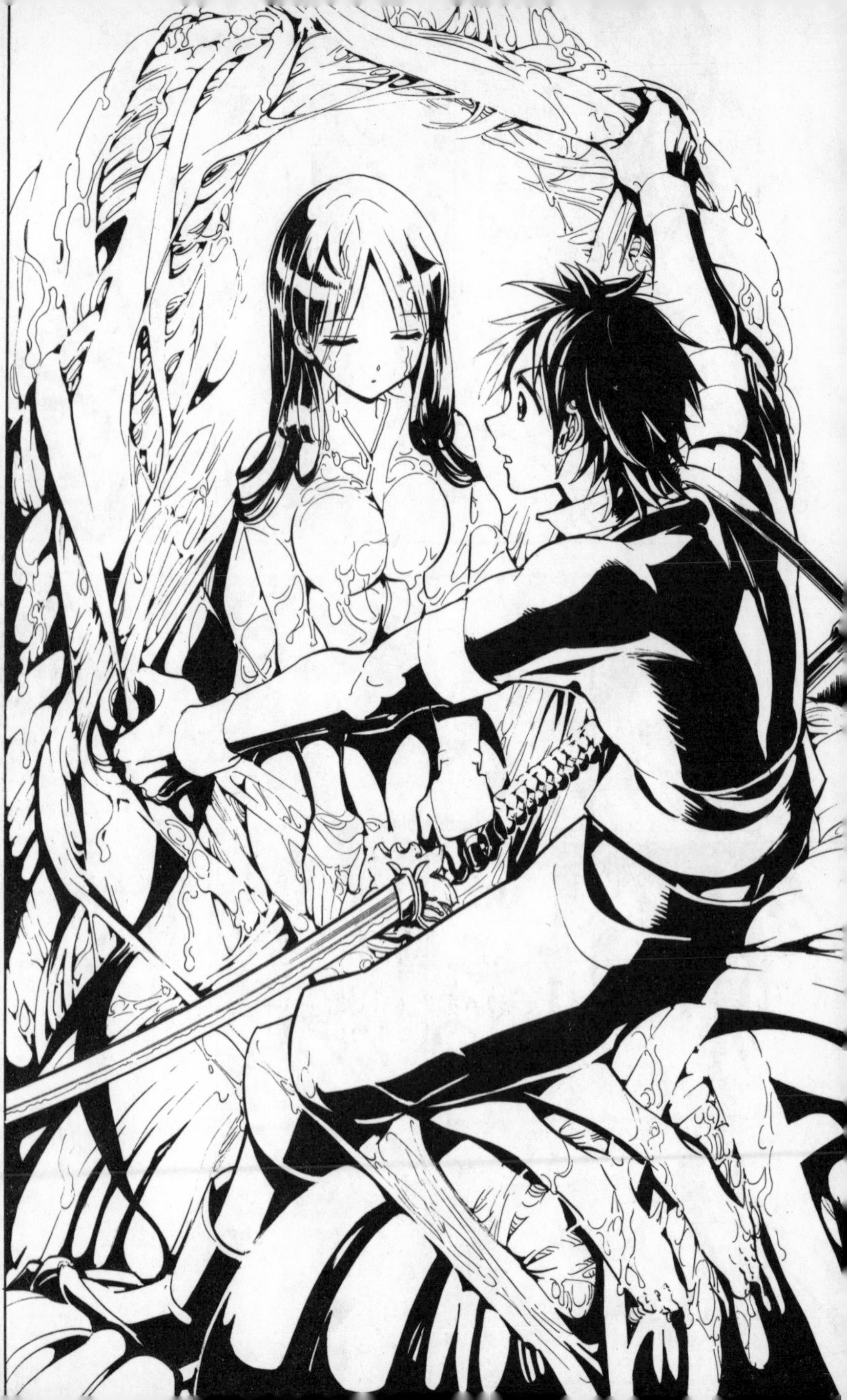

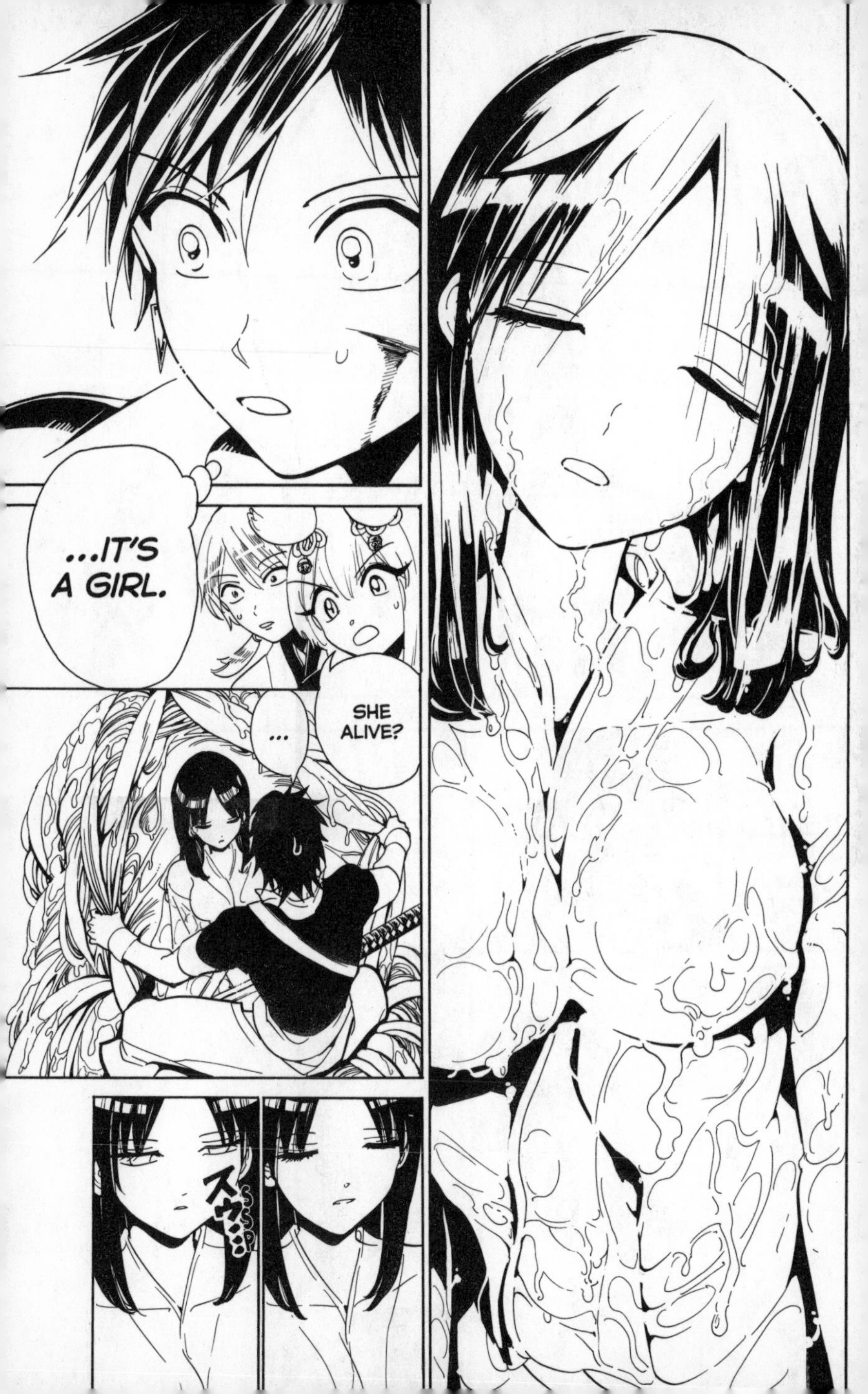
...IT'S A GIRL.
SHE ALIVE?
...
スゥ...
SSSP

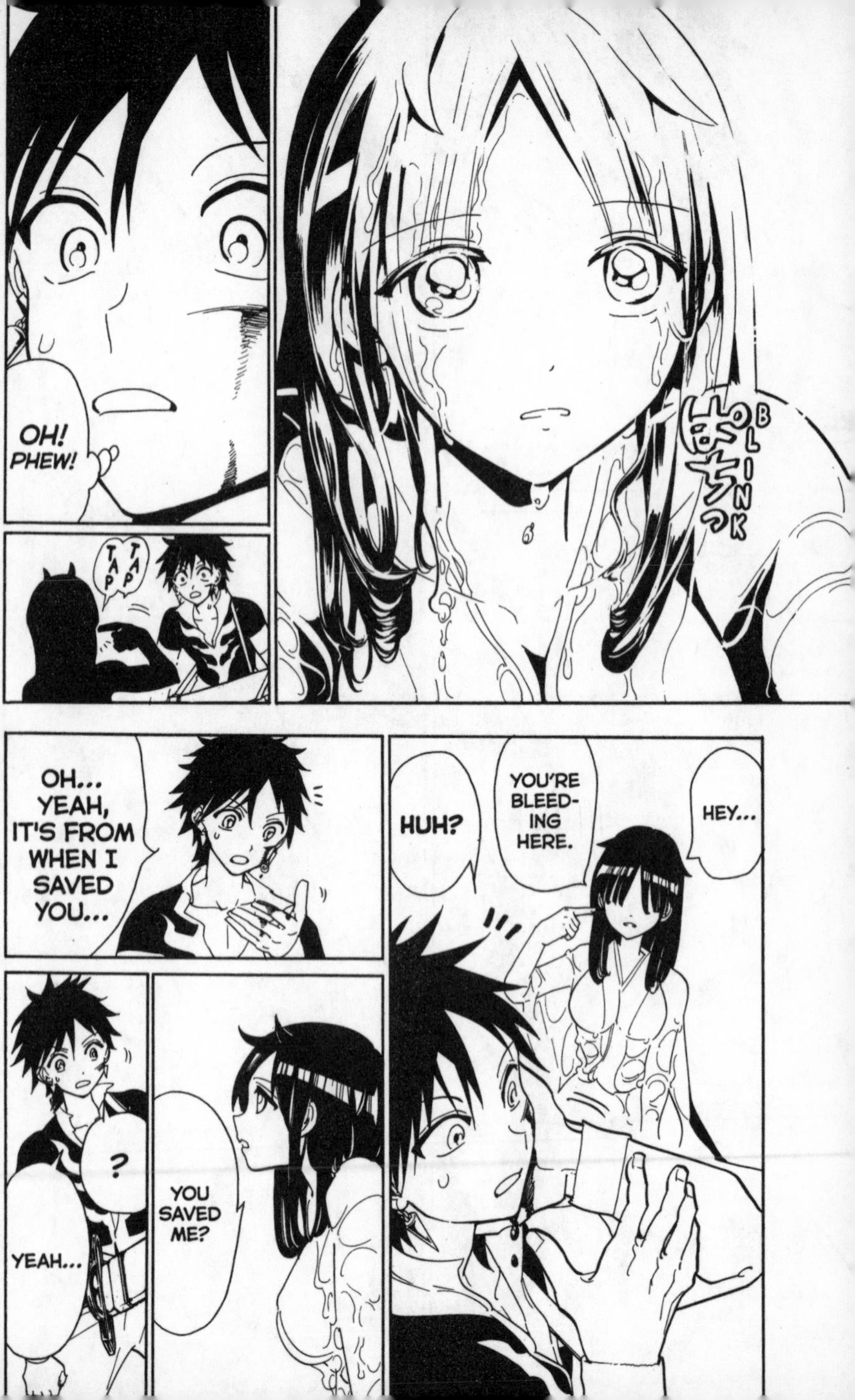
はちっ
BLINK
OH! PHEW!
TAP TAP
HEY...
YOU'RE BLEEDING HERE.
HUH?
OH... YEAH, IT'S FROM WHEN I SAVED YOU...
YOU SAVED ME?
?
YEAH...

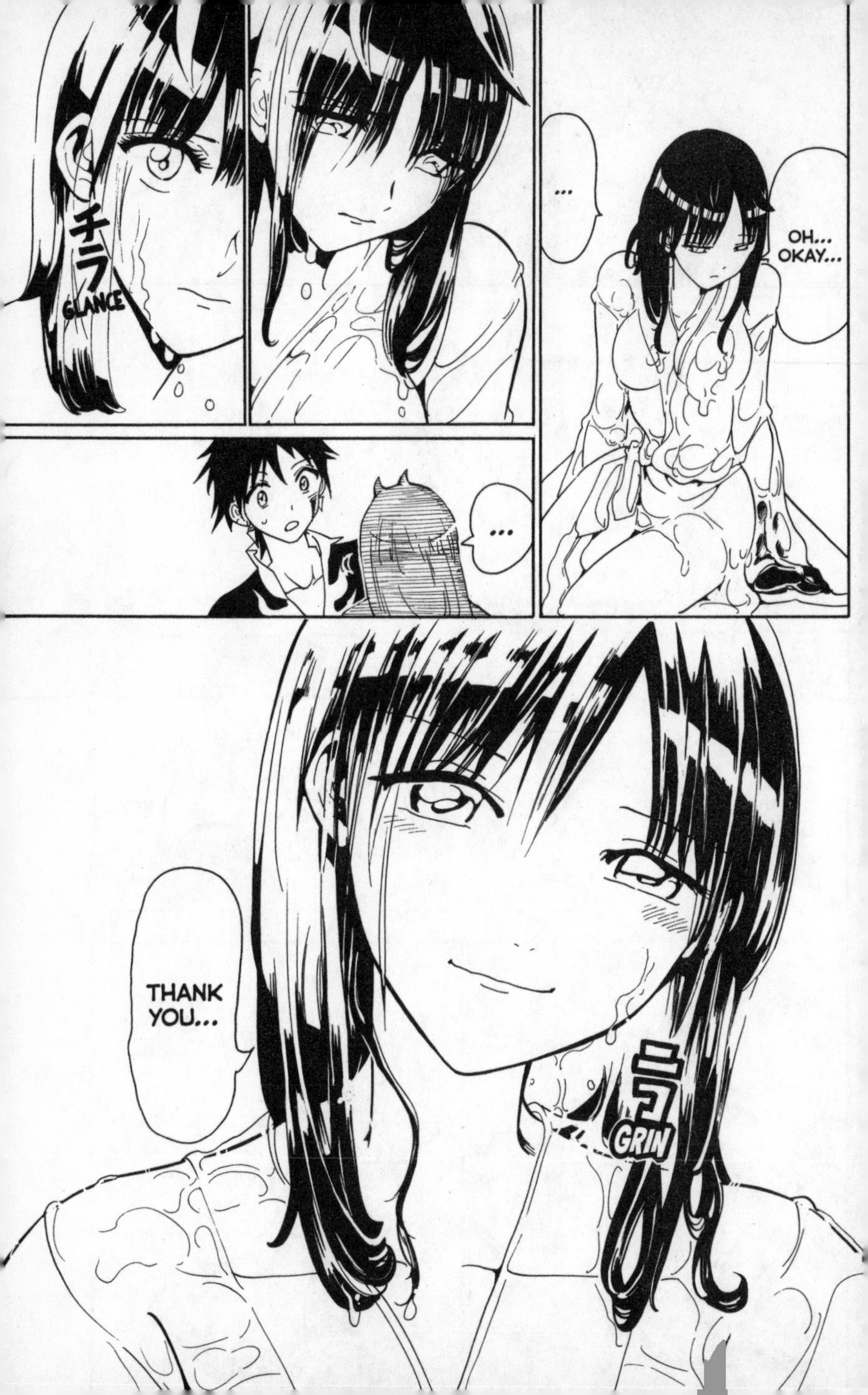

OH... OKAY...
...
チラ
GLANCE
...
ニコ
GRIN
THANK YOU...

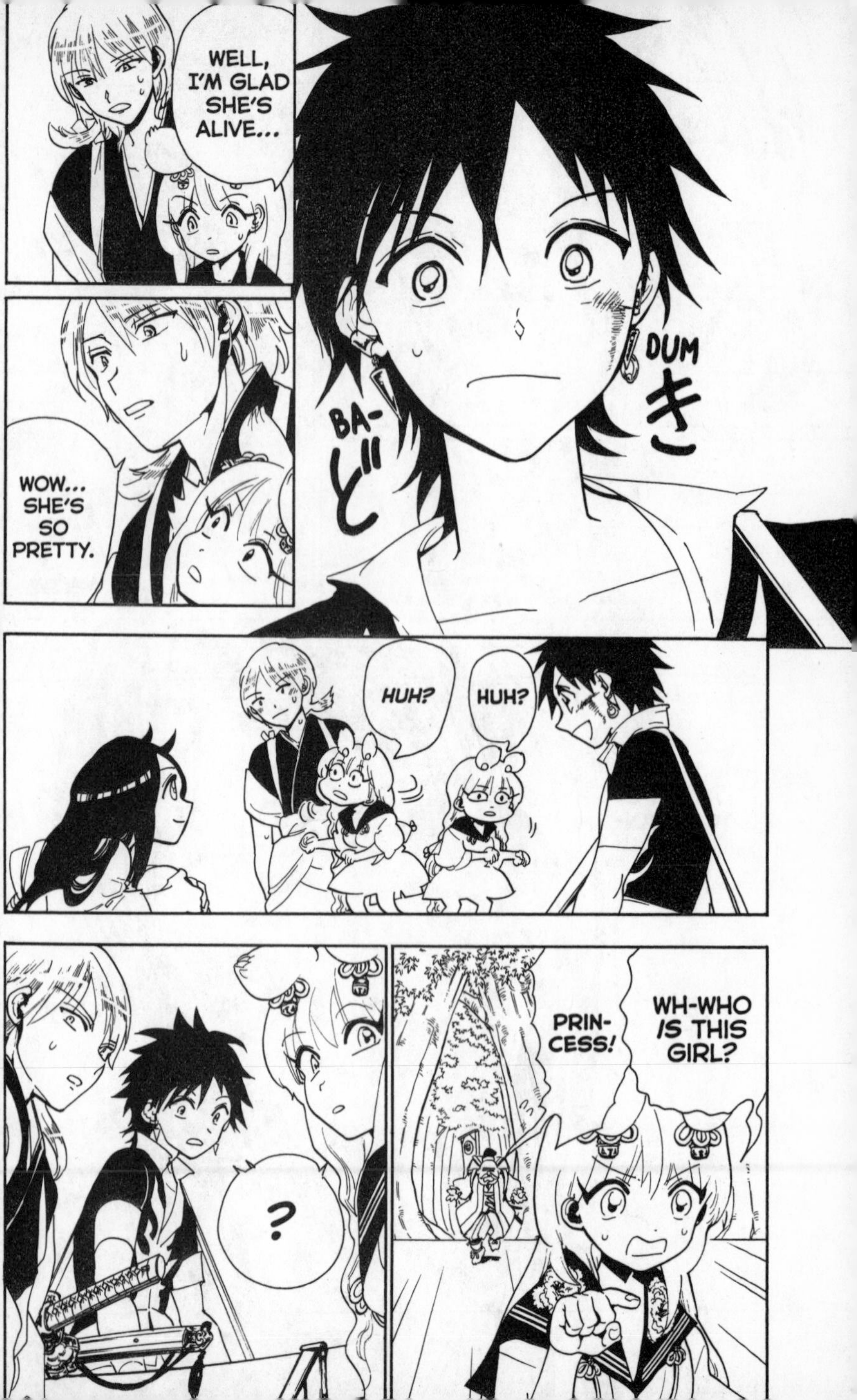
DUM
き
BA-
ど
WELL, I'M GLAD SHE'S ALIVE...
WOW... SHE'S SO PRETTY.
HUH?
HUH?
WH-WHO IS THIS GIRL?
PRIN-CESS!
?

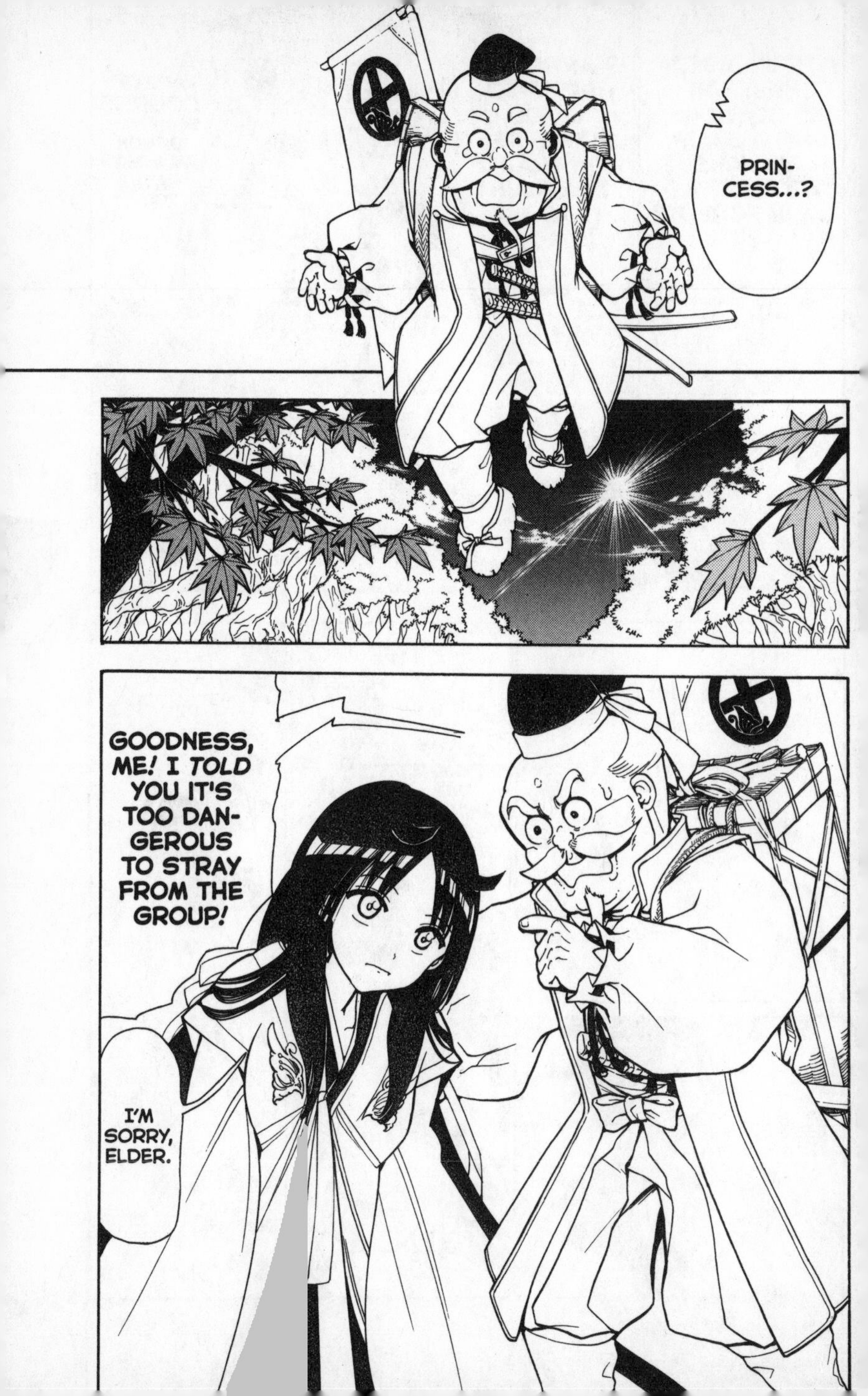
PRIN-
CESS...?
GOODNESS, ME! I *TOLD* YOU IT'S TOO DANGEROUS TO STRAY FROM THE GROUP!
I'M SORRY, ELDER.

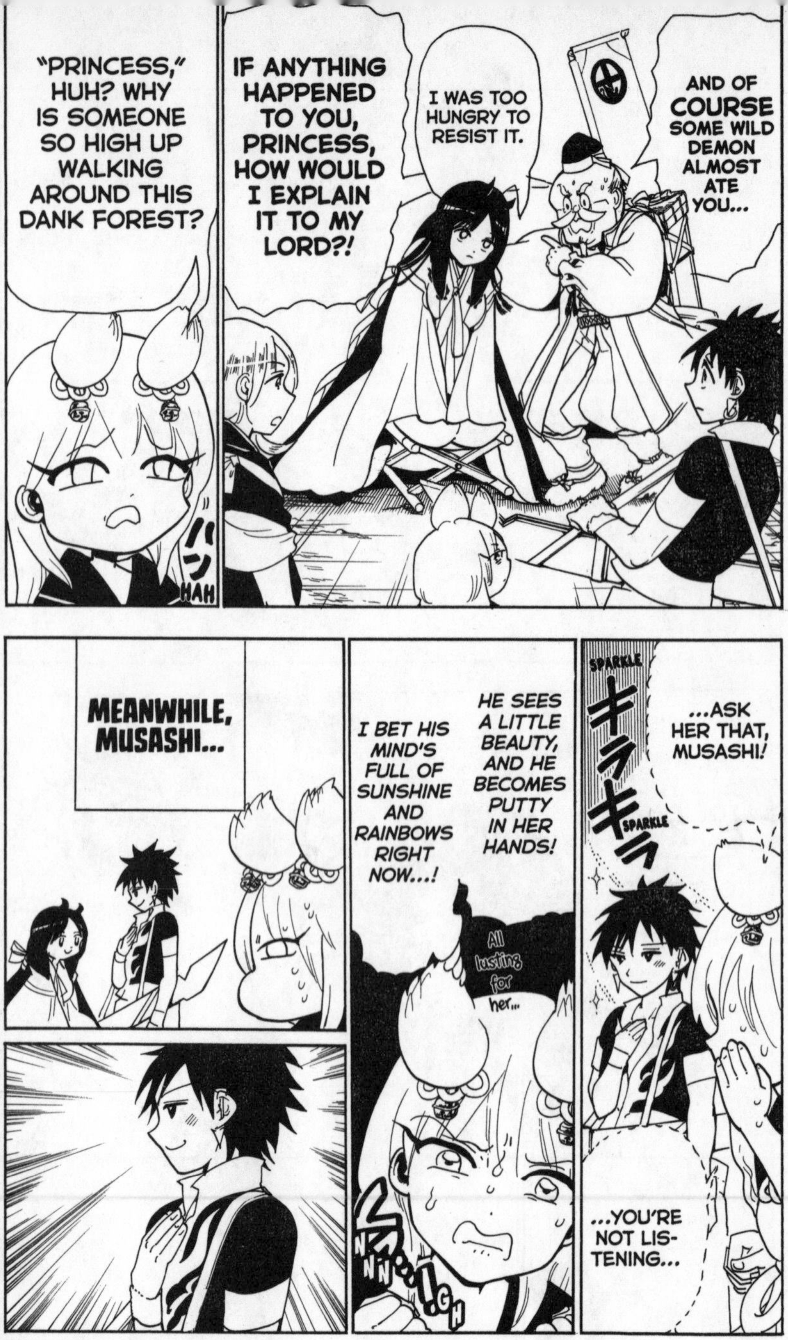
AND OF COURSE SOME WILD DEMON ALMOST ATE YOU...
I WAS TOO HUNGRY TO RESIST IT.
IF ANYTHING HAPPENED TO YOU, PRINCESS, HOW WOULD I EXPLAIN IT TO MY LORD?!
"PRINCESS," HUH? WHY IS SOMEONE SO HIGH UP WALKING AROUND THIS DANK FOREST?
HAH
SPARKLE
SPARKLE
...ASK HER THAT, MUSASHI!
...YOU'RE NOT LIS-TENING...
HE SEES A LITTLE BEAUTY, AND HE BECOMES PUTTY IN HER HANDS!
I BET HIS MIND'S FULL OF SUNSHINE AND RAINBOWS RIGHT NOW...!
All lusting for her...
MEANWHILE, MUSASHI...

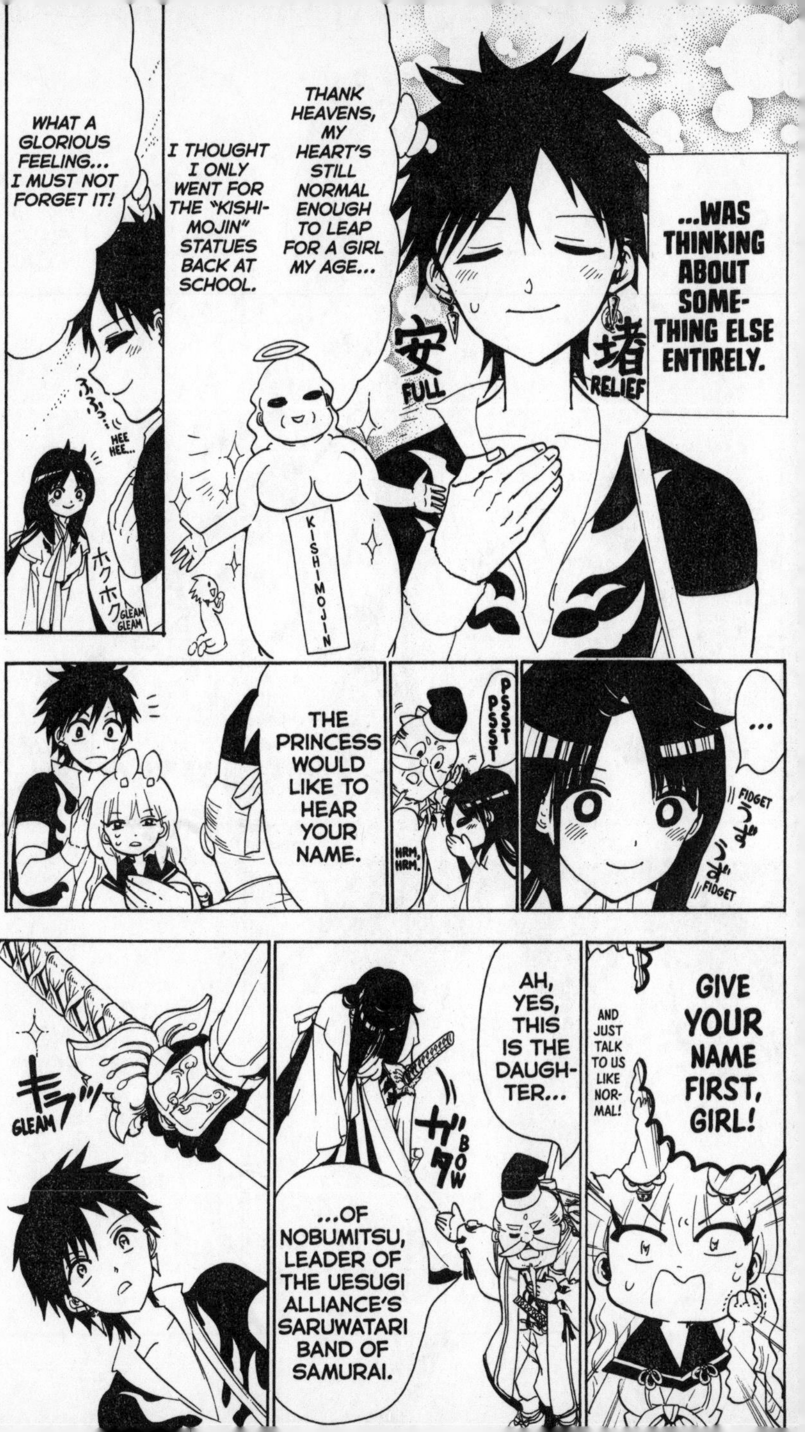
...WAS THINKING ABOUT SOME-THING ELSE ENTIRELY.
THANK HEAVENS, MY HEART'S STILL NORMAL ENOUGH TO LEAP FOR A GIRL MY AGE...
I THOUGHT I ONLY WENT FOR THE "KISHI-MOJIN" STATUES BACK AT SCHOOL.
堵 RELIEF
安 FULL
KISHIMOJIN
WHAT A GLORIOUS FEELING... I MUST NOT FORGET IT!
ふふっ HEE HEE...
ホクホク GLEAM GLEAM
...
うずうず FIDGET FIDGET
PSST PSST PSST
HRM, HRM.
THE PRINCESS WOULD LIKE TO HEAR YOUR NAME.
GIVE YOUR NAME FIRST, GIRL!
AND JUST TALK TO US LIKE NOR-MAL!
AH, YES, THIS IS THE DAUGH-TER...
...OF NOBUMITSU, LEADER OF THE UESUGI ALLIANCE'S SARUWATARI BAND OF SAMURAI.
ガタ BOW
キラッ GLEAM

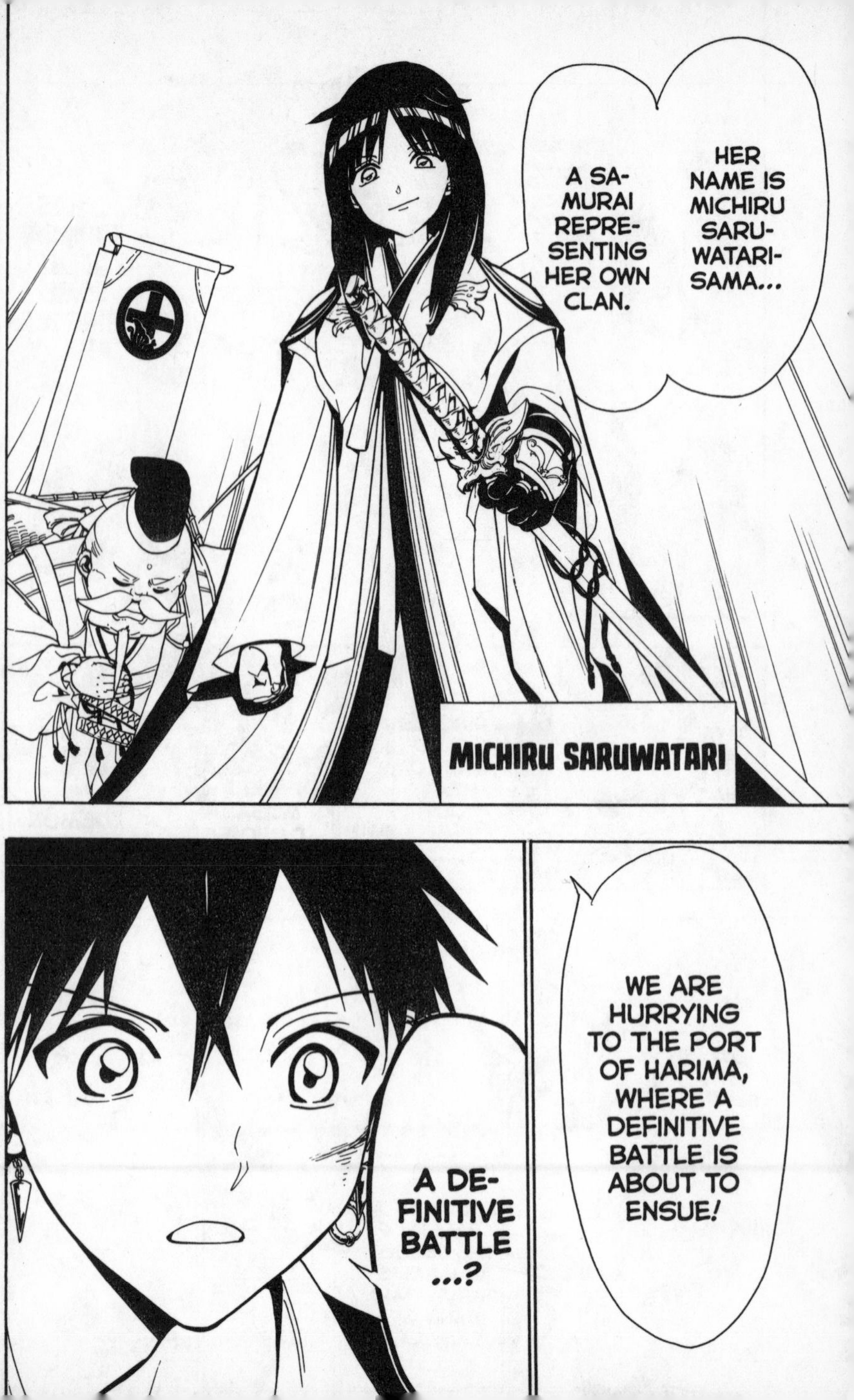
HER NAME IS MICHIRU SARUWATARI-SAMA...
A SAMURAI REPRESENTING HER OWN CLAN.
MICHIRU SARUWATARI
WE ARE HURRYING TO THE PORT OF HARIMA, WHERE A DEFINITIVE BATTLE IS ABOUT TO ENSUE!
A DEFINITIVE BATTLE ...?

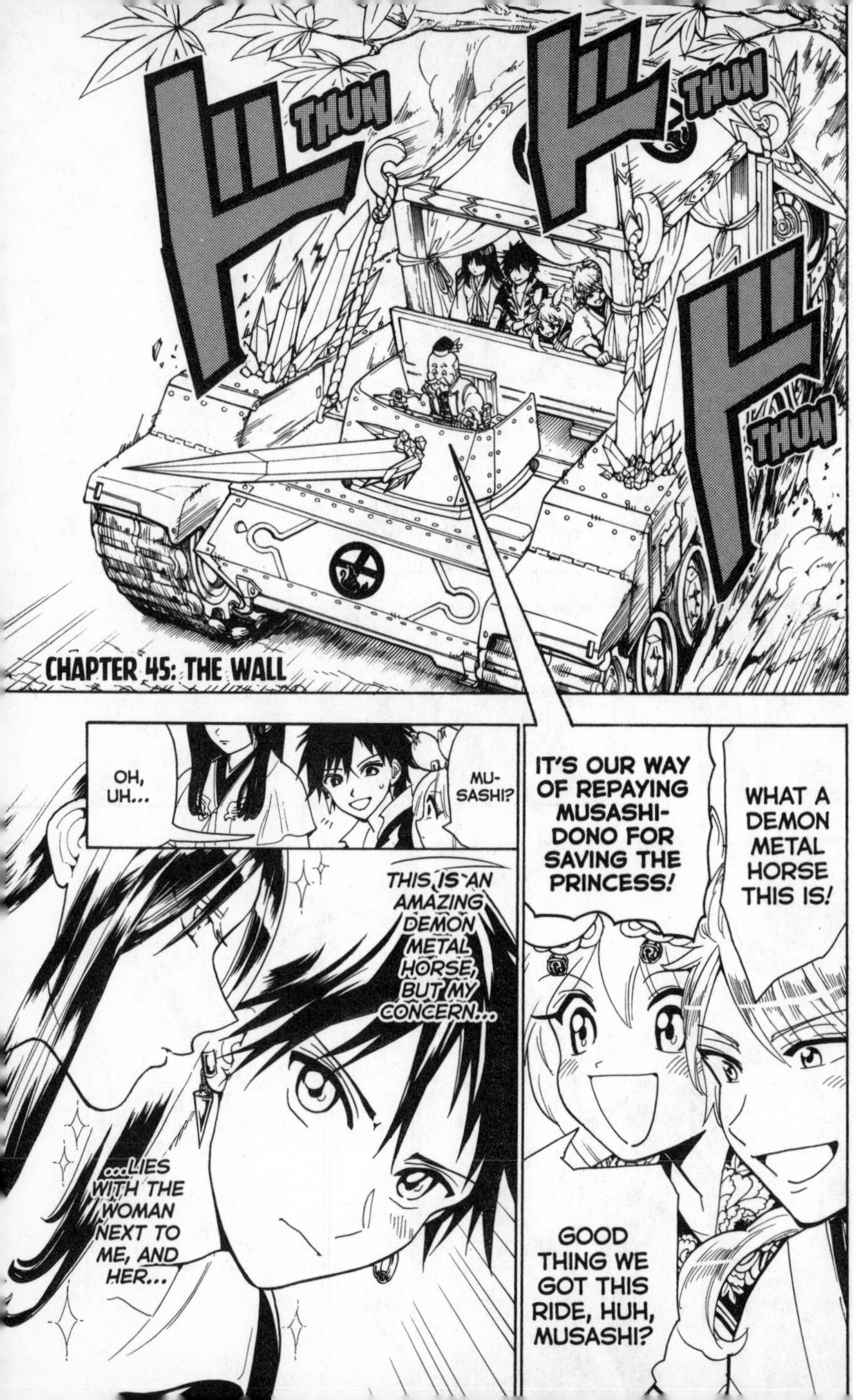
THUN
THUN
THUN
CHAPTER 45: THE WALL
WHAT A DEMON METAL HORSE THIS IS!
IT'S OUR WAY OF REPAYING MUSASHI-DONO FOR SAVING THE PRINCESS!
GOOD THING WE GOT THIS RIDE, HUH, MUSASHI?
MU-SASHI?
OH, UH...
THIS IS AN AMAZING DEMON METAL HORSE, BUT MY CONCERN...
...LIES WITH THE WOMAN NEXT TO ME, AND HER...

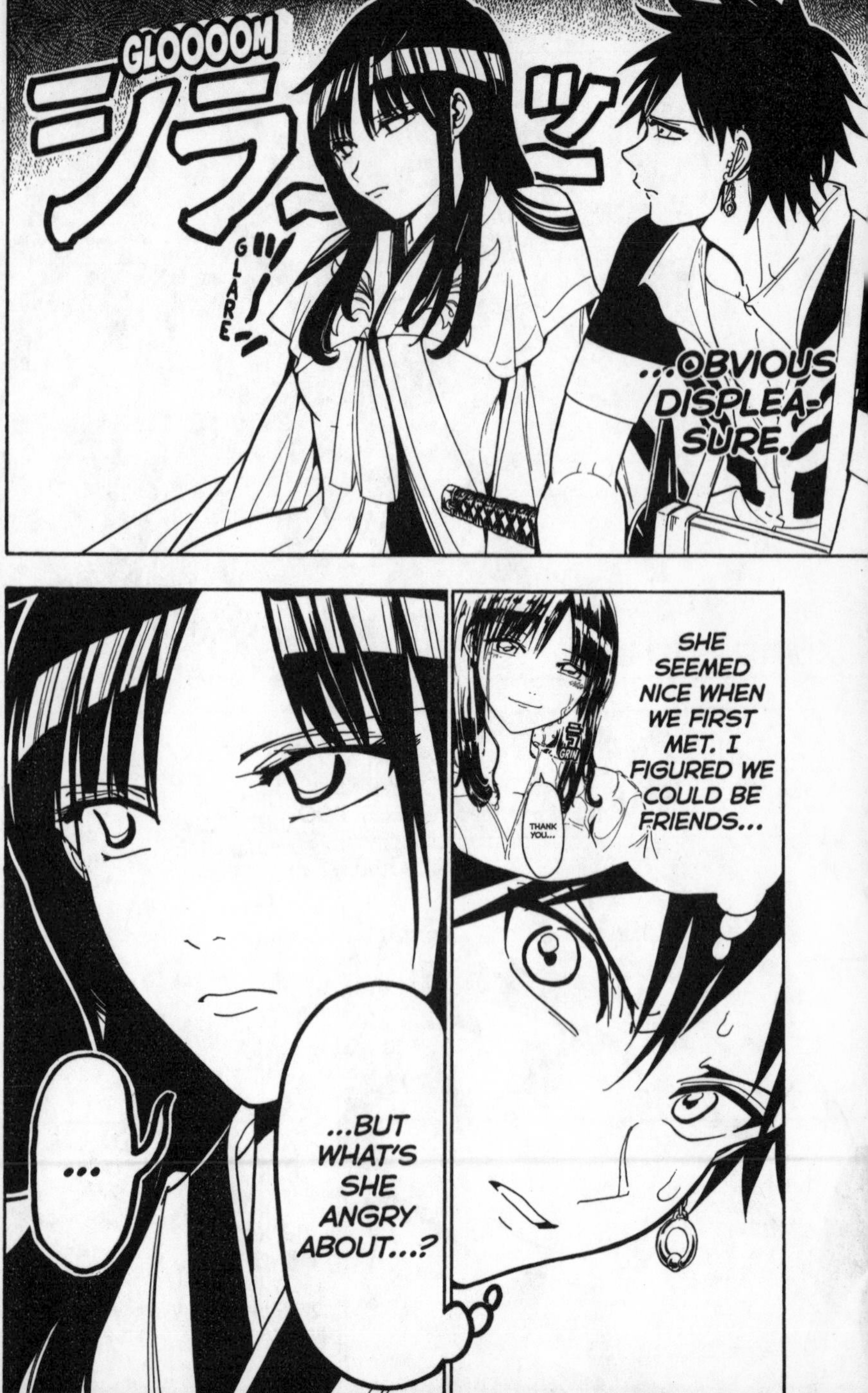
GLOOOM
シラ～ッ
GLARE
...OBVIOUS DISPLEA-SURE.
SHE SEEMED NICE WHEN WE FIRST MET. I FIGURED WE COULD BE FRIENDS...
GRIN
THANK YOU...
...BUT WHAT'S SHE ANGRY ABOUT...?
...

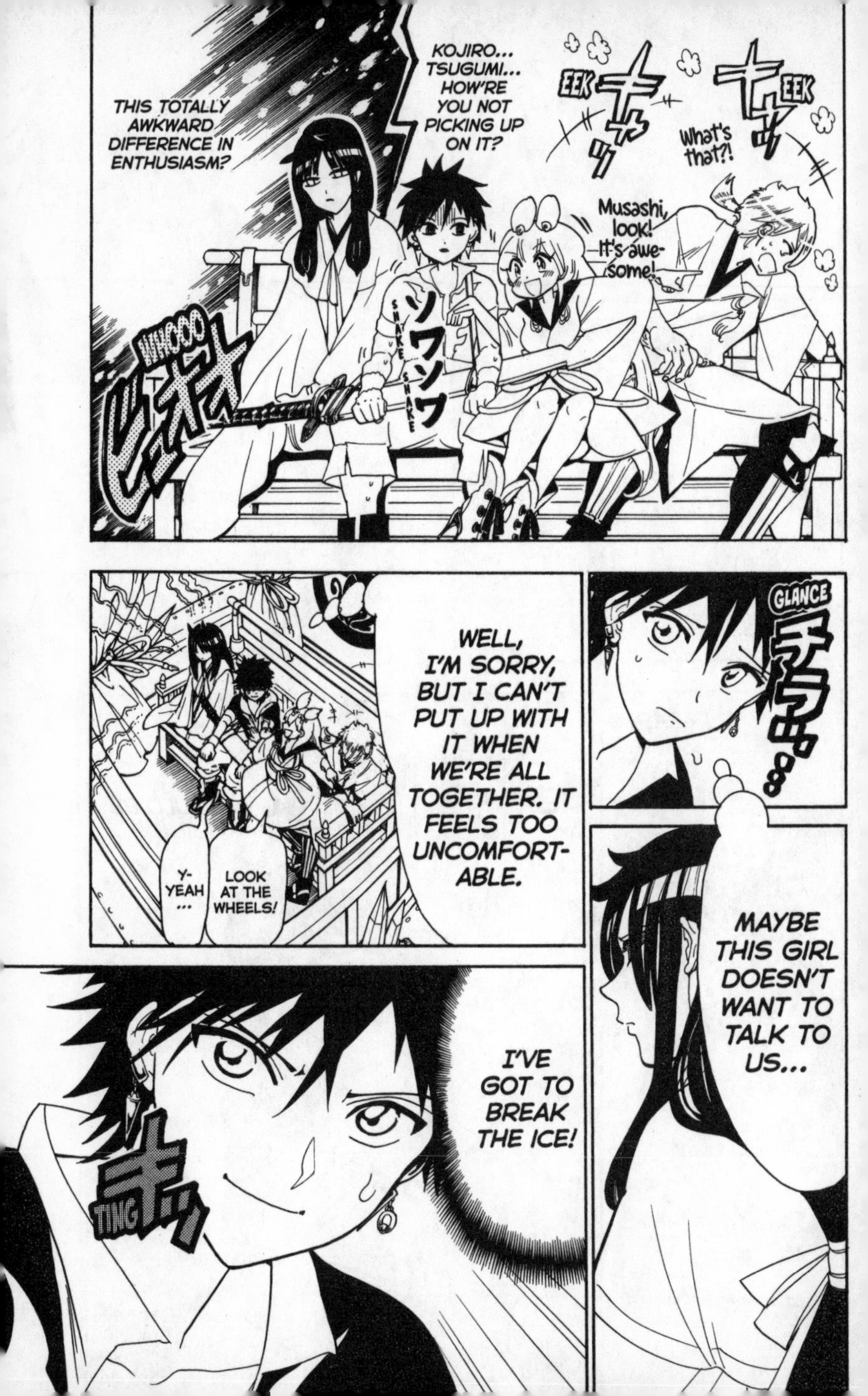
EEK
EEK
What's that?!
Musashi, look! It's awe-some!
KOJIRO... TSUGUMI... HOW'RE YOU NOT PICKING UP ON IT?
THIS TOTALLY AWKWARD DIFFERENCE IN ENTHUSIASM?
SNAKE SNAKE
WHOOO
GLANCE
WELL, I'M SORRY, BUT I CAN'T PUT UP WITH IT WHEN WE'RE ALL TOGETHER. IT FEELS TOO UNCOMFORT-ABLE.
LOOK AT THE WHEELS!
Y-YEAH...
MAYBE THIS GIRL DOESN'T WANT TO TALK TO US...
I'VE GOT TO BREAK THE ICE!
TING

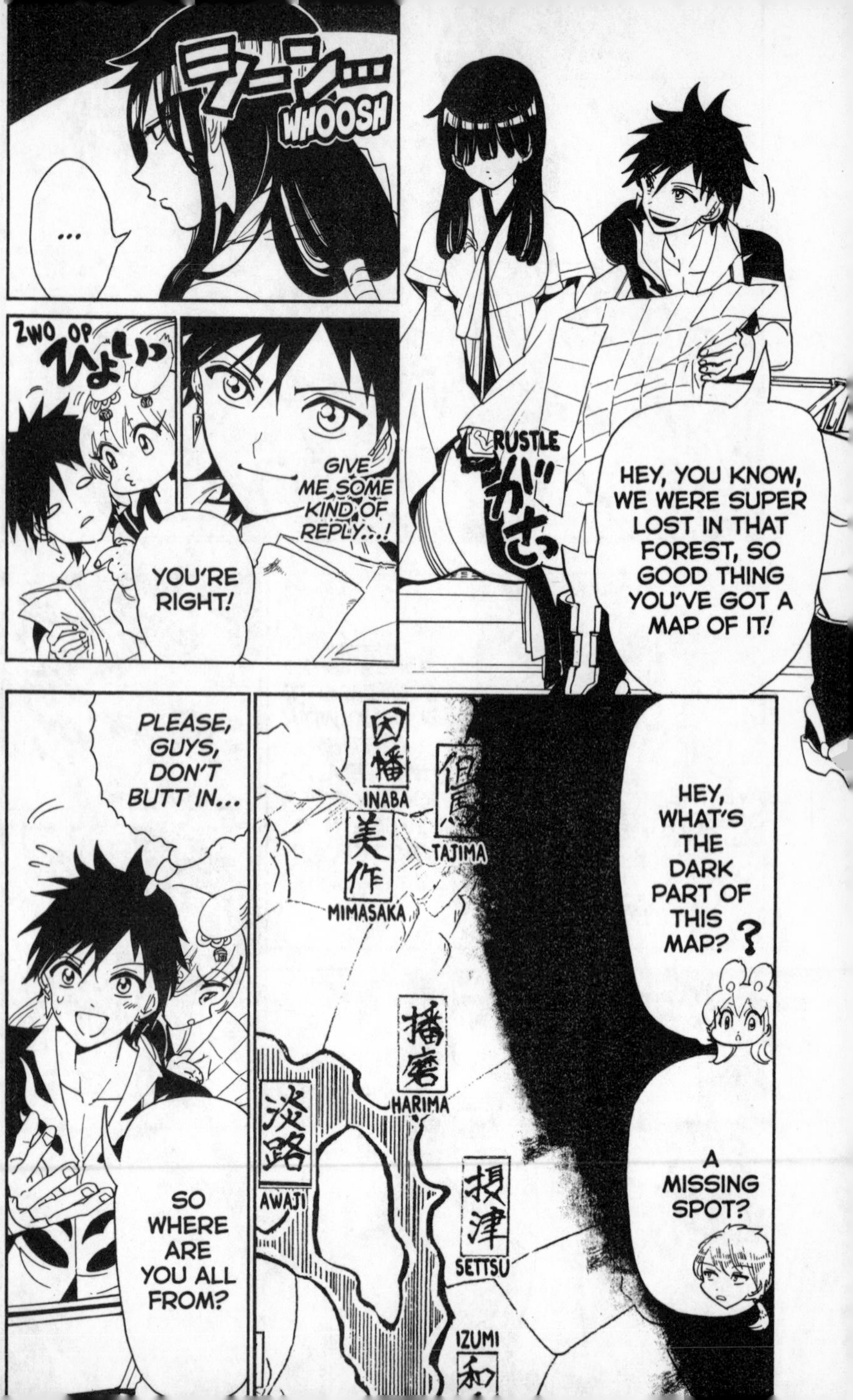
HEY, YOU KNOW, WE WERE SUPER LOST IN THAT FOREST, SO GOOD THING YOU'VE GOT A MAP OF IT!
RUSTLE
がさっ
WHOOSH
...
GIVE ME SOME KIND OF REPLY...!
ZWO OP
YOU'RE RIGHT!
HEY, WHAT'S THE DARK PART OF THIS MAP?
A MISSING SPOT?
但馬
TAJIMA
因幡
INABA
美作
MIMASAKA
播磨
HARIMA
摂津
SETTSU
淡路
AWAJI
IZUMI
PLEASE, GUYS, DON'T BUTT IN...
SO WHERE ARE YOU ALL FROM?

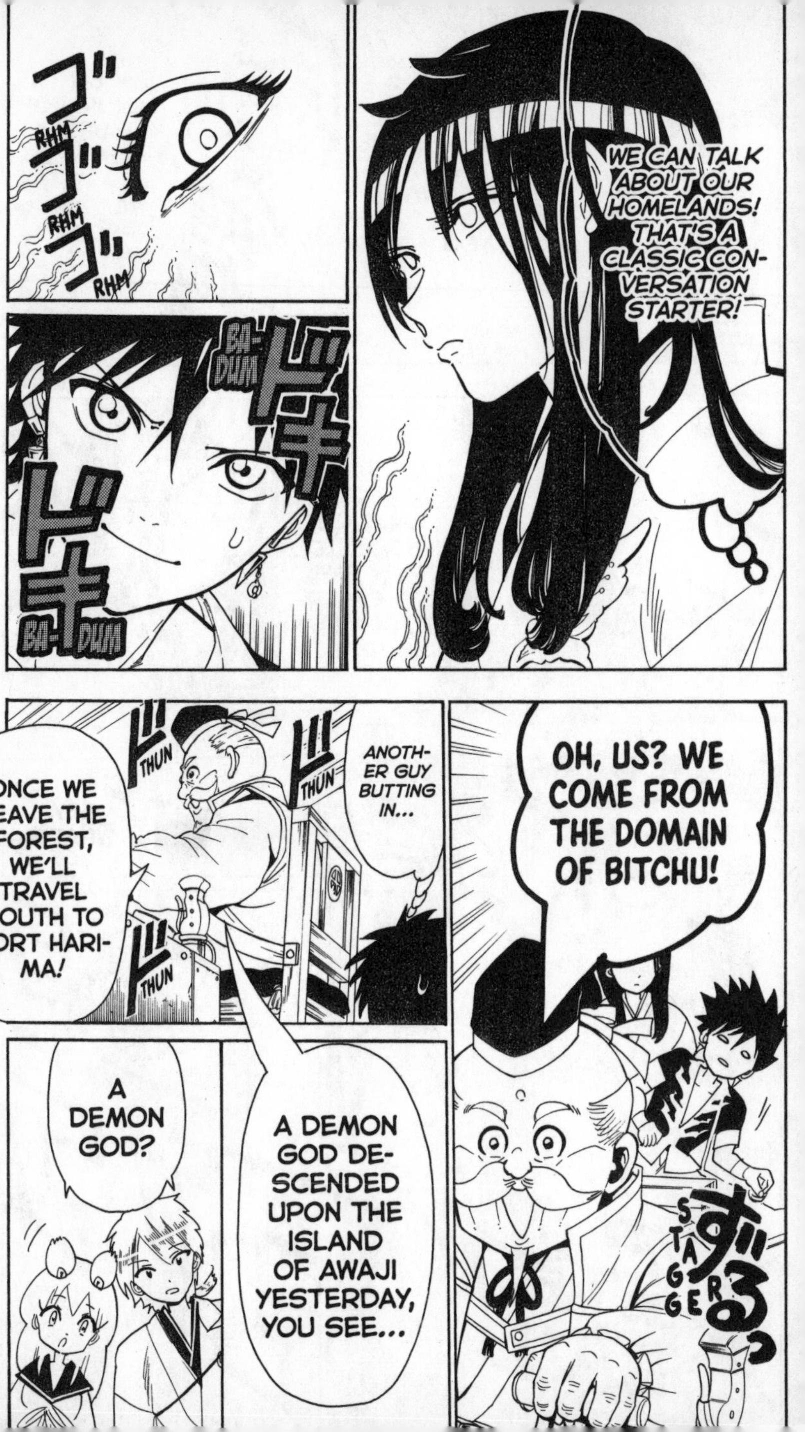
WE CAN TALK ABOUT OUR HOMELANDS! THAT'S A CLASSIC CON-VERSATION STARTER!
ゴゴゴ
RHM RHM RHM
ドキドキ
BA-DUM BA-DUM
OH, US? WE COME FROM THE DOMAIN OF BITCHU!
ドドド
THUN THUN THUN
ANOTH-ER GUY BUTTING IN...
ONCE WE LEAVE THE FOREST, WE'LL TRAVEL SOUTH TO PORT HARI-MA!
ずるっ
STAGGER
A DEMON GOD DE-SCENDED UPON THE ISLAND OF AWAJI YESTERDAY, YOU SEE...
A DEMON GOD?

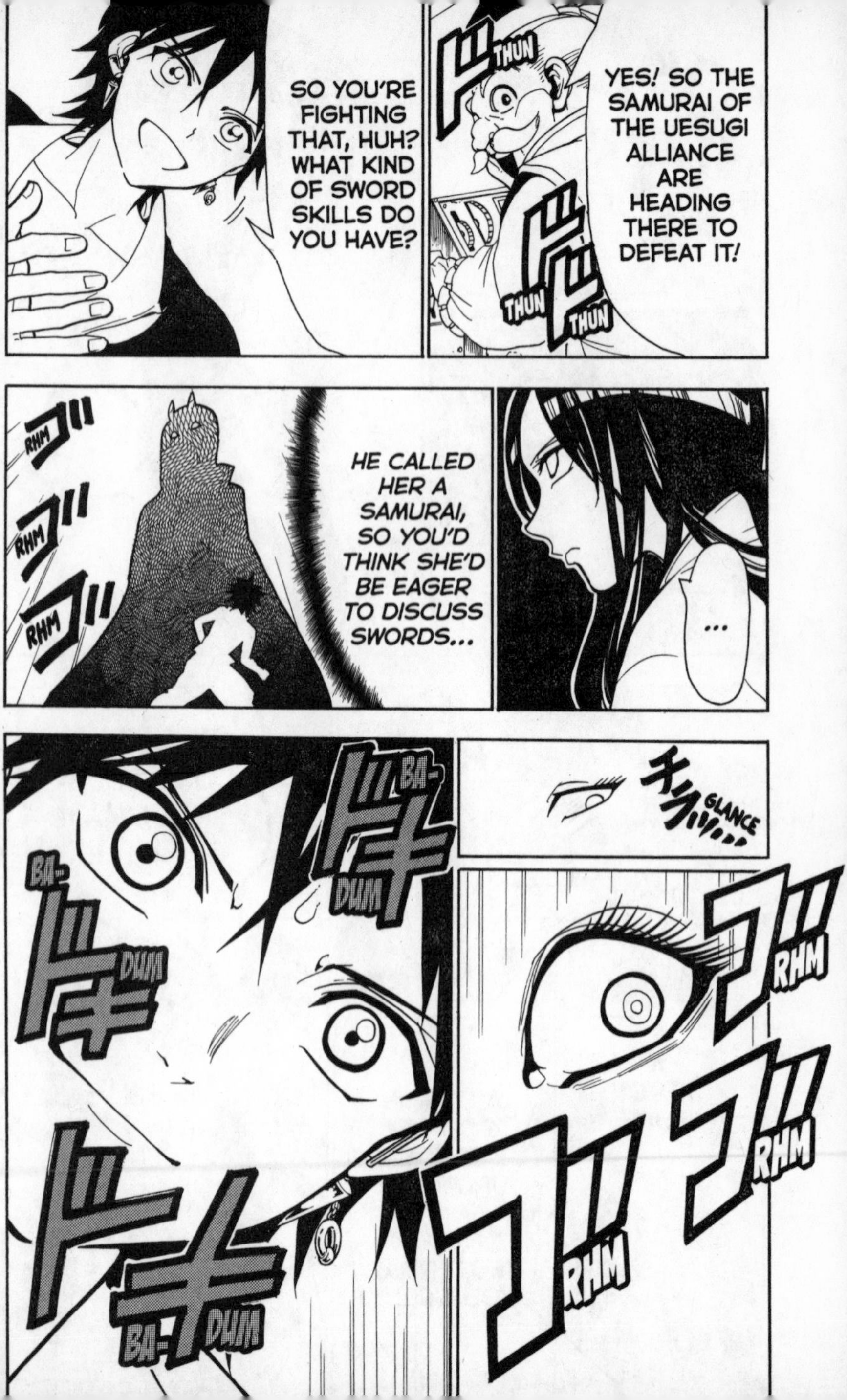
THUN
YES! SO THE SAMURAI OF THE UESUGI ALLIANCE ARE HEADING THERE TO DEFEAT IT!
THUN
THUN
SO YOU'RE FIGHTING THAT, HUH? WHAT KIND OF SWORD SKILLS DO YOU HAVE?
...
HE CALLED HER A SAMURAI, SO YOU'D THINK SHE'D BE EAGER TO DISCUSS SWORDS...
RHM
RHM
RHM
GLANCE
RHM
RHM
RHM
BA-DUM
BA-DUM
BA-DUM

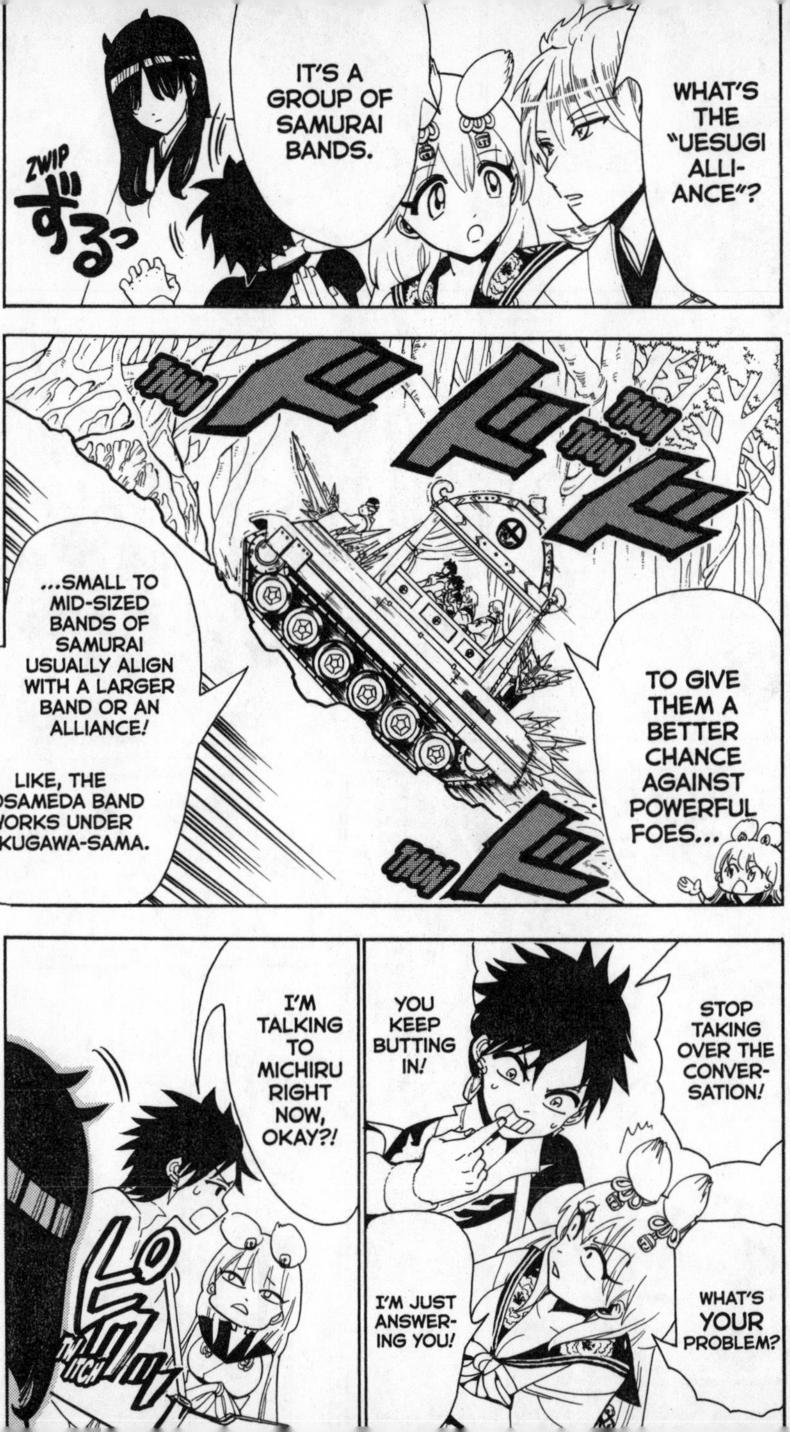
WHAT'S THE "UESUGI ALLI-ANCE"?
IT'S A GROUP OF SAMURAI BANDS.
ZWIP
ずるっ
THUD
THUD
THUD
THUD
TO GIVE THEM A BETTER CHANCE AGAINST POWERFUL FOES...
...SMALL TO MID-SIZED BANDS OF SAMURAI USUALLY ALIGN WITH A LARGER BAND OR AN ALLIANCE!
LIKE, THE KOSAMEDA BAND WORKS UNDER TOKUGAWA-SAMA.
STOP TAKING OVER THE CONVER-SATION!
YOU KEEP BUTTING IN!
WHAT'S YOUR PROBLEM?
I'M JUST ANSWER-ING YOU!
I'M TALKING TO MICHIRU RIGHT NOW, OKAY?!
TWITCH

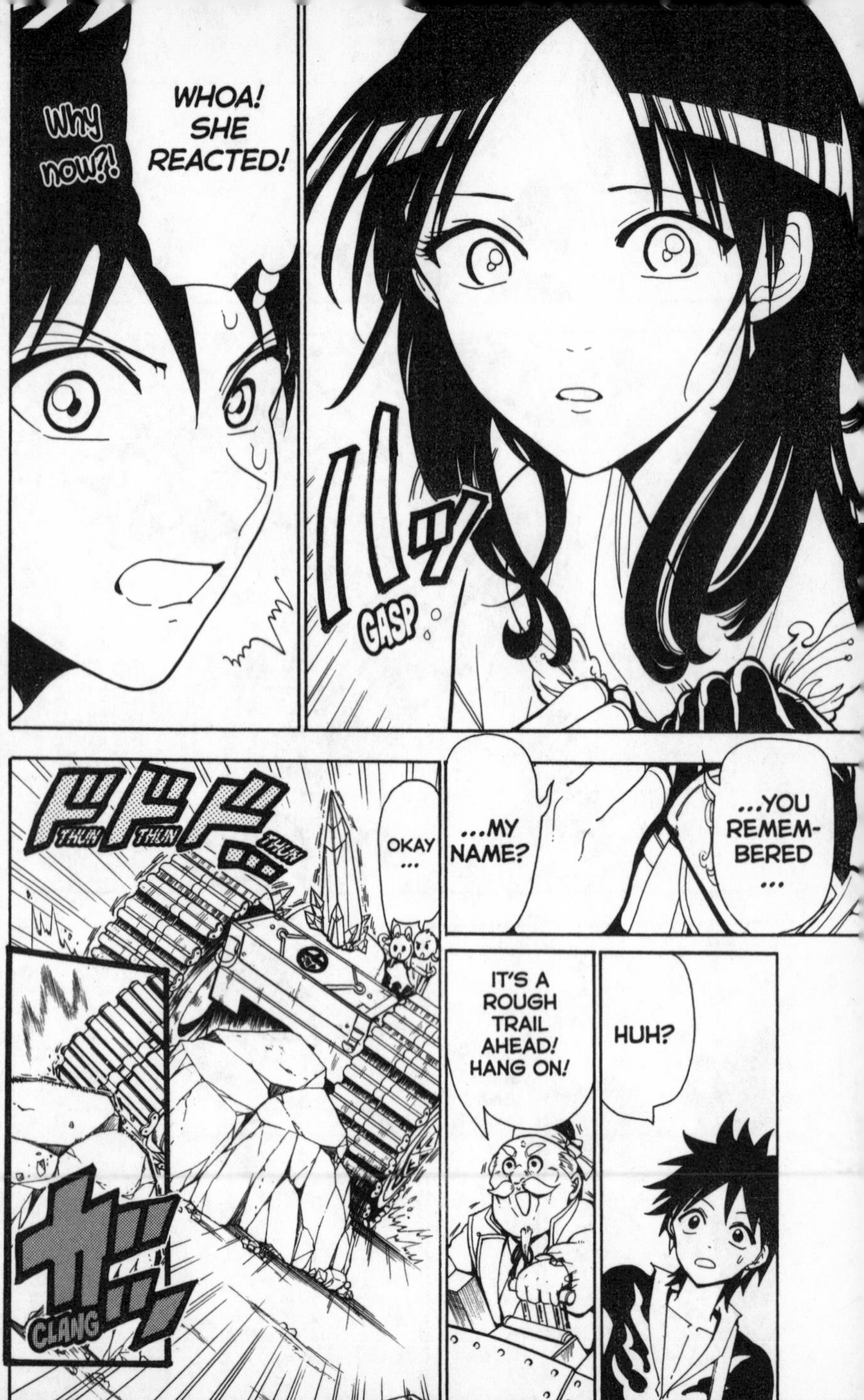
GASP
WHOA! SHE REACTED!
Why now?!
...YOU REMEMBERED...
...MY NAME?
OKAY...
HUH?
IT'S A ROUGH TRAIL AHEAD! HANG ON!
THUN THUN THUN
CLANG

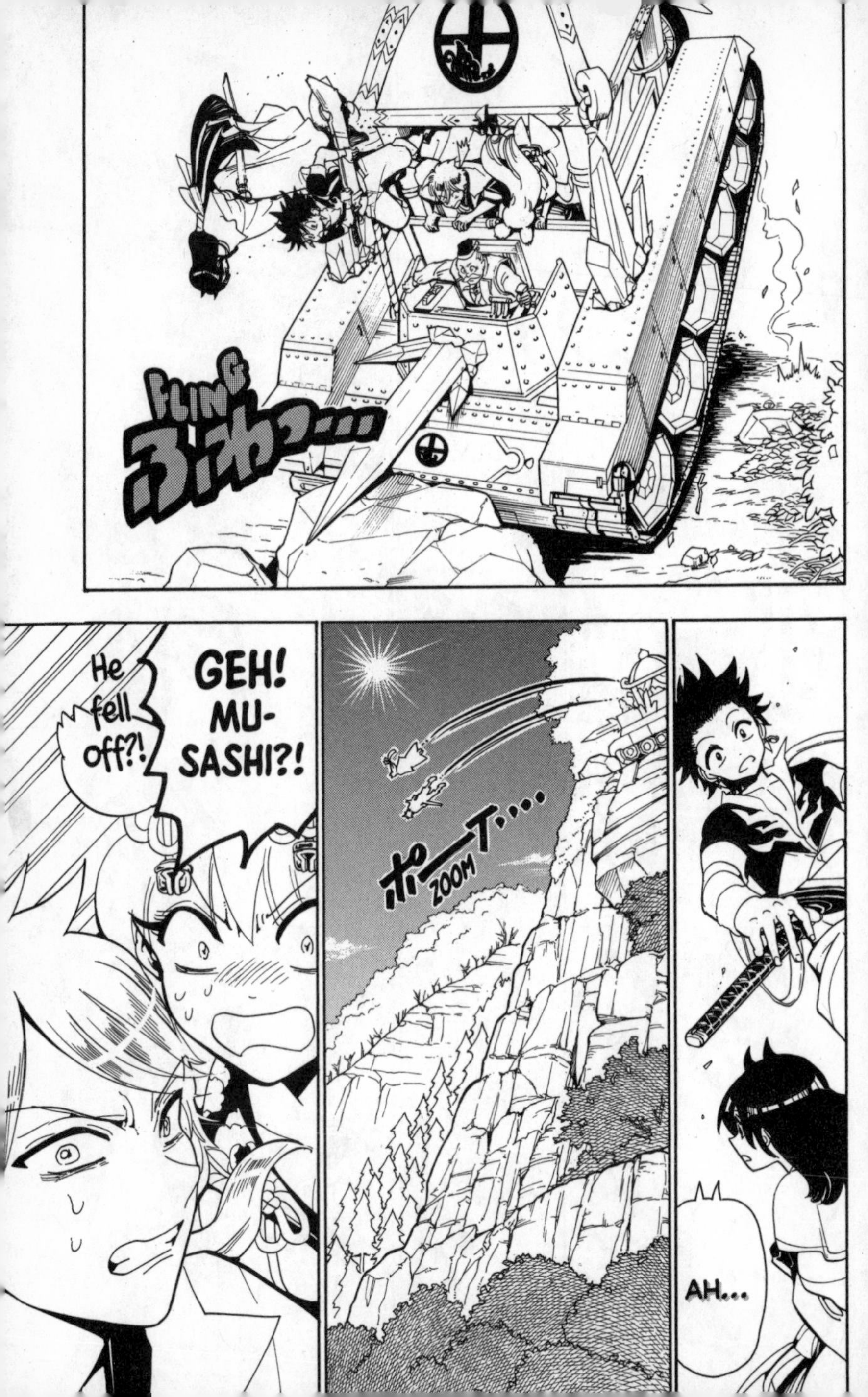
FLING
ふわっ…
AH...
ポ—ン…
ZOOM
GEH! MU-SASHI?!
He fell off?!

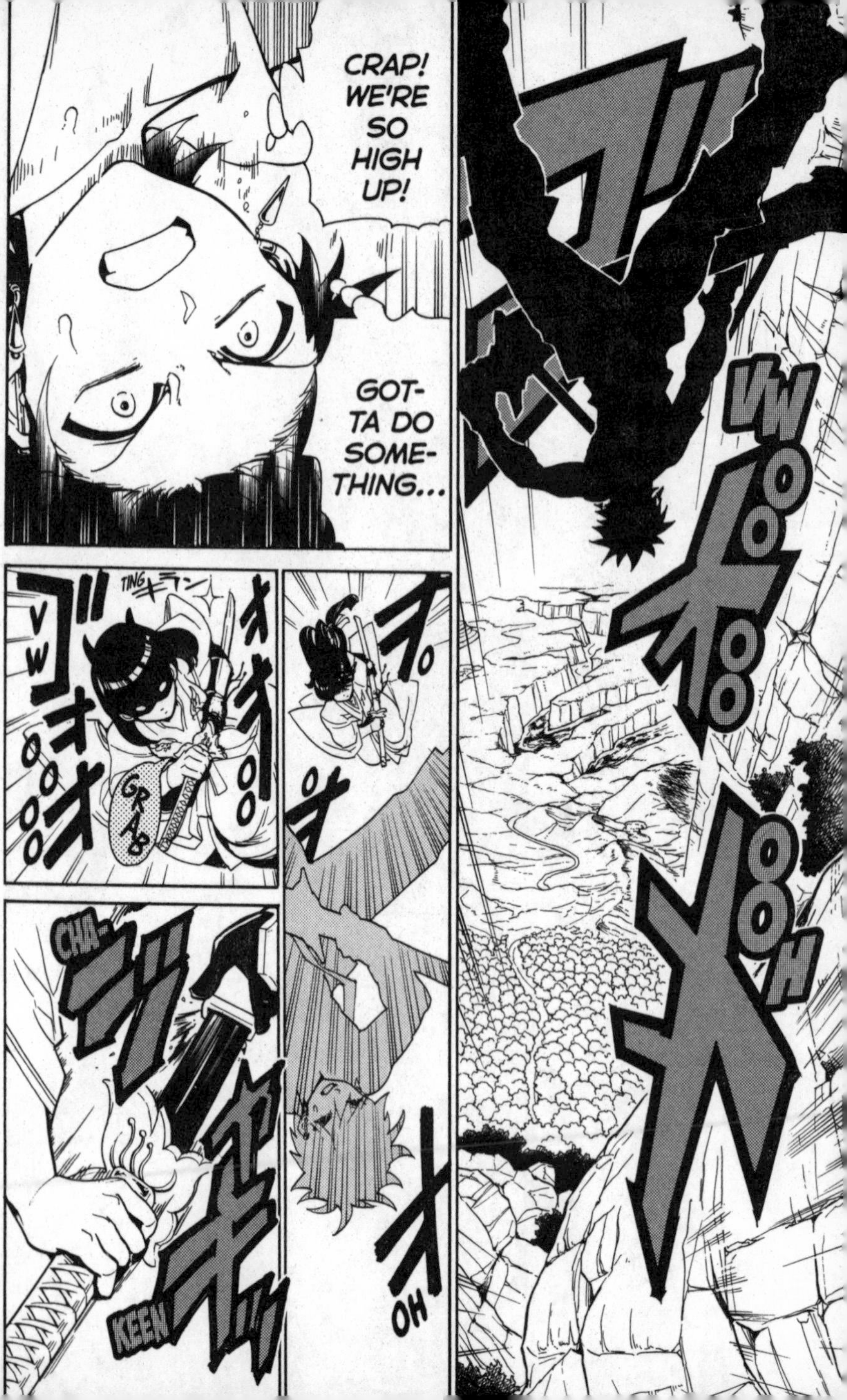
VWOOOOOOOOH
CRAP! WE'RE SO HIGH UP!
GOT-TA DO SOME-THING...
OH
TING
VWOOOOOOO
GRAB
CHA-
KEEN

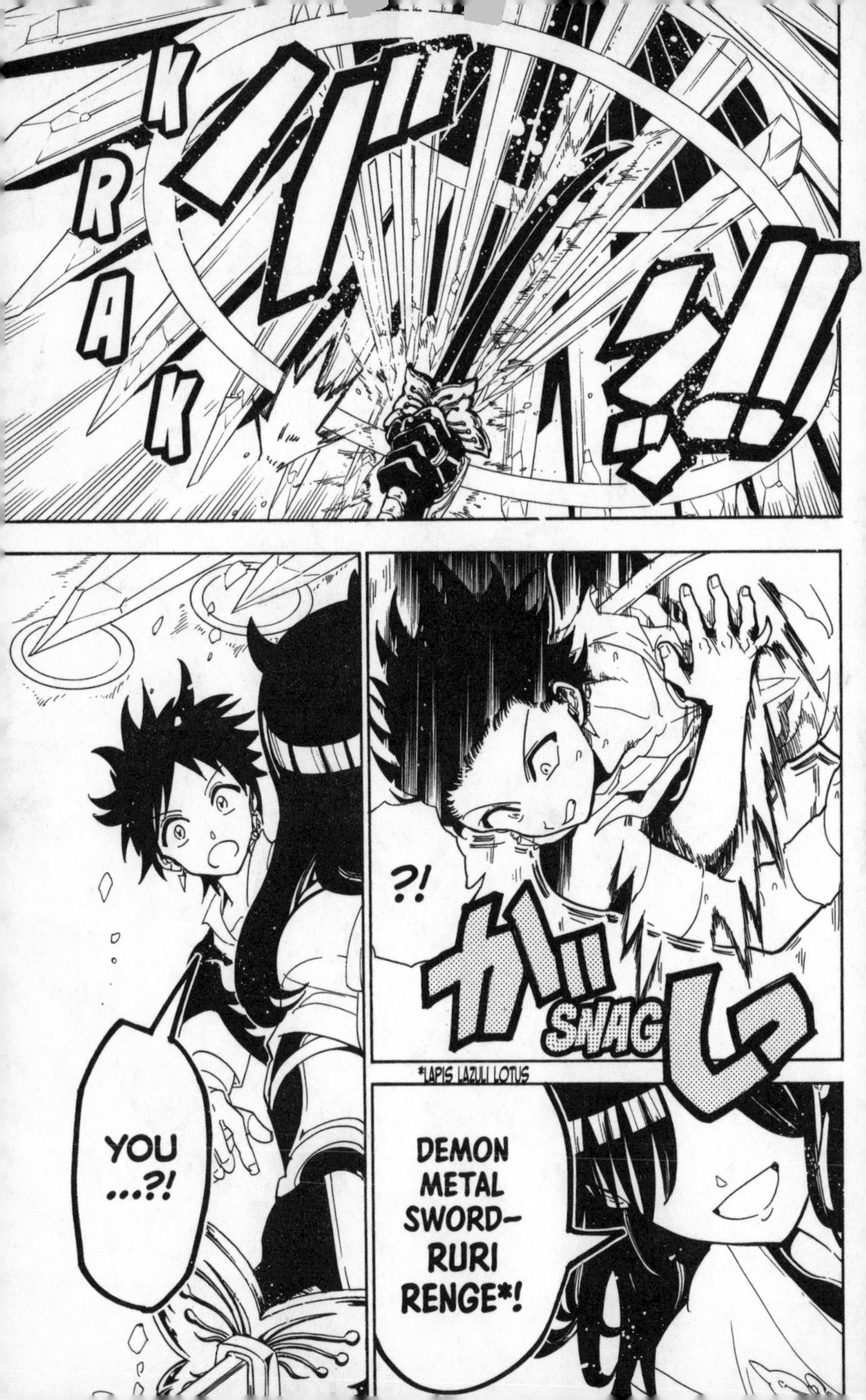
KRAK
?!
SNAG
DEMON METAL SWORD-RURI RENGE*!
*LAPIS LAZULI LOTUS
YOU ...?!

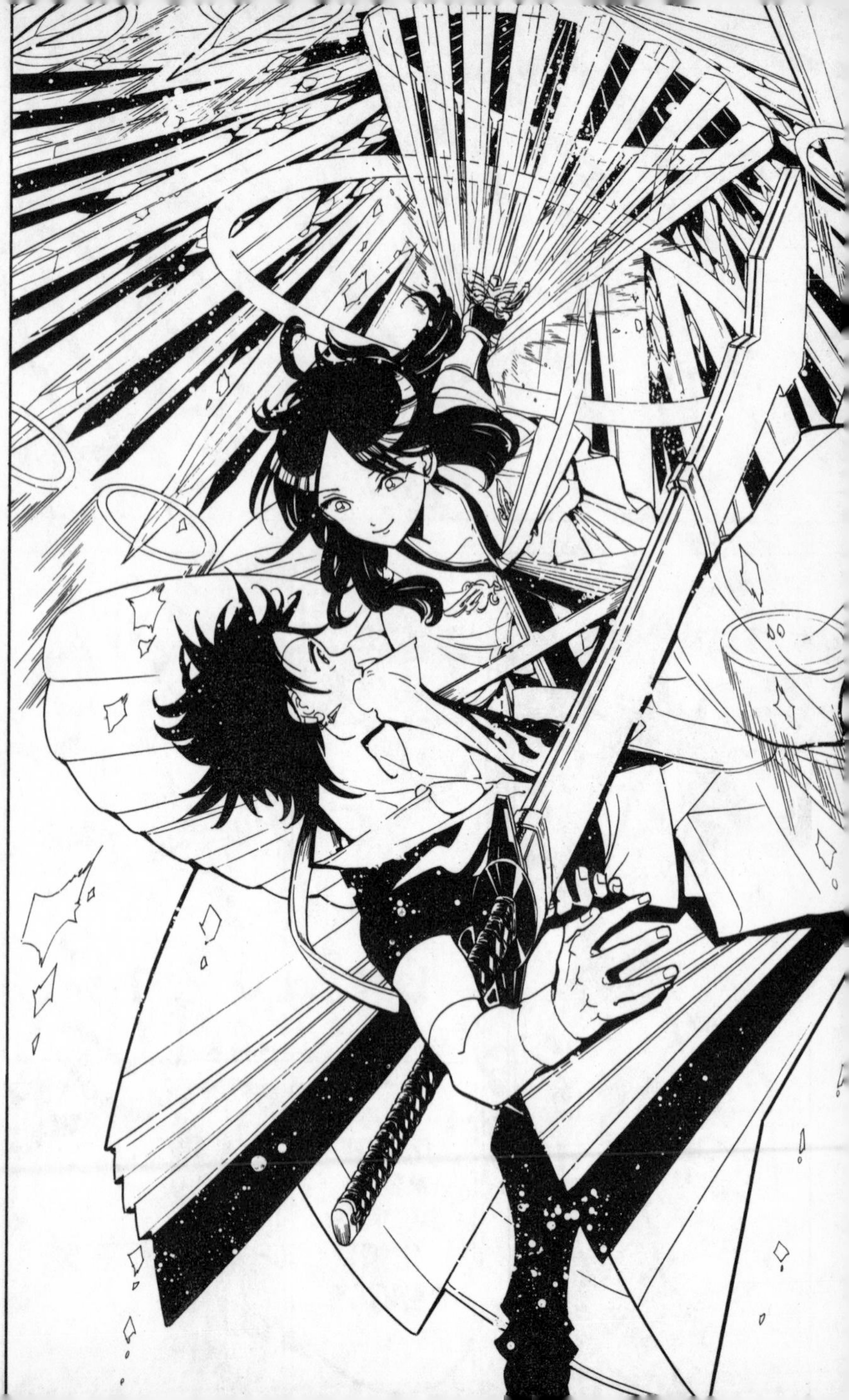

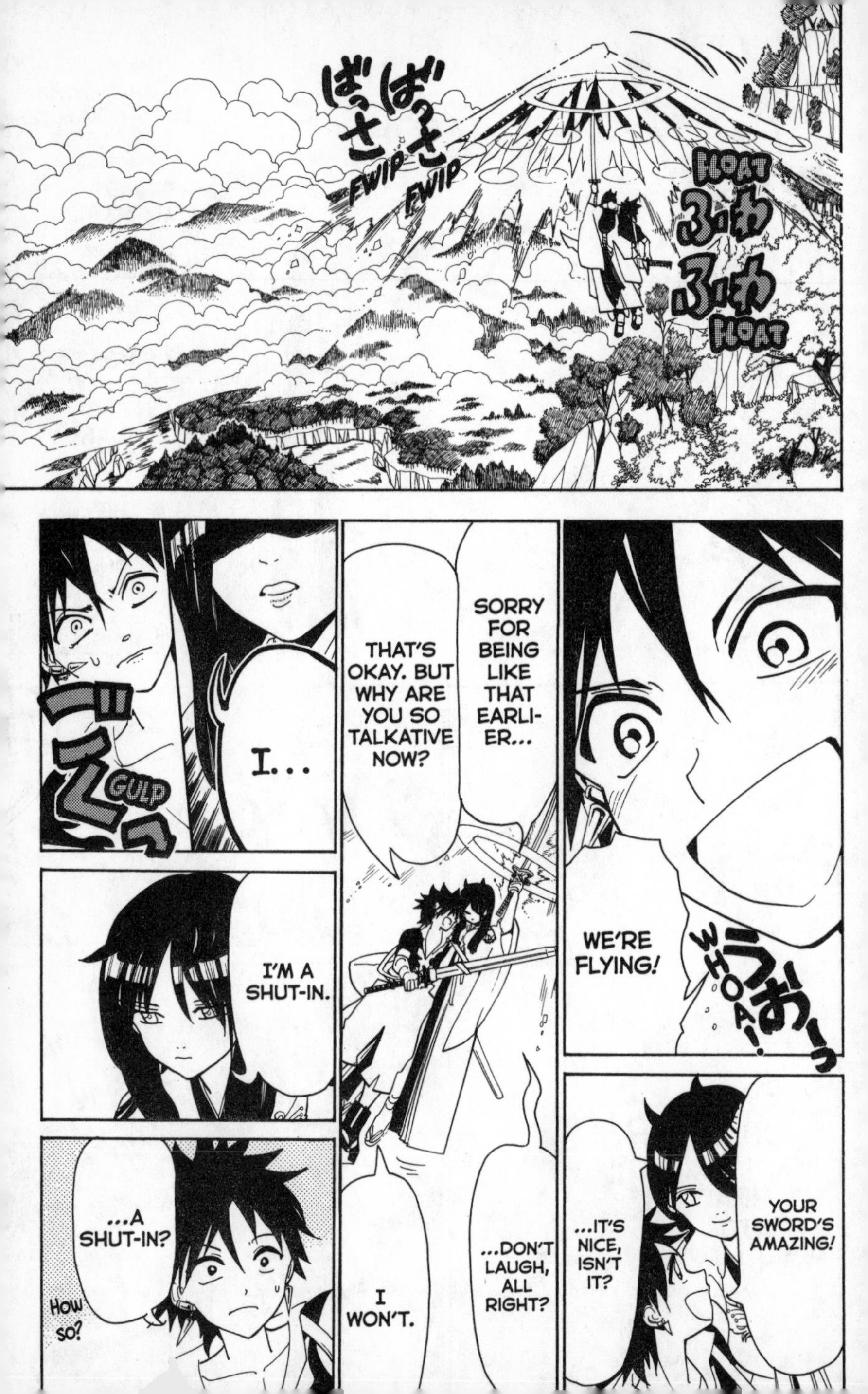
FLOAT
ふわ
ふわ
FLOAT
ばっさ
ばっさ
FWIP
FWIP
WE'RE FLYING!
うおーっ
WHOA!
YOUR SWORD'S AMAZING!
...IT'S NICE, ISN'T IT?
SORRY FOR BEING LIKE THAT EARLIER...
THAT'S OKAY. BUT WHY ARE YOU SO TALKATIVE NOW?
...DON'T LAUGH, ALL RIGHT?
I WON'T.
I...
ごくっ
GULP
I'M A SHUT-IN.
...A SHUT-IN?
HOW SO?

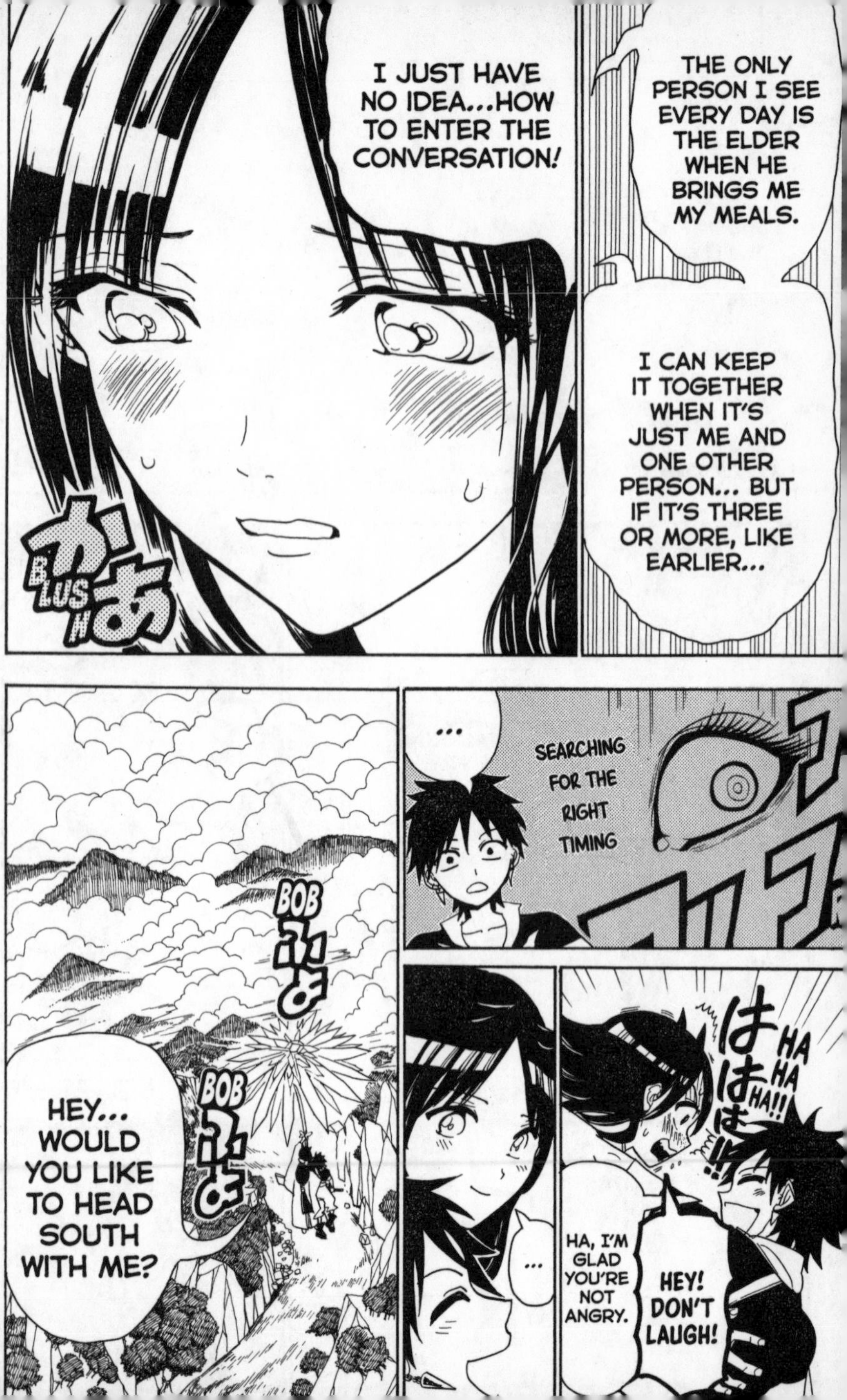
THE ONLY PERSON I SEE EVERY DAY IS THE ELDER WHEN HE BRINGS ME MY MEALS.
I CAN KEEP IT TOGETHER WHEN IT'S JUST ME AND ONE OTHER PERSON... BUT IF IT'S THREE OR MORE, LIKE EARLIER...
I JUST HAVE NO IDEA...HOW TO ENTER THE CONVERSATION!
かあ
BLUSH
...
SEARCHING FOR THE RIGHT TIMING
ははは!!
HA HA HA!!
HEY! DON'T LAUGH!
HA, I'M GLAD YOU'RE NOT ANGRY.
...
BOB
ふよ
BOB
ふよ
HEY... WOULD YOU LIKE TO HEAD SOUTH WITH ME?

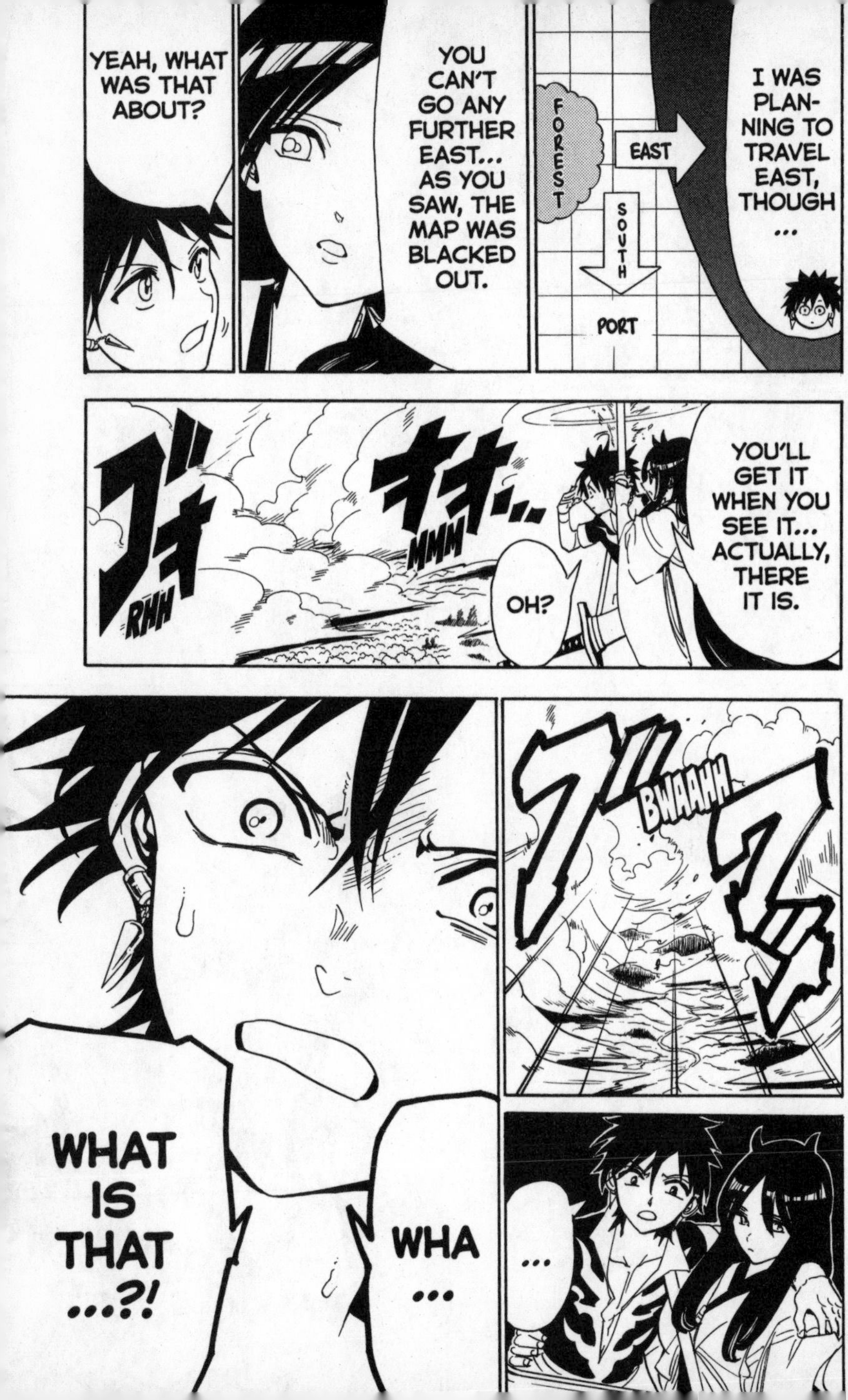
I WAS PLAN-NING TO TRAVEL EAST, THOUGH ...
FOREST
EAST
SOUTH
PORT
YOU CAN'T GO ANY FURTHER EAST... AS YOU SAW, THE MAP WAS BLACKED OUT.
YEAH, WHAT WAS THAT ABOUT?
YOU'LL GET IT WHEN YOU SEE IT... ACTUALLY, THERE IT IS.
OH?
MMM
RHH
BWAAHH
...
WHA ...
WHAT IS THAT ...?!

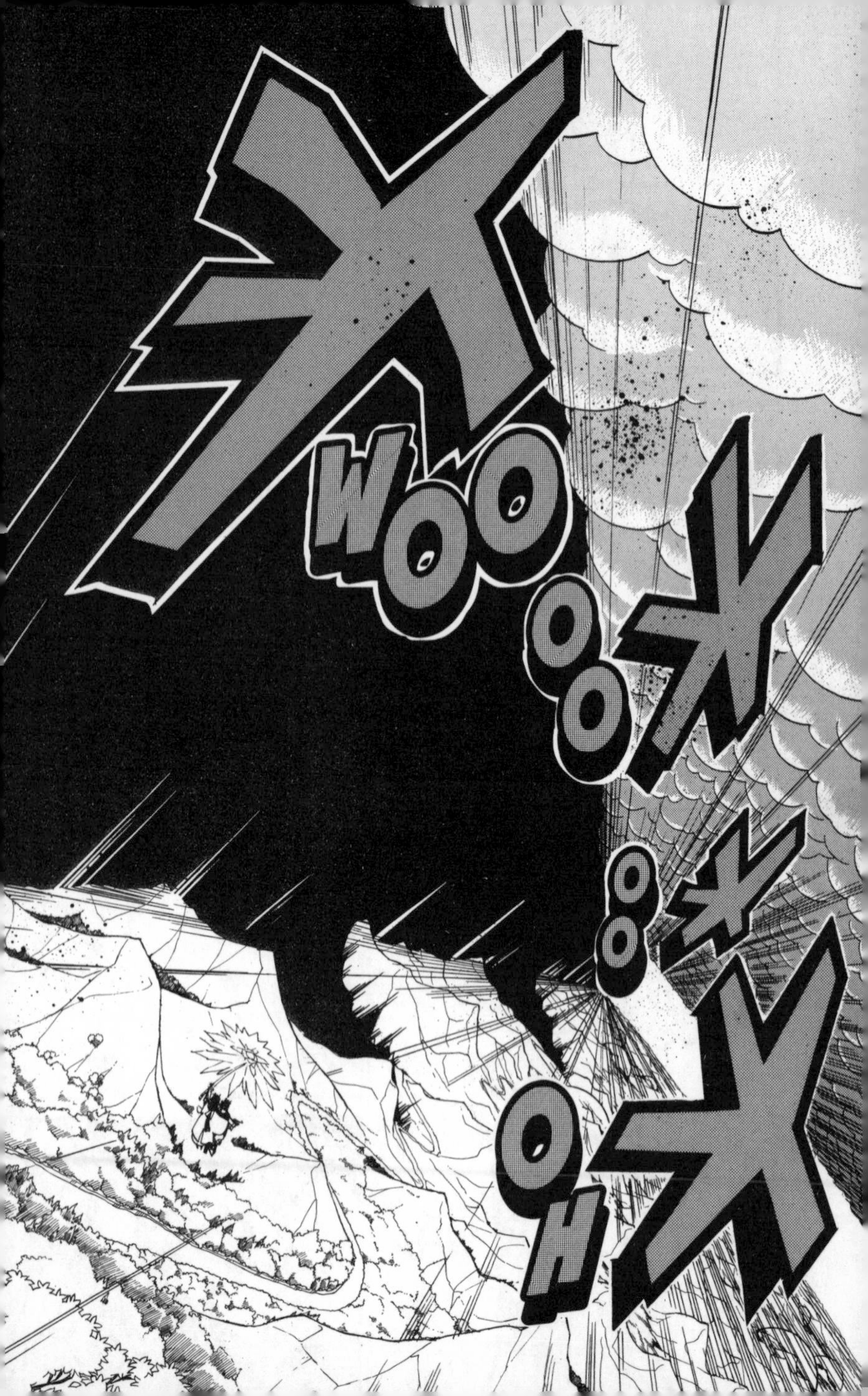
WOOOOOOOOH

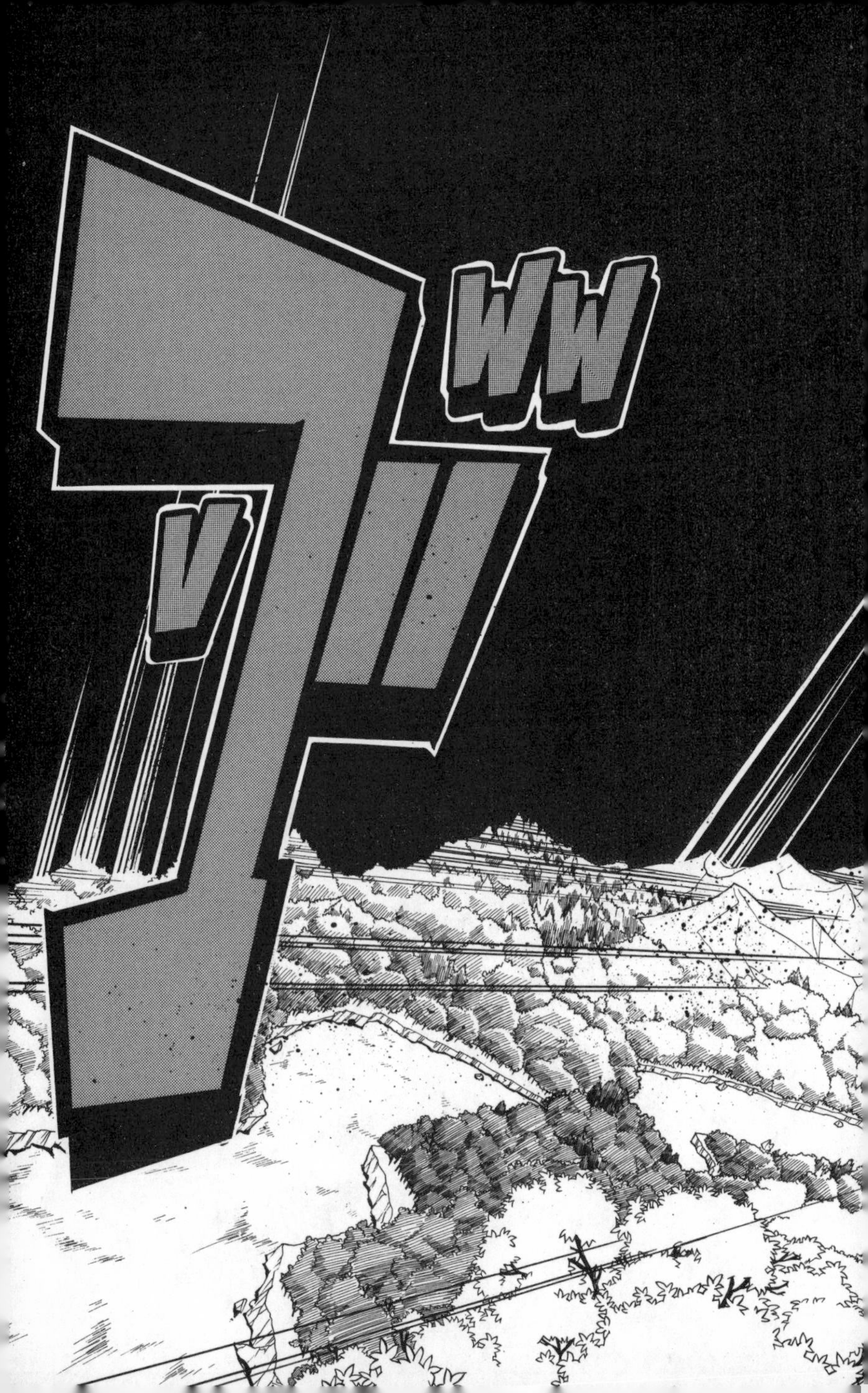
VWW

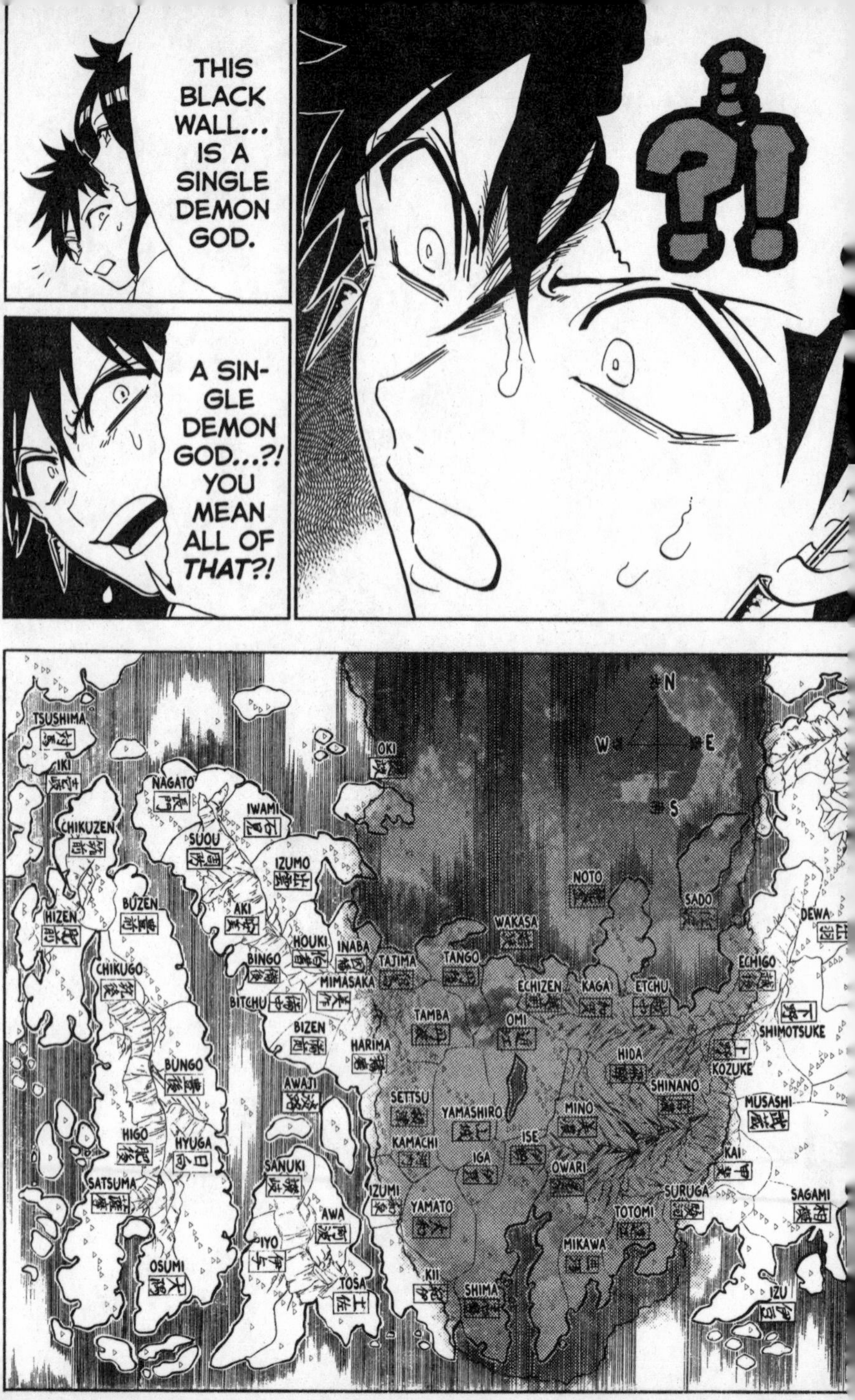
?!
THIS BLACK WALL... IS A SINGLE DEMON GOD.
A SINGLE DEMON GOD...?! YOU MEAN ALL OF *THAT*?!
N
W
E
S
DEWA
SADO
NOTO
SHIMOTSUKE
ECHIGO
ETCHU
KAGA
ECHIZEN
WAKASA
TANGO
TAJIMA
OKI
KOZUKE
HIDA
OMI
TAMBA
MUSASHI
SHINANO
MINO
YAMASHIRO
SETTSU
KAI
ISE
IGA
KAMACHI
SAGAMI
SURUGA
OWARI
TOTOMI
MIKAWA
YAMATO
IZUMI
IZU
SHIMA
KII
INABA
HOUKI
MIMASAKA
HARIMA
BIZEN
BITCHU
BINGO
IZUMO
IWAMI
AKI
SUOU
NAGATO
AWAJI
SANUKI
AWA
IYO
TOSA
BUZEN
BUNGO
HYUGA
HIGO
OSUMI
SATSUMA
CHIKUGO
HIZEN
CHIKUZEN
IKI
TSUSHIMA

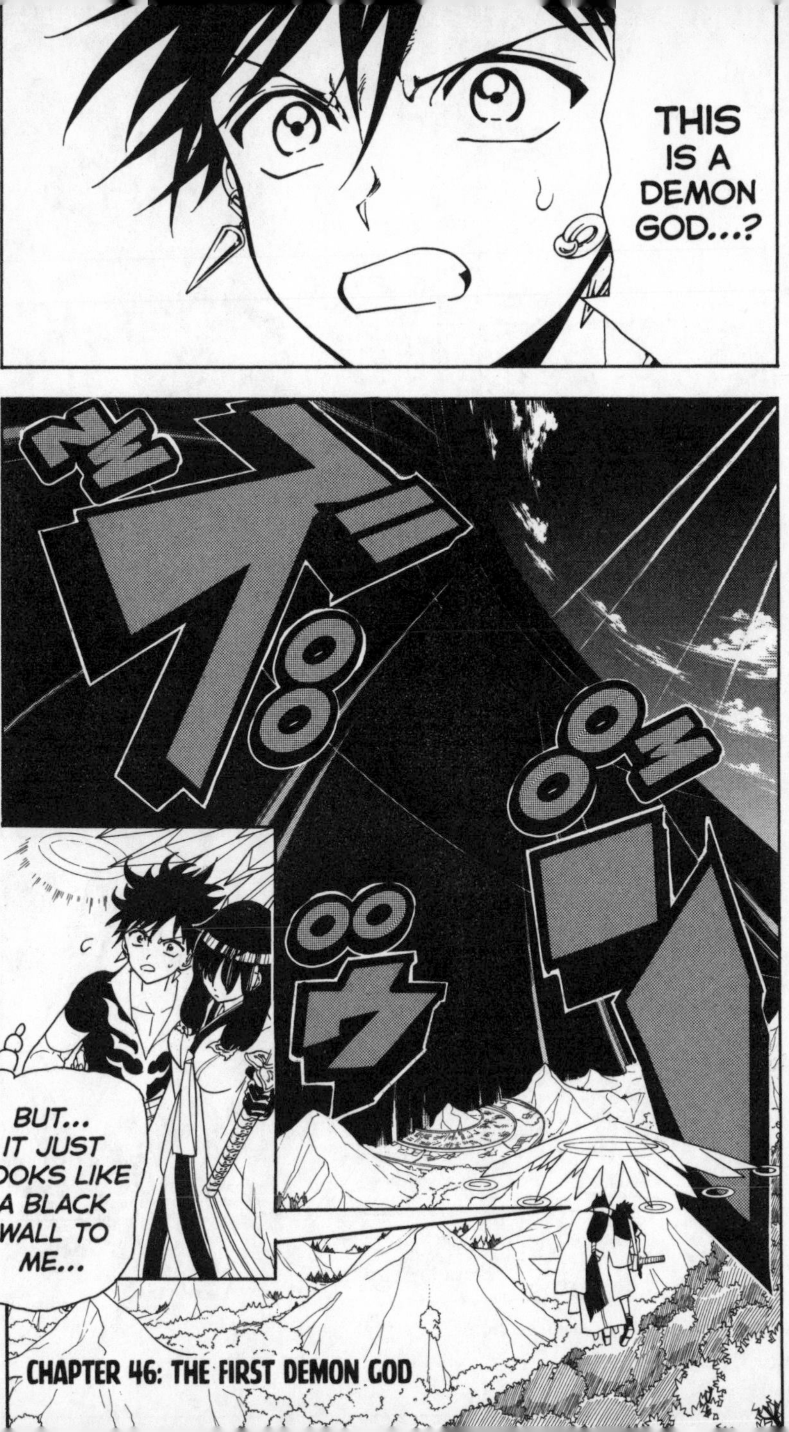
THIS IS A DEMON GOD...?
ZZOOOOM
BUT... IT JUST LOOKS LIKE A BLACK WALL TO ME...
CHAPTER 46: THE FIRST DEMON GOD

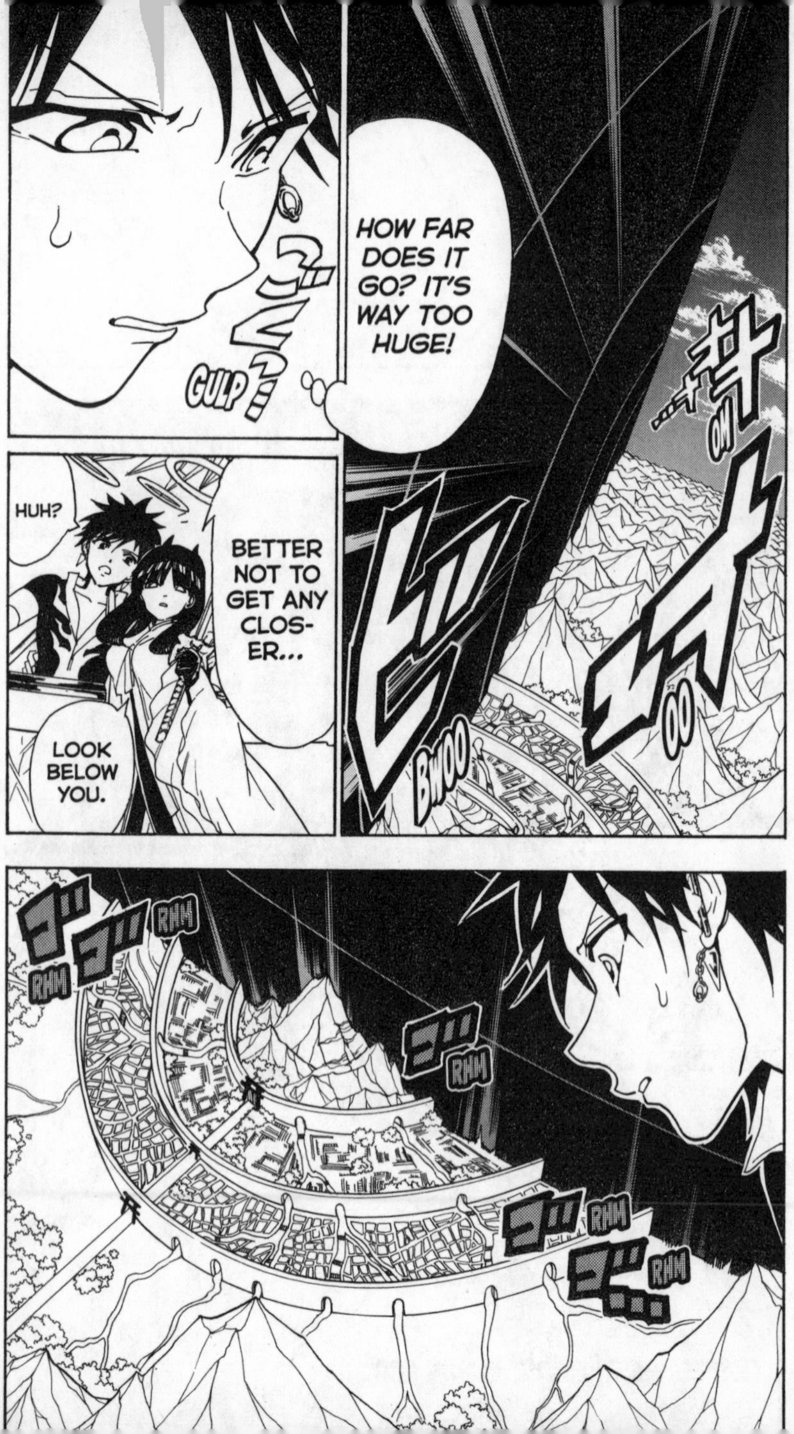
HOW FAR DOES IT GO? IT'S WAY TOO HUGE!
OM
BWOO
GULP
BETTER NOT TO GET ANY CLOS-ER...
HUH?
LOOK BELOW YOU.
RMM
RMM
RMM
RMM
RMM
RMM

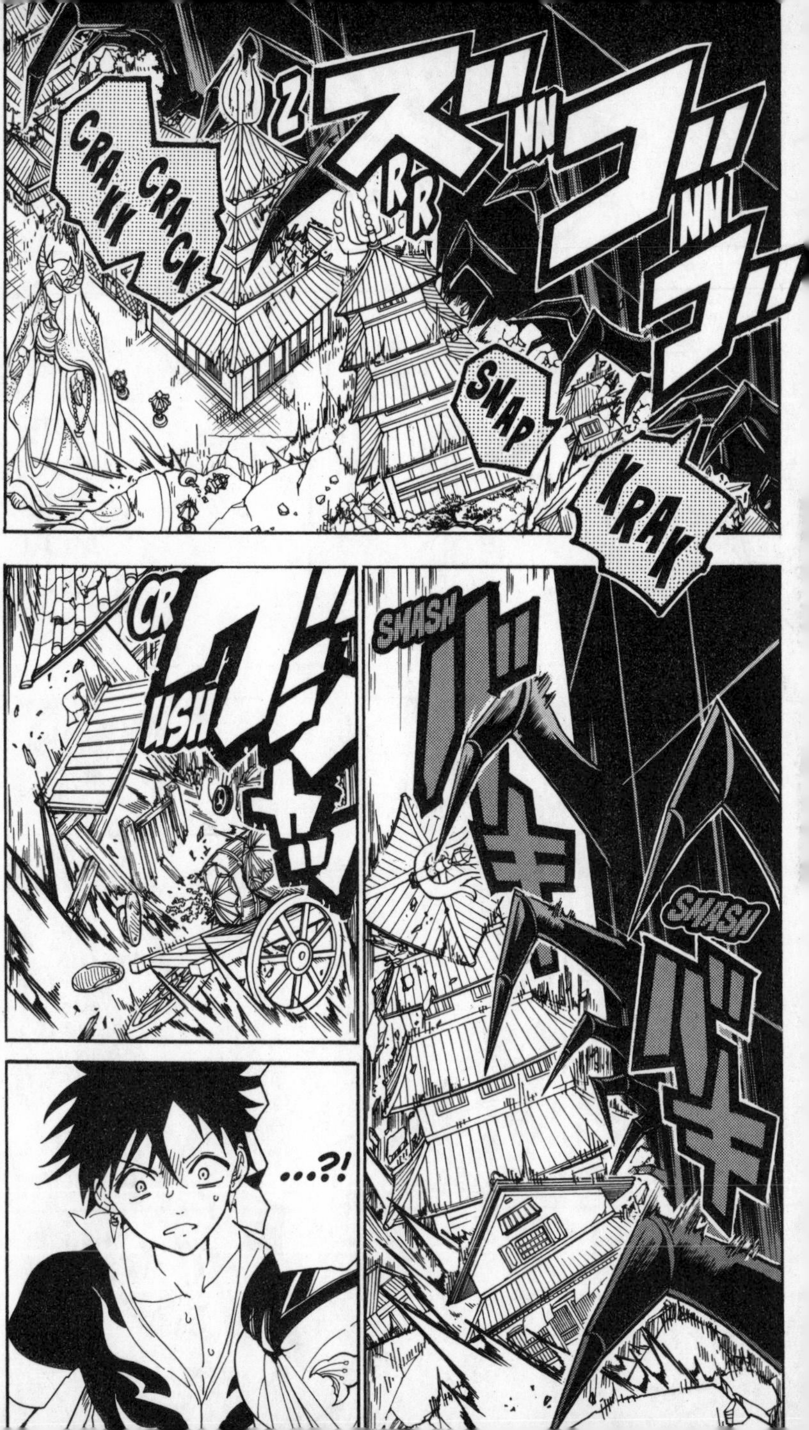
Z
RR
NN
NN
SNAP
KRAK
CRACK CRACK
SMASH
SMASH
CR
USH
...?!

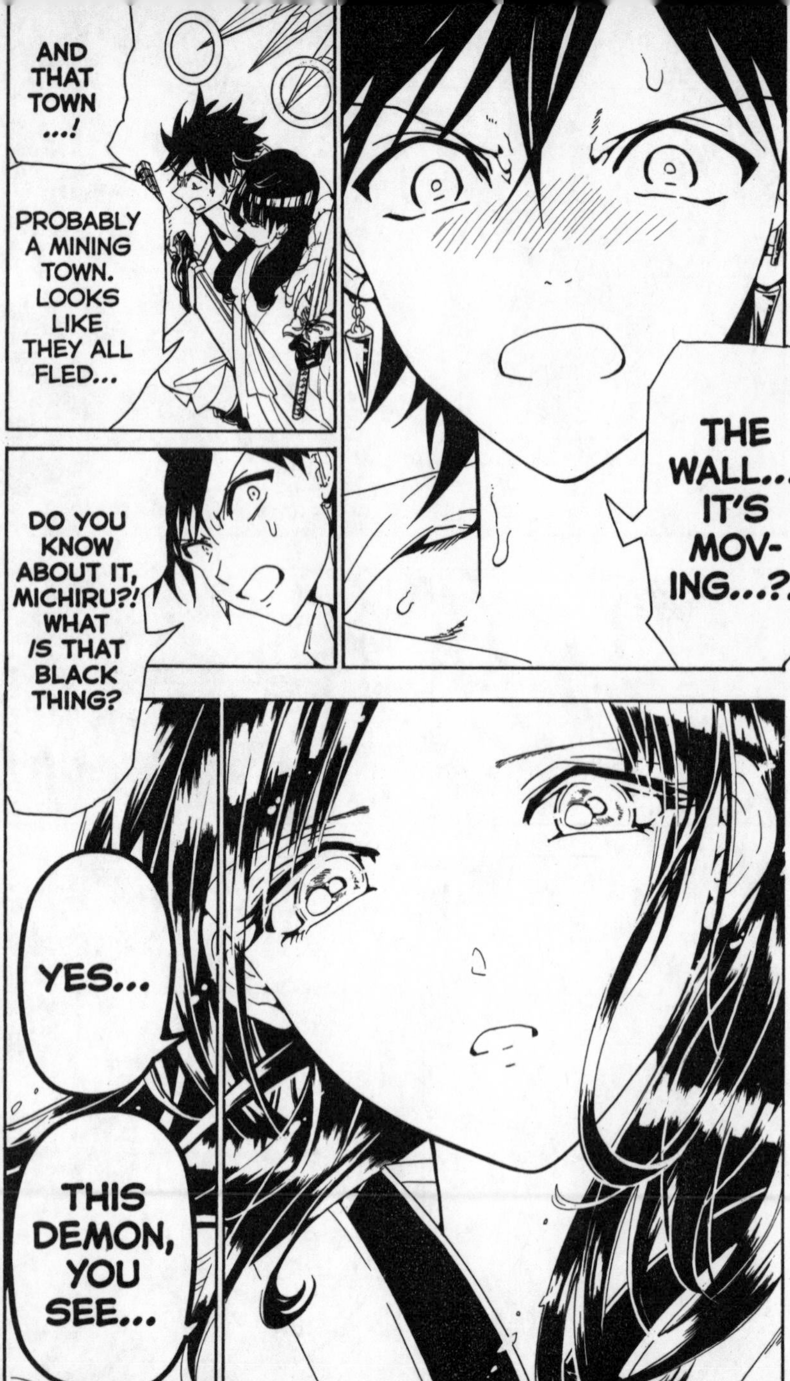
THE WALL... IT'S MOVING...?!
AND THAT TOWN ...!
PROBABLY A MINING TOWN. LOOKS LIKE THEY ALL FLED...
DO YOU KNOW ABOUT IT, MICHIRU?! WHAT IS THAT BLACK THING?
YES...
THIS DEMON, YOU SEE...

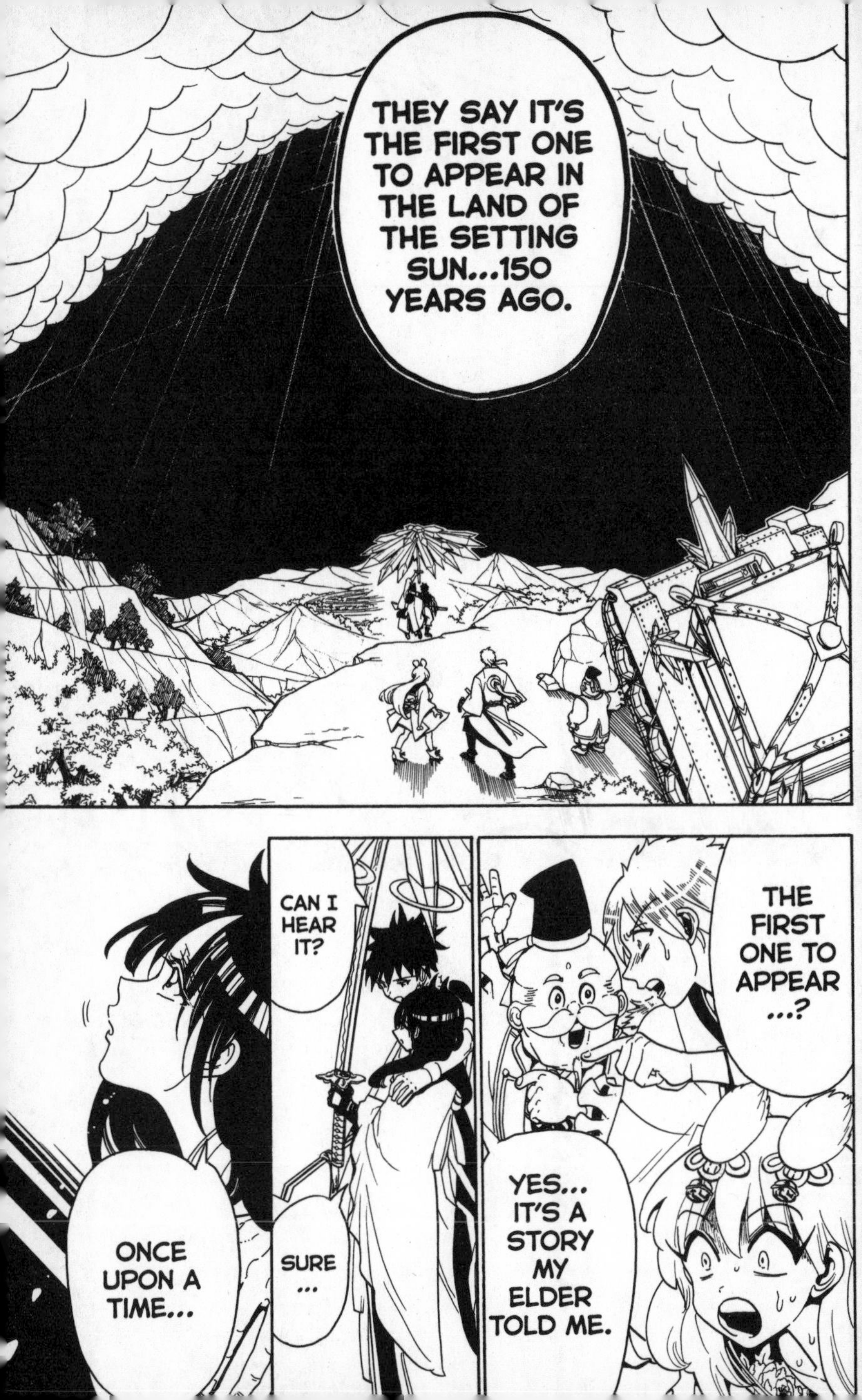
THEY SAY IT'S THE FIRST ONE TO APPEAR IN THE LAND OF THE SETTING SUN...150 YEARS AGO.
THE FIRST ONE TO APPEAR ...?
YES... IT'S A STORY MY ELDER TOLD ME.
CAN I HEAR IT?
SURE ...
ONCE UPON A TIME...

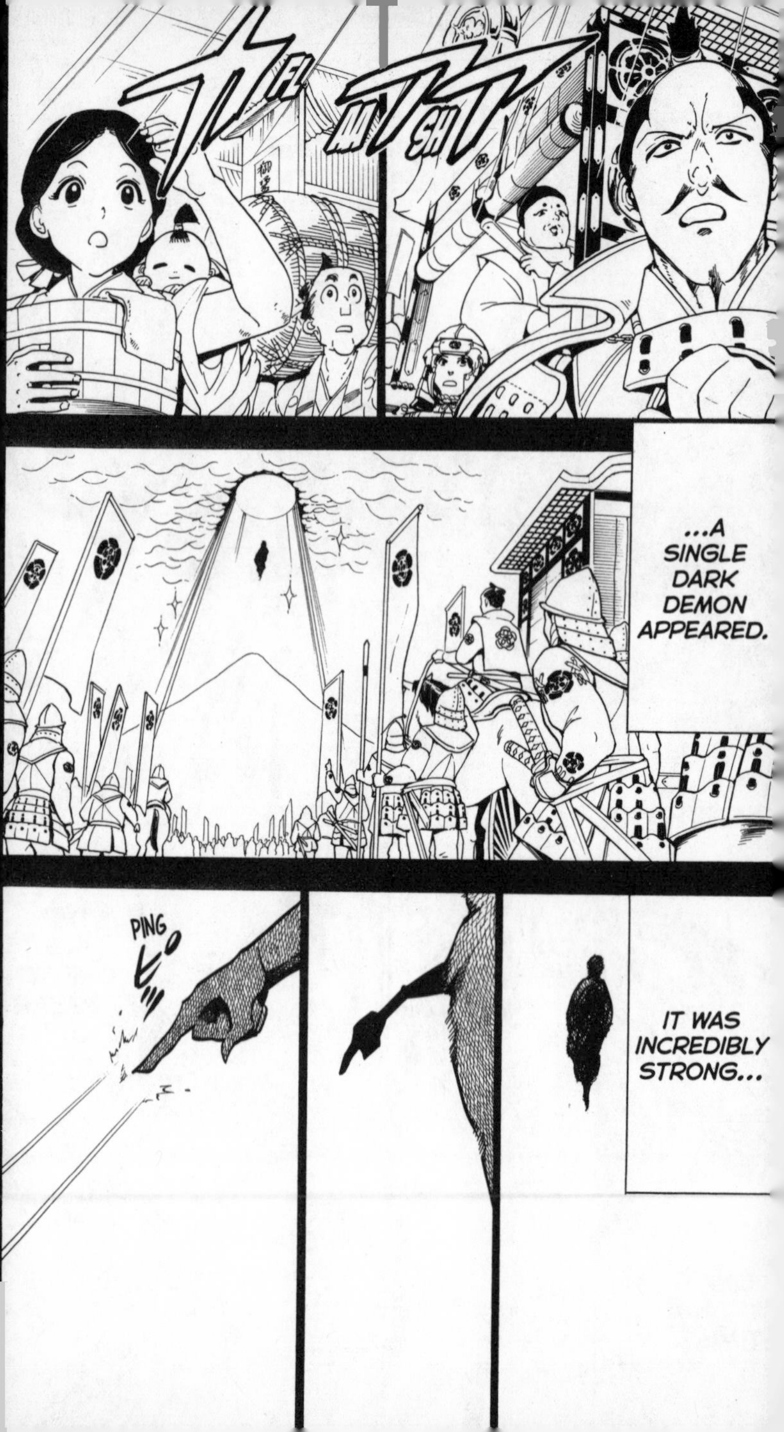

SH
FL
A
...A SINGLE DARK DEMON APPEARED.
IT WAS INCREDIBLY STRONG...
PING

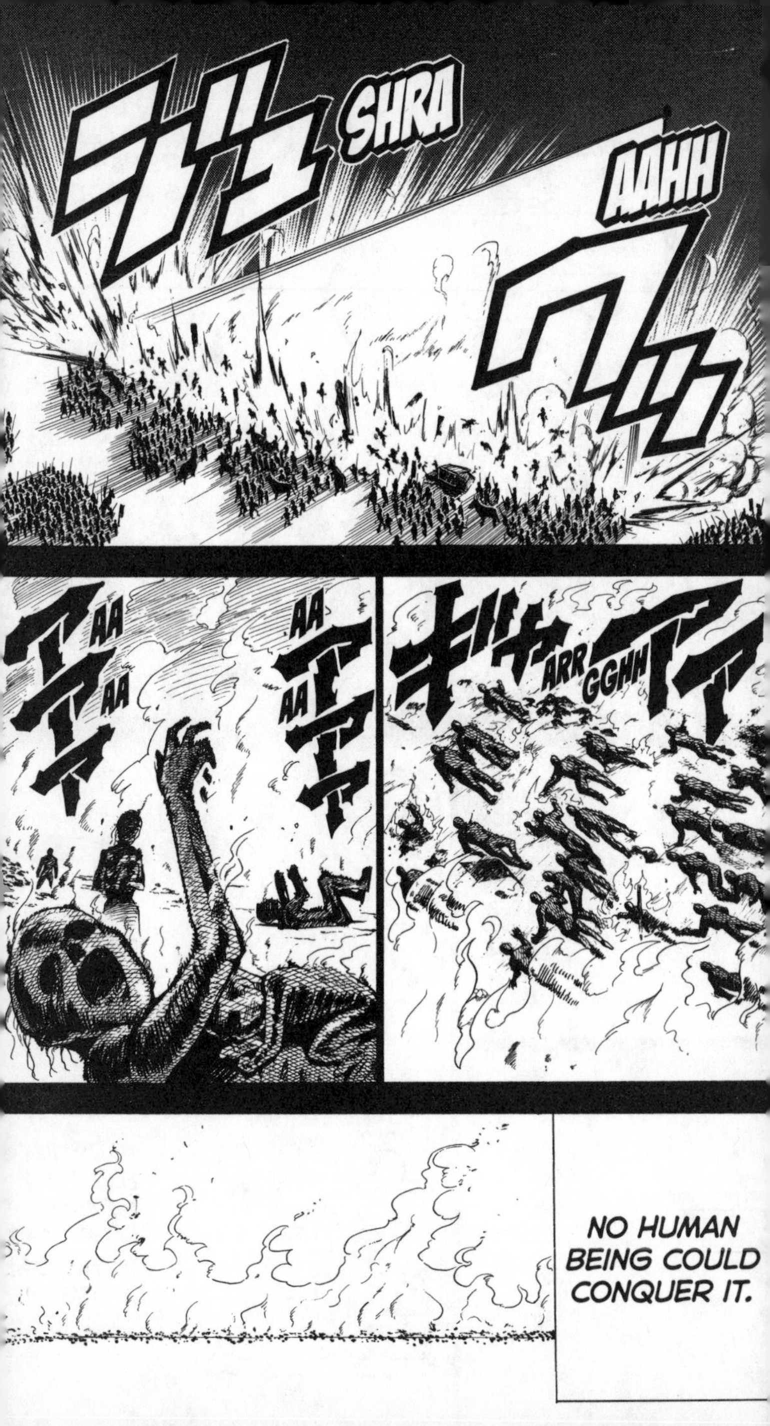
SHRA
AAHH
ARR
GGHH
AA
AA
AA
AA
NO HUMAN BEING COULD CONQUER IT.

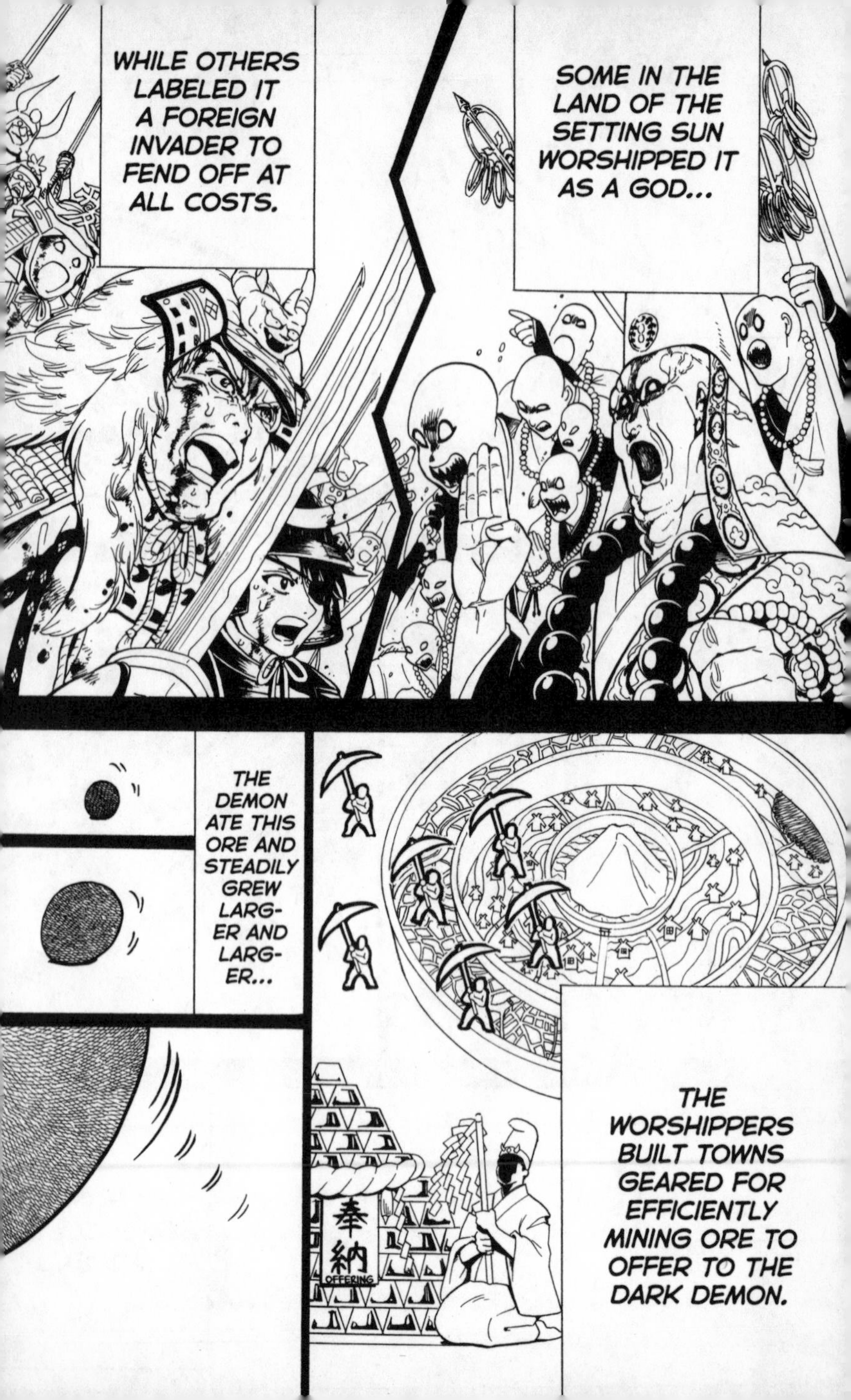
SOME IN THE LAND OF THE SETTING SUN WORSHIPPED IT AS A GOD...
WHILE OTHERS LABELED IT A FOREIGN INVADER TO FEND OFF AT ALL COSTS.
THE WORSHIPPERS BUILT TOWNS GEARED FOR EFFICIENTLY MINING ORE TO OFFER TO THE DARK DEMON.
奉納
OFFERING
THE DEMON ATE THIS ORE AND STEADILY GREW LARG-ER AND LARG-ER...

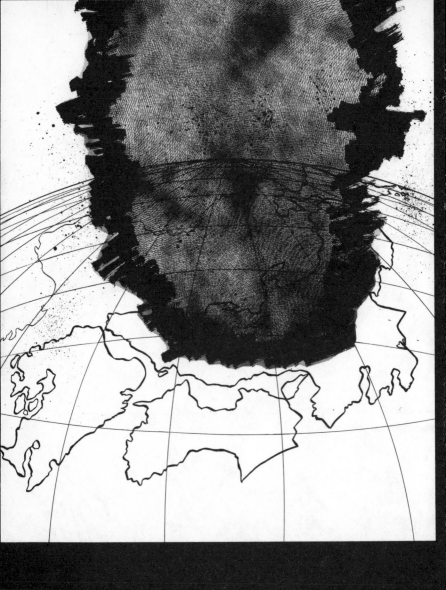

AND NOW, IT IS BIG ENOUGH TO ENVELOP
HALF OF THE LAND OF THE SETTING SUN.

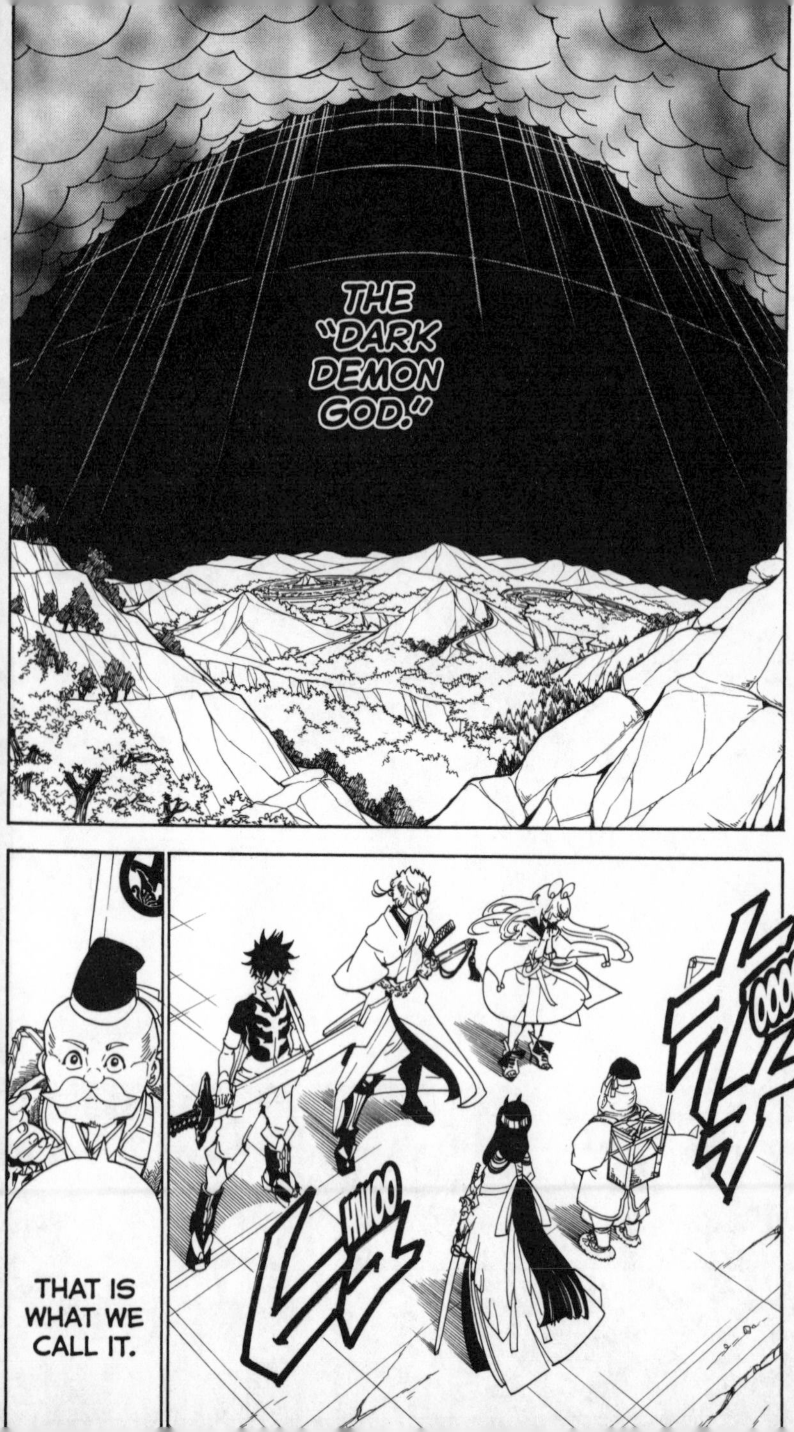
THE "DARK DEMON GOD."
OOOOH
HWOO
THAT IS WHAT WE CALL IT.

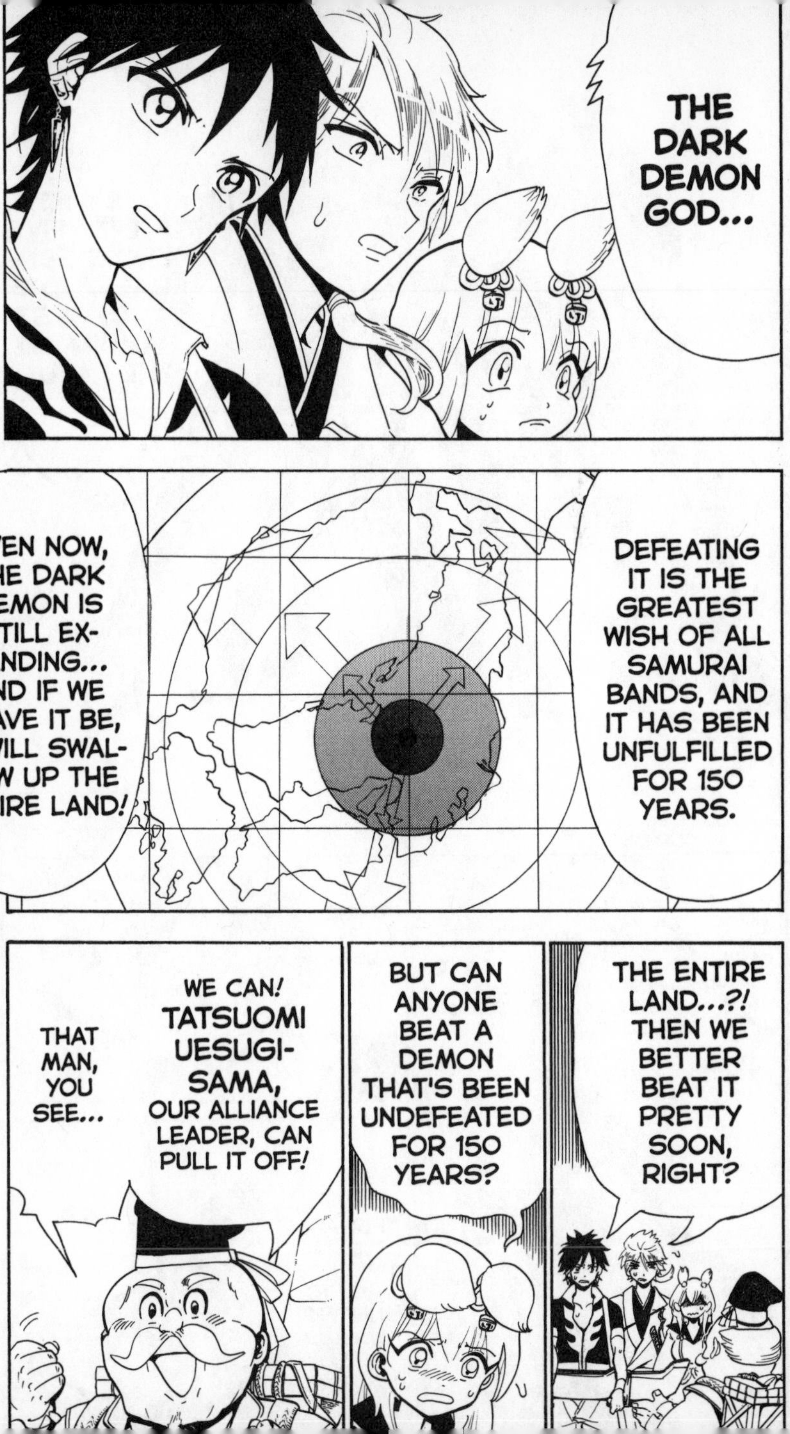
THE DARK DEMON GOD...
DEFEATING IT IS THE GREATEST WISH OF ALL SAMURAI BANDS, AND IT HAS BEEN UNFULFILLED FOR 150 YEARS.
EVEN NOW, THE DARK DEMON IS STILL EX-PANDING... AND IF WE LEAVE IT BE, IT WILL SWAL-LOW UP THE ENTIRE LAND!
THE ENTIRE LAND...?! THEN WE BETTER BEAT IT PRETTY SOON, RIGHT?
BUT CAN ANYONE BEAT A DEMON THAT'S BEEN UNDEFEATED FOR 150 YEARS?
WE CAN! TATSUOMI UESUGI-SAMA, OUR ALLIANCE LEADER, CAN PULL IT OFF!
THAT MAN, YOU SEE...

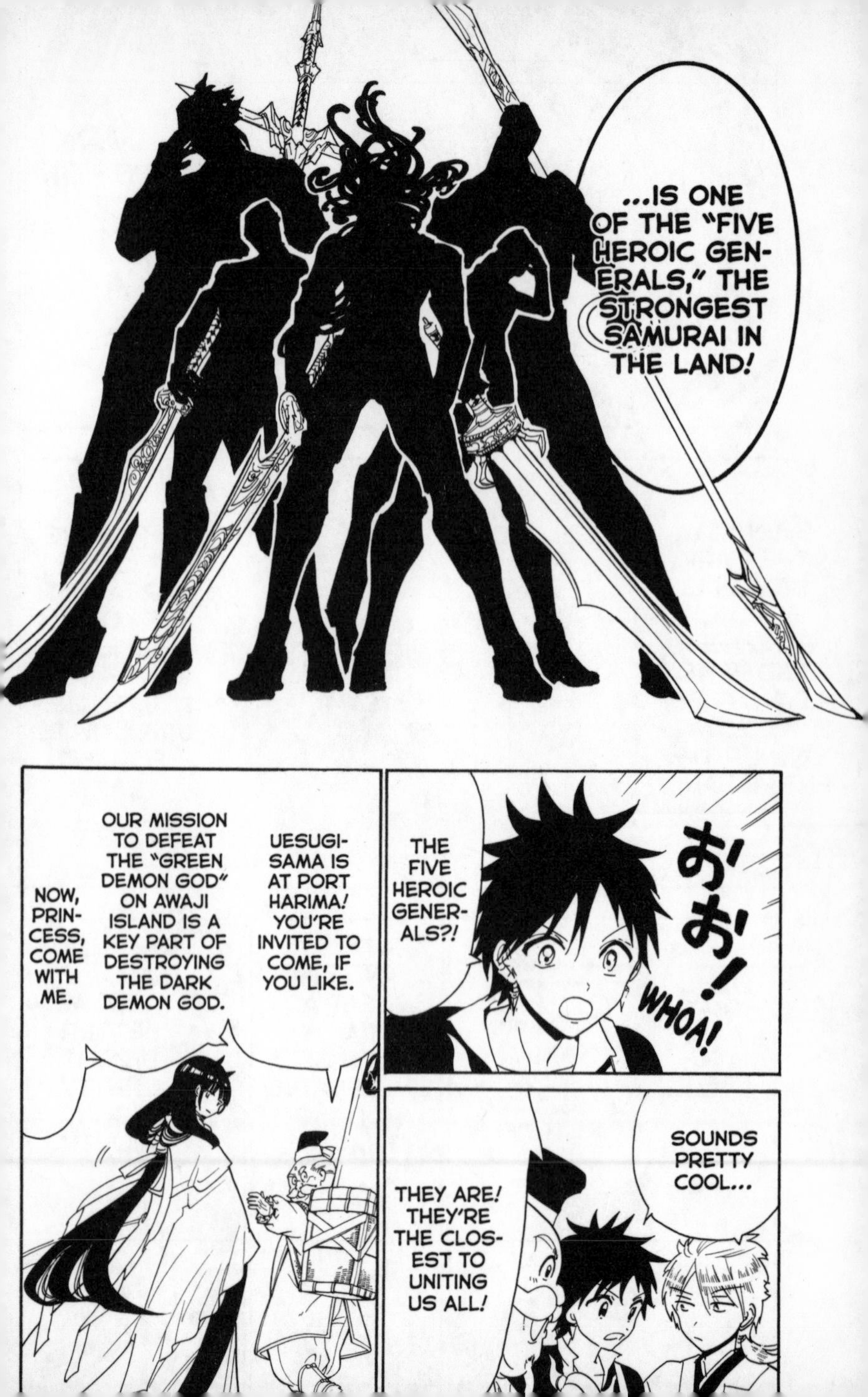

...IS ONE OF THE "FIVE HEROIC GENERALS," THE STRONGEST SAMURAI IN THE LAND!
おお!
WHOA!
THE FIVE HEROIC GENERALS?!
SOUNDS PRETTY COOL...
THEY ARE! THEY'RE THE CLOSEST TO UNITING US ALL!
UESUGI-SAMA IS AT PORT HARIMA! YOU'RE INVITED TO COME, IF YOU LIKE.
OUR MISSION TO DEFEAT THE "GREEN DEMON GOD" ON AWAJI ISLAND IS A KEY PART OF DESTROYING THE DARK DEMON GOD.
NOW, PRINCESS, COME WITH ME.

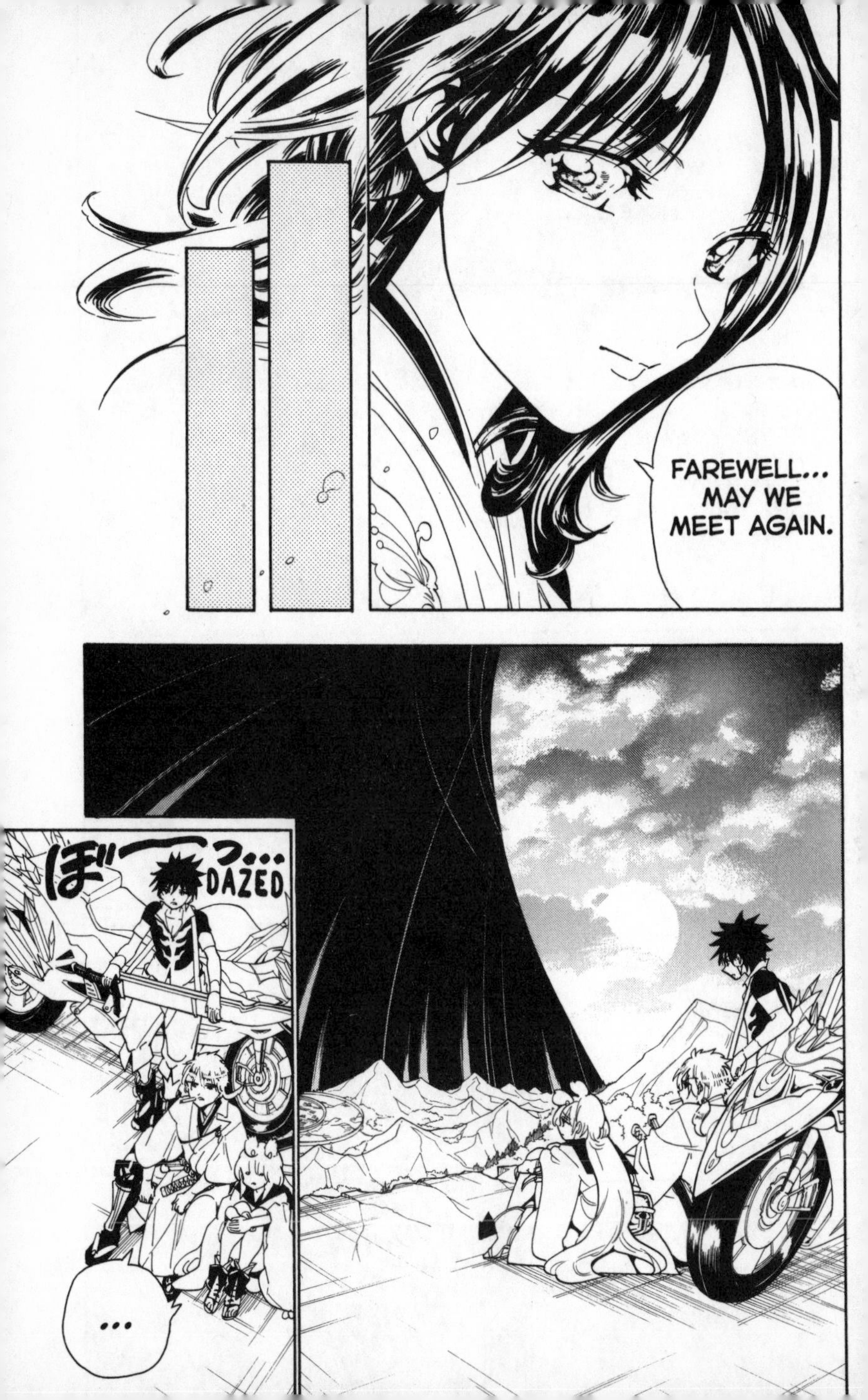
FAREWELL... MAY WE MEET AGAIN.
ぼーっ...
DAZED
...

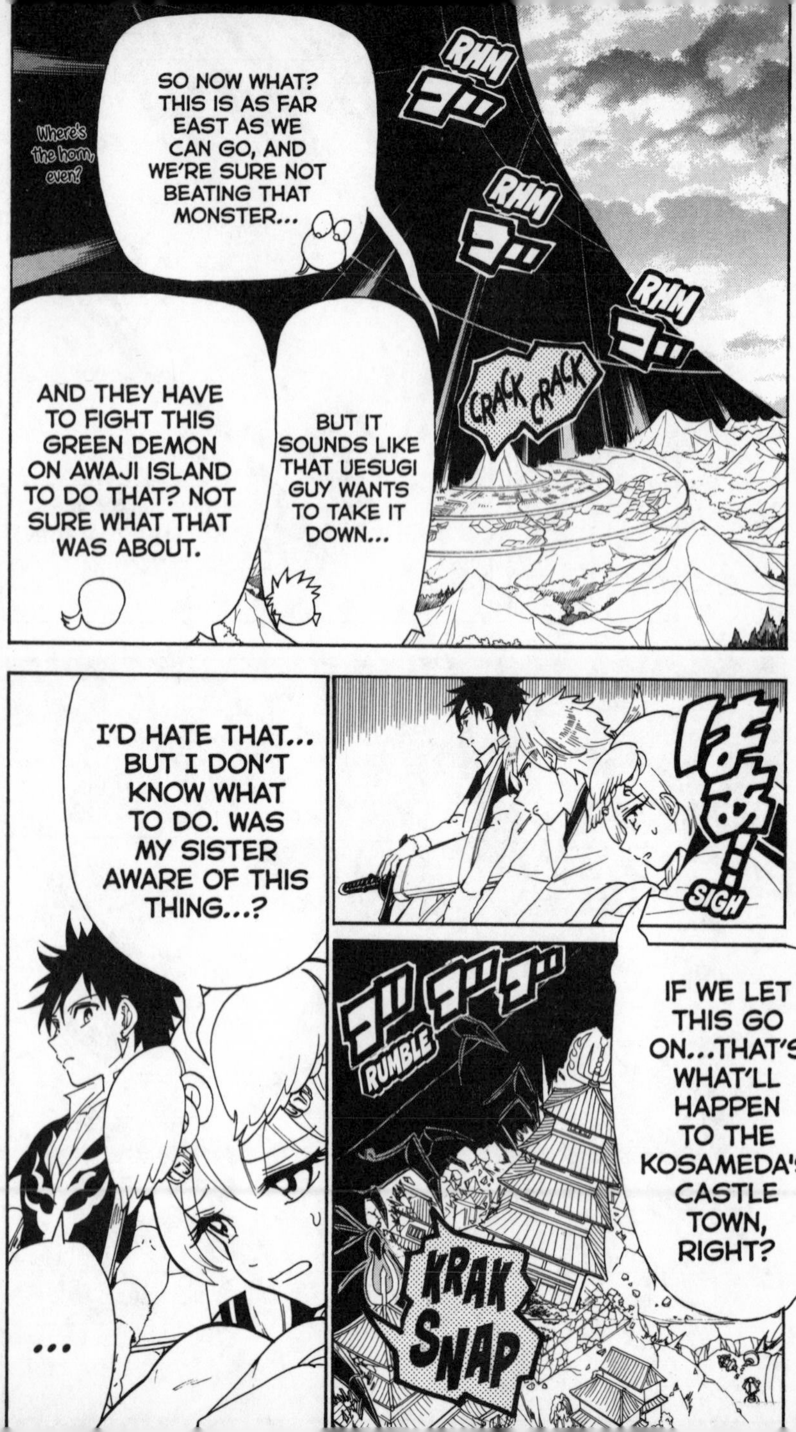
RHM
ゴッ
RHM
ゴッ
RHM
ゴッ
SO NOW WHAT? THIS IS AS FAR EAST AS WE CAN GO, AND WE'RE SURE NOT BEATING THAT MONSTER...
Where's the horn, even?
CRACK CRACK
BUT IT SOUNDS LIKE THAT UESUGI GUY WANTS TO TAKE IT DOWN...
AND THEY HAVE TO FIGHT THIS GREEN DEMON ON AWAJI ISLAND TO DO THAT? NOT SURE WHAT THAT WAS ABOUT.
はぁ…
SIGH
IF WE LET THIS GO ON...THAT'S WHAT'LL HAPPEN TO THE KOSAMEDA'S CASTLE TOWN, RIGHT?
ゴッゴッゴッ
RUMBLE
KRAK SNAP
I'D HATE THAT... BUT I DON'T KNOW WHAT TO DO. WAS MY SISTER AWARE OF THIS THING...?
...

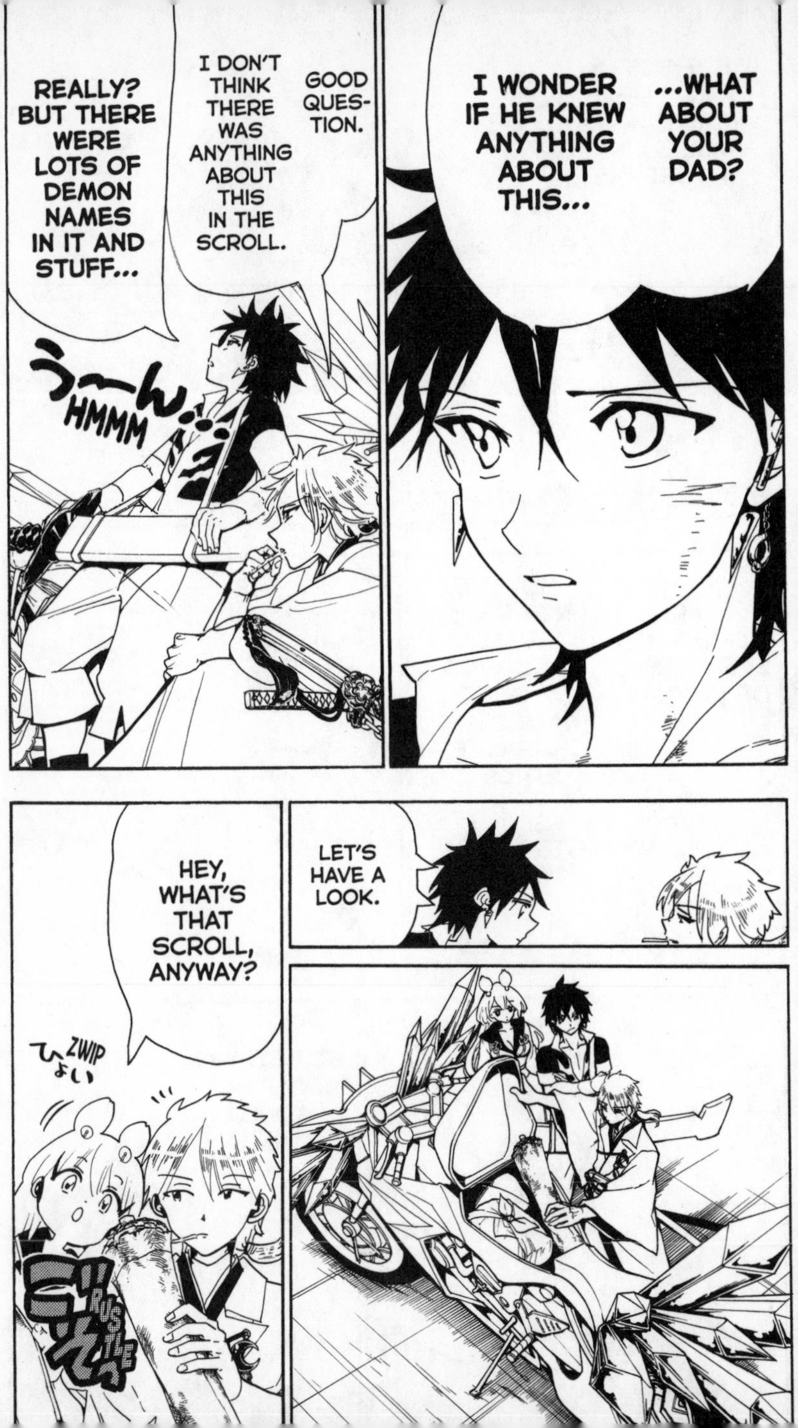

...WHAT ABOUT YOUR DAD?
I WONDER IF HE KNEW ANYTHING ABOUT THIS...
GOOD QUES-TION.
I DON'T THINK THERE WAS ANYTHING ABOUT THIS IN THE SCROLL.
REALLY? BUT THERE WERE LOTS OF DEMON NAMES IN IT AND STUFF...
うーん HMMM
LET'S HAVE A LOOK.
HEY, WHAT'S THAT SCROLL, ANYWAY?
ひょい ZWIP
ごそっ RUSTLE

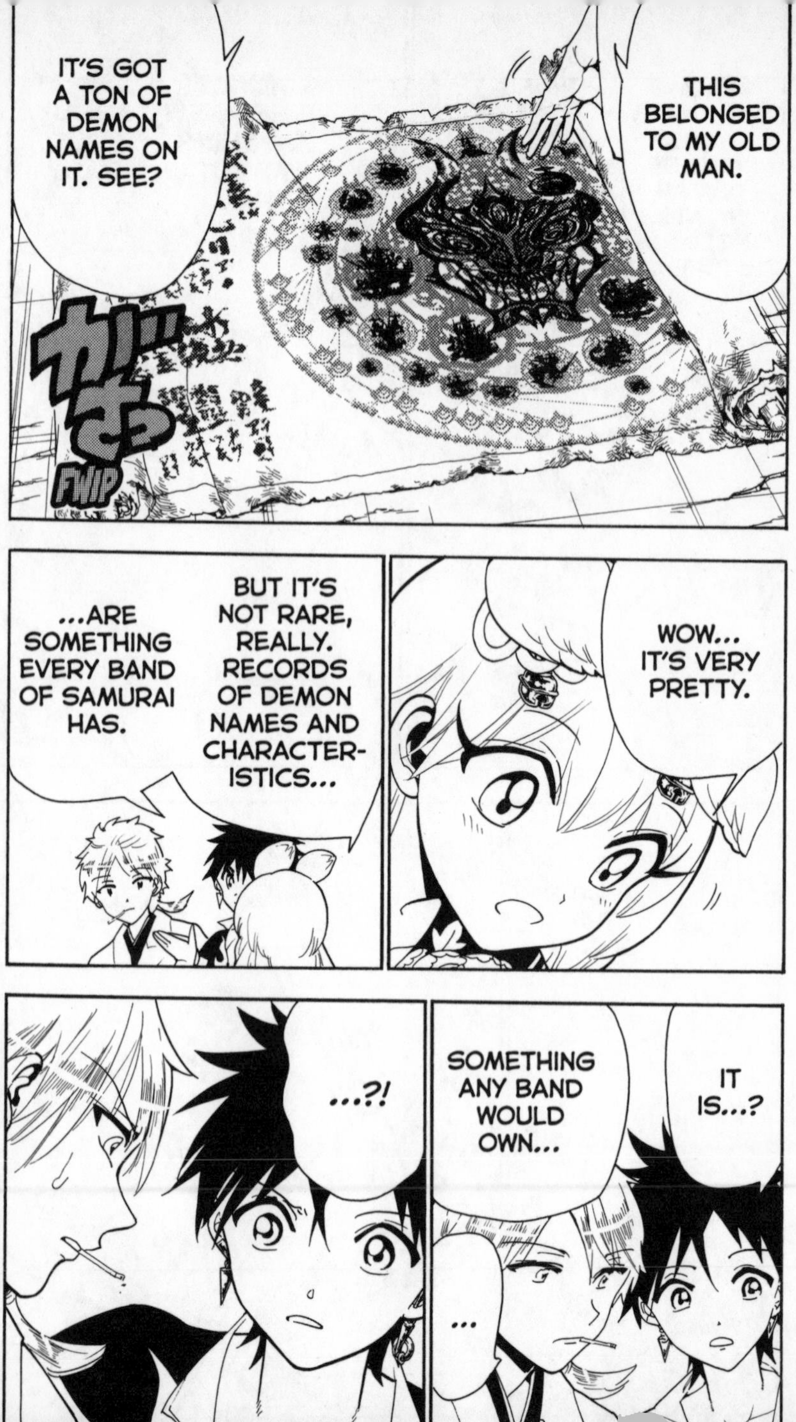
THIS BELONGED TO MY OLD MAN.
IT'S GOT A TON OF DEMON NAMES ON IT. SEE?
がさっ
FWIP
WOW... IT'S VERY PRETTY.
BUT IT'S NOT RARE, REALLY. RECORDS OF DEMON NAMES AND CHARACTER-ISTICS...
...ARE SOMETHING EVERY BAND OF SAMURAI HAS.
IT IS...?
SOMETHING ANY BAND WOULD OWN...
...
...?!

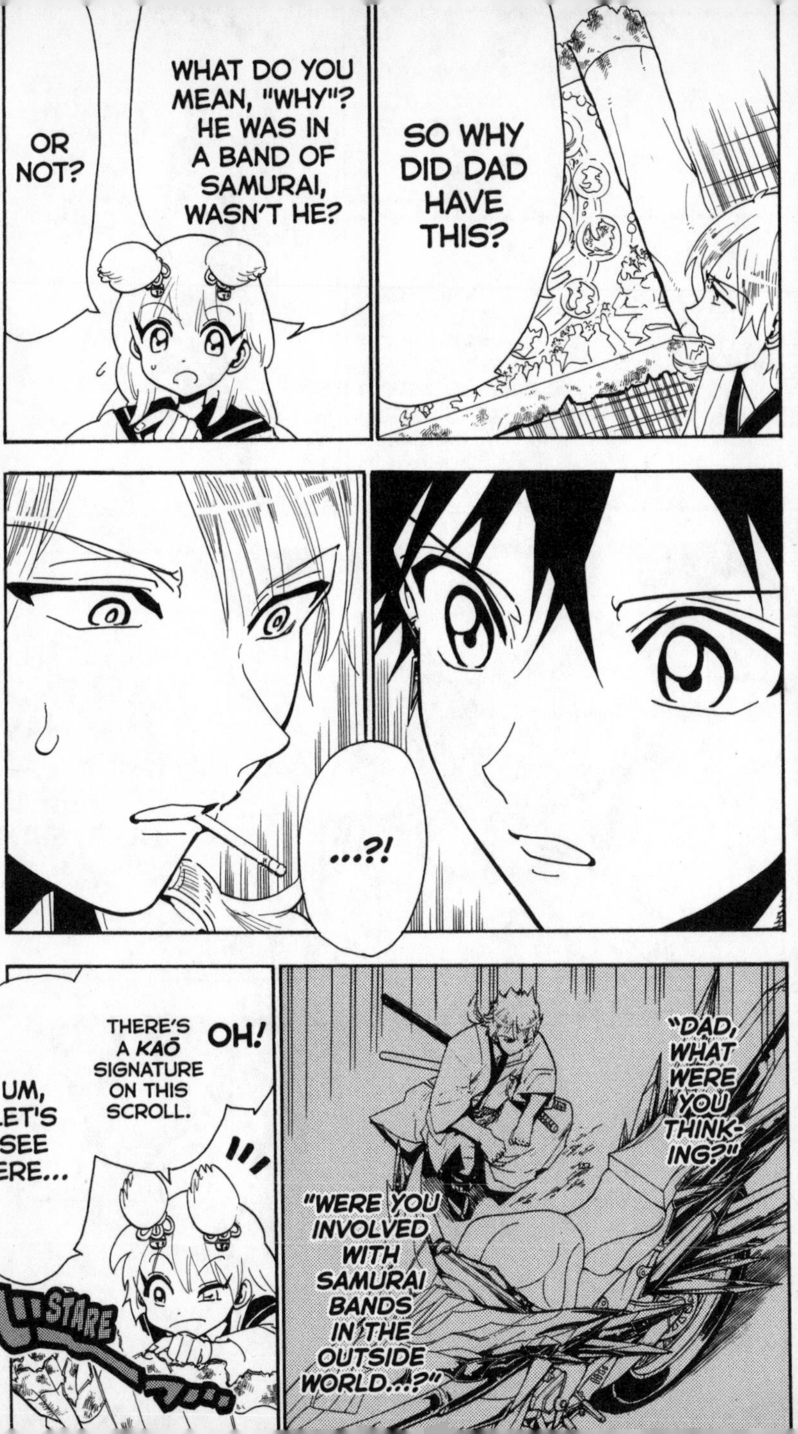
SO WHY DID DAD HAVE THIS?
WHAT DO YOU MEAN, "WHY"? HE WAS IN A BAND OF SAMURAI, WASN'T HE?
OR NOT?
...?!
"DAD, WHAT WERE YOU THINKING?"
"WERE YOU INVOLVED WITH SAMURAI BANDS IN THE OUTSIDE WORLD...?"
OH!
THERE'S A *KAŌ* SIGNATURE ON THIS SCROLL.
UM, LET'S SEE HERE...
STARE

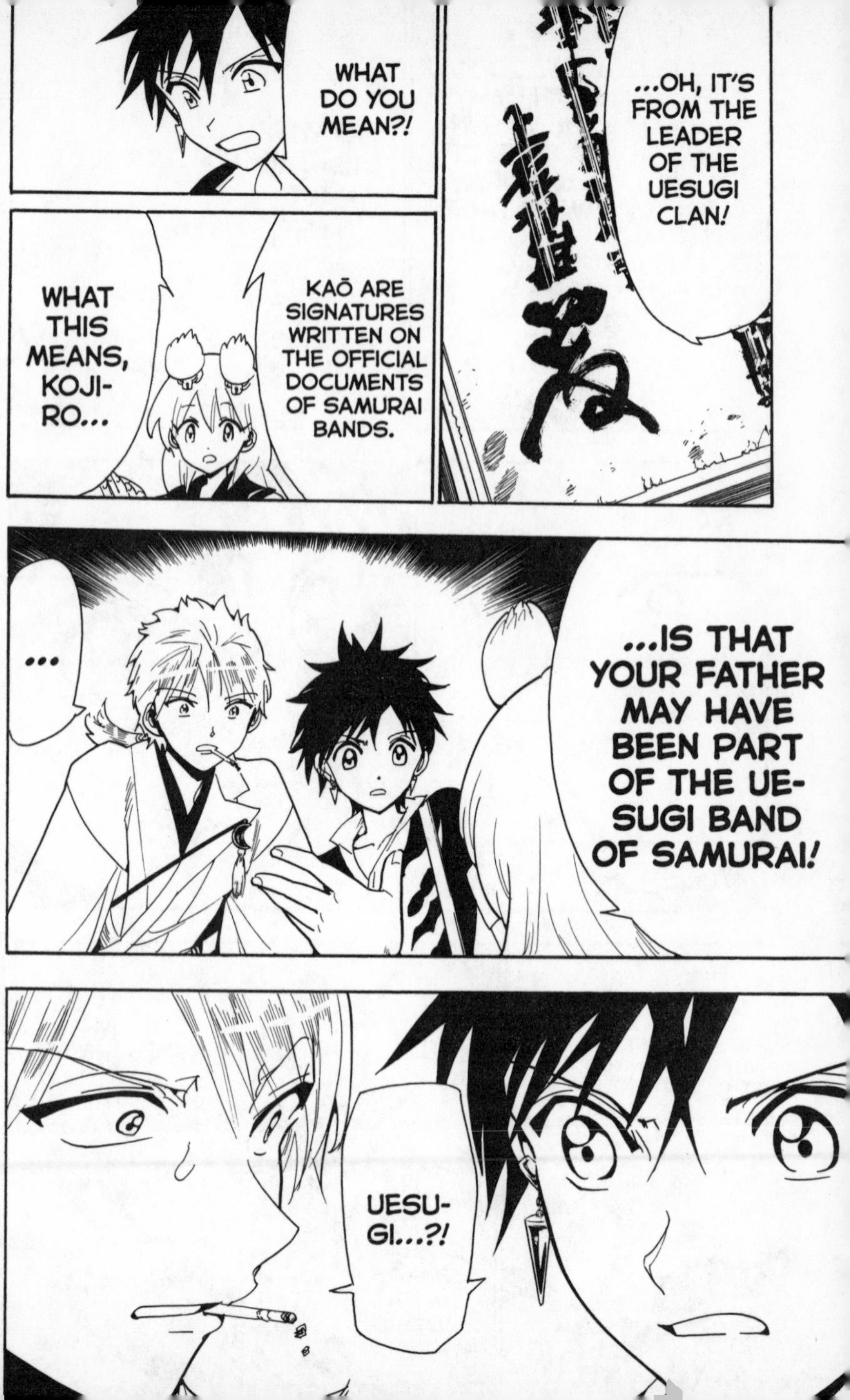
...OH, IT'S FROM THE LEADER OF THE UESUGI CLAN!
WHAT DO YOU MEAN?!
KAŌ ARE SIGNATURES WRITTEN ON THE OFFICIAL DOCUMENTS OF SAMURAI BANDS.
WHAT THIS MEANS, KOJI-RO...
...IS THAT YOUR FATHER MAY HAVE BEEN PART OF THE UE-SUGI BAND OF SAMURAI!
...
UESU-GI...?!

ORIENT

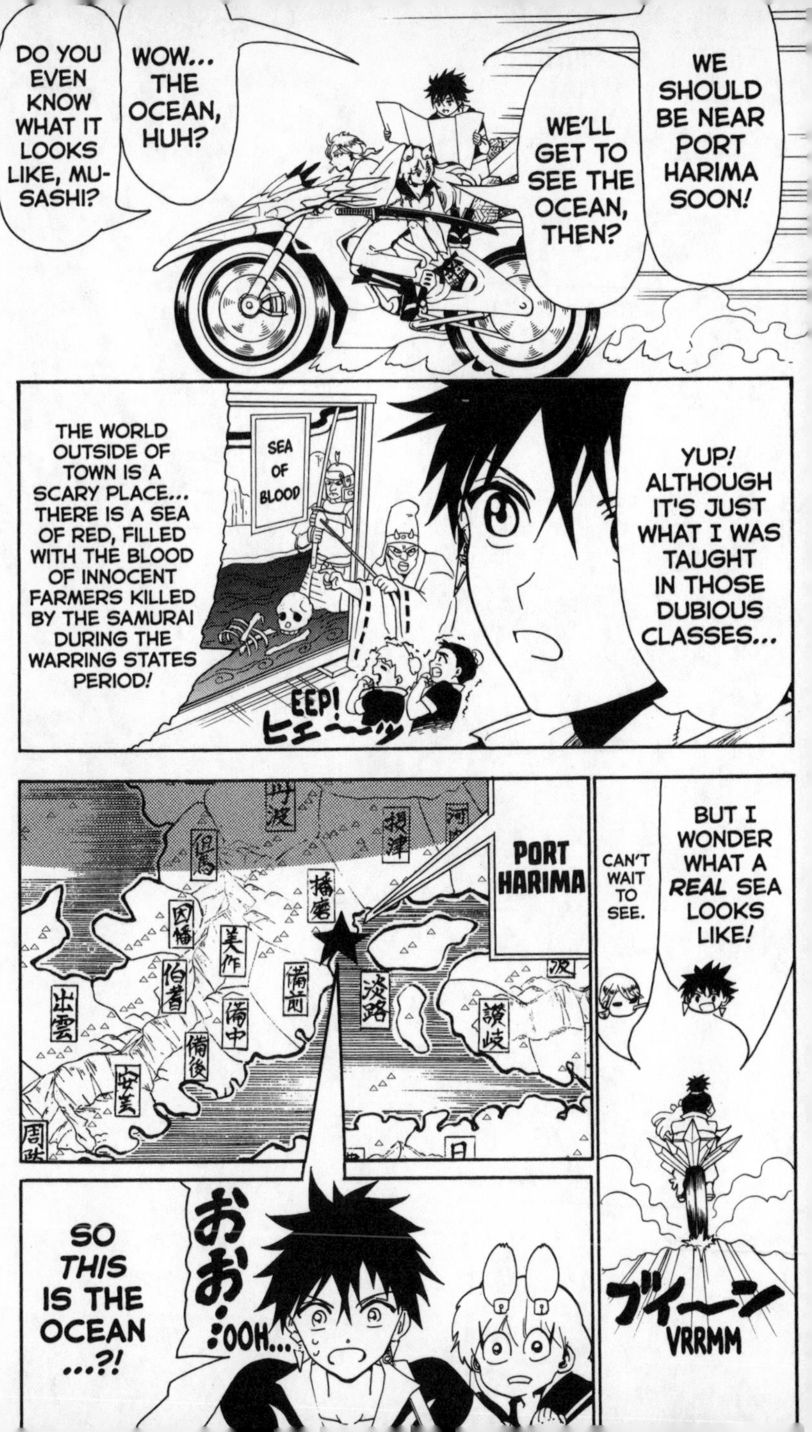
WE SHOULD BE NEAR PORT HARIMA SOON!
WE'LL GET TO SEE THE OCEAN, THEN?
WOW... THE OCEAN, HUH?
DO YOU EVEN KNOW WHAT IT LOOKS LIKE, MU-SASHI?
YUP! ALTHOUGH IT'S JUST WHAT I WAS TAUGHT IN THOSE DUBIOUS CLASSES...
THE WORLD OUTSIDE OF TOWN IS A SCARY PLACE... THERE IS A SEA OF RED, FILLED WITH THE BLOOD OF INNOCENT FARMERS KILLED BY THE SAMURAI DURING THE WARRING STATES PERIOD!
SEA OF BLOOD
EEP!
ヒエ〜〜ッ
BUT I WONDER WHAT A *REAL* SEA LOOKS LIKE!
CAN'T WAIT TO SEE.
ブイーン
VRRMM
PORT HARIMA
丹波
摂津
但馬
播磨
因幡
美作
備前
伯耆
淡路
備中
出雲
讃岐
備後
安芸
周防
おお…
OOH...
SO *THIS* IS THE OCEAN...?!

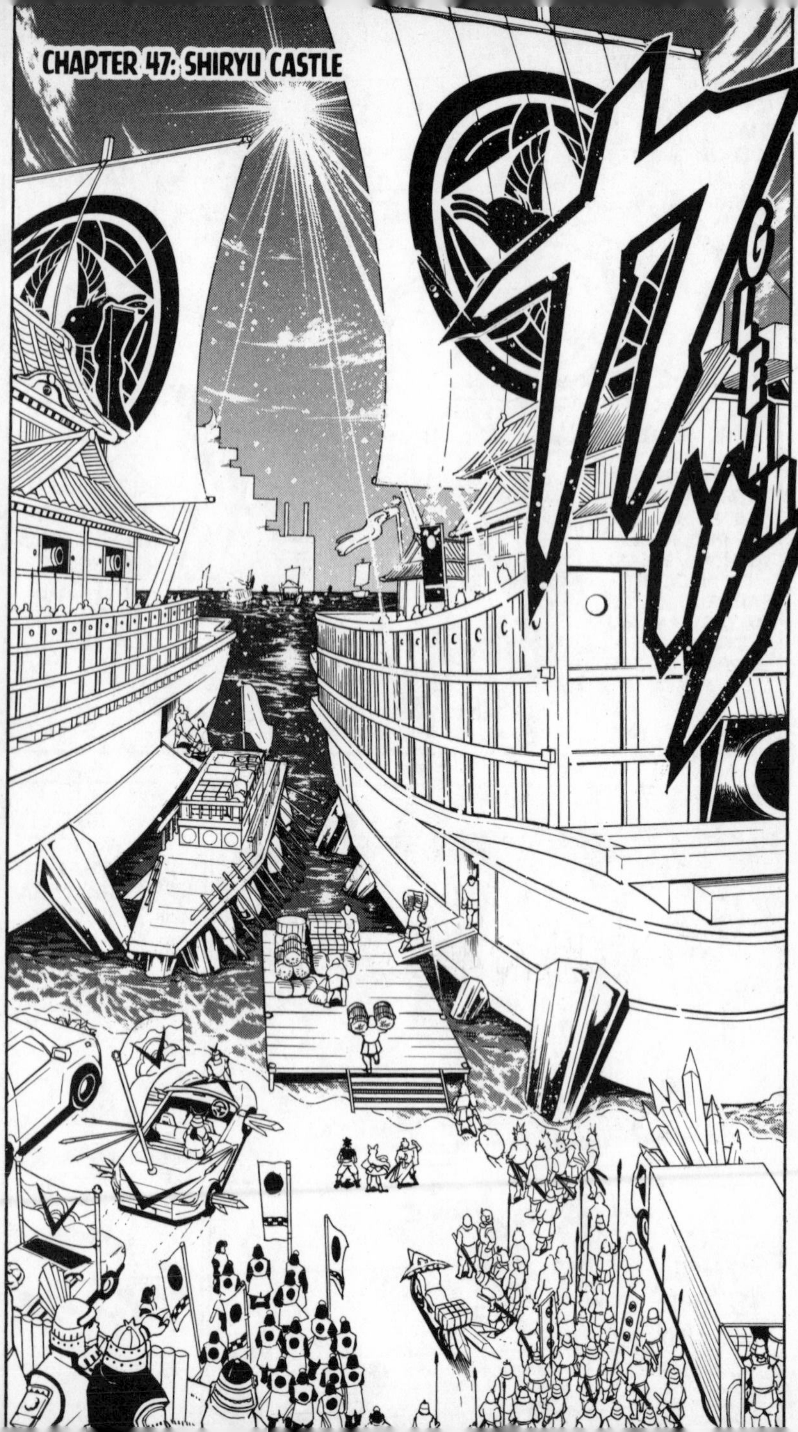
CHAPTER 47: SHIRYU CASTLE
GLEAM

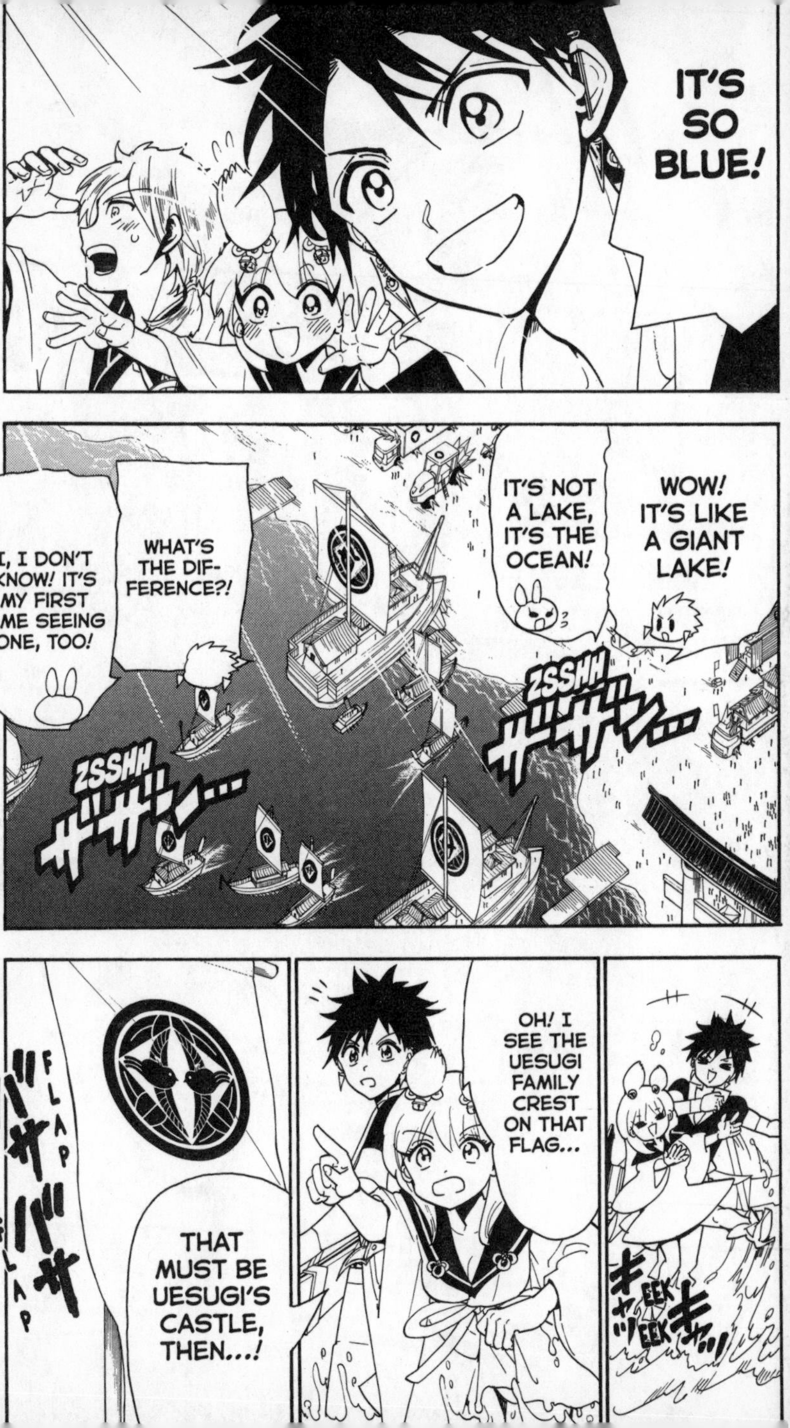
IT'S SO BLUE!
WOW! IT'S LIKE A GIANT LAKE!
IT'S NOT A LAKE, IT'S THE OCEAN!
ZSSHH
WHAT'S THE DIF-FERENCE?!
I, I DON'T KNOW! IT'S MY FIRST TIME SEEING ONE, TOO!
ZSSHH
EEK EEK
OH! I SEE THE UESUGI FAMILY CREST ON THAT FLAG...
FLAP FLAP
THAT MUST BE UESUGI'S CASTLE, THEN...!

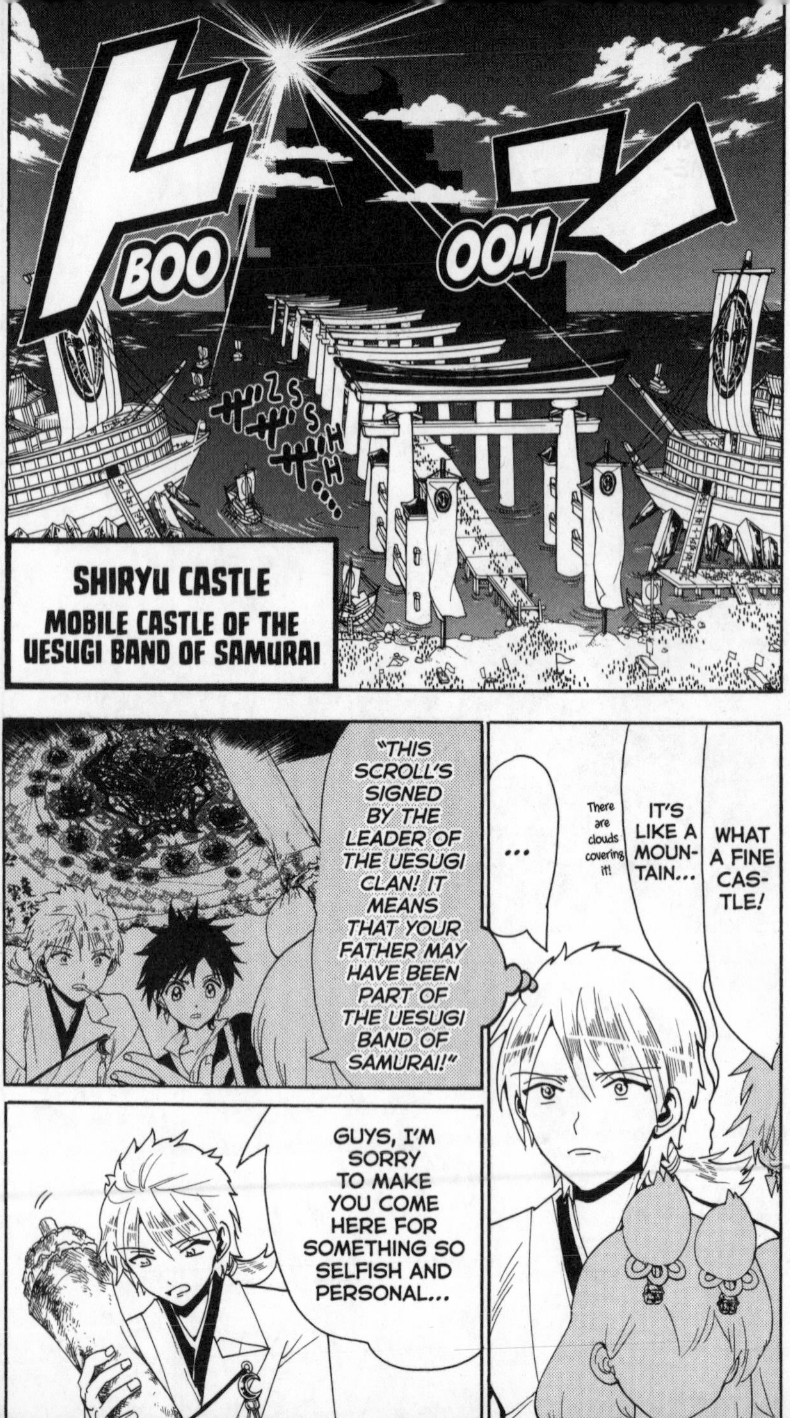
ド
BOO
ー
OOM
ン
ザザザ
ZSSHH...
SHIRYU CASTLE
MOBILE CASTLE OF THE UESUGI BAND OF SAMURAI
WHAT A FINE CASTLE!
IT'S LIKE A MOUNTAIN...
There are clouds covering it!
...
"THIS SCROLL'S SIGNED BY THE LEADER OF THE UESUGI CLAN! IT MEANS THAT YOUR FATHER MAY HAVE BEEN PART OF THE UESUGI BAND OF SAMURAI!"
GUYS, I'M SORRY TO MAKE YOU COME HERE FOR SOMETHING SO SELFISH AND PERSONAL...

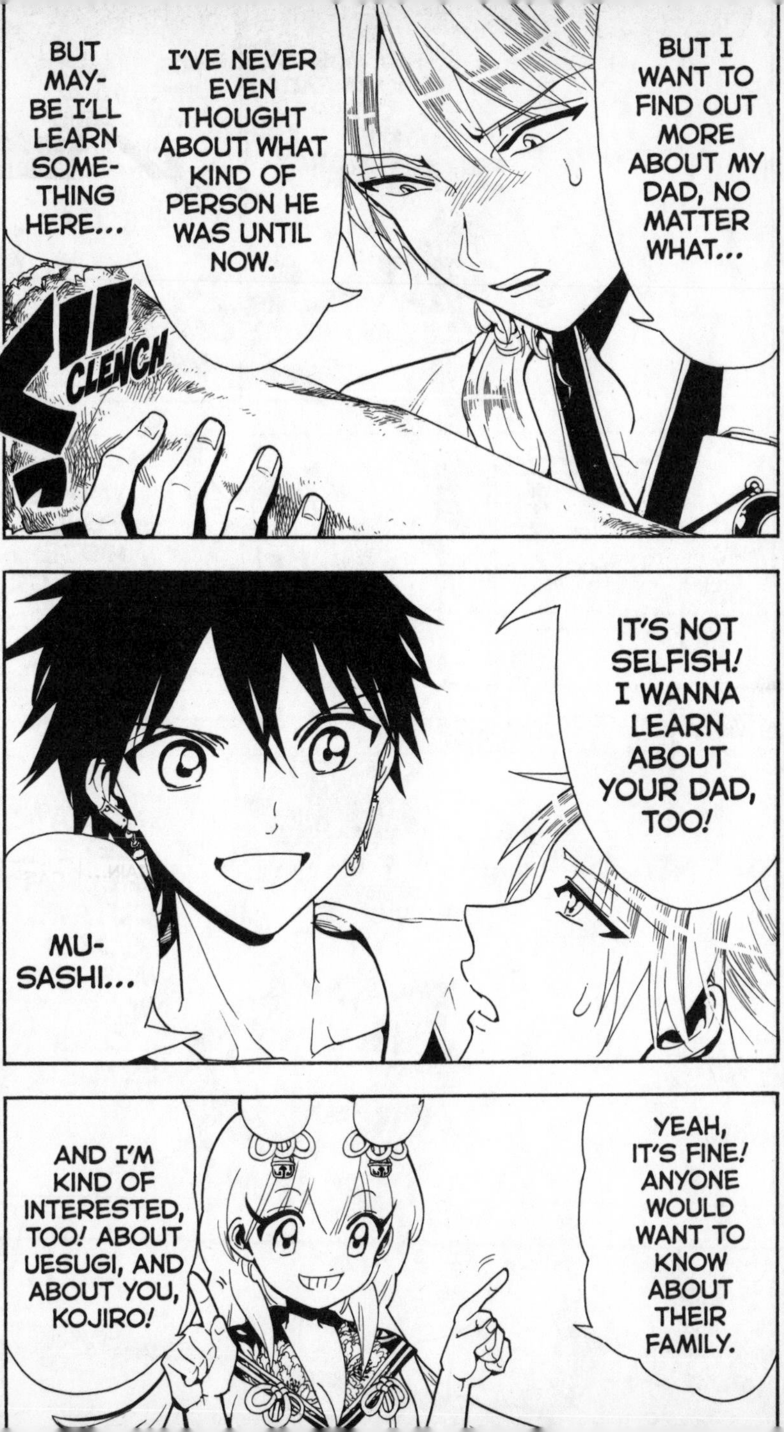
BUT I WANT TO FIND OUT MORE ABOUT MY DAD, NO MATTER WHAT...
I'VE NEVER EVEN THOUGHT ABOUT WHAT KIND OF PERSON HE WAS UNTIL NOW.
BUT MAY-BE I'LL LEARN SOME-THING HERE...
CLENCH
IT'S NOT SELFISH! I WANNA LEARN ABOUT YOUR DAD, TOO!
MU-SASHI...
YEAH, IT'S FINE! ANYONE WOULD WANT TO KNOW ABOUT THEIR FAMILY.
AND I'M KIND OF INTERESTED, TOO! ABOUT UESUGI, AND ABOUT YOU, KOJIRO!

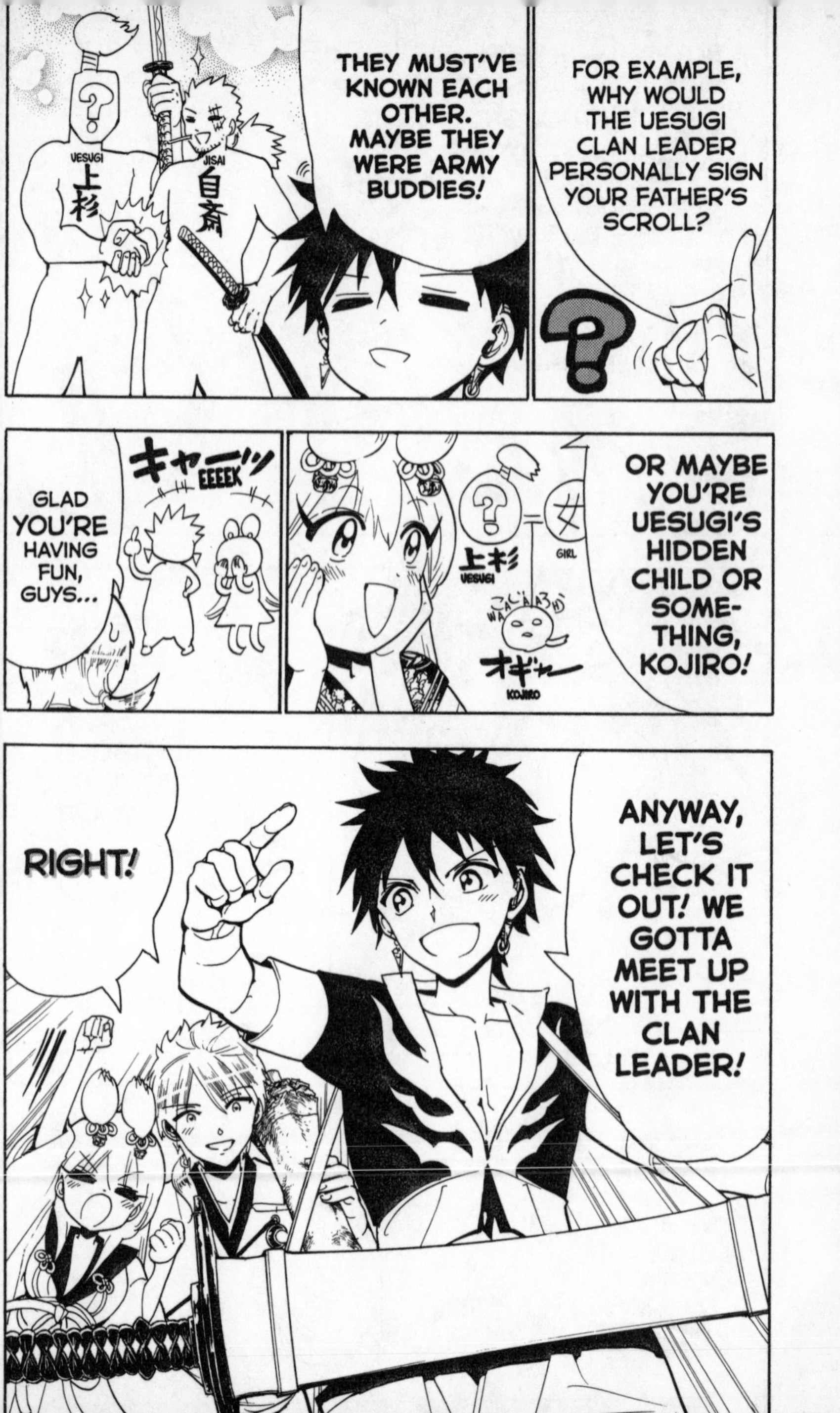
FOR EXAMPLE, WHY WOULD THE UESUGI CLAN LEADER PERSONALLY SIGN YOUR FATHER'S SCROLL?
THEY MUST'VE KNOWN EACH OTHER. MAYBE THEY WERE ARMY BUDDIES!
UESUGI
上杉
JISAI
自斎
OR MAYBE YOU'RE UESUGI'S HIDDEN CHILD OR SOME-THING, KOJIRO!
女
GIRL
上杉
UESUGI
オギャー
KOJIRO
キャーッ
EEEEK
GLAD YOU'RE HAVING FUN, GUYS...
ANYWAY, LET'S CHECK IT OUT! WE GOTTA MEET UP WITH THE CLAN LEADER!
RIGHT!

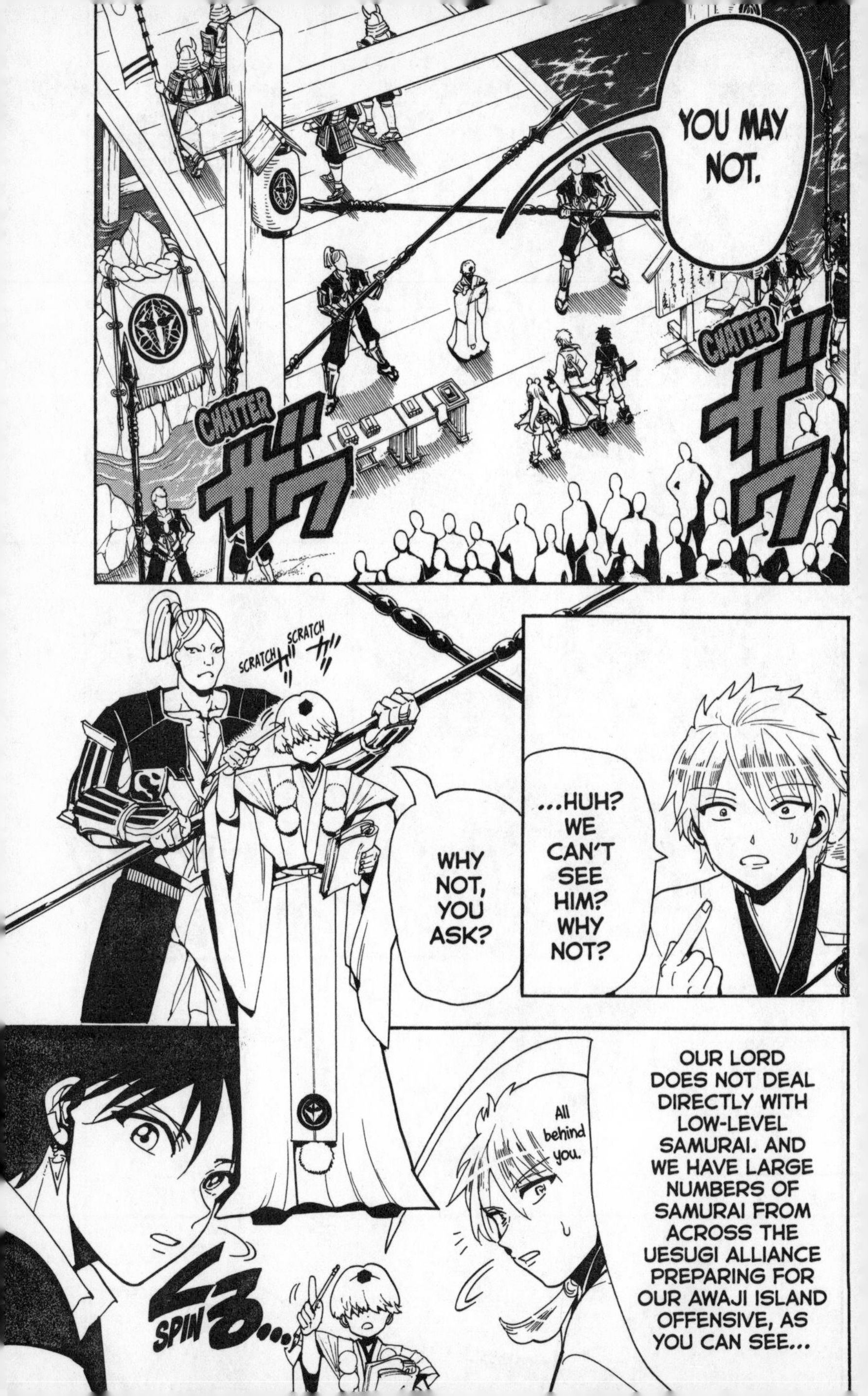
YOU MAY NOT.
CHATTER
CHATTER
...HUH? WE CAN'T SEE HIM? WHY NOT?
WHY NOT, YOU ASK?
SCRATCH SCRATCH
OUR LORD DOES NOT DEAL DIRECTLY WITH LOW-LEVEL SAMURAI. AND WE HAVE LARGE NUMBERS OF SAMURAI FROM ACROSS THE UESUGI ALLIANCE PREPARING FOR OUR AWAJI ISLAND OFFENSIVE, AS YOU CAN SEE...
All behind you.
SPIN

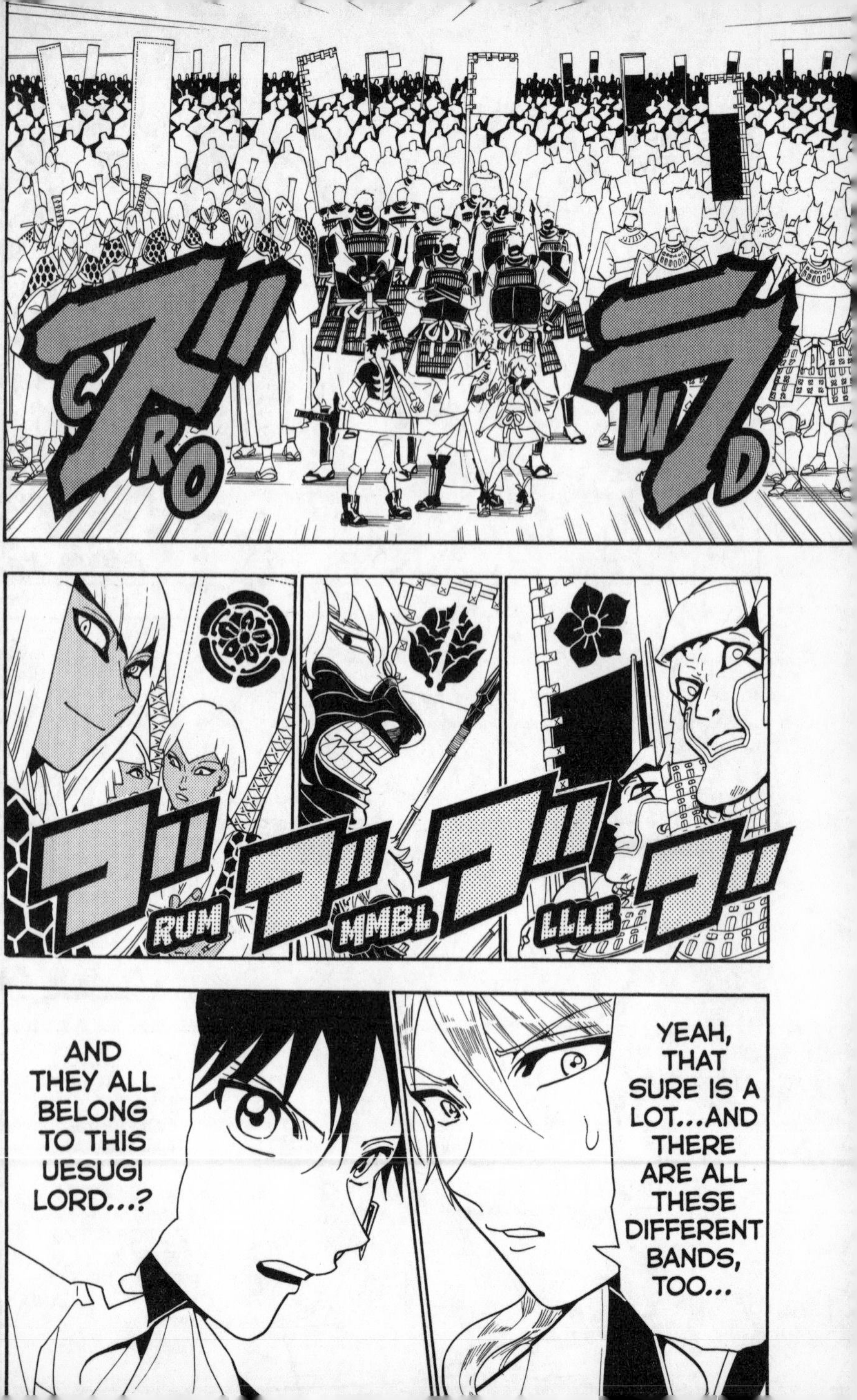
CROWD
RUM
MMBL
LLLE
YEAH, THAT SURE IS A LOT...AND THERE ARE ALL THESE DIFFERENT BANDS, TOO...
AND THEY ALL BELONG TO THIS UESUGI LORD...?

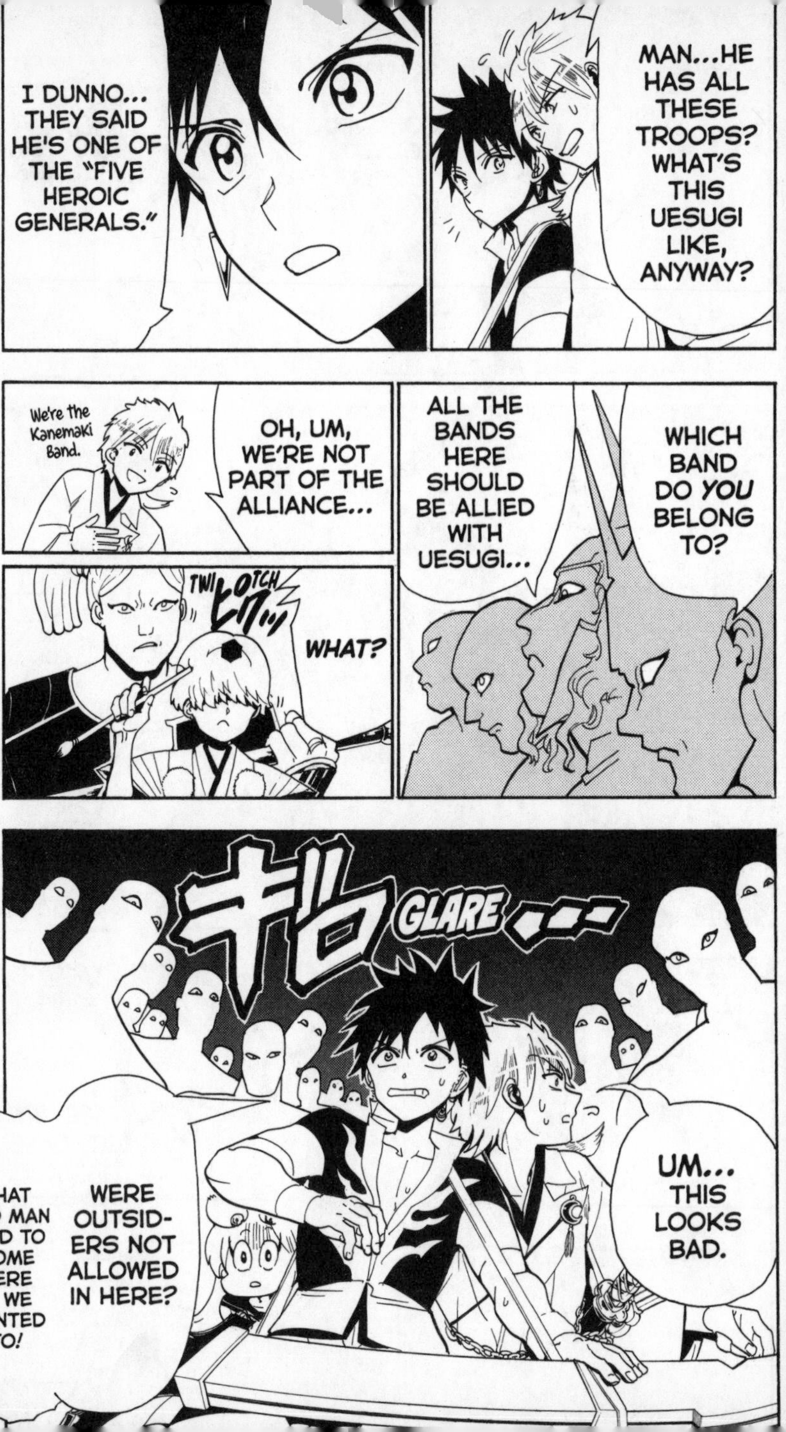
MAN...HE HAS ALL THESE TROOPS? WHAT'S THIS UESUGI LIKE, ANYWAY?
I DUNNO... THEY SAID HE'S ONE OF THE "FIVE HEROIC GENERALS."
WHICH BAND DO *YOU* BELONG TO?
ALL THE BANDS HERE SHOULD BE ALLIED WITH UESUGI...
OH, UM, WE'RE NOT PART OF THE ALLIANCE...
We're the Kanemaki Band.
ビクッ TWITCH
WHAT?
ギロ GLARE...
UM... THIS LOOKS BAD.
WERE OUTSIDERS NOT ALLOWED IN HERE?
THAT OLD MAN SAID TO COME HERE IF WE WANTED TO!

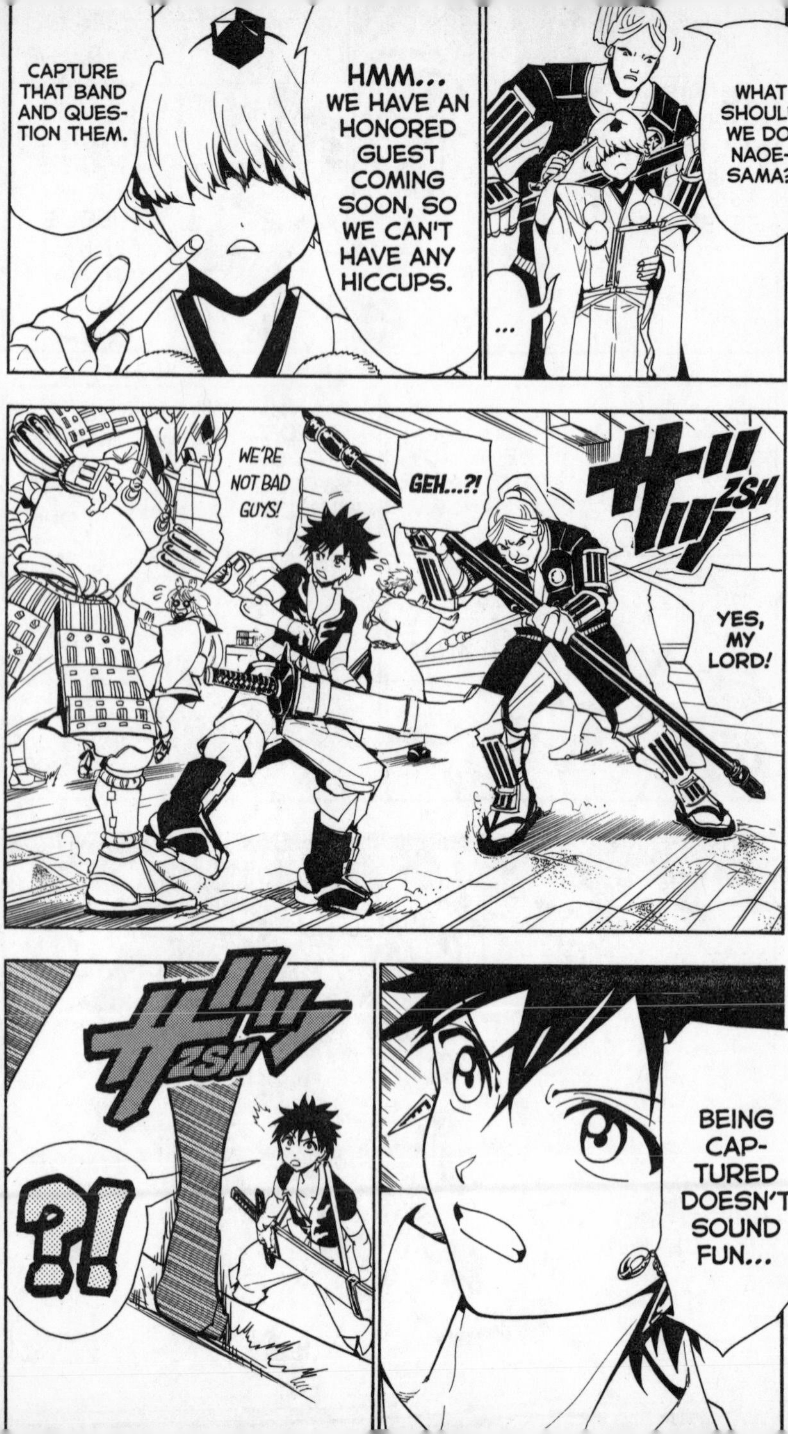
WHAT SHOULD WE DO, NAOE-SAMA?
...
HMM... WE HAVE AN HONORED GUEST COMING SOON, SO WE CAN'T HAVE ANY HICCUPS.
CAPTURE THAT BAND AND QUES-TION THEM.
YES, MY LORD!
ZSH
GEH...?!
WE'RE NOT BAD GUYS!
BEING CAP-TURED DOESN'T SOUND FUN...
ZSH
?!

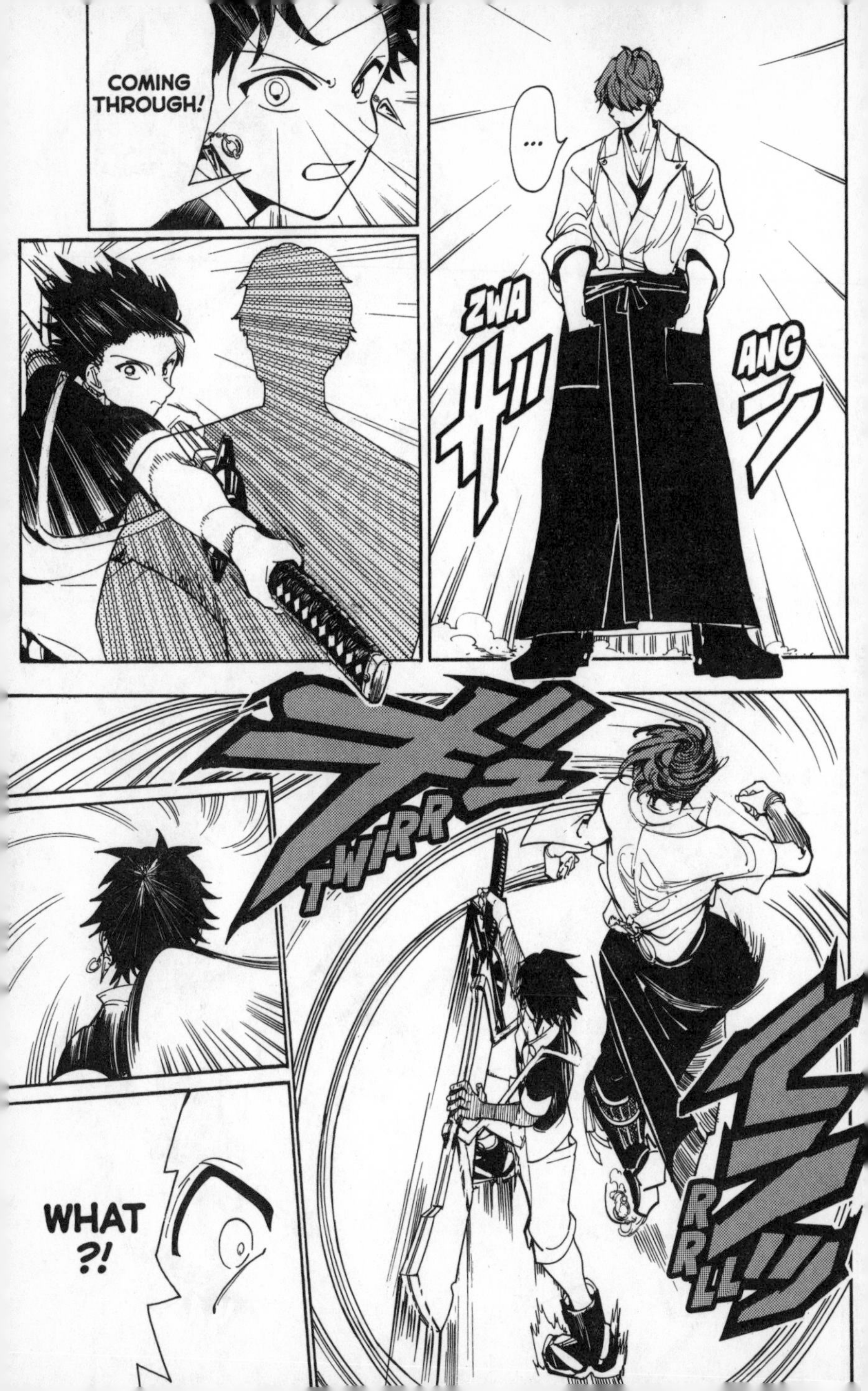
...
ZWA
ANG
COMING THROUGH!
TWIRR
RRLL
WHAT ?!

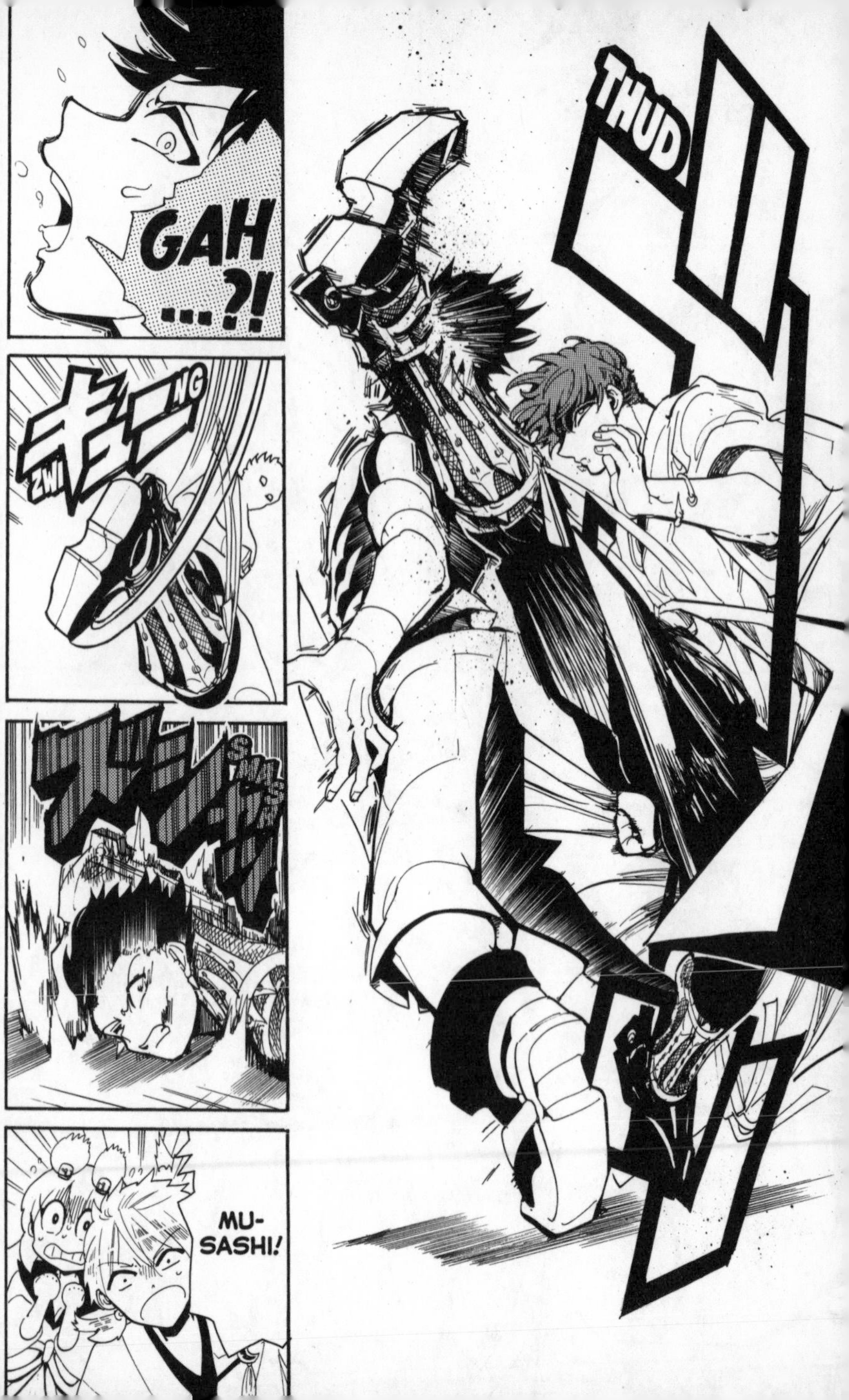
THUD
GAH ...?!
キーン
ZWING
SMASH
MU-SASHI!

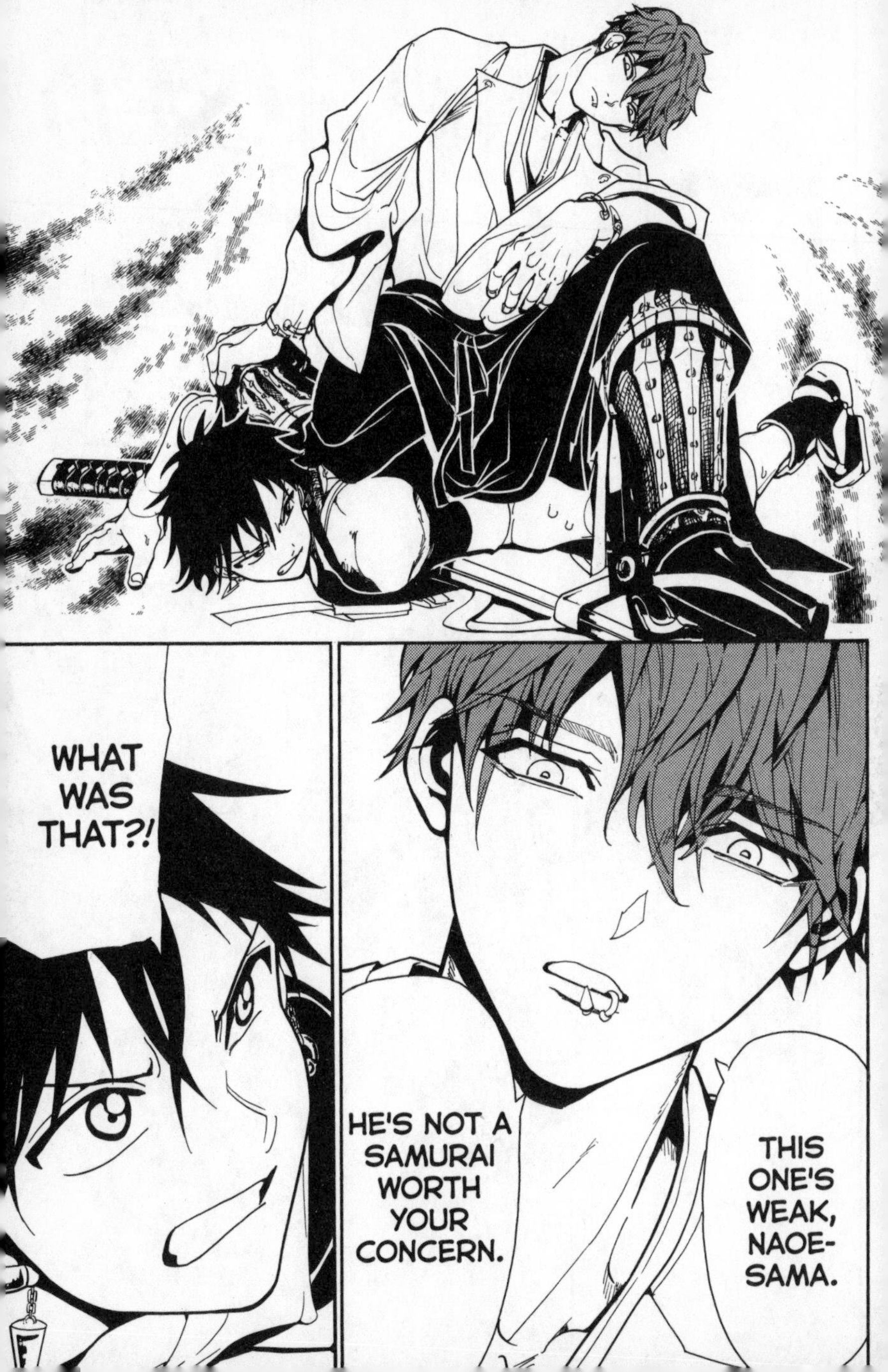
THIS ONE'S WEAK, NAOE-SAMA.
HE'S NOT A SAMURAI WORTH YOUR CONCERN.
WHAT WAS THAT?!

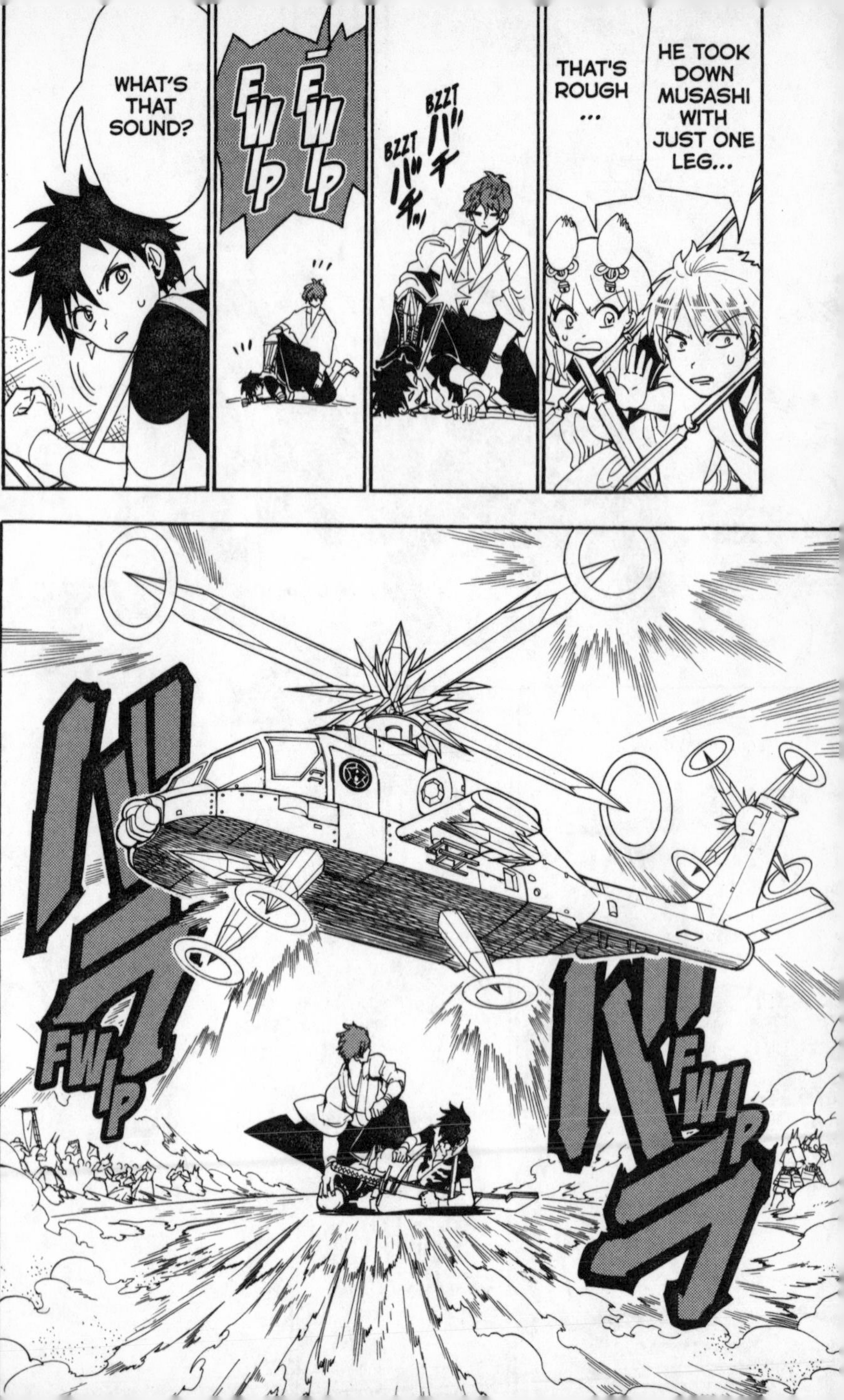
HE TOOK DOWN MUSASHI WITH JUST ONE LEG...
THAT'S ROUGH ...
BZZT
バチ
BZZT
バチッ
FWIP
FWIP
WHAT'S THAT SOUND?
FWIP
FWIP

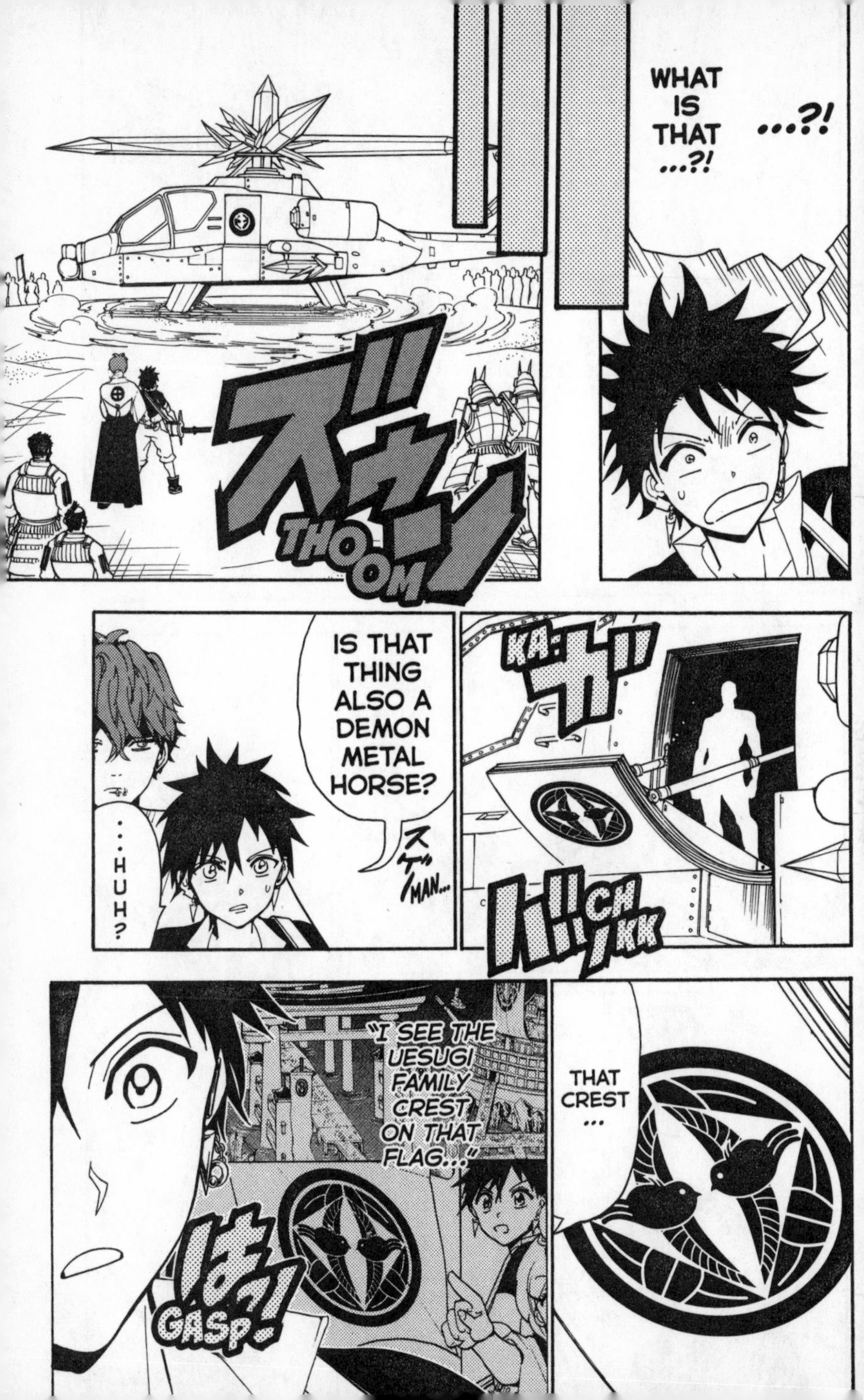
WHAT IS THAT ...?!
...?!
THOOM
KA-
IS THAT THING ALSO A DEMON METAL HORSE?
MAN...
...HUH?
CH IKK
THAT CREST ...
"I SEE THE UESUGI FAMILY CREST ON THAT FLAG..."
GASP!

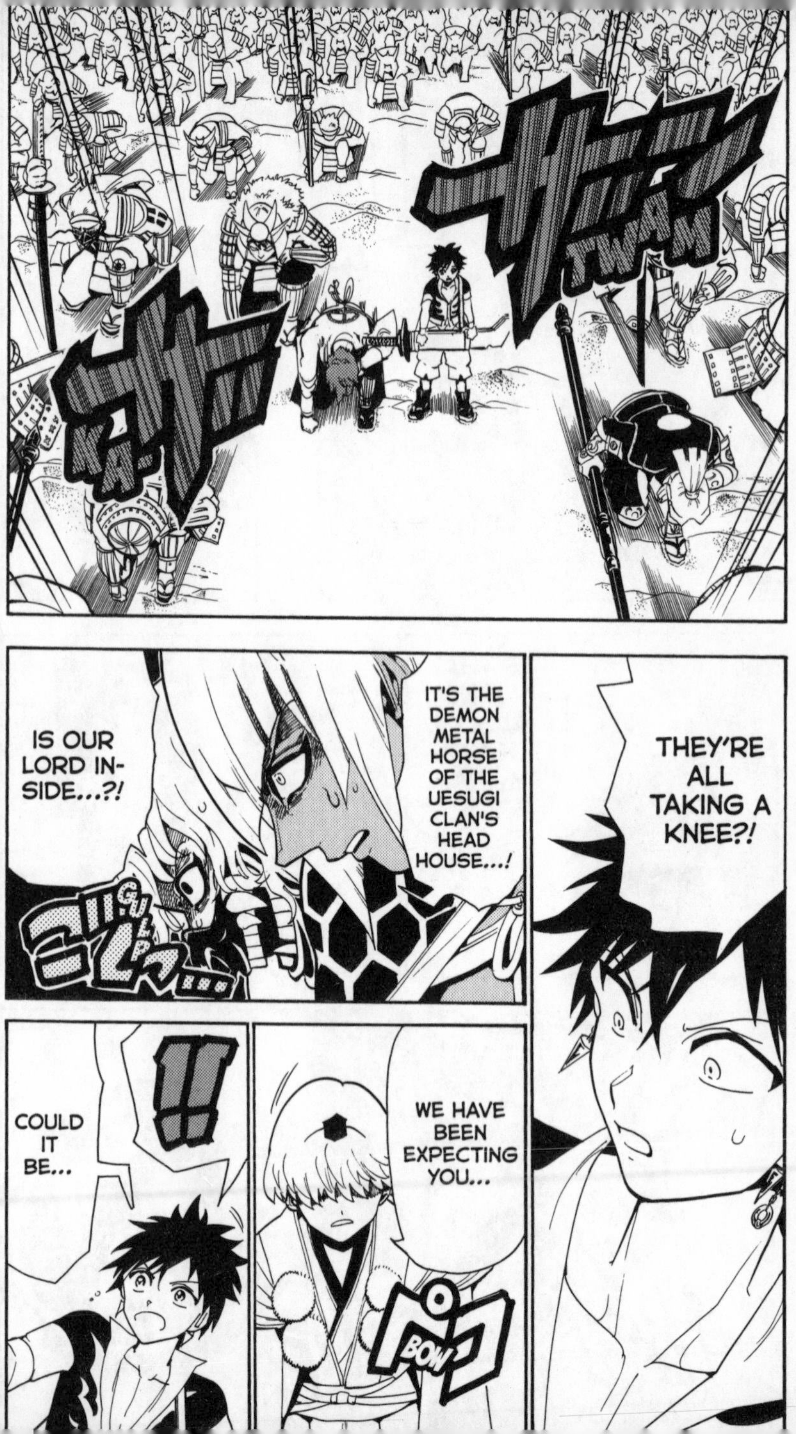
TWAM
THEY'RE ALL TAKING A KNEE?!
IT'S THE DEMON METAL HORSE OF THE UESUGI CLAN'S HEAD HOUSE...!
IS OUR LORD IN- SIDE...?!
GULP
WE HAVE BEEN EXPECTING YOU...
BOW
COULD IT BE...

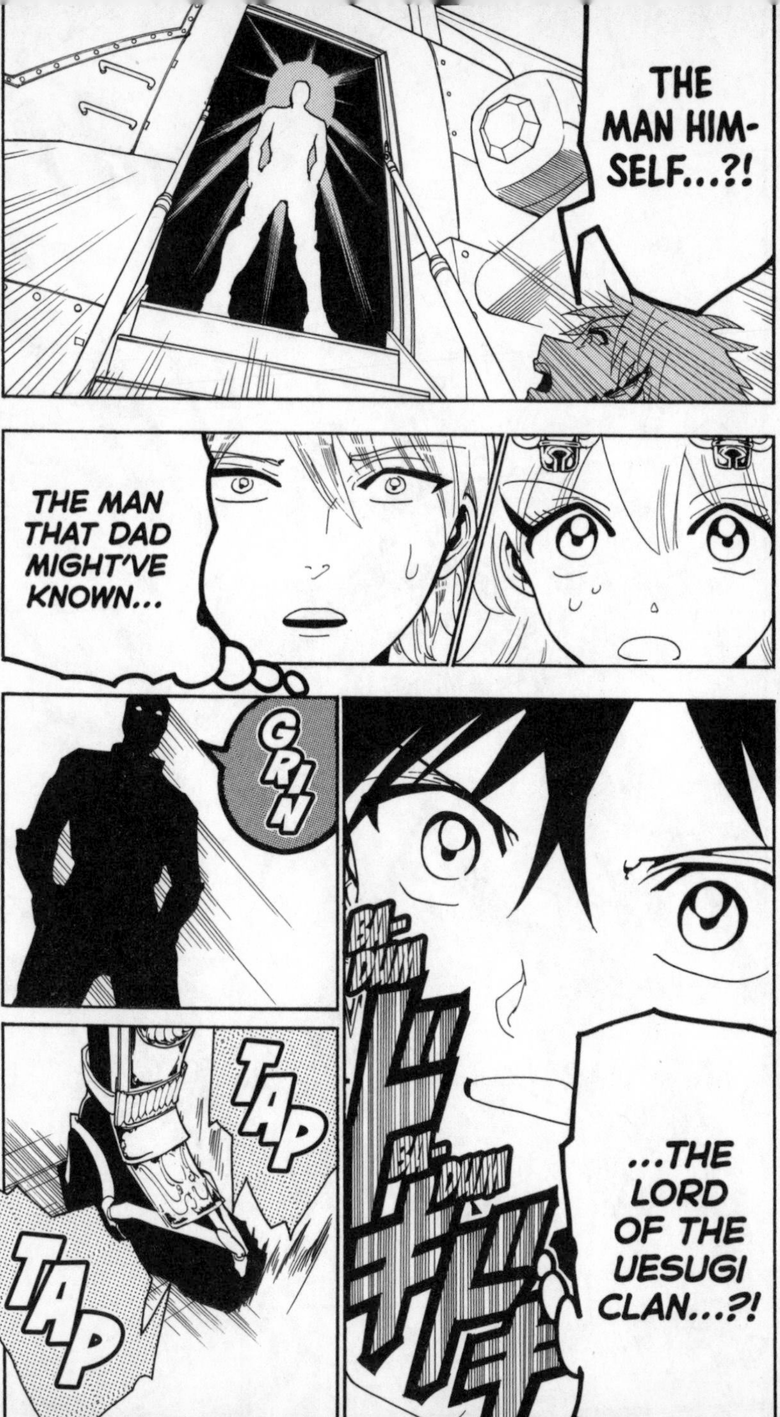
THE MAN HIM-SELF...?!
THE MAN THAT DAD MIGHT'VE KNOWN...
BA-DMMM
BA-DMMM
...THE LORD OF THE UESUGI CLAN...?!
GRIN
TAP
TAP

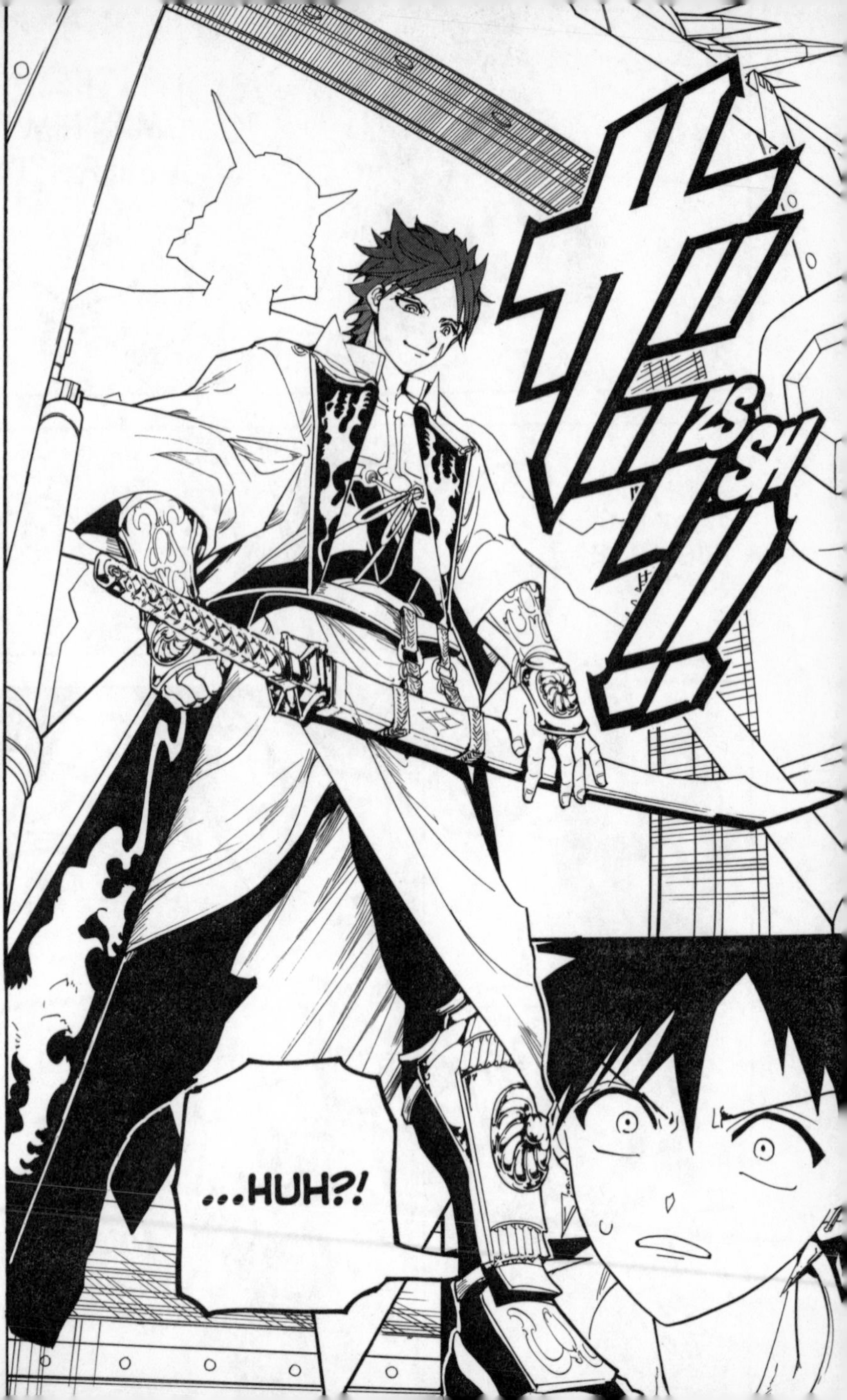
ZSSH
...HUH?!

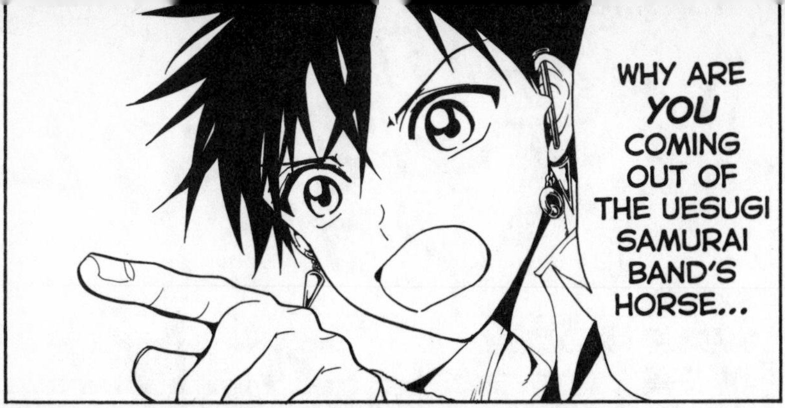
WHY ARE *YOU* COMING OUT OF THE UESUGI SAMURAI BAND'S HORSE...
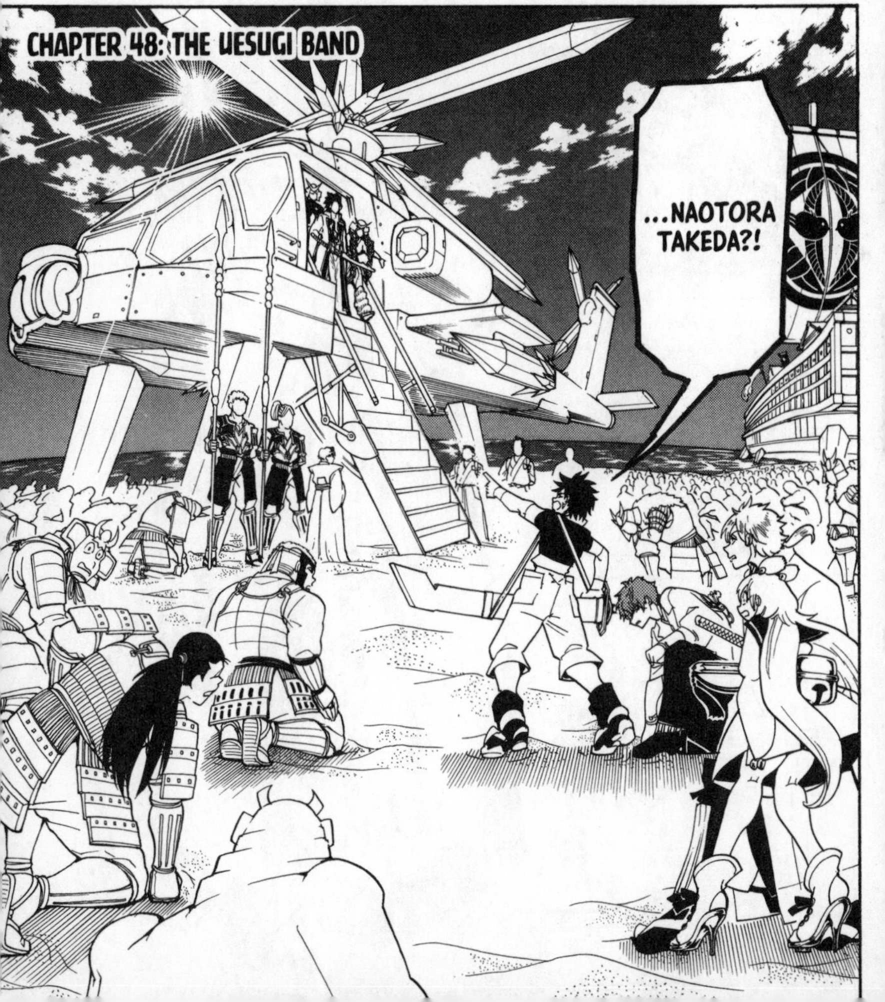
CHAPTER 48: THE UESUGI BAND
...NAOTORA TAKEDA?!

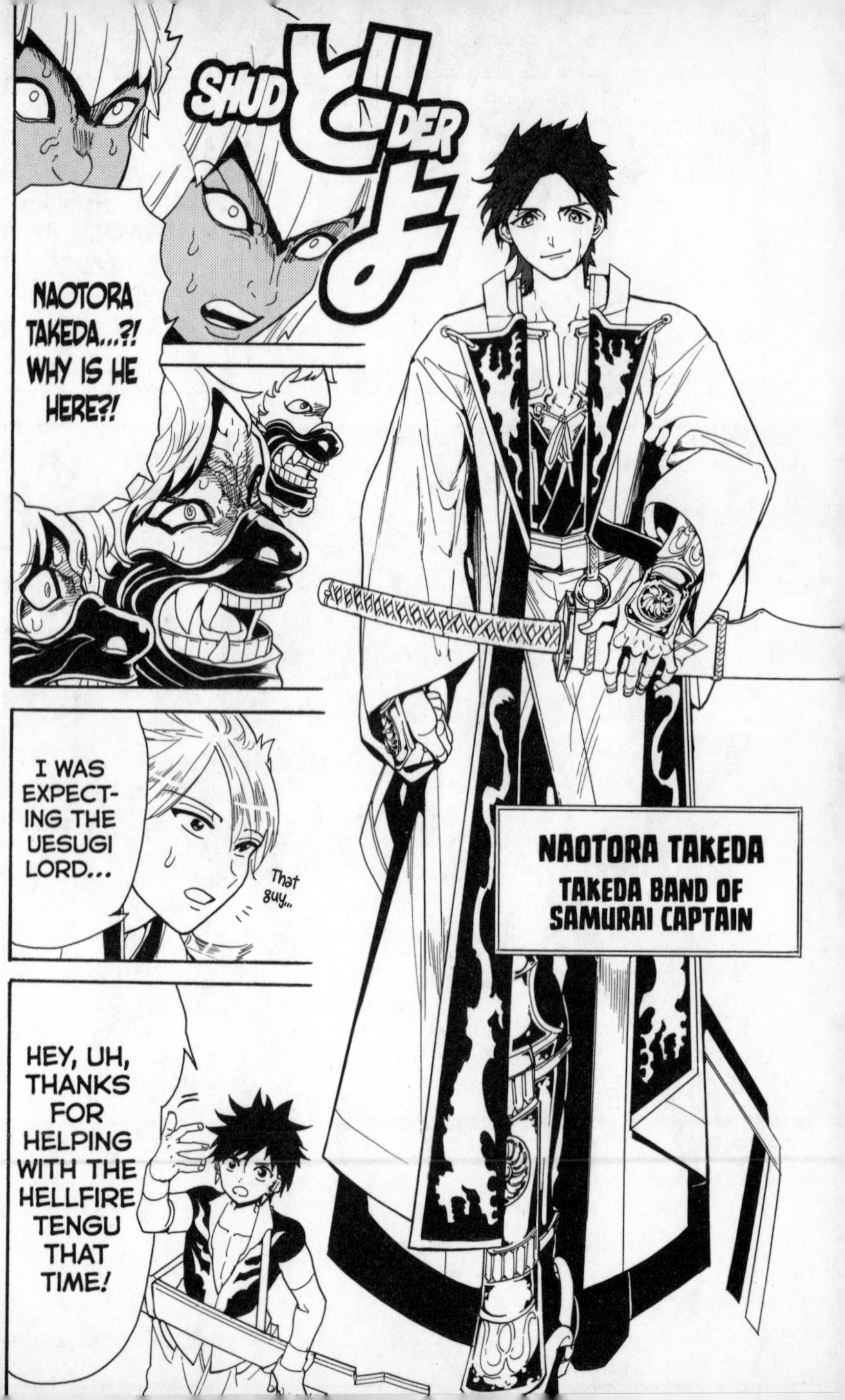
NAOTORA TAKEDA
TAKEDA BAND OF SAMURAI CAPTAIN
SHUDDER
NAOTORA TAKEDA...?! WHY IS HE HERE?!
I WAS EXPECTING THE UESUGI LORD...
That guy...
HEY, UH, THANKS FOR HELPING WITH THE HELLFIRE TENGU THAT TIME!

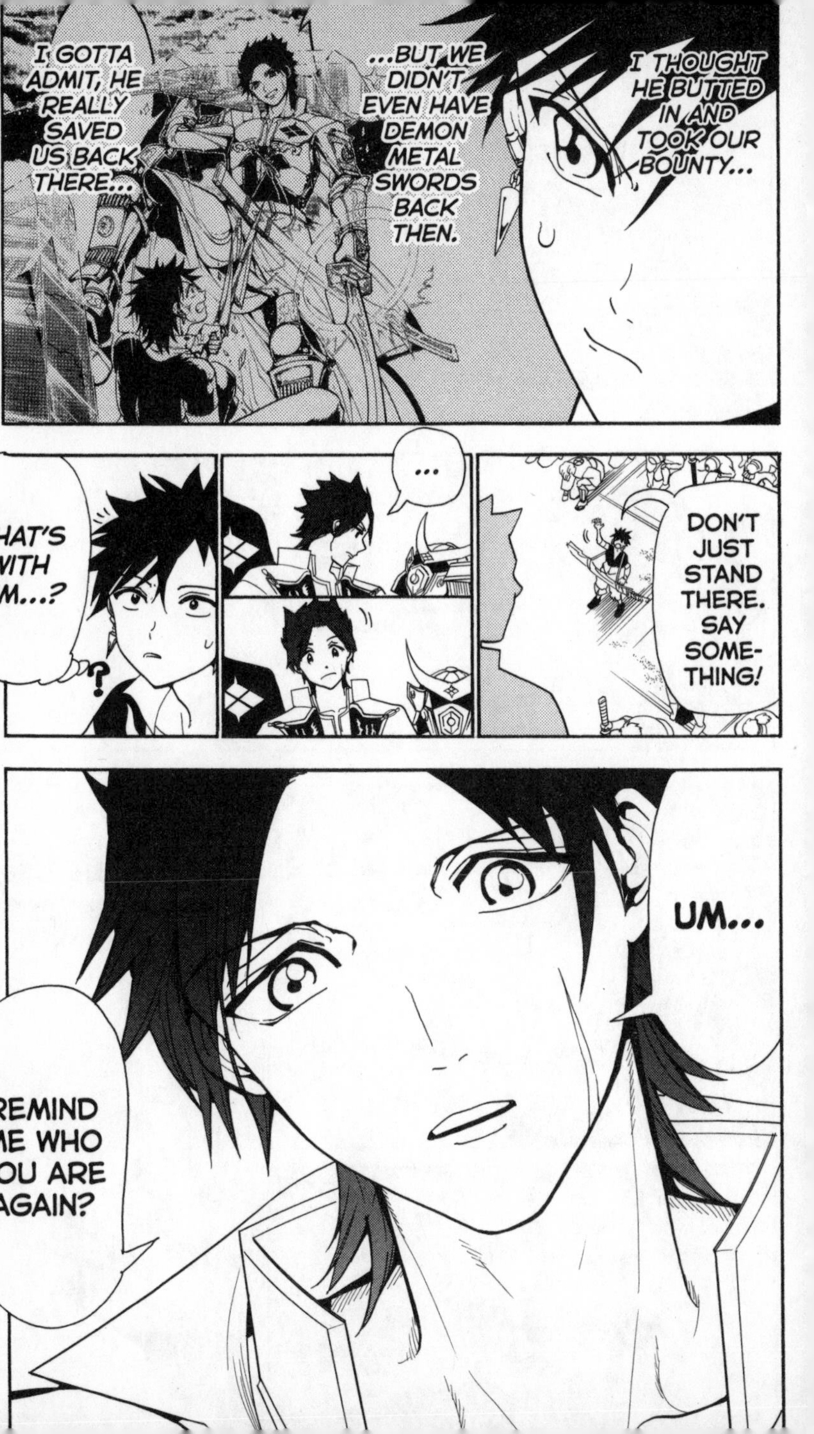
I THOUGHT HE BUTTED IN AND TOOK OUR BOUNTY...
...BUT WE DIDN'T EVEN HAVE DEMON METAL SWORDS BACK THEN.
I GOTTA ADMIT, HE REALLY SAVED US BACK THERE...
DON'T JUST STAND THERE. SAY SOME-THING!
...
WHAT'S WITH HIM...?
?
UM...
REMIND ME WHO YOU ARE AGAIN?

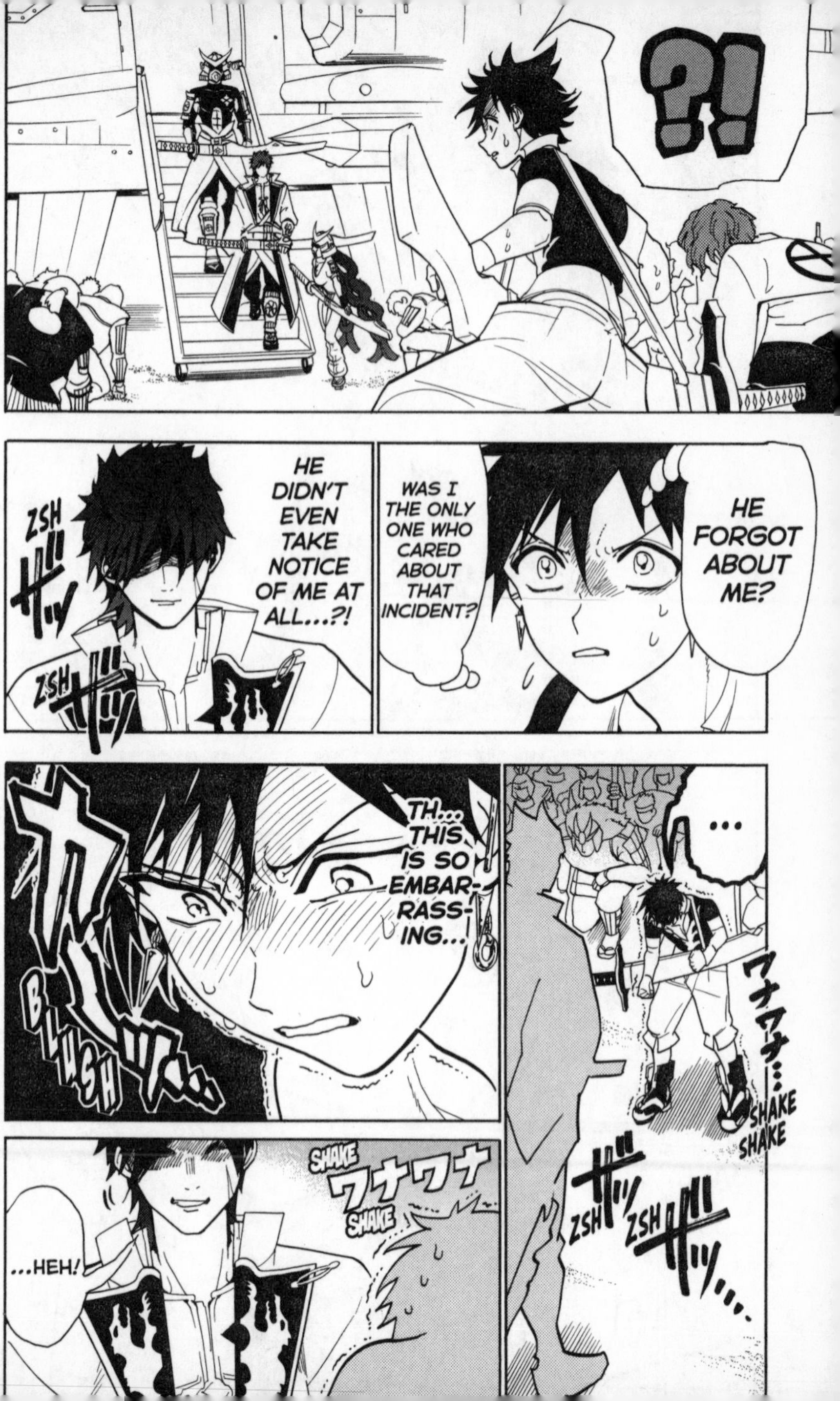
?!
HE FORGOT ABOUT ME?
WAS I THE ONLY ONE WHO CARED ABOUT THAT INCIDENT?
HE DIDN'T EVEN TAKE NOTICE OF ME AT ALL...?!
ZSH
ザッ
ZSH
ザッ
...
ワナワナ...
SHAKE SHAKE
ZSH
ザッ
ZSH
ザッ...
TH... THIS IS SO EMBARRASSING...!
BLUSH
...HEH!
SHAKE
ワナワナ
SHAKE

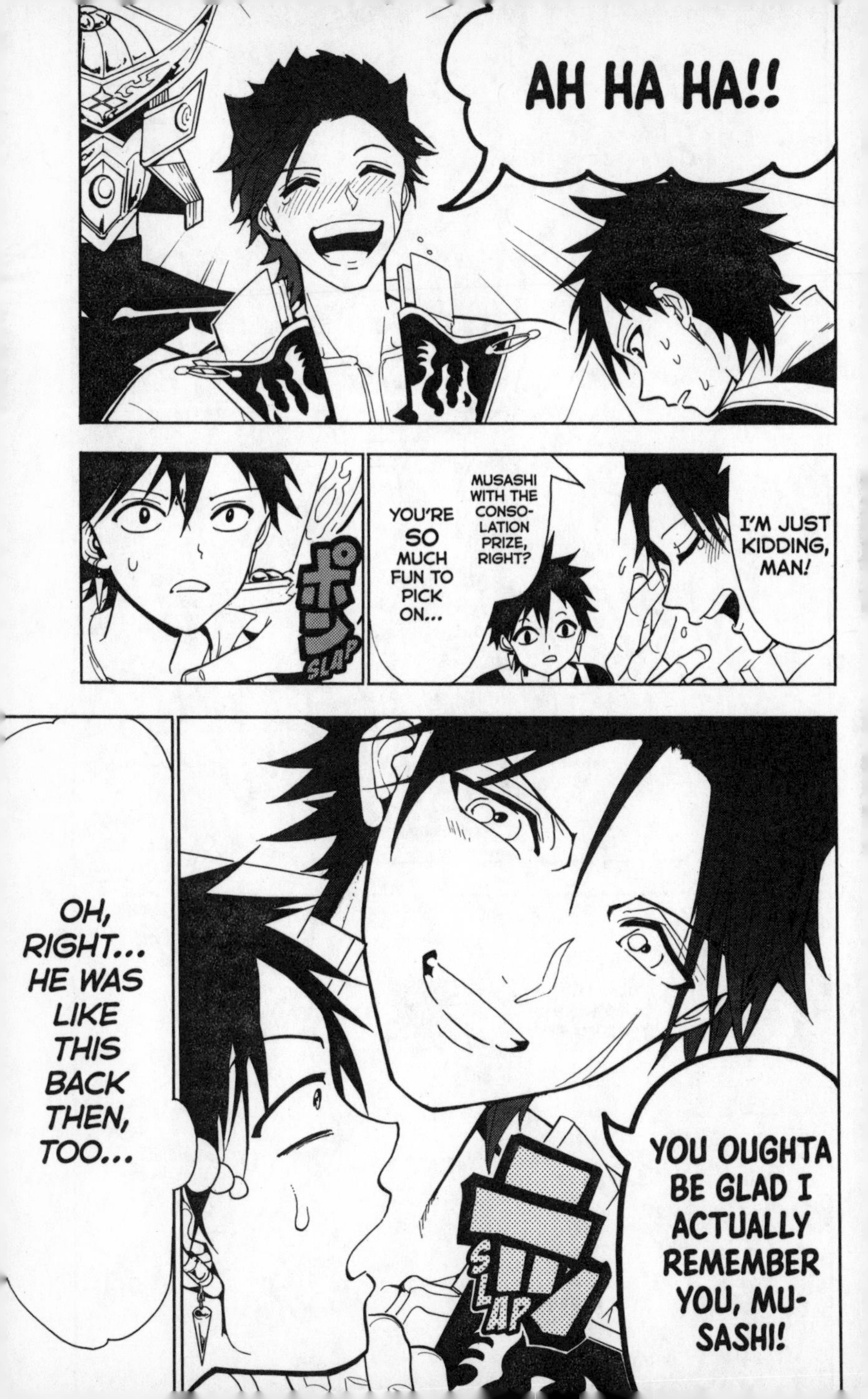
AH HA HA!!
I'M JUST KIDDING, MAN!
MUSASHI WITH THE CONSO-LATION PRIZE, RIGHT?
YOU'RE SO MUCH FUN TO PICK ON...
ポン
SLAP
YOU OUGHTA BE GLAD I ACTUALLY REMEMBER YOU, MU-SASHI!
SLAP
OH, RIGHT... HE WAS LIKE THIS BACK THEN, TOO...

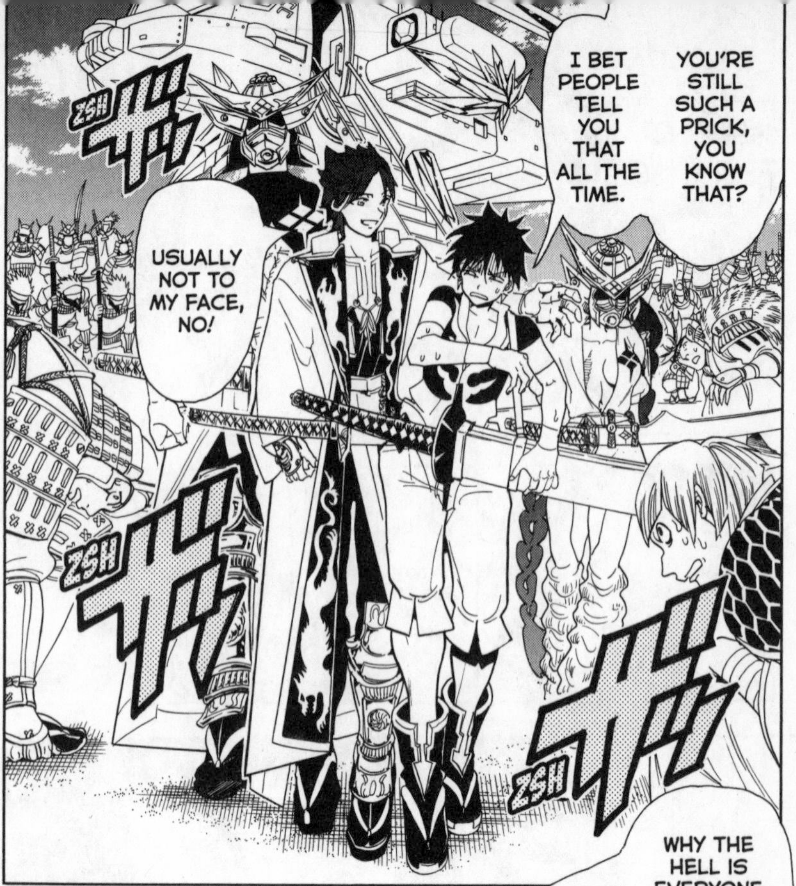
ZSH
YOU'RE STILL SUCH A PRICK, YOU KNOW THAT?
I BET PEOPLE TELL YOU THAT ALL THE TIME.
USUALLY NOT TO MY FACE, NO!
ZSH
ZSH
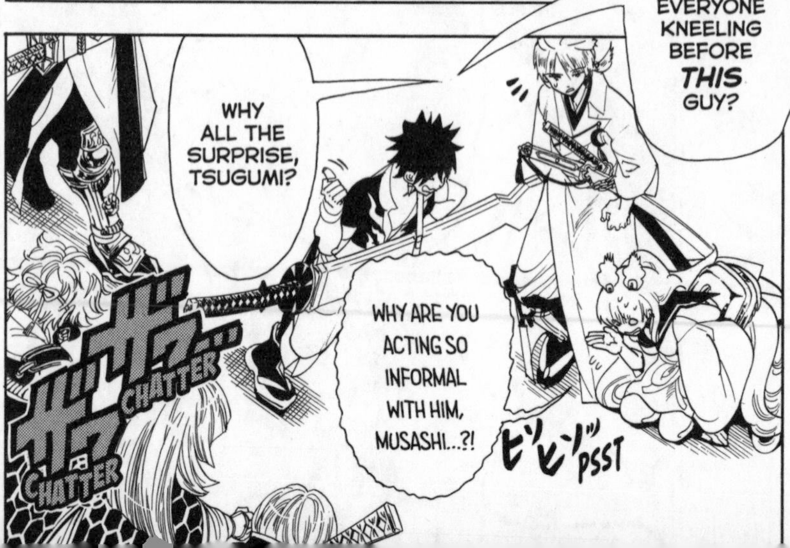
WHY THE HELL IS EVERYONE KNEELING BEFORE THIS GUY?
WHY ALL THE SURPRISE, TSUGUMI?
PSST
WHY ARE YOU ACTING SO INFORMAL WITH HIM, MUSASHI...?!
CHATTER
CHATTER

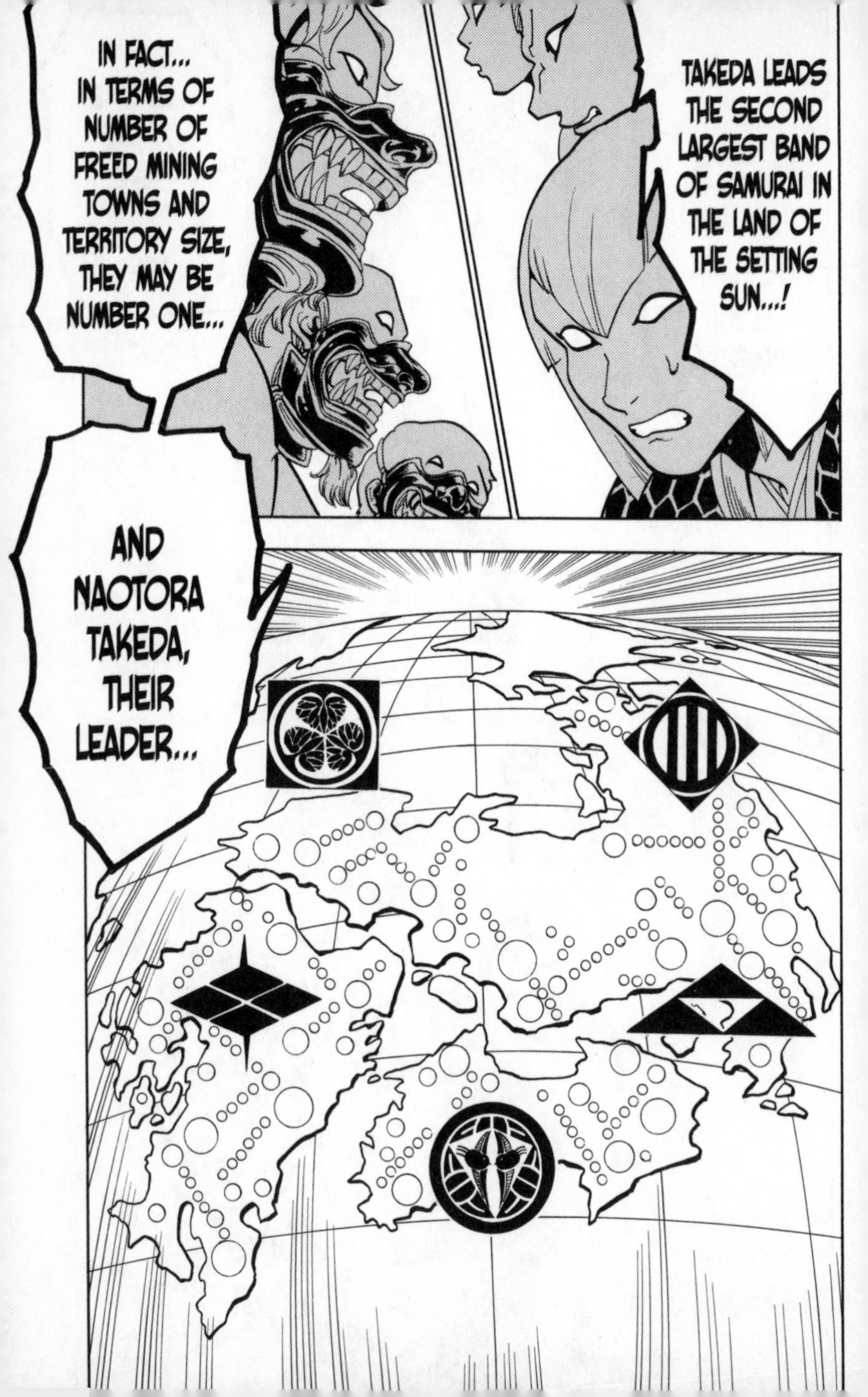
TAKEDA LEADS THE SECOND LARGEST BAND OF SAMURAI IN THE LAND OF THE SETTING SUN...!
IN FACT... IN TERMS OF NUMBER OF FREED MINING TOWNS AND TERRITORY SIZE, THEY MAY BE NUMBER ONE...
AND NAOTORA TAKEDA, THEIR LEADER...

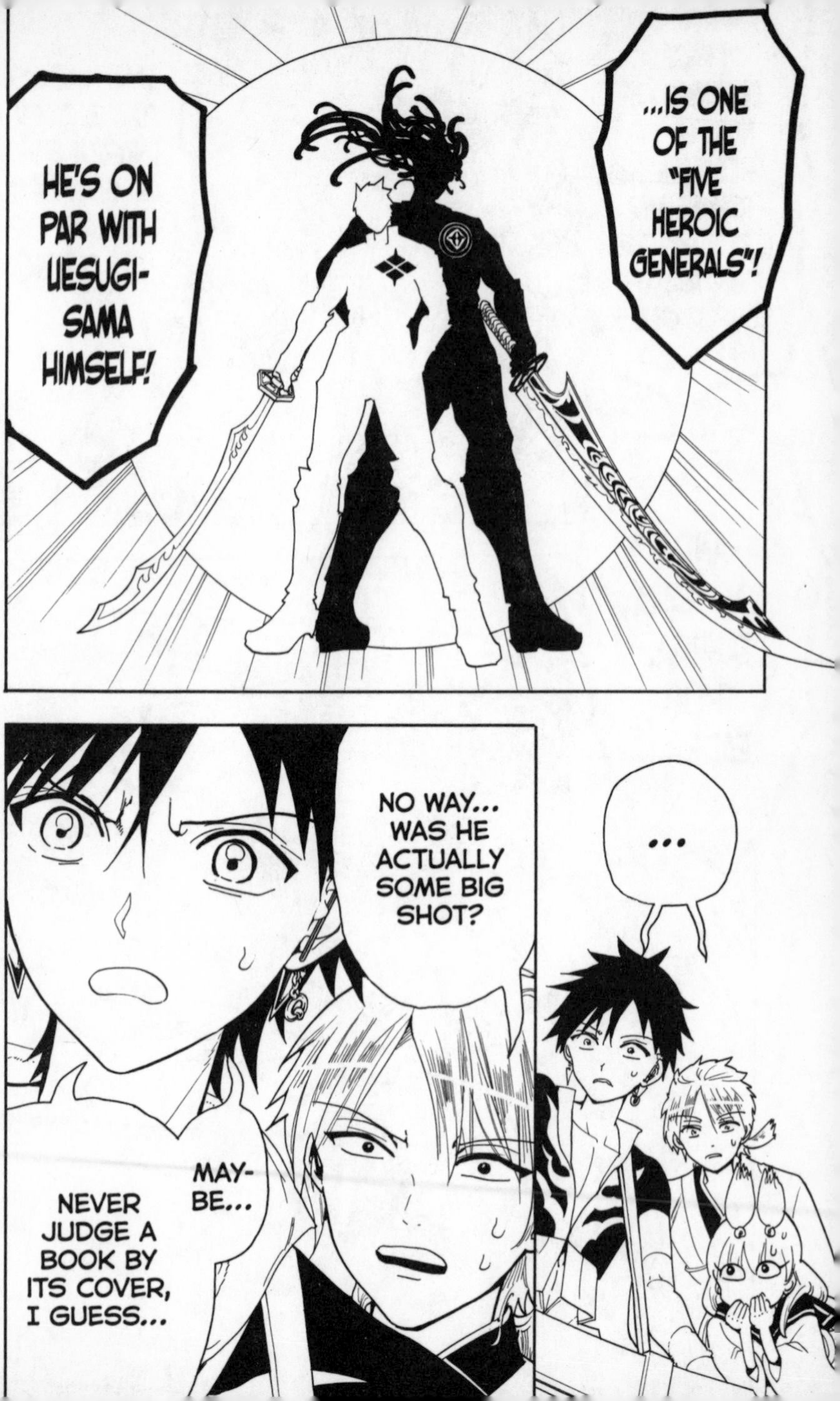
...IS ONE OF THE "FIVE HEROIC GENERALS"!
HE'S ON PAR WITH UESUGI-SAMA HIMSELF!
...
NO WAY... WAS HE ACTUALLY SOME BIG SHOT?
MAY-BE...
NEVER JUDGE A BOOK BY ITS COVER, I GUESS...

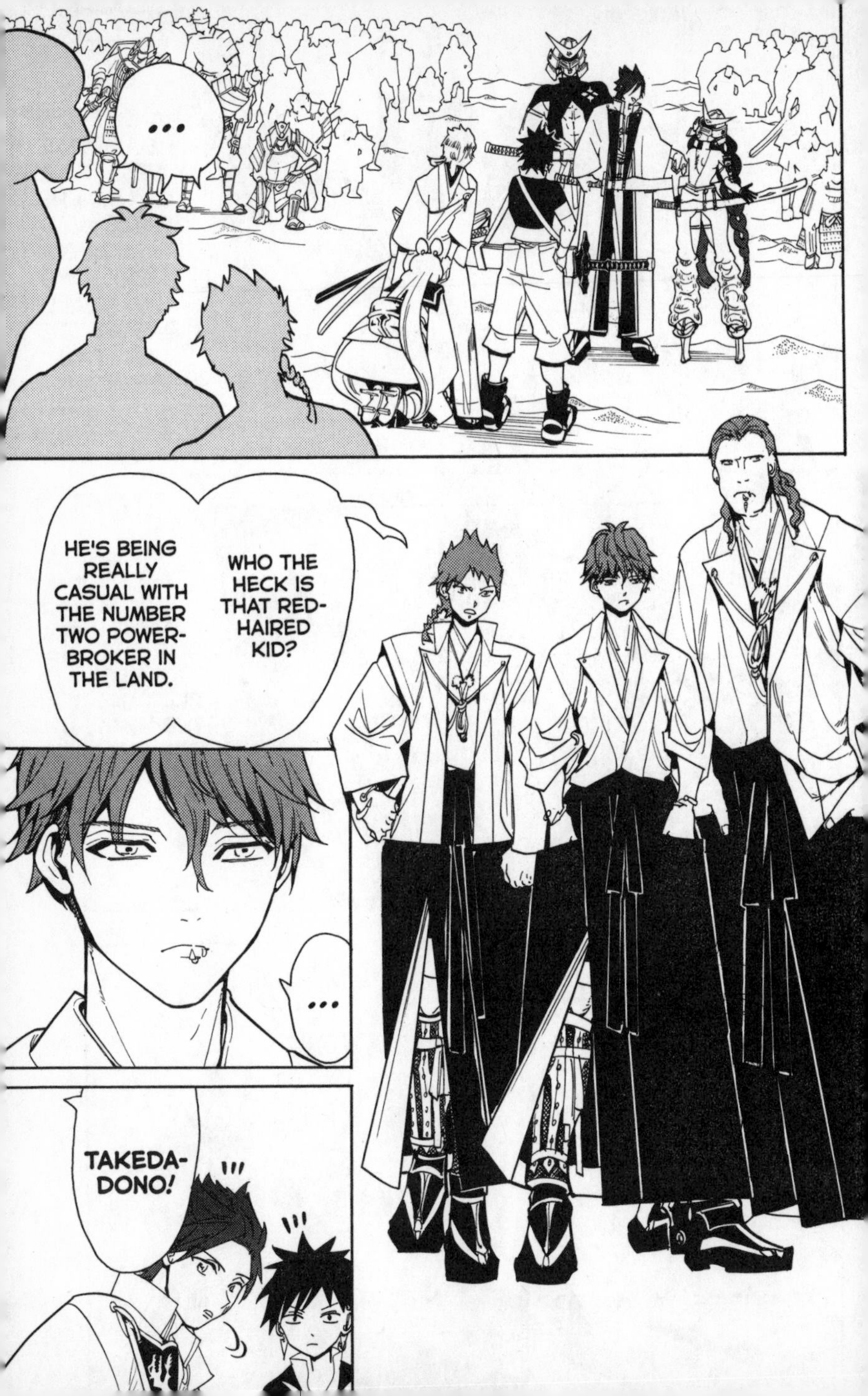
...
WHO THE HECK IS THAT RED-HAIRED KID?
HE'S BEING REALLY CASUAL WITH THE NUMBER TWO POWER-BROKER IN THE LAND.
...
TAKEDA-DONO!
!!!
!!!

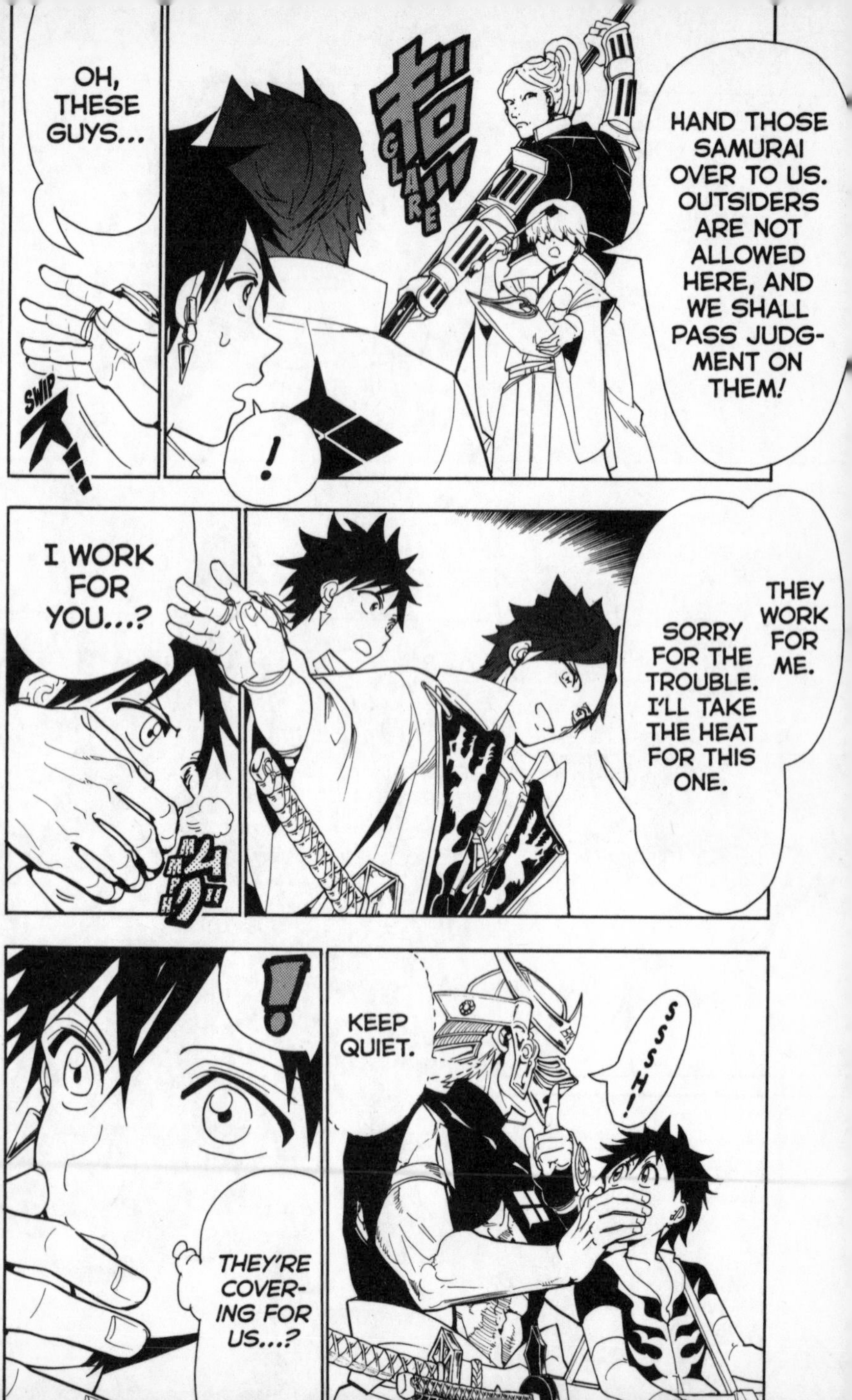
GLARE
HAND THOSE SAMURAI OVER TO US. OUTSIDERS ARE NOT ALLOWED HERE, AND WE SHALL PASS JUDGMENT ON THEM!
!
OH, THESE GUYS...
SWIP
THEY WORK FOR ME.
SORRY FOR THE TROUBLE. I'LL TAKE THE HEAT FOR THIS ONE.
I WORK FOR YOU...?
KEEP QUIET.
SSSSH!
!
THEY'RE COVERING FOR US...?

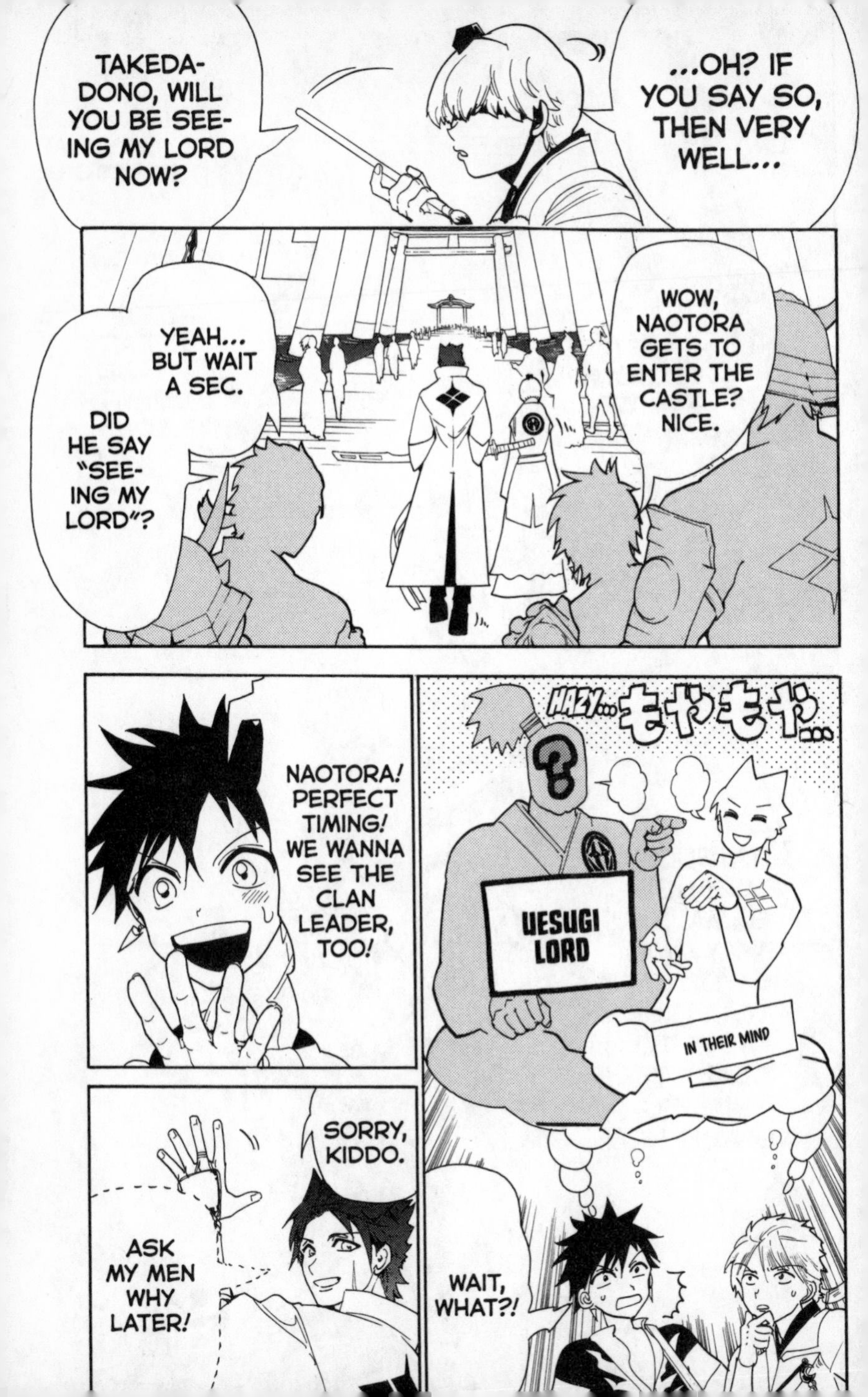
...OH? IF YOU SAY SO, THEN VERY WELL...
TAKEDA-DONO, WILL YOU BE SEE-ING MY LORD NOW?
WOW, NAOTORA GETS TO ENTER THE CASTLE? NICE.
YEAH... BUT WAIT A SEC.
DID HE SAY "SEE-ING MY LORD"?
HAZY... もやもや...
UESUGI LORD
IN THEIR MIND
WAIT, WHAT?!
NAOTORA! PERFECT TIMING! WE WANNA SEE THE CLAN LEADER, TOO!
SORRY, KIDDO.
ASK MY MEN WHY LATER!

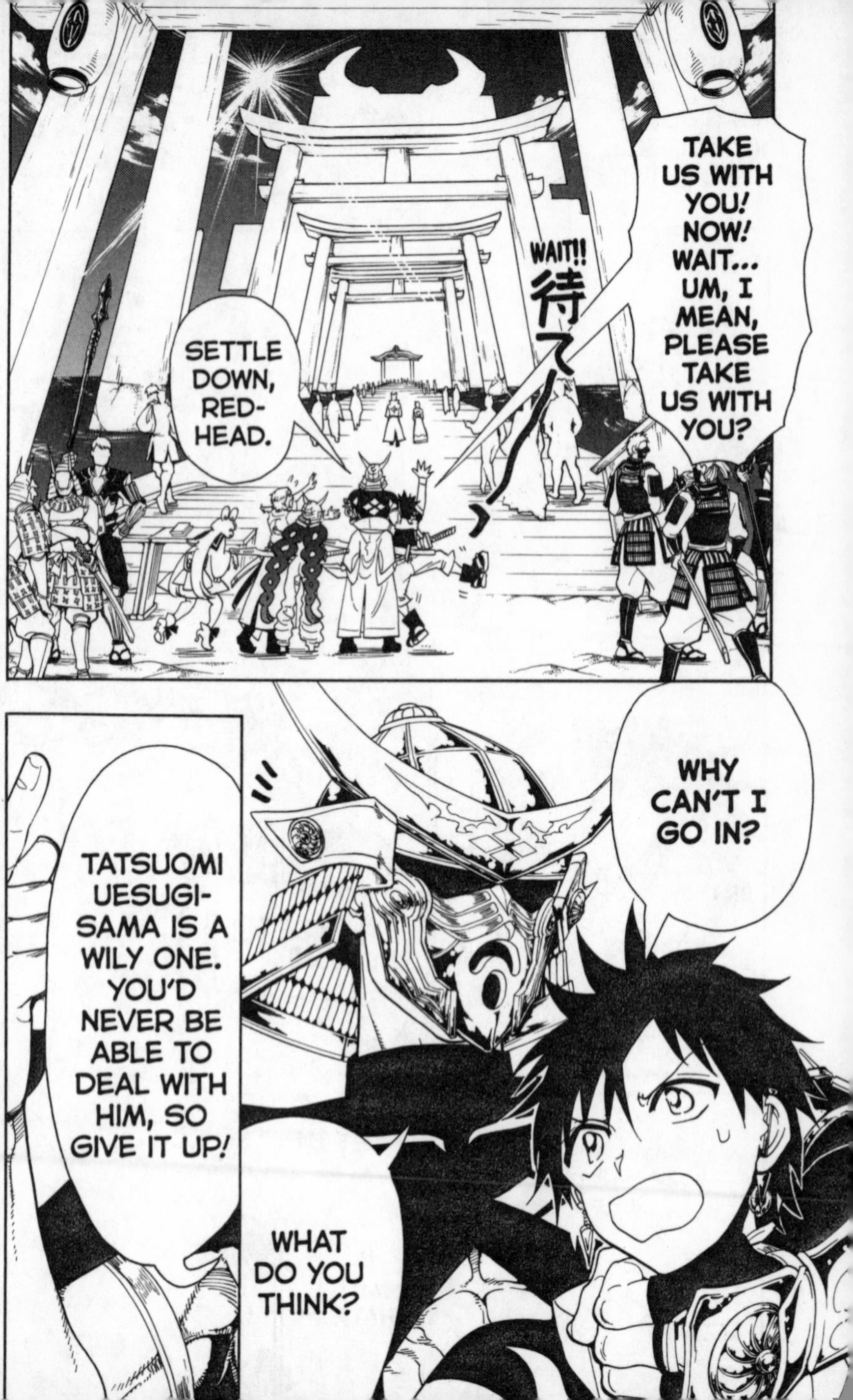
TAKE US WITH YOU! NOW! WAIT... UM, I MEAN, PLEASE TAKE US WITH YOU?
WAIT!!
待て
SETTLE DOWN, RED-HEAD.
WHY CAN'T I GO IN?
WHAT DO YOU THINK?
TATSUOMI UESUGI-SAMA IS A WILY ONE. YOU'D NEVER BE ABLE TO DEAL WITH HIM, SO GIVE IT UP!

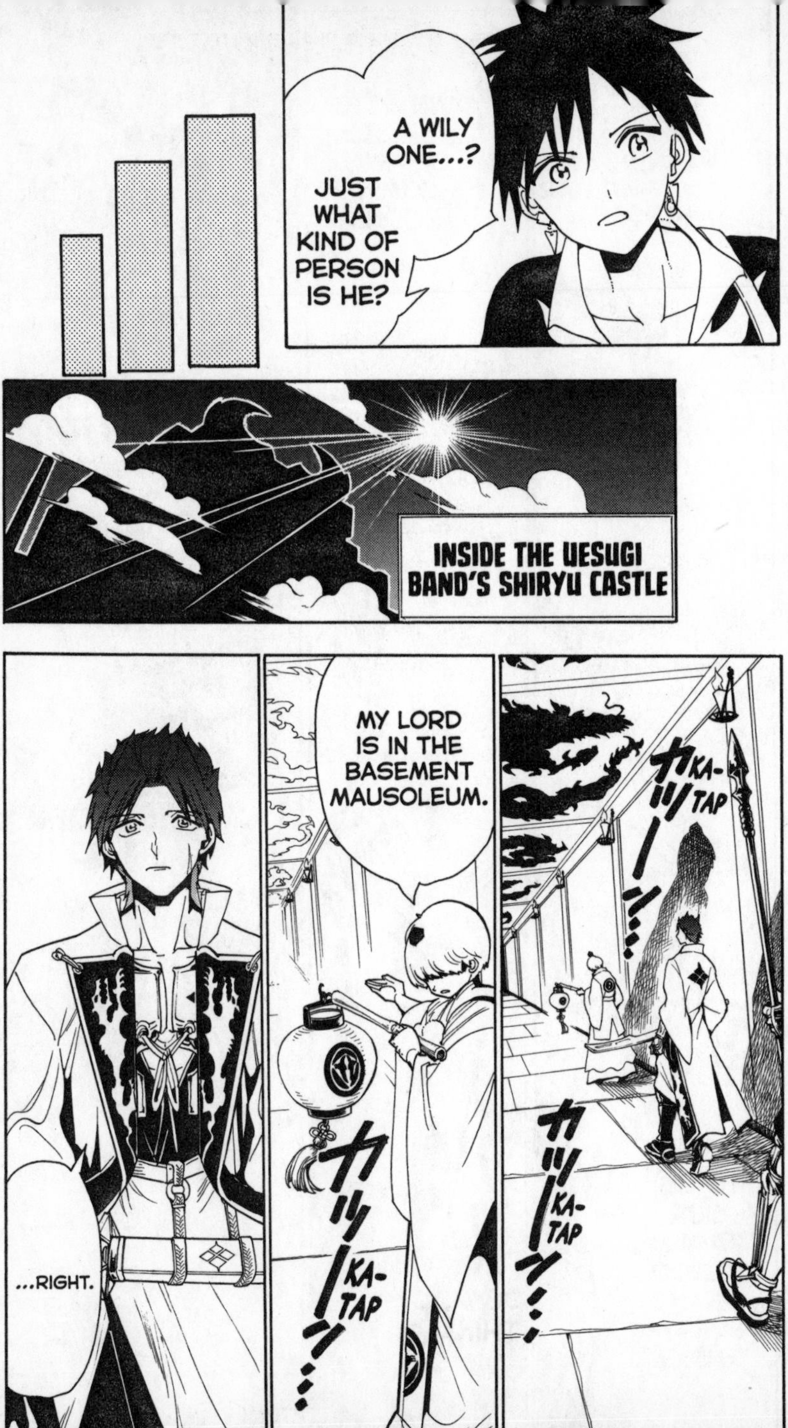
A WILY ONE...?
JUST WHAT KIND OF PERSON IS HE?
INSIDE THE UESUGI BAND'S SHIRYU CASTLE
KA-TAP
KA-TAP
MY LORD IS IN THE BASEMENT MAUSOLEUM.
KA-TAP
...RIGHT.

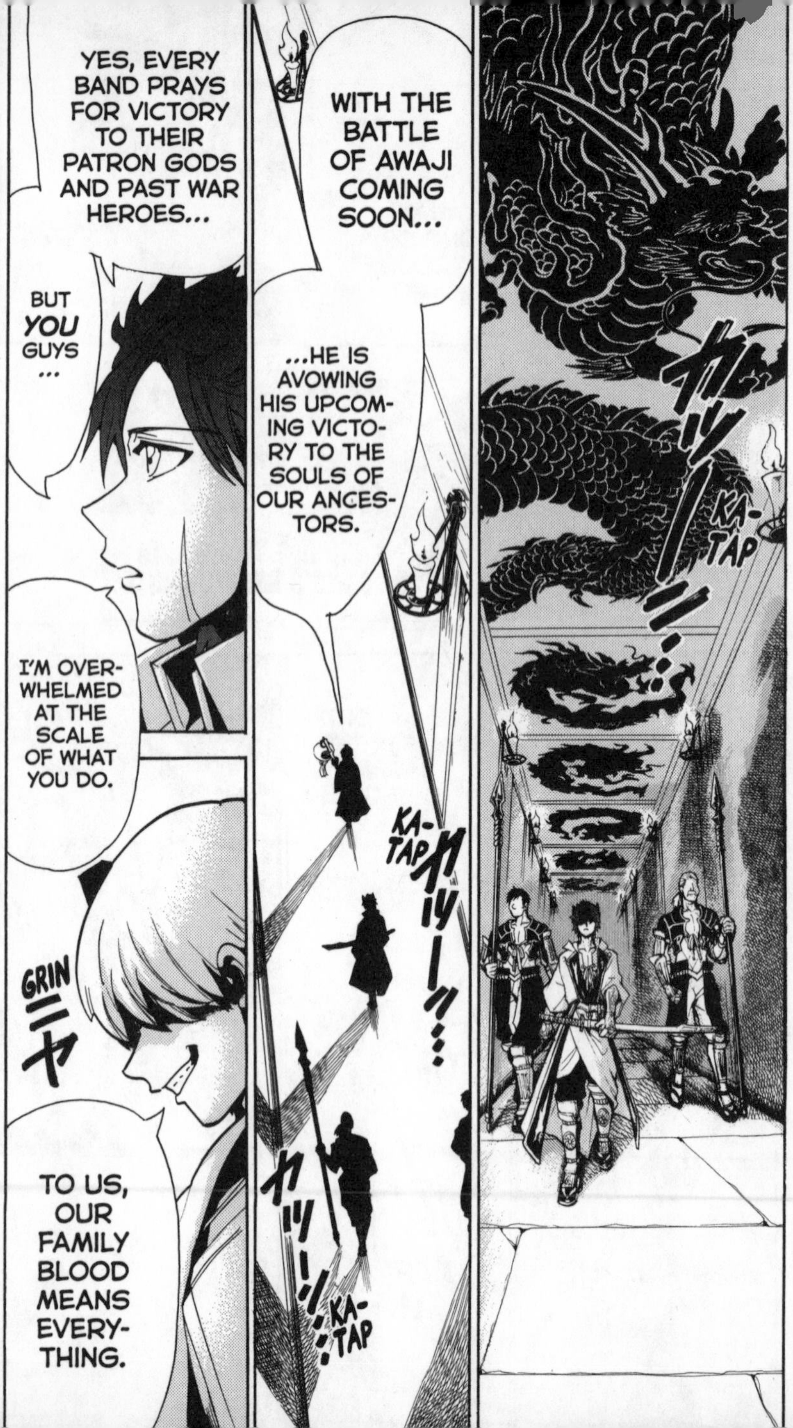

KA-TAP
WITH THE BATTLE OF AWAJI COMING SOON...
...HE IS AVOWING HIS UPCOMING VICTORY TO THE SOULS OF OUR ANCESTORS.
KA-TAP
KA-TAP
YES, EVERY BAND PRAYS FOR VICTORY TO THEIR PATRON GODS AND PAST WAR HEROES...
BUT *YOU* GUYS ...
I'M OVERWHELMED AT THE SCALE OF WHAT YOU DO.
GRIN ニヤ
TO US, OUR FAMILY BLOOD MEANS EVERYTHING.

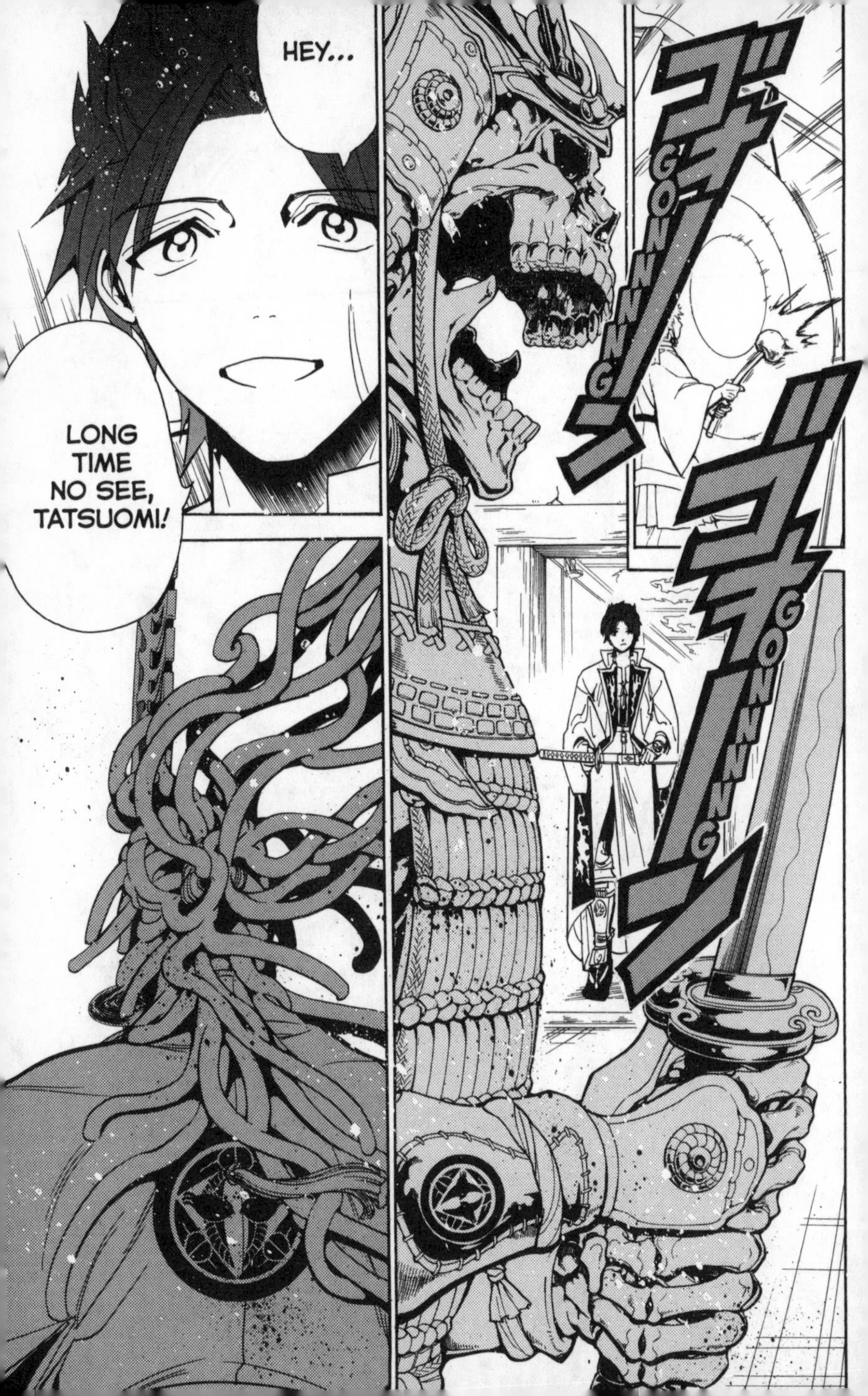
ゴォーン
GONNNNNG
ゴォーン
GONNNNNG
HEY...
LONG TIME NO SEE, TATSUOMI!

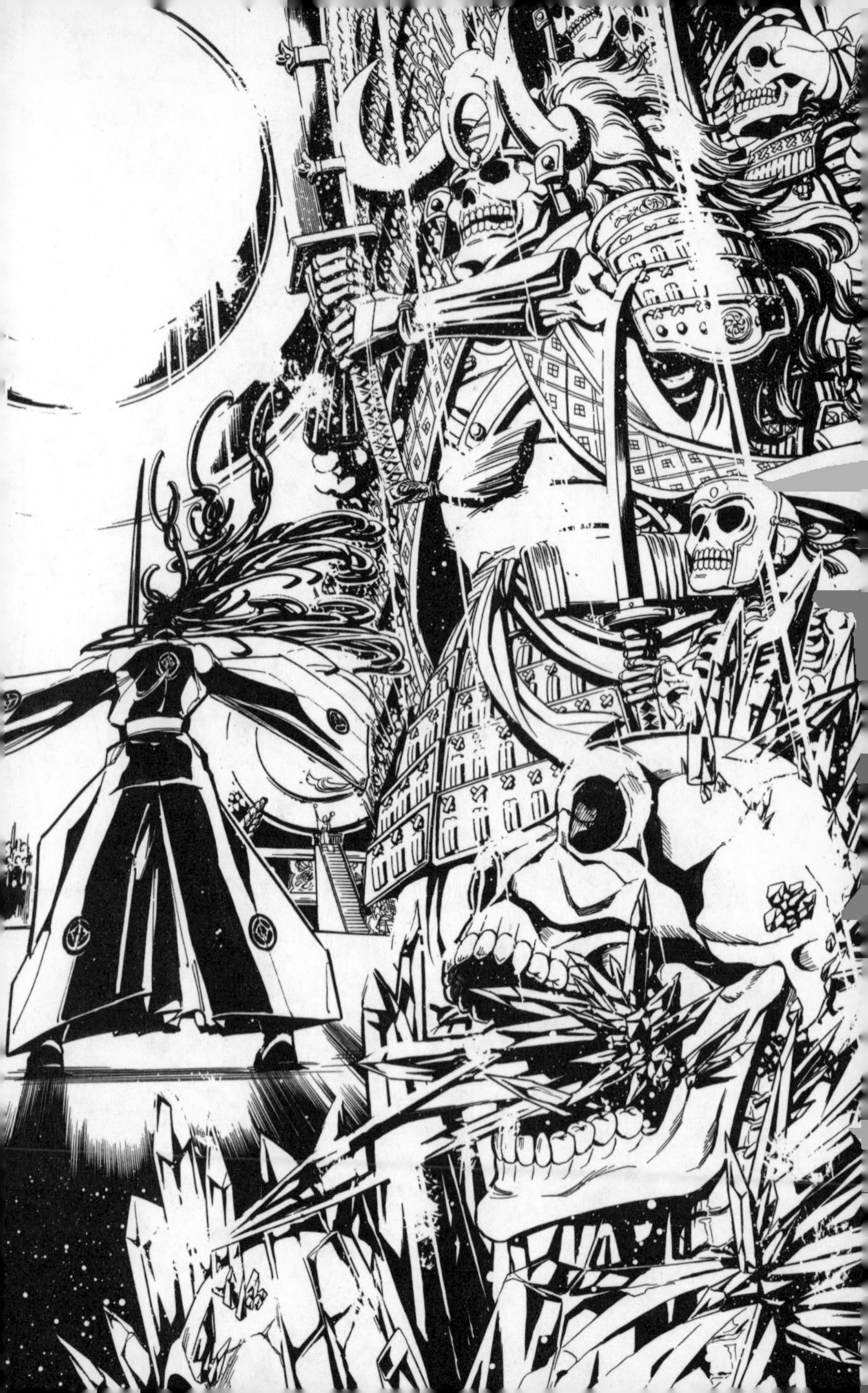

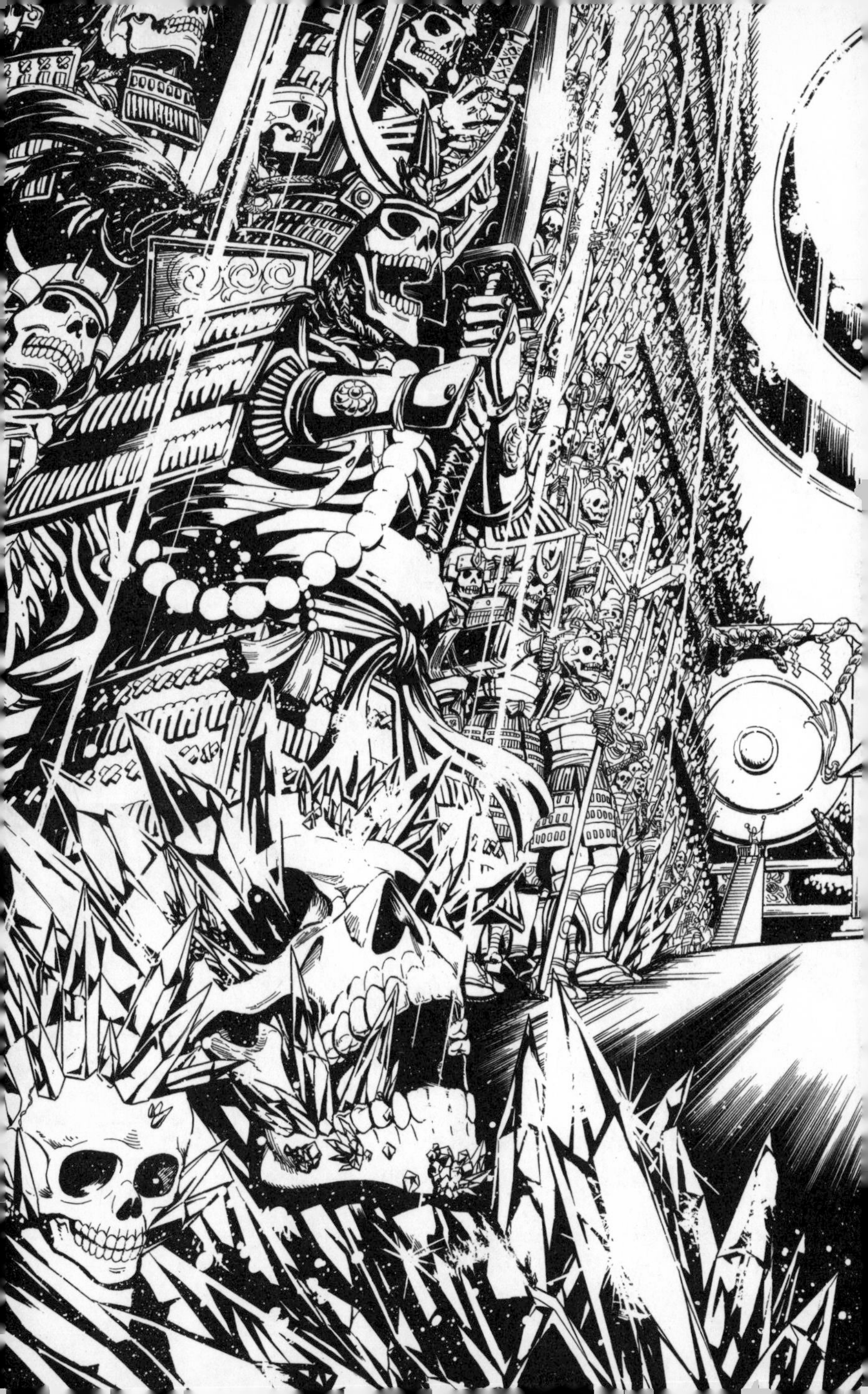

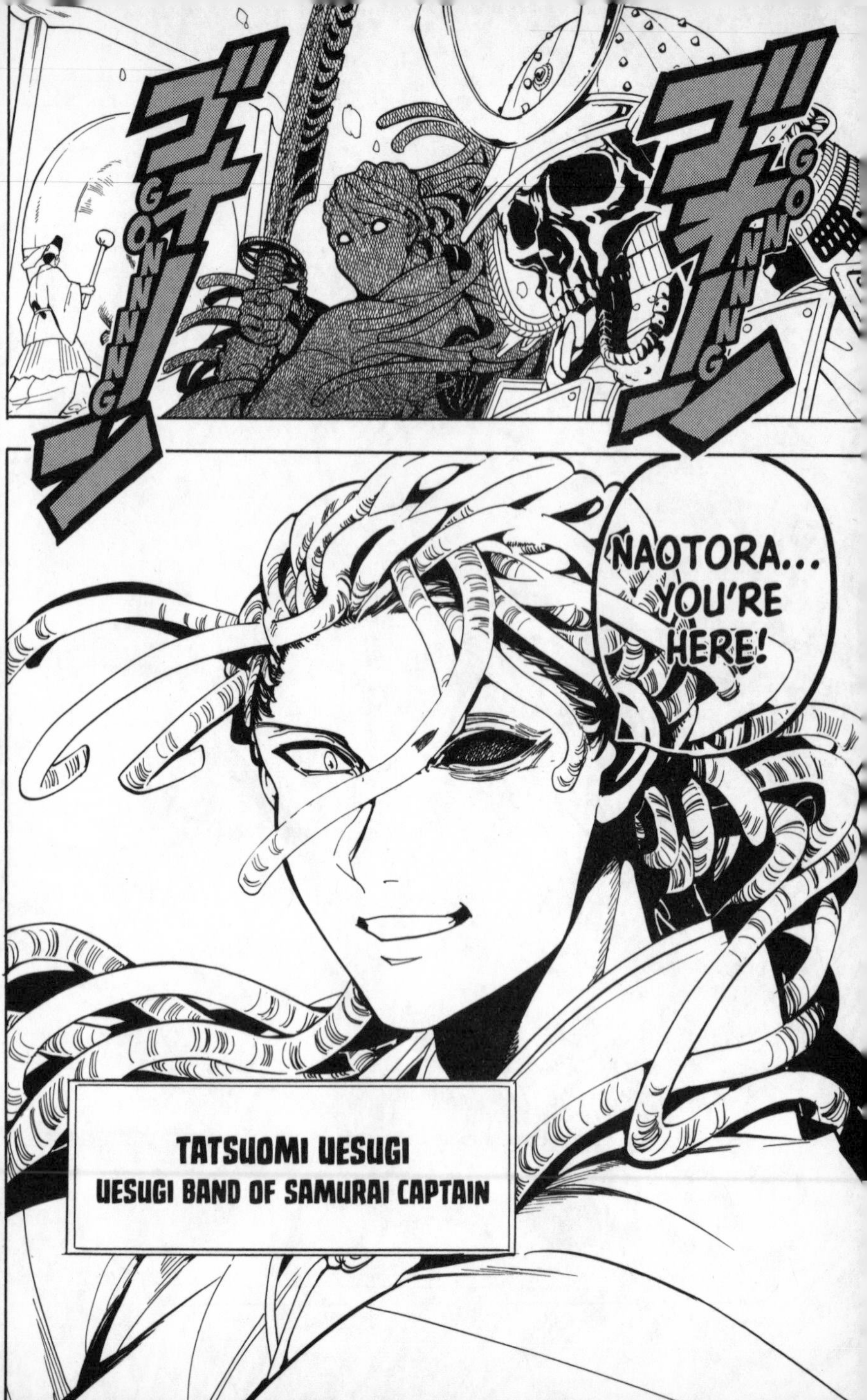
GONNNNG
GONNNNG
NAOTORA... YOU'RE HERE!
TATSUOMI UESUGI
UESUGI BAND OF SAMURAI CAPTAIN

CHAPTER 49: THE DEMON HAUNTING AWAJI

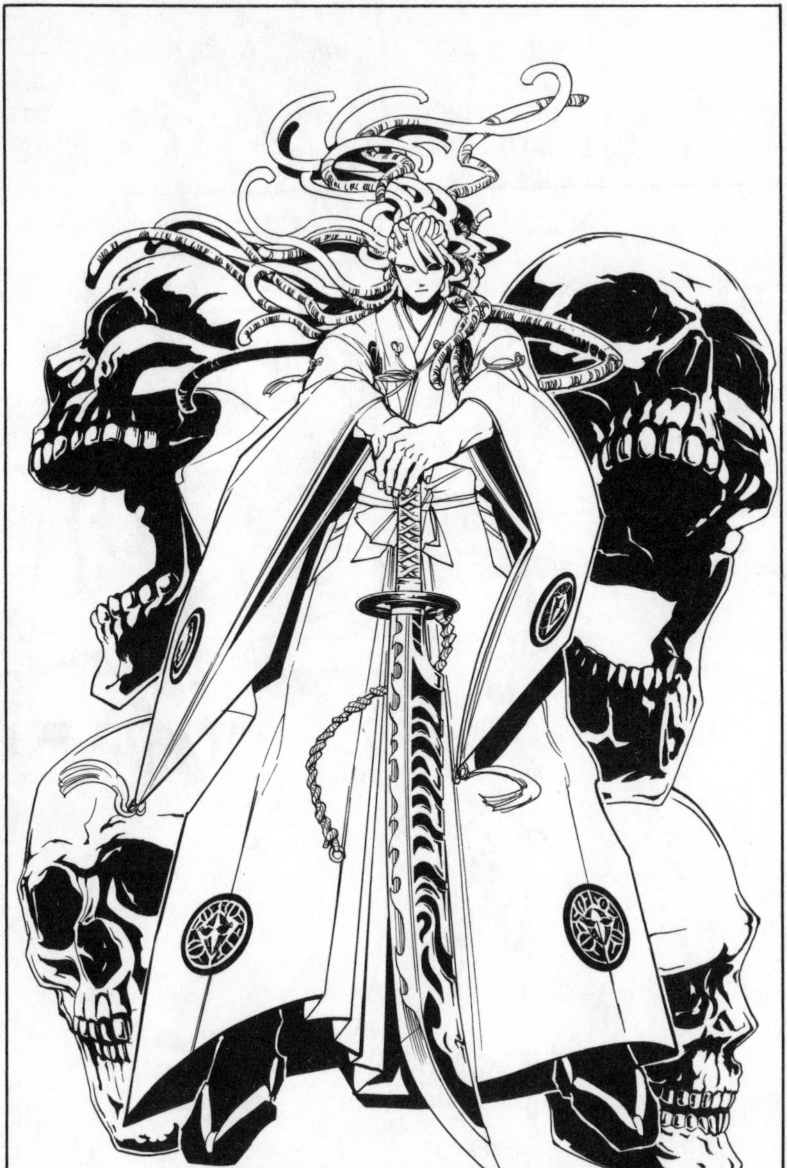

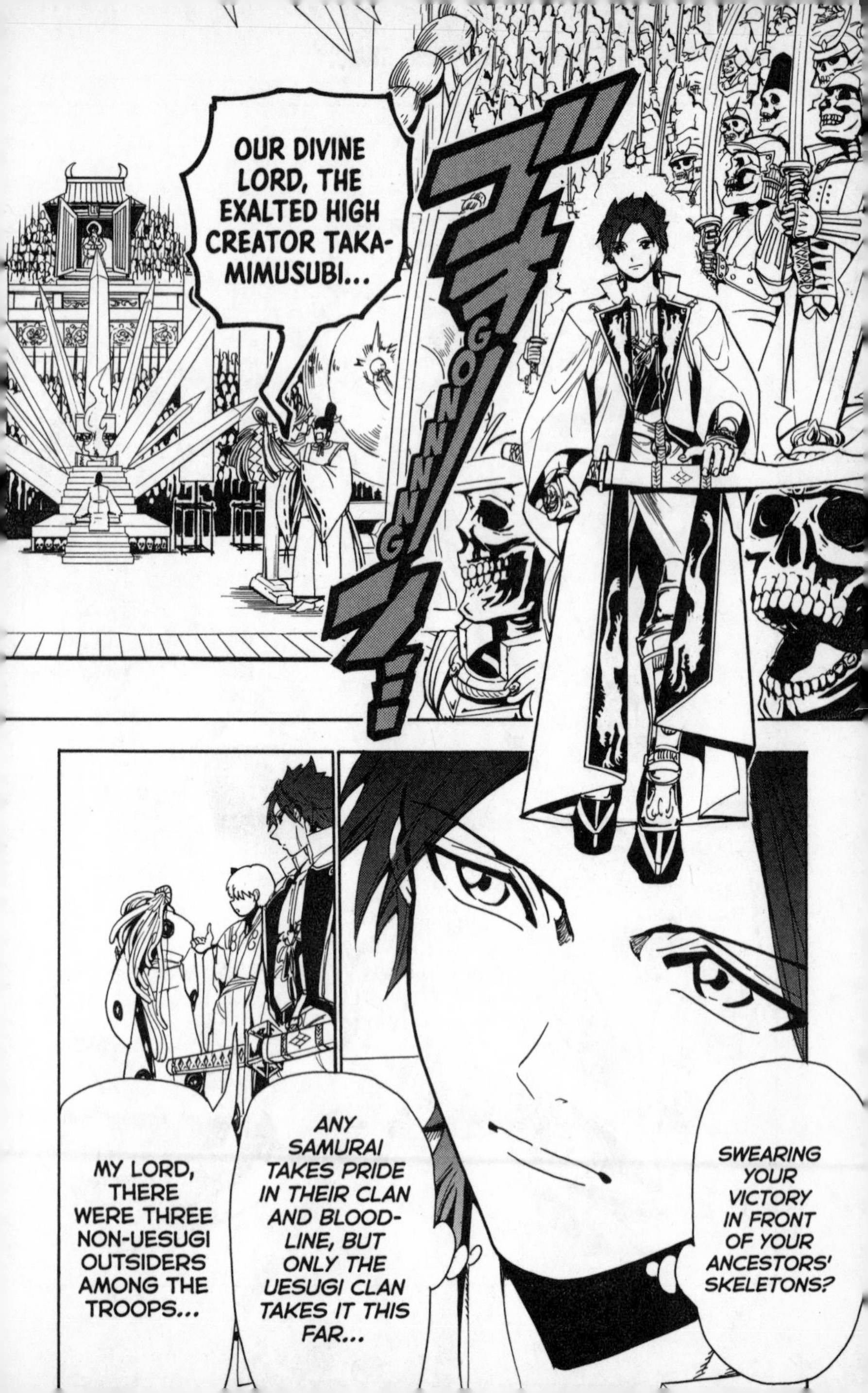
GOOONNNG!!
OUR DIVINE LORD, THE EXALTED HIGH CREATOR TAKA-MIMUSUBI...
SWEARING YOUR VICTORY IN FRONT OF YOUR ANCESTORS' SKELETONS?
ANY SAMURAI TAKES PRIDE IN THEIR CLAN AND BLOOD-LINE, BUT ONLY THE UESUGI CLAN TAKES IT THIS FAR...
MY LORD, THERE WERE THREE NON-UESUGI OUTSIDERS AMONG THE TROOPS...

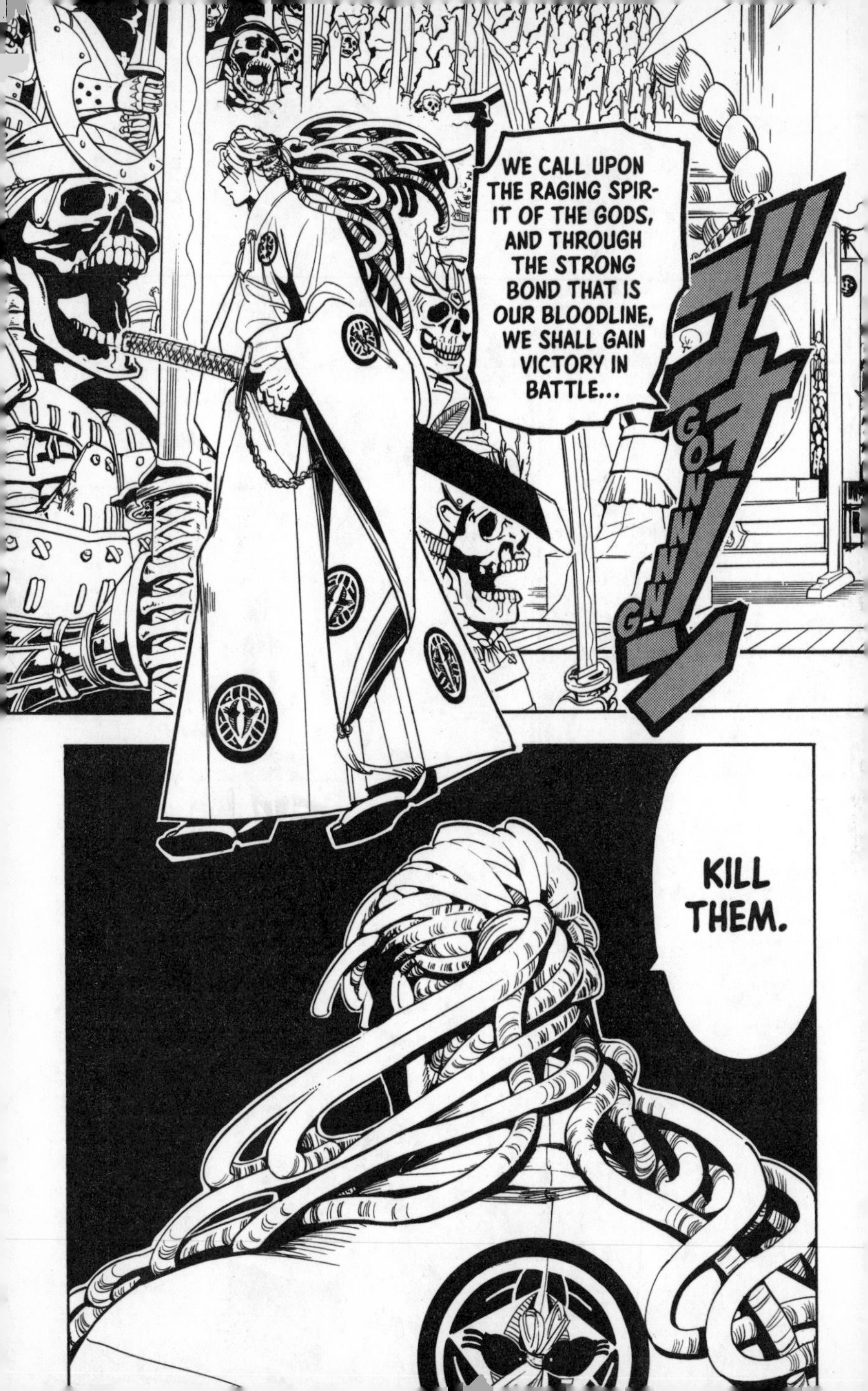
WE CALL UPON THE RAGING SPIRIT OF THE GODS, AND THROUGH THE STRONG BOND THAT IS OUR BLOODLINE, WE SHALL GAIN VICTORY IN BATTLE...
GONNNNG
KILL THEM.

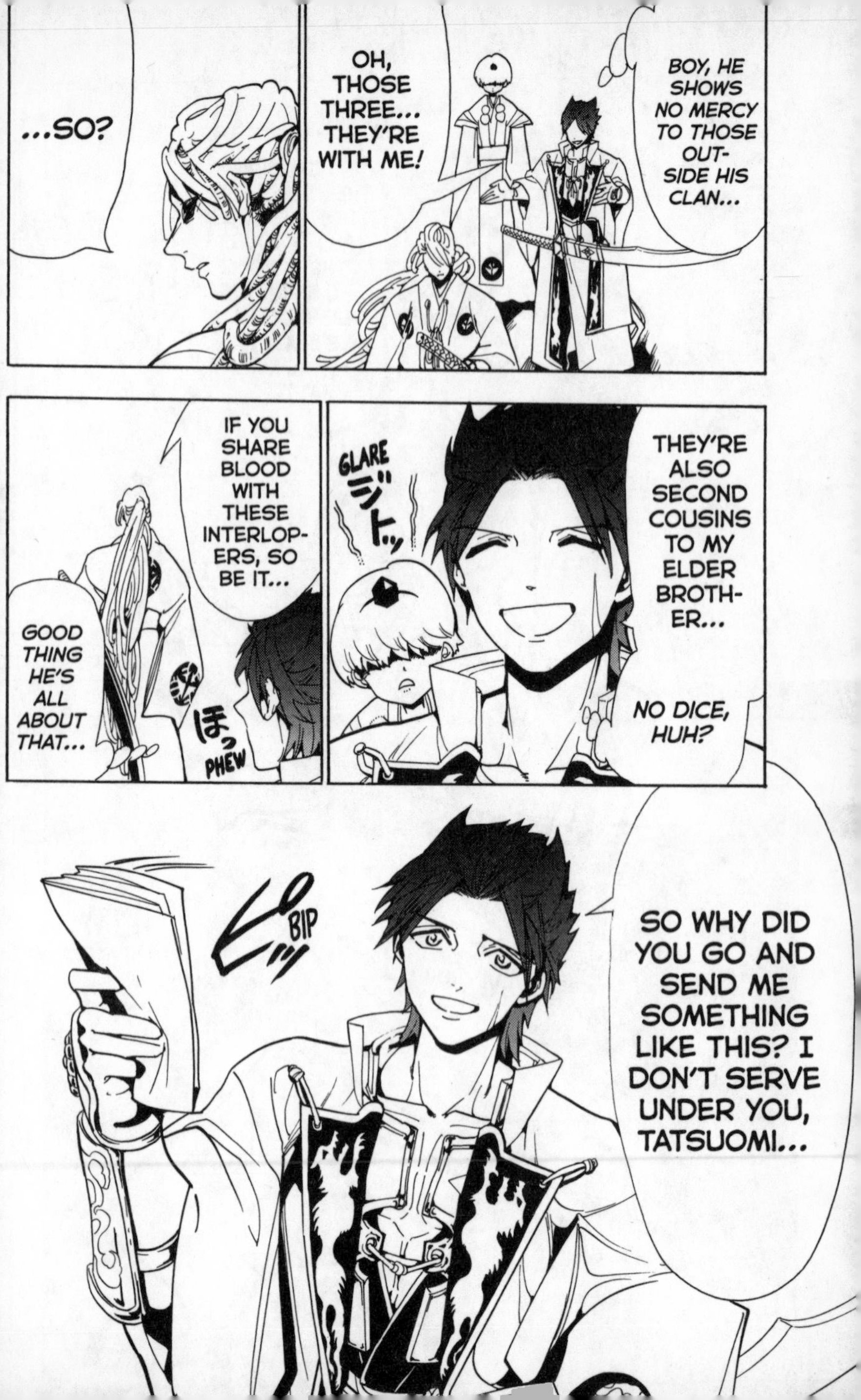
BOY, HE SHOWS NO MERCY TO THOSE OUT-SIDE HIS CLAN...
OH, THOSE THREE... THEY'RE WITH ME!
...SO?
THEY'RE ALSO SECOND COUSINS TO MY ELDER BROTH-ER...
GLARE ジトッ
NO DICE, HUH?
IF YOU SHARE BLOOD WITH THESE INTERLOP-ERS, SO BE IT...
GOOD THING HE'S ALL ABOUT THAT...
ほっ PHEW
SO WHY DID YOU GO AND SEND ME SOMETHING LIKE THIS? I DON'T SERVE UNDER YOU, TATSUOMI...
ピッ BIP

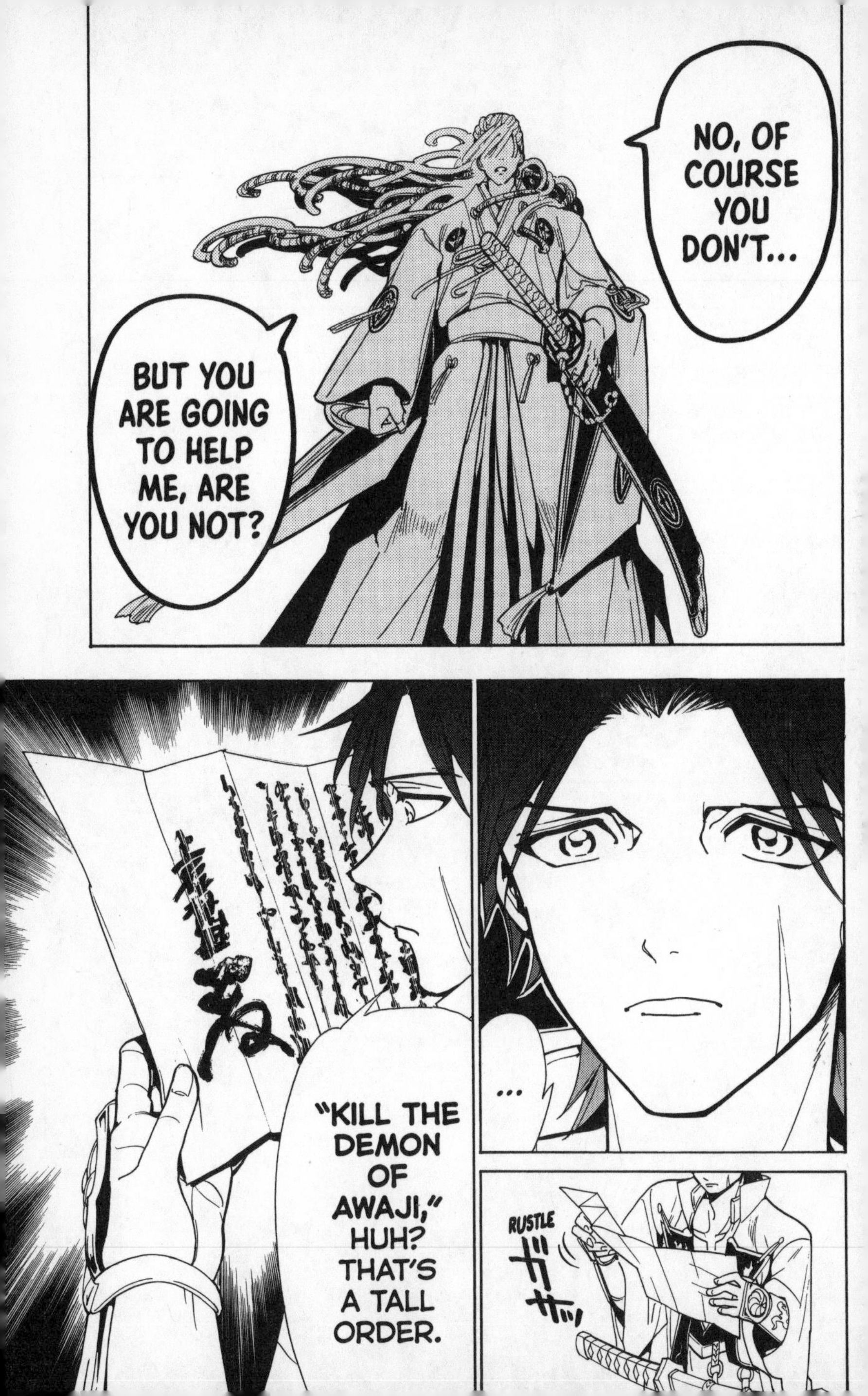
NO, OF COURSE YOU DON'T...
BUT YOU ARE GOING TO HELP ME, ARE YOU NOT?
...
RUSTLE
"KILL THE DEMON OF AWAJI," HUH? THAT'S A TALL ORDER.

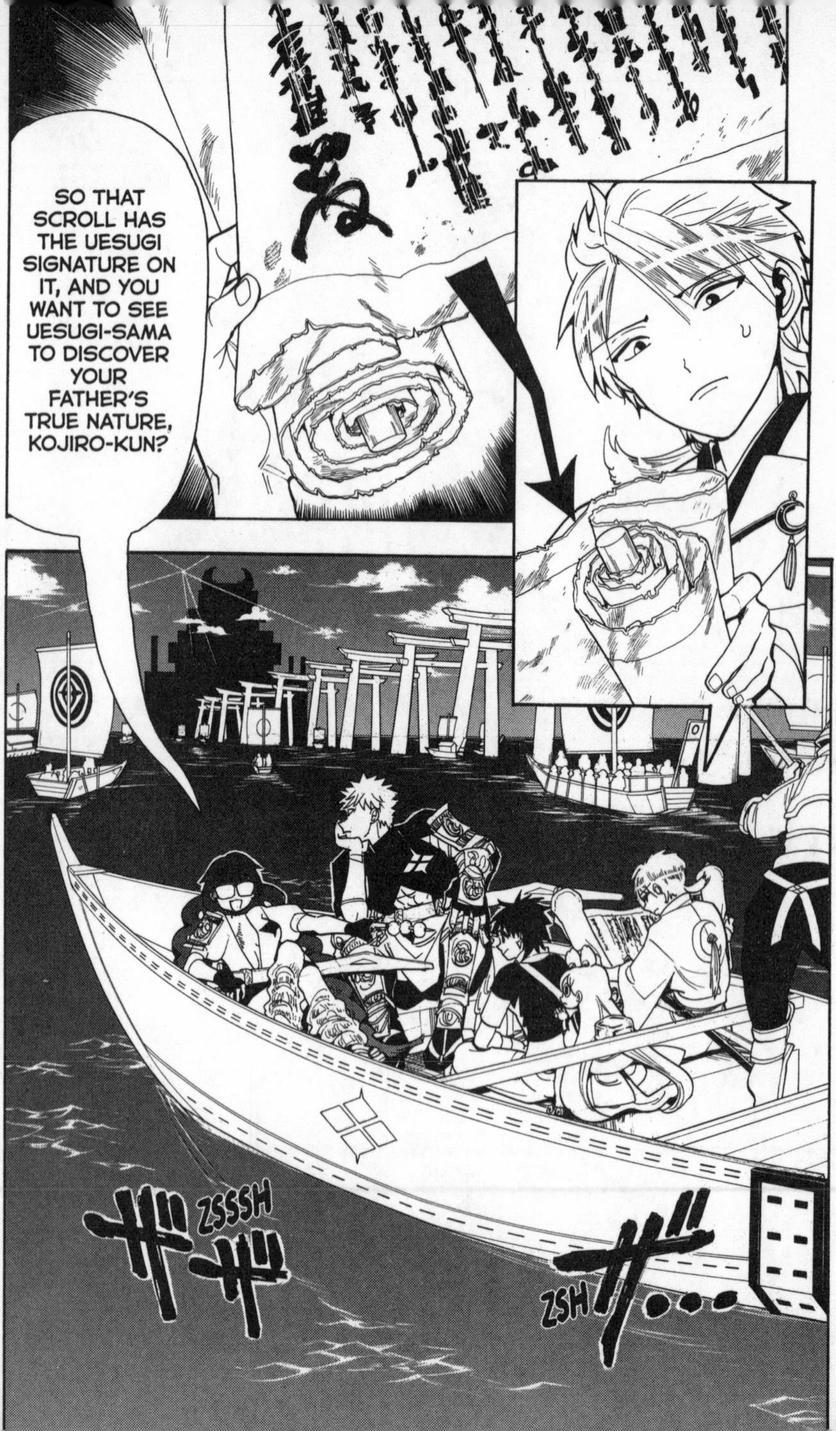
SO THAT SCROLL HAS THE UESUGI SIGNATURE ON IT, AND YOU WANT TO SEE UESUGI-SAMA TO DISCOVER YOUR FATHER'S TRUE NATURE, KOJIRO-KUN?
ZSSSH
ZSH

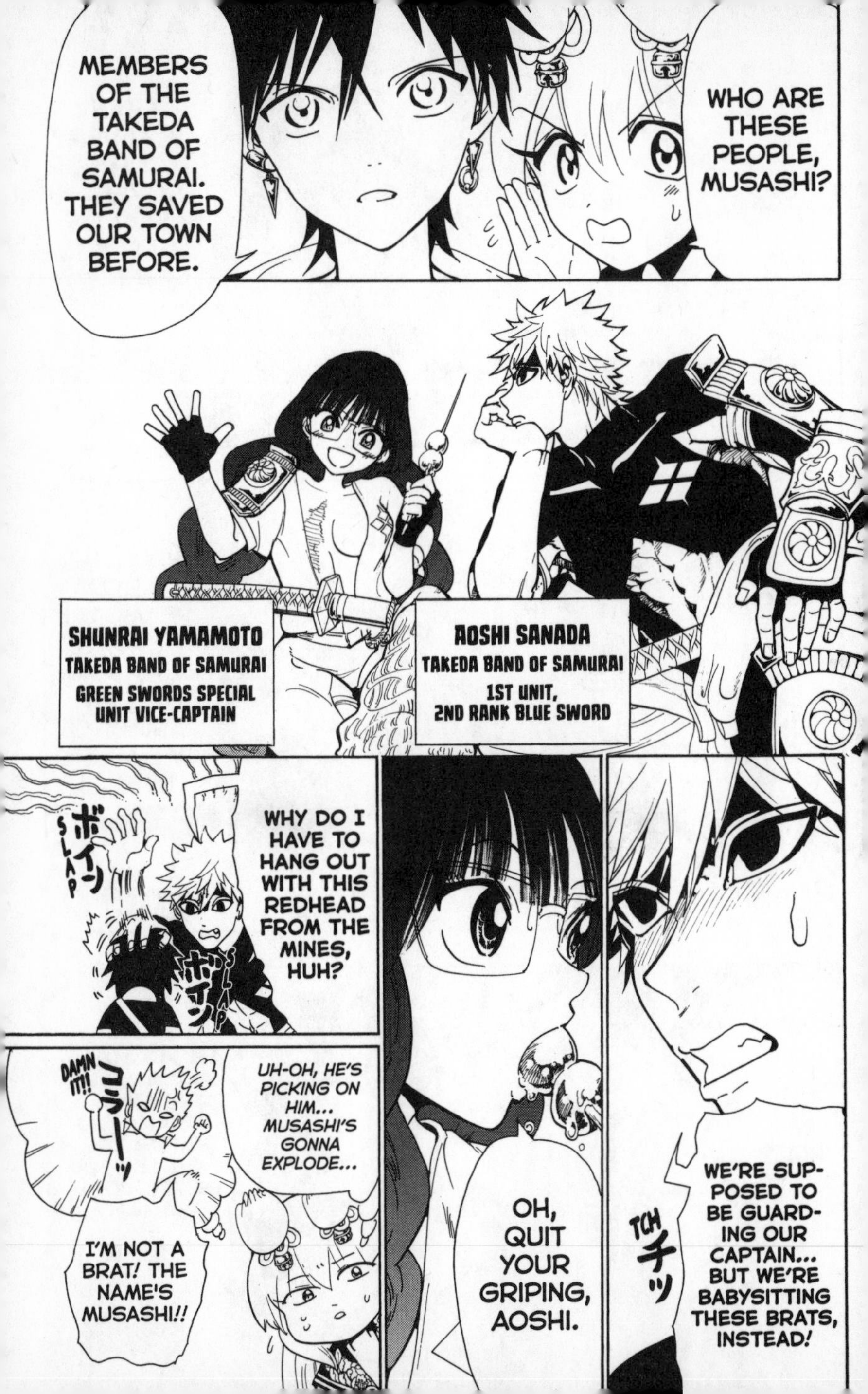
WHO ARE THESE PEOPLE, MUSASHI?
MEMBERS OF THE TAKEDA BAND OF SAMURAI. THEY SAVED OUR TOWN BEFORE.
AOSHI SANADA
TAKEDA BAND OF SAMURAI
1ST UNIT, 2ND RANK BLUE SWORD
SHUNRAI YAMAMOTO
TAKEDA BAND OF SAMURAI
GREEN SWORDS SPECIAL UNIT VICE-CAPTAIN
WE'RE SUP-POSED TO BE GUARD-ING OUR CAPTAIN... BUT WE'RE BABYSITTING THESE BRATS, INSTEAD!
TCH
チッ
OH, QUIT YOUR GRIPING, AOSHI.
WHY DO I HAVE TO HANG OUT WITH THIS REDHEAD FROM THE MINES, HUH?
ボイン
SLAP
ボイン
SLAP
UH-OH, HE'S PICKING ON HIM... MUSASHI'S GONNA EXPLODE...
DAMN IT!!
コラーーッ
I'M NOT A BRAT! THE NAME'S MUSASHI!!

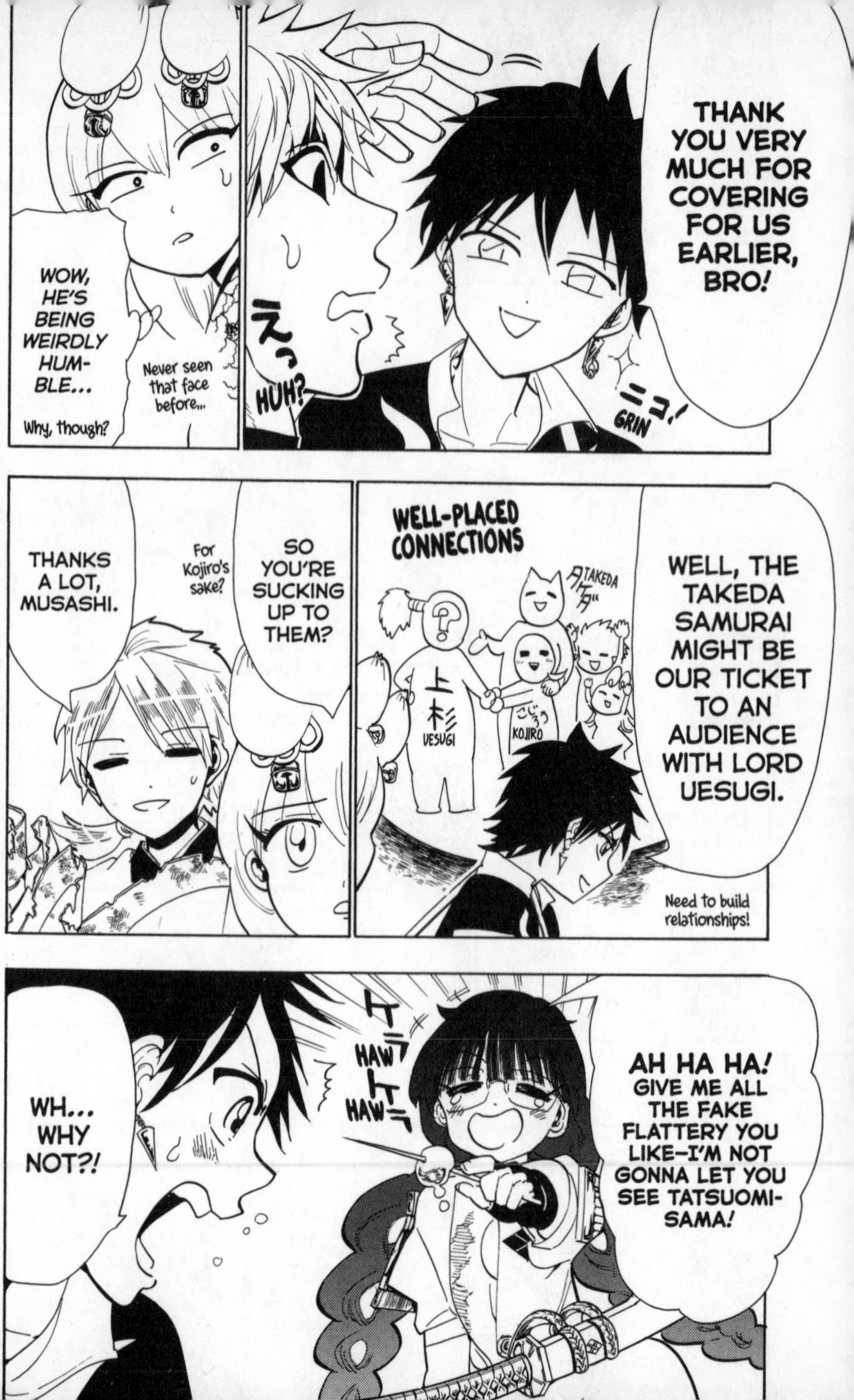
THANK YOU VERY MUCH FOR COVERING FOR US EARLIER, BRO!
ニコ!
GRIN
えっ
HUH?
WOW, HE'S BEING WEIRDLY HUM-BLE...
Never seen that face before...
Why, though?
WELL-PLACED CONNECTIONS
WELL, THE TAKEDA SAMURAI MIGHT BE OUR TICKET TO AN AUDIENCE WITH LORD UESUGI.
タケダ
TAKEDA
上杉
UESUGI
こじろう
KOJIRO
Need to build relationships!
SO YOU'RE SUCKING UP TO THEM?
For Kojiro's sake?
THANKS A LOT, MUSASHI.
AH HA HA! GIVE ME ALL THE FAKE FLATTERY YOU LIKE—I'M NOT GONNA LET YOU SEE TATSUOMI-SAMA!
ケラ
HAW
ケラ
HAW
WH... WHY NOT?!

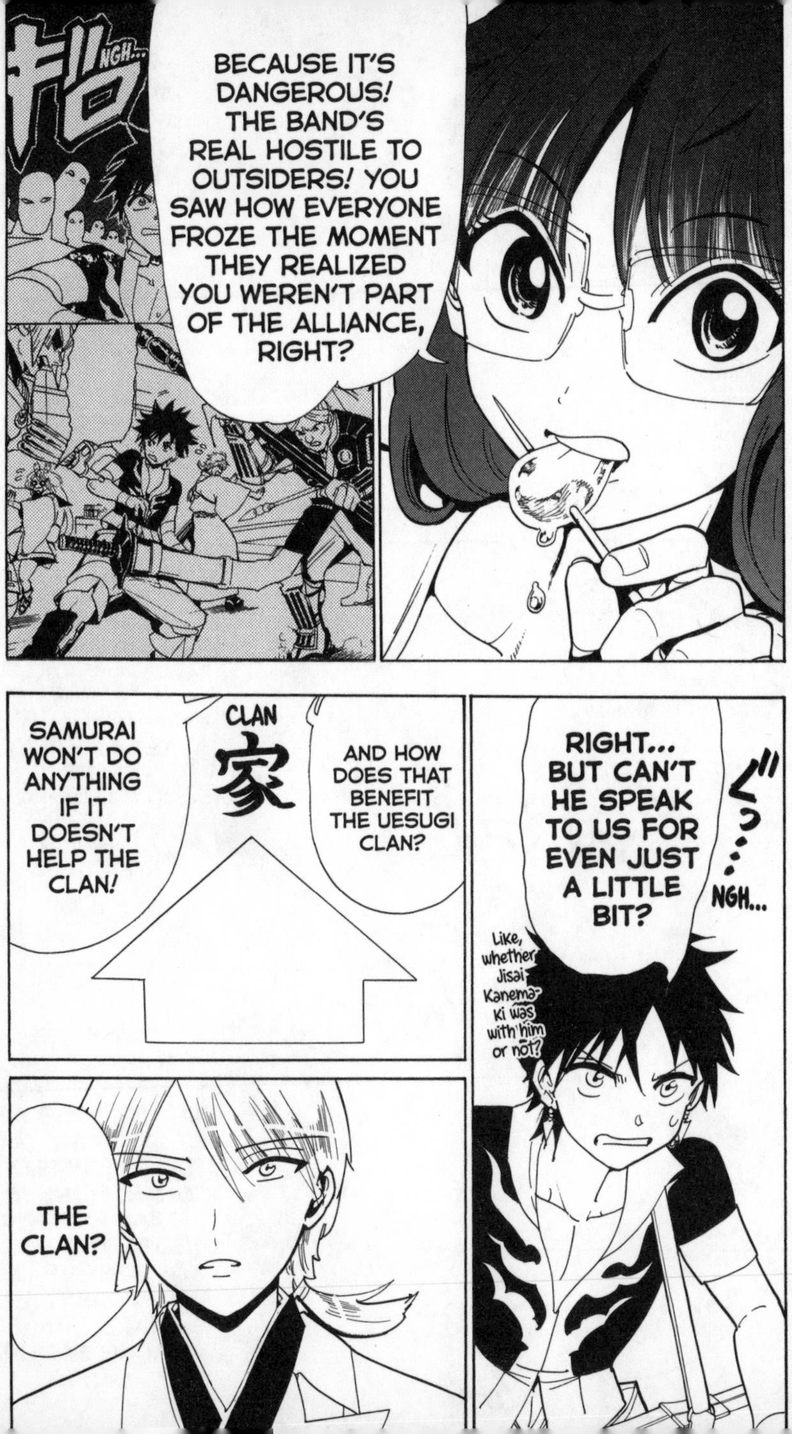
BECAUSE IT'S DANGEROUS! THE BAND'S REAL HOSTILE TO OUTSIDERS! YOU SAW HOW EVERYONE FROZE THE MOMENT THEY REALIZED YOU WEREN'T PART OF THE ALLIANCE, RIGHT?
NGH...
RIGHT... BUT CAN'T HE SPEAK TO US FOR EVEN JUST A LITTLE BIT?
NGH...
Like, whether Jisai Kanema-Ki was with him or not?
AND HOW DOES THAT BENEFIT THE UESUGI CLAN?
CLAN
家
SAMURAI WON'T DO ANYTHING IF IT DOESN'T HELP THE CLAN!
THE CLAN?

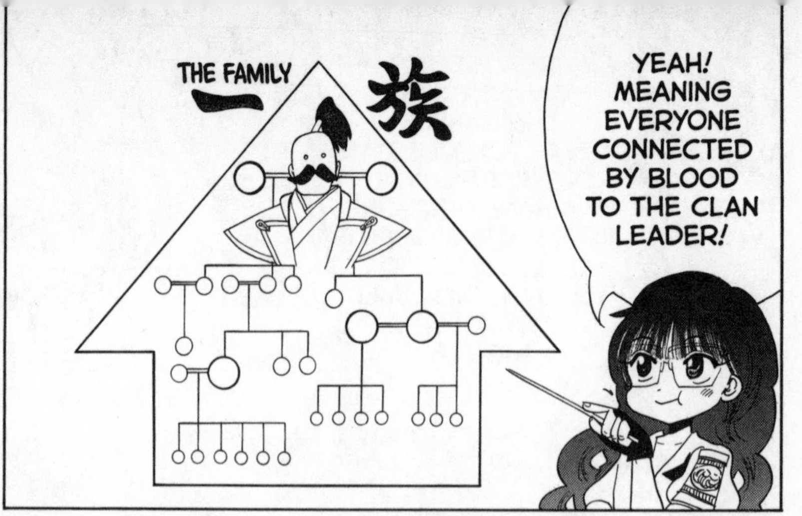
THE FAMILY
一族
YEAH! MEANING EVERYONE CONNECTED BY BLOOD TO THE CLAN LEADER!
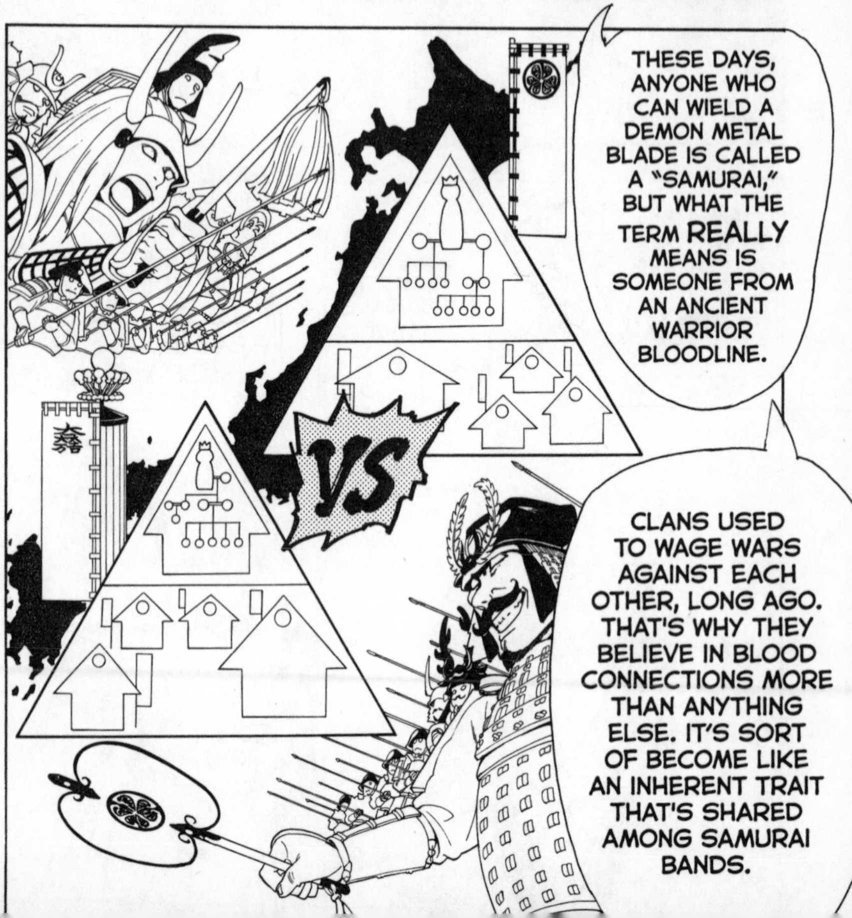
THESE DAYS, ANYONE WHO CAN WIELD A DEMON METAL BLADE IS CALLED A "SAMURAI," BUT WHAT THE TERM REALLY MEANS IS SOMEONE FROM AN ANCIENT WARRIOR BLOODLINE.
CLANS USED TO WAGE WARS AGAINST EACH OTHER, LONG AGO. THAT'S WHY THEY BELIEVE IN BLOOD CONNECTIONS MORE THAN ANYTHING ELSE. IT'S SORT OF BECOME LIKE AN INHERENT TRAIT THAT'S SHARED AMONG SAMURAI BANDS.
VS

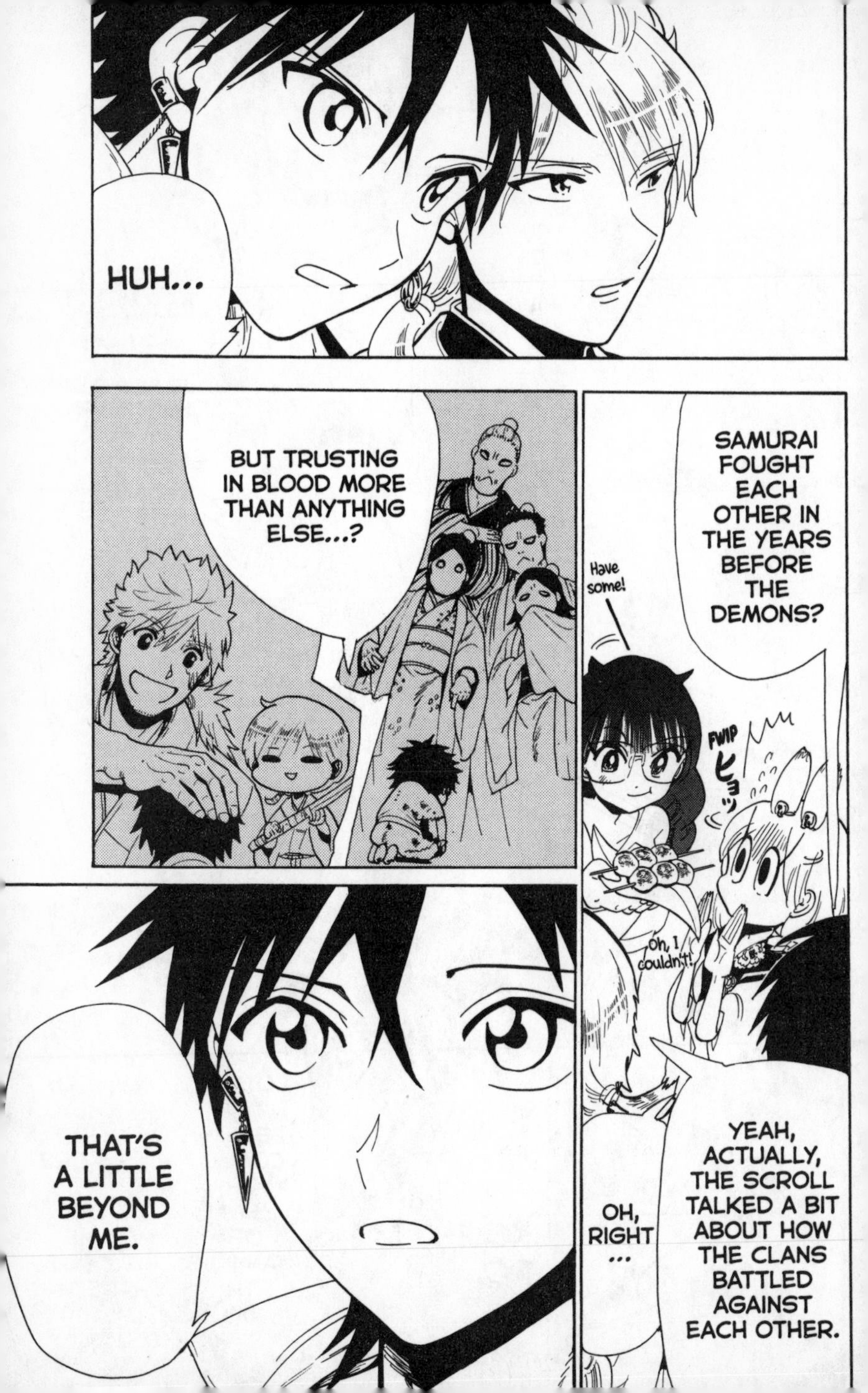
HUH...
SAMURAI FOUGHT EACH OTHER IN THE YEARS BEFORE THE DEMONS?
Have some!
FWIP
ヒョッ
Oh, I couldn't!
YEAH, ACTUALLY, THE SCROLL TALKED A BIT ABOUT HOW THE CLANS BATTLED AGAINST EACH OTHER.
OH, RIGHT...
BUT TRUSTING IN BLOOD MORE THAN ANYTHING ELSE...?
THAT'S A LITTLE BEYOND ME.

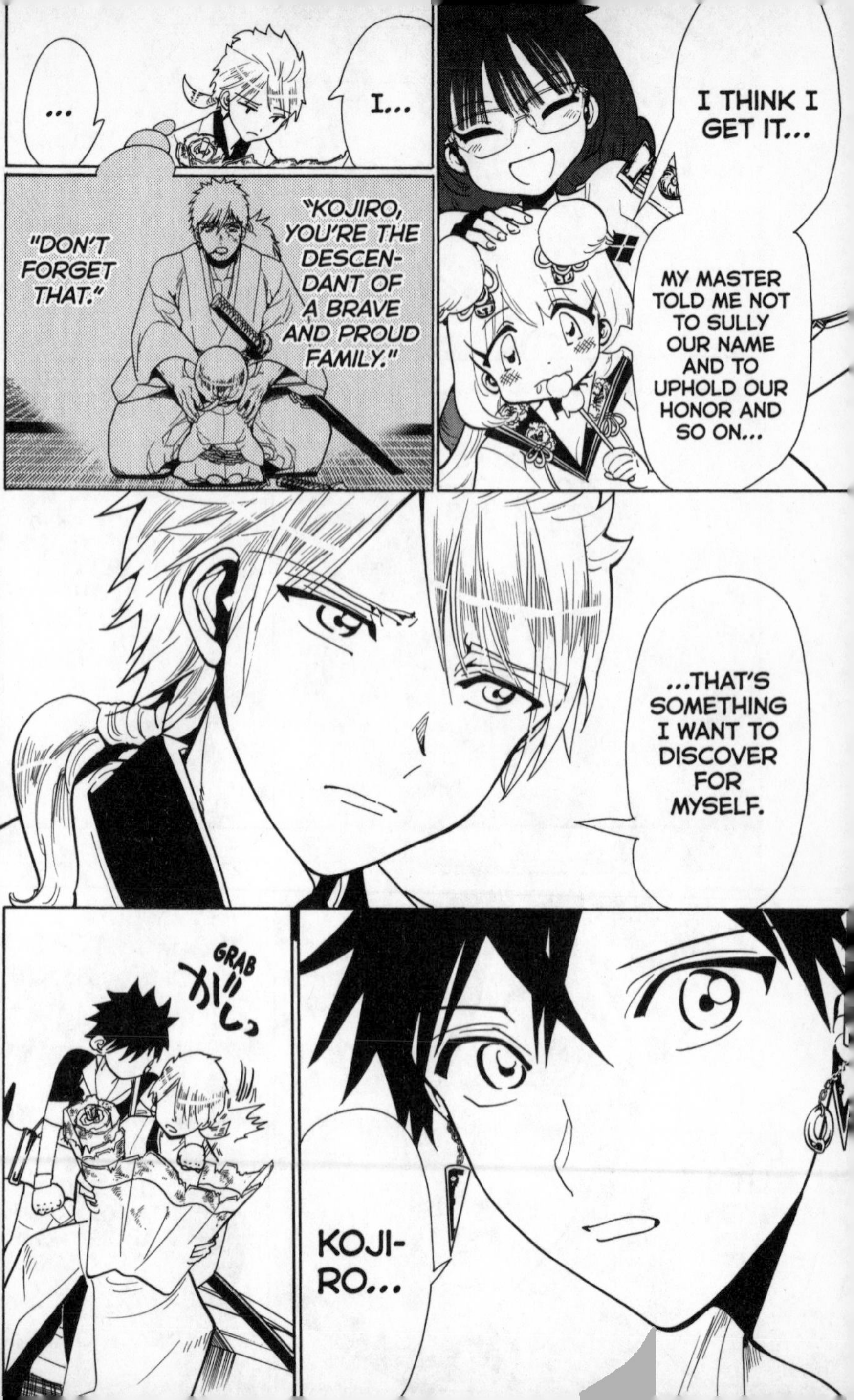
I THINK I GET IT...
MY MASTER TOLD ME NOT TO SULLY OUR NAME AND TO UPHOLD OUR HONOR AND SO ON...
I...
...
"KOJIRO, YOU'RE THE DESCEN-DANT OF A BRAVE AND PROUD FAMILY."
"DON'T FORGET THAT."
...THAT'S SOMETHING I WANT TO DISCOVER FOR MYSELF.
KOJI-RO...
GRAB

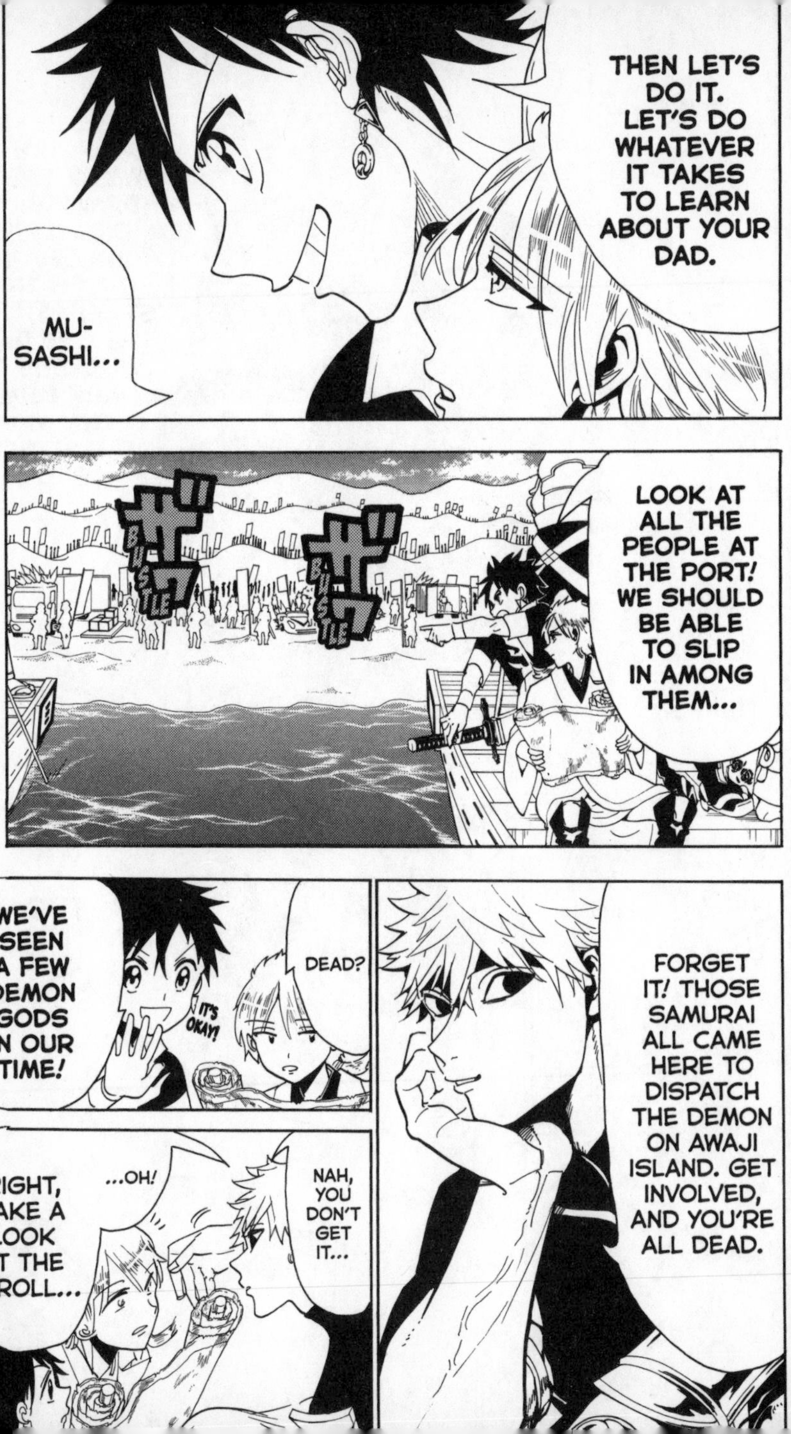
THEN LET'S DO IT. LET'S DO WHATEVER IT TAKES TO LEARN ABOUT YOUR DAD.
MU-SASHI...
LOOK AT ALL THE PEOPLE AT THE PORT! WE SHOULD BE ABLE TO SLIP IN AMONG THEM...
BUSTLE
BUSTLE
FORGET IT! THOSE SAMURAI ALL CAME HERE TO DISPATCH THE DEMON ON AWAJI ISLAND. GET INVOLVED, AND YOU'RE ALL DEAD.
DEAD?
IT'S OKAY!
WE'VE SEEN A FEW DEMON GODS IN OUR TIME!
NAH, YOU DON'T GET IT...
...OH!
RIGHT, TAKE A LOOK AT THE SCROLL...

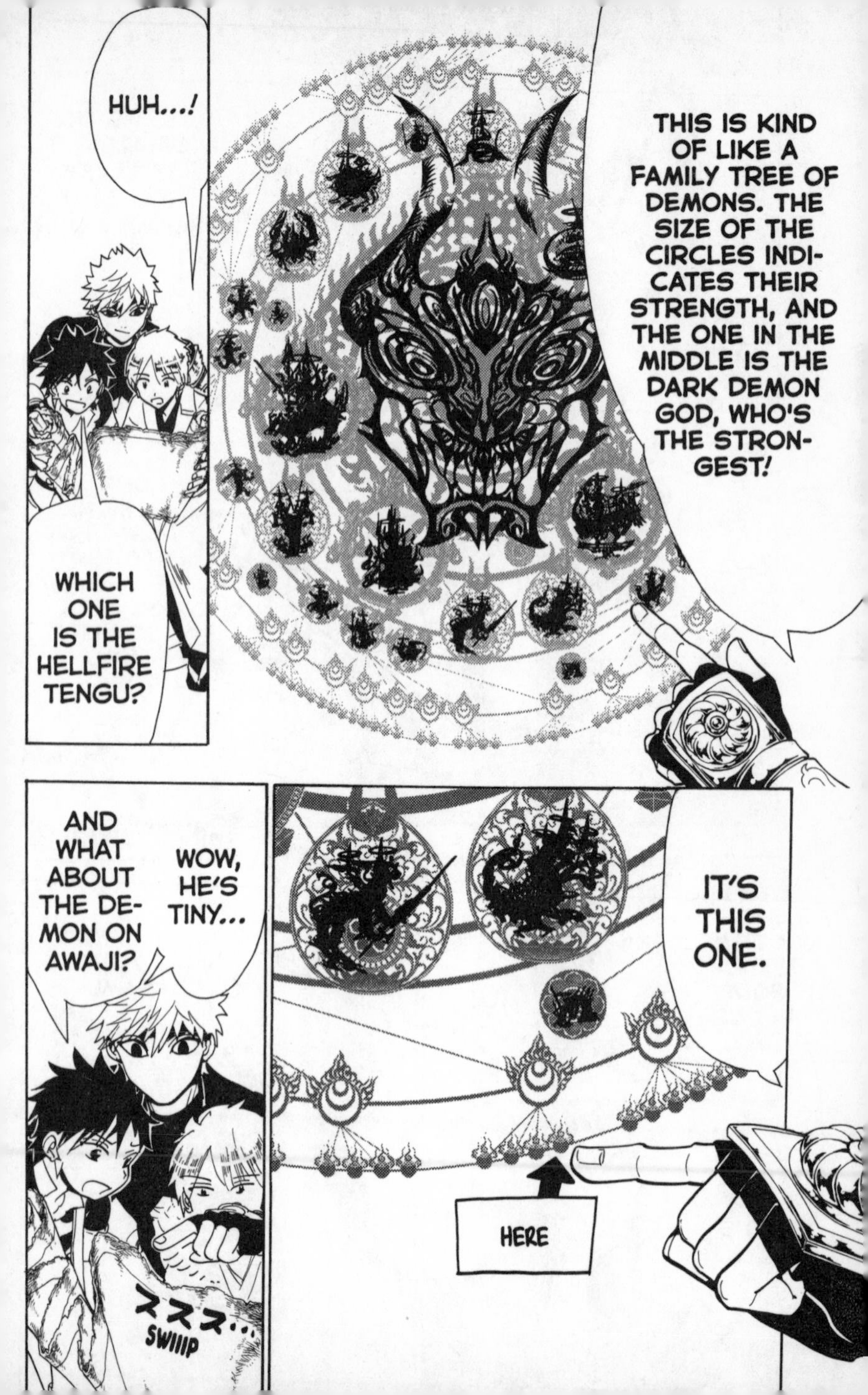
THIS IS KIND OF LIKE A FAMILY TREE OF DEMONS. THE SIZE OF THE CIRCLES INDICATES THEIR STRENGTH, AND THE ONE IN THE MIDDLE IS THE DARK DEMON GOD, WHO'S THE STRONGEST!
HUH...!
WHICH ONE IS THE HELLFIRE TENGU?
IT'S THIS ONE.
HERE
WOW, HE'S TINY...
AND WHAT ABOUT THE DEMON ON AWAJI?
スススッ…
SWIIIP

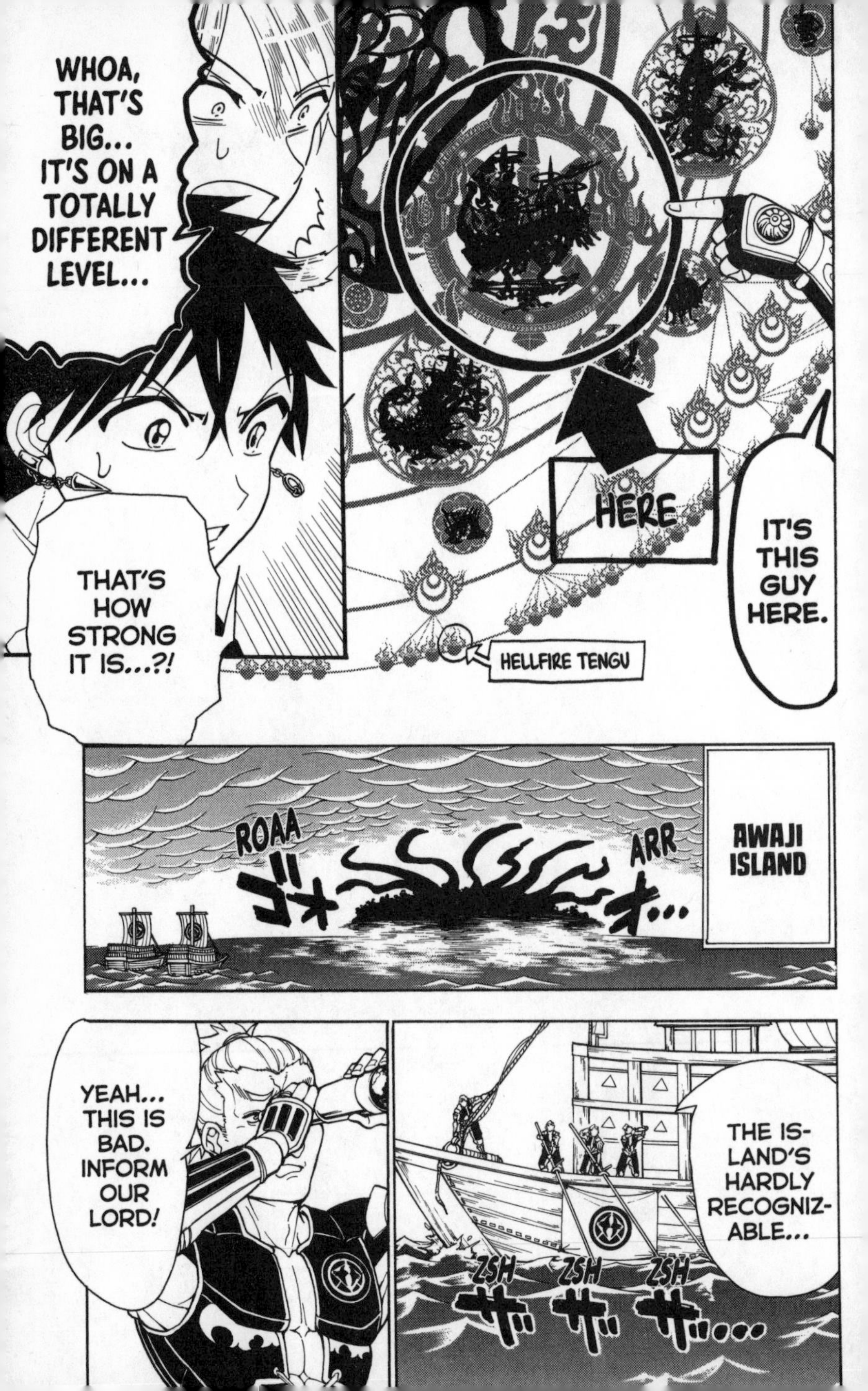
IT'S THIS GUY HERE.
HERE
HELLFIRE TENGU
WHOA, THAT'S BIG... IT'S ON A TOTALLY DIFFERENT LEVEL...
THAT'S HOW STRONG IT IS...?!
AWAJI ISLAND
ROAA
ARR
THE IS-LAND'S HARDLY RECOGNIZ-ABLE...
ZSH ZSH ZSH
YEAH... THIS IS BAD. INFORM OUR LORD!

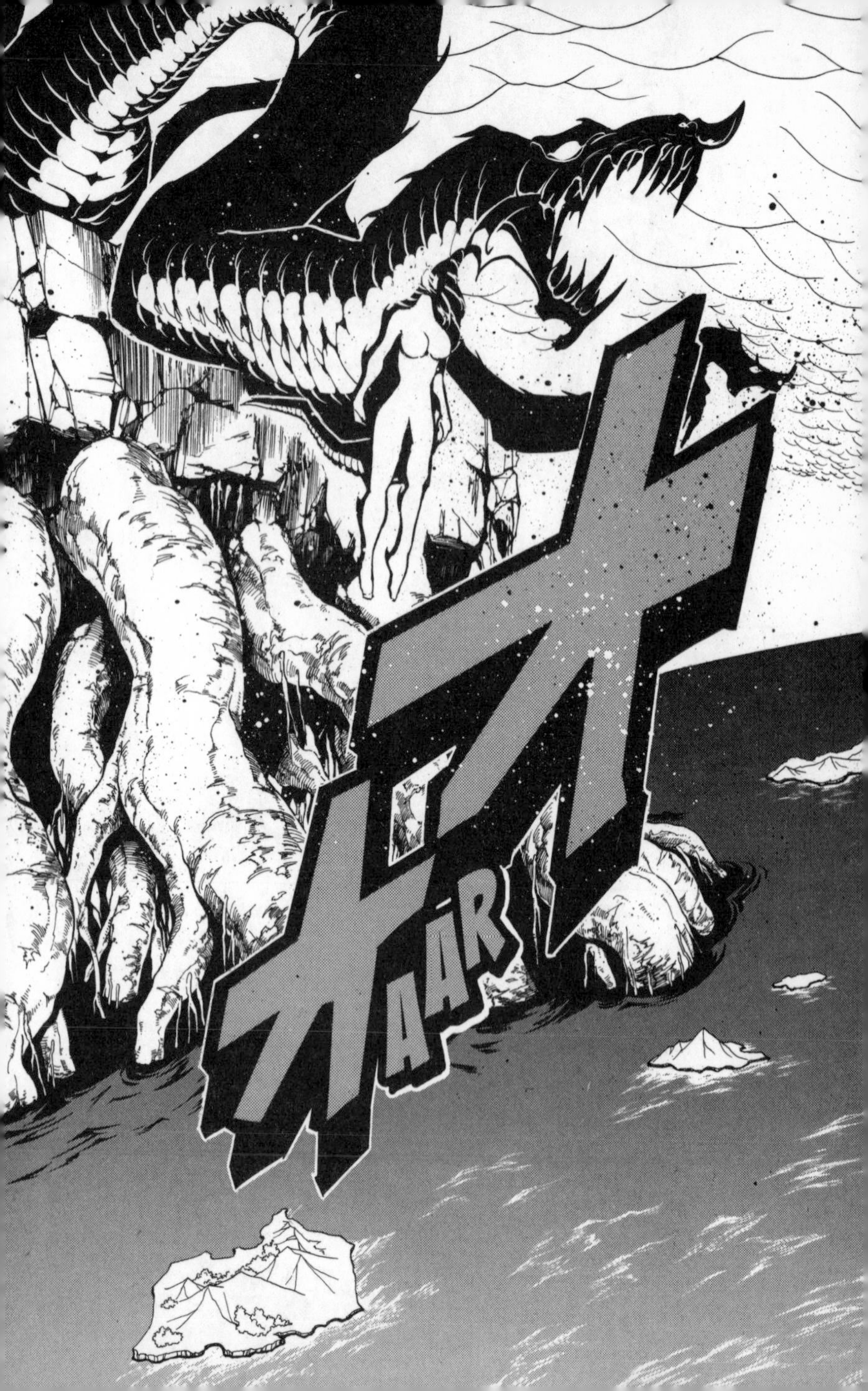
AAR

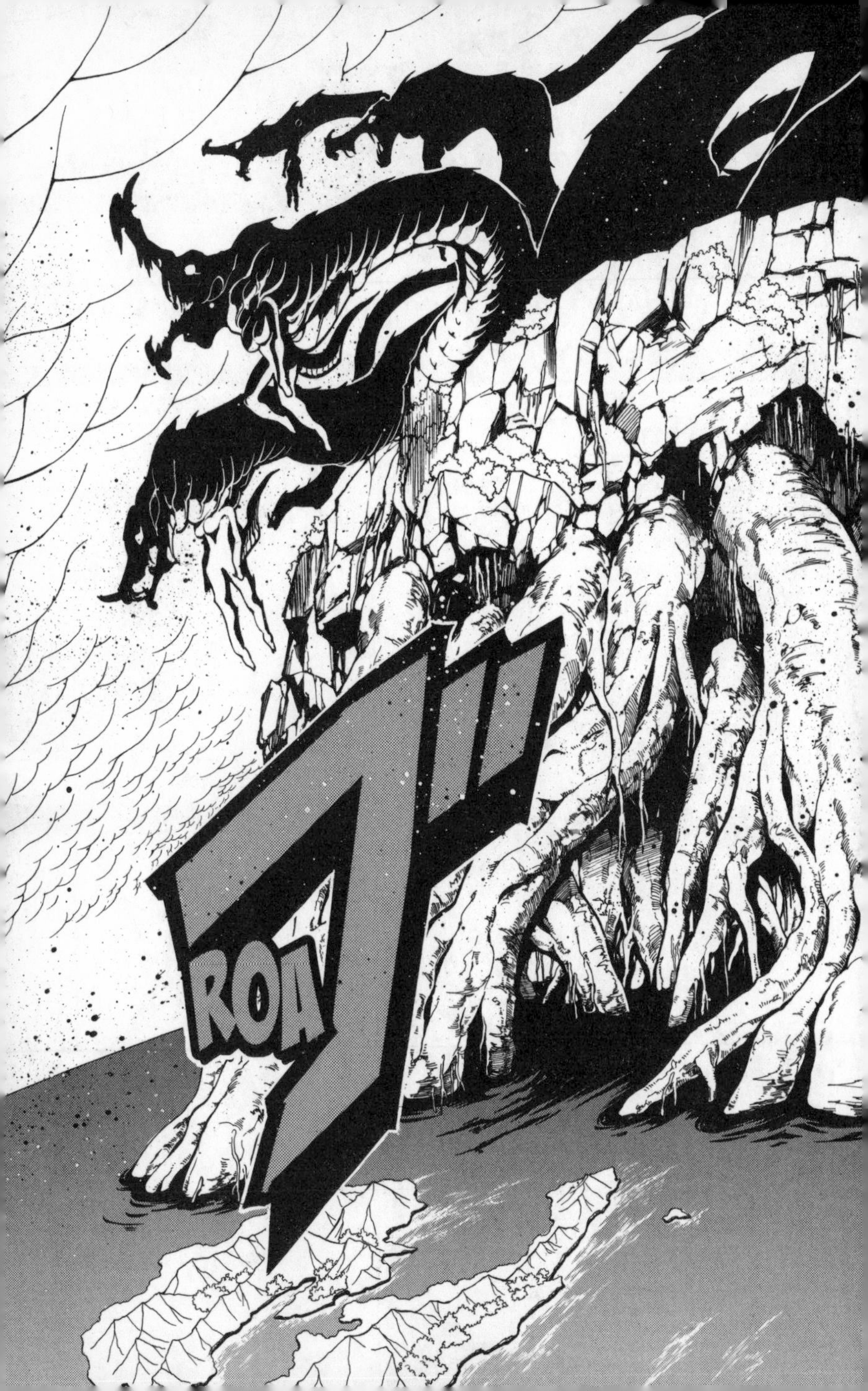
ROA

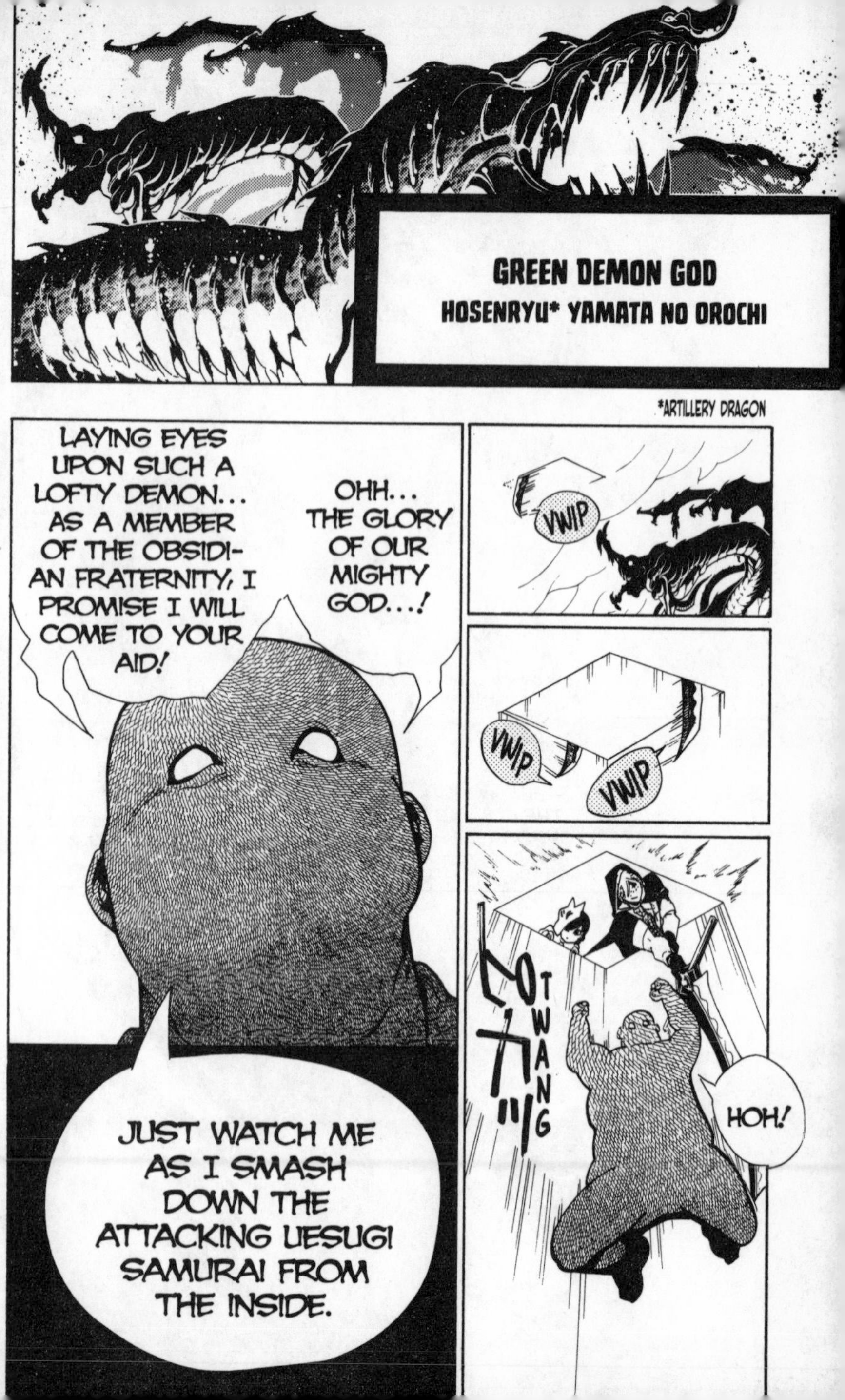

GREEN DEMON GOD
HOSENRYU* YAMATA NO OROCHI
*ARTILLERY DRAGON
VWIP
VWIP
VWIP
TWANG
HOH!
OHH... THE GLORY OF OUR MIGHTY GOD...!
LAYING EYES UPON SUCH A LOFTY DEMON... AS A MEMBER OF THE OBSIDIAN FRATERNITY, I PROMISE I WILL COME TO YOUR AID!
JUST WATCH ME AS I SMASH DOWN THE ATTACKING UESUGI SAMURAI FROM THE INSIDE.

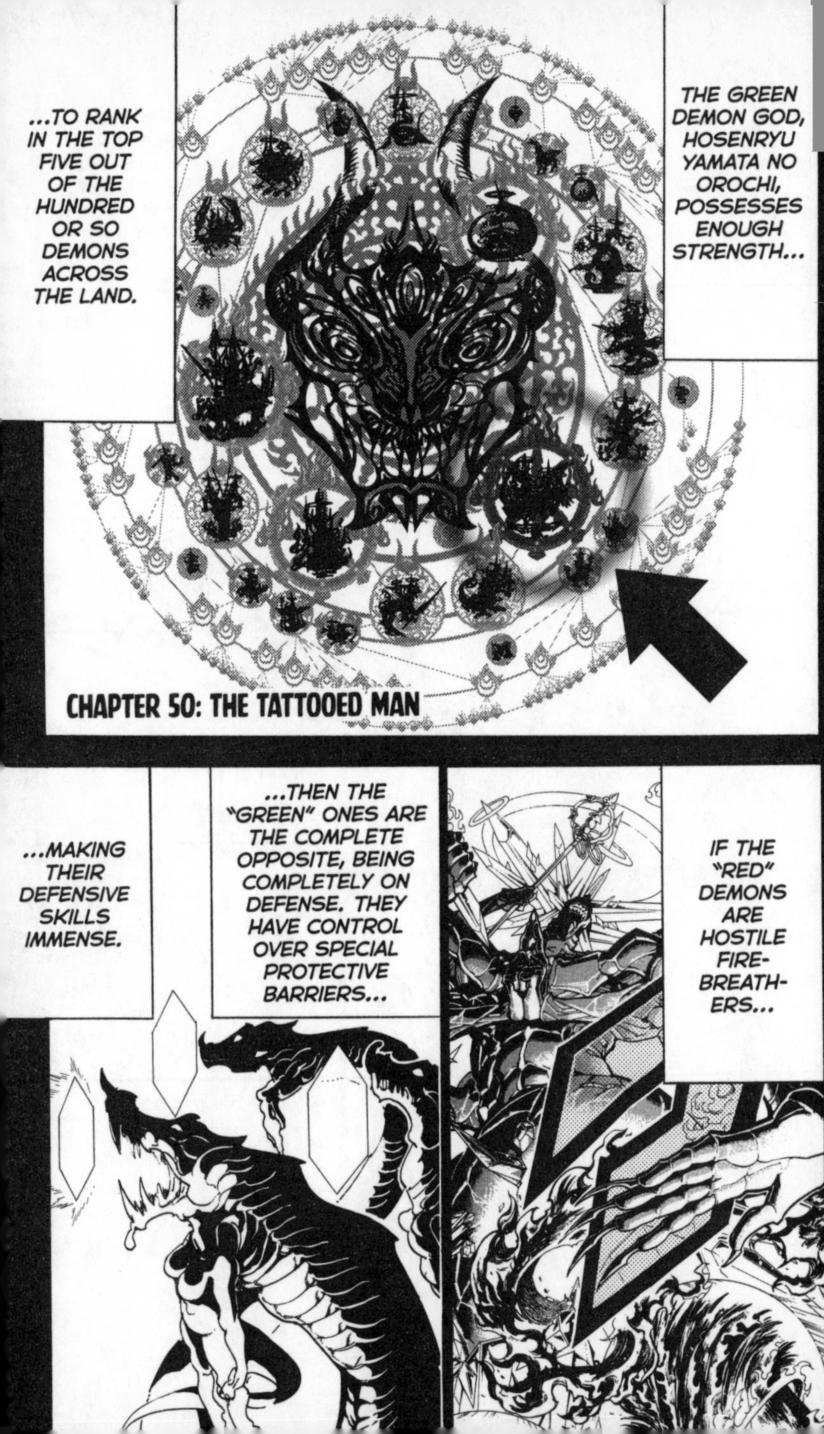
THE GREEN DEMON GOD, HOSENRYU YAMATA NO OROCHI, POSSESSES ENOUGH STRENGTH...
...TO RANK IN THE TOP FIVE OUT OF THE HUNDRED OR SO DEMONS ACROSS THE LAND.
CHAPTER 50: THE TATTOOED MAN
IF THE "RED" DEMONS ARE HOSTILE FIRE-BREATHERS...
...THEN THE "GREEN" ONES ARE THE COMPLETE OPPOSITE, BEING COMPLETELY ON DEFENSE. THEY HAVE CONTROL OVER SPECIAL PROTECTIVE BARRIERS...
...MAKING THEIR DEFENSIVE SKILLS IMMENSE.

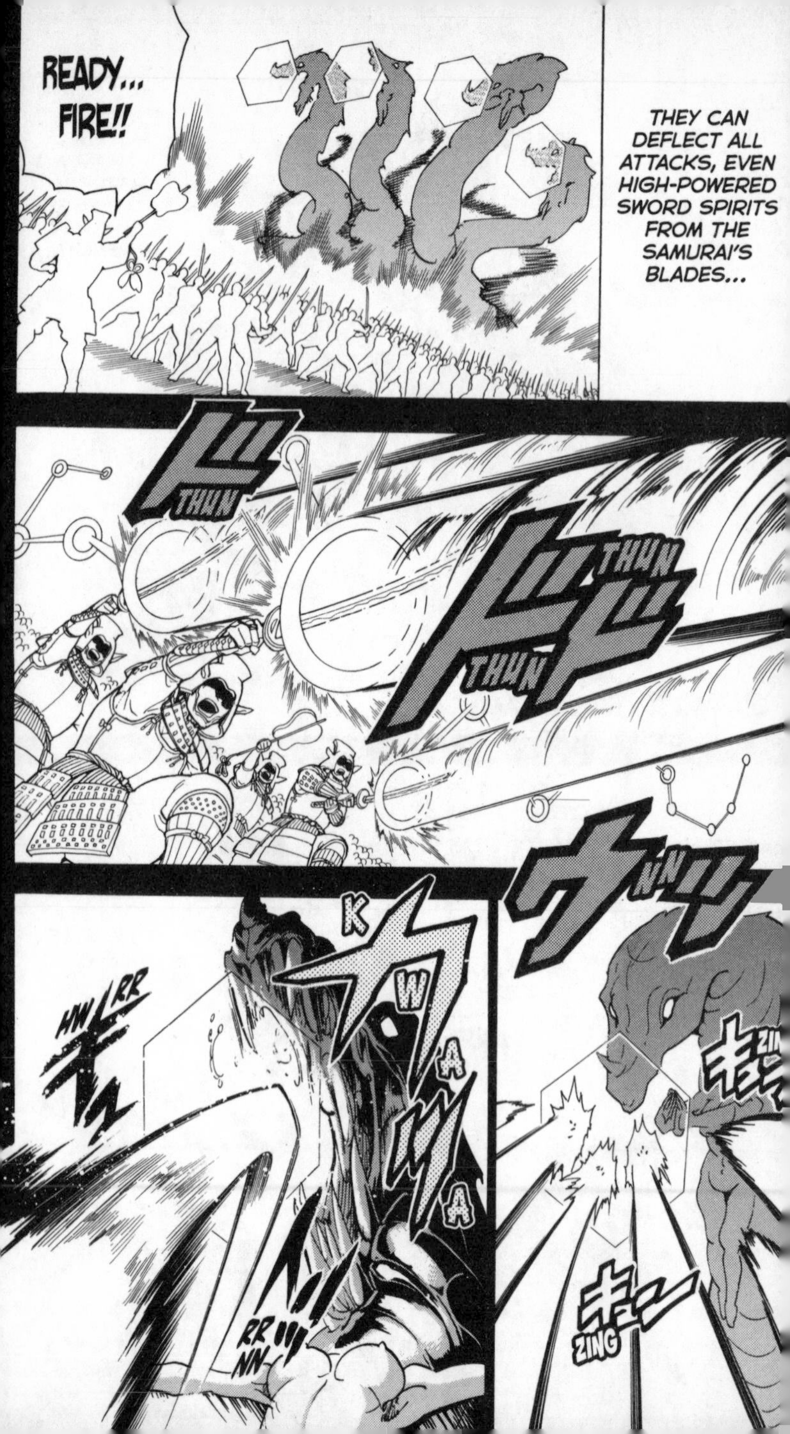

THEY CAN DEFLECT ALL ATTACKS, EVEN HIGH-POWERED SWORD SPIRITS FROM THE SAMURAI'S BLADES...
READY... FIRE!!
THUN
THUN
THUN
ZING
K
W
A
A
RR
NN-

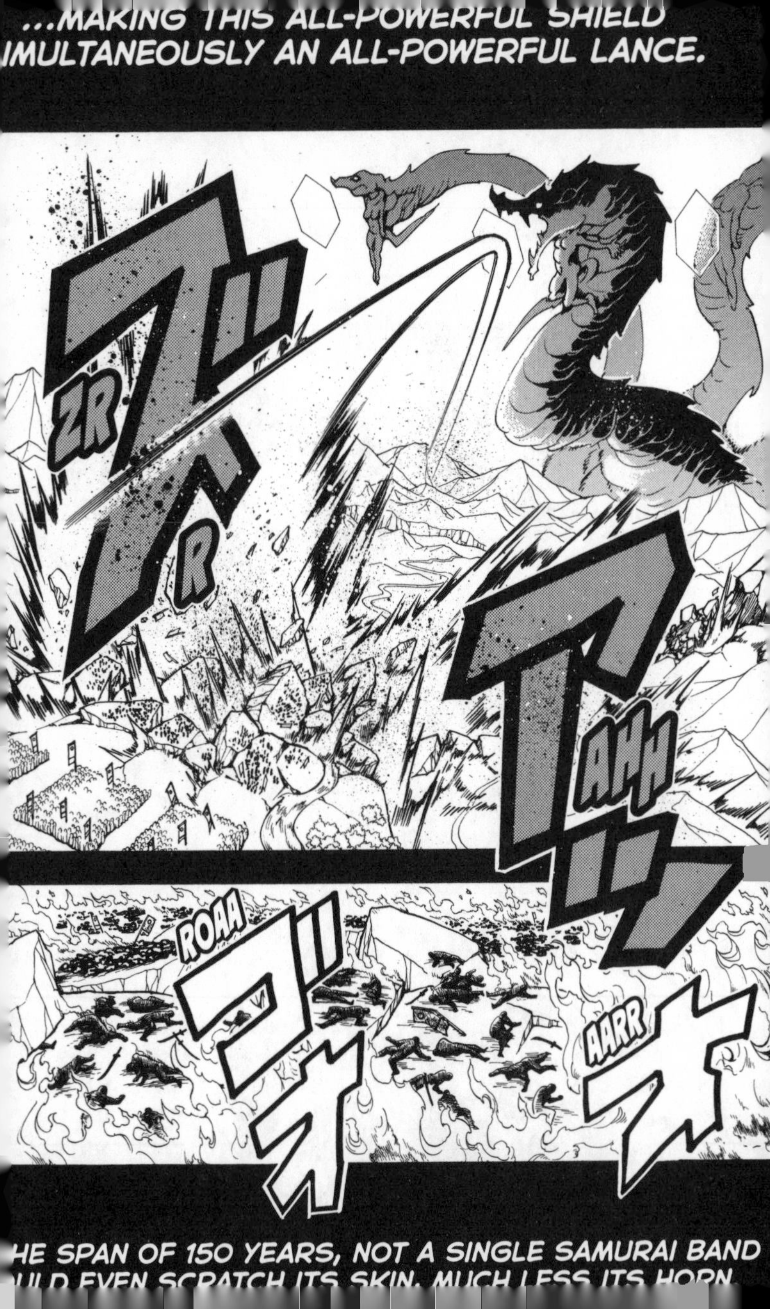
…MAKING THIS ALL-POWERFUL SHIELD
IMULTANEOUSLY AN ALL-POWERFUL LANCE.
ZR
R
AHH
ROAA
AARR
HE SPAN OF 150 YEARS, NOT A SINGLE SAMURAI BAND
ULD EVEN SCRATCH ITS SKIN, MUCH LESS ITS HORN.

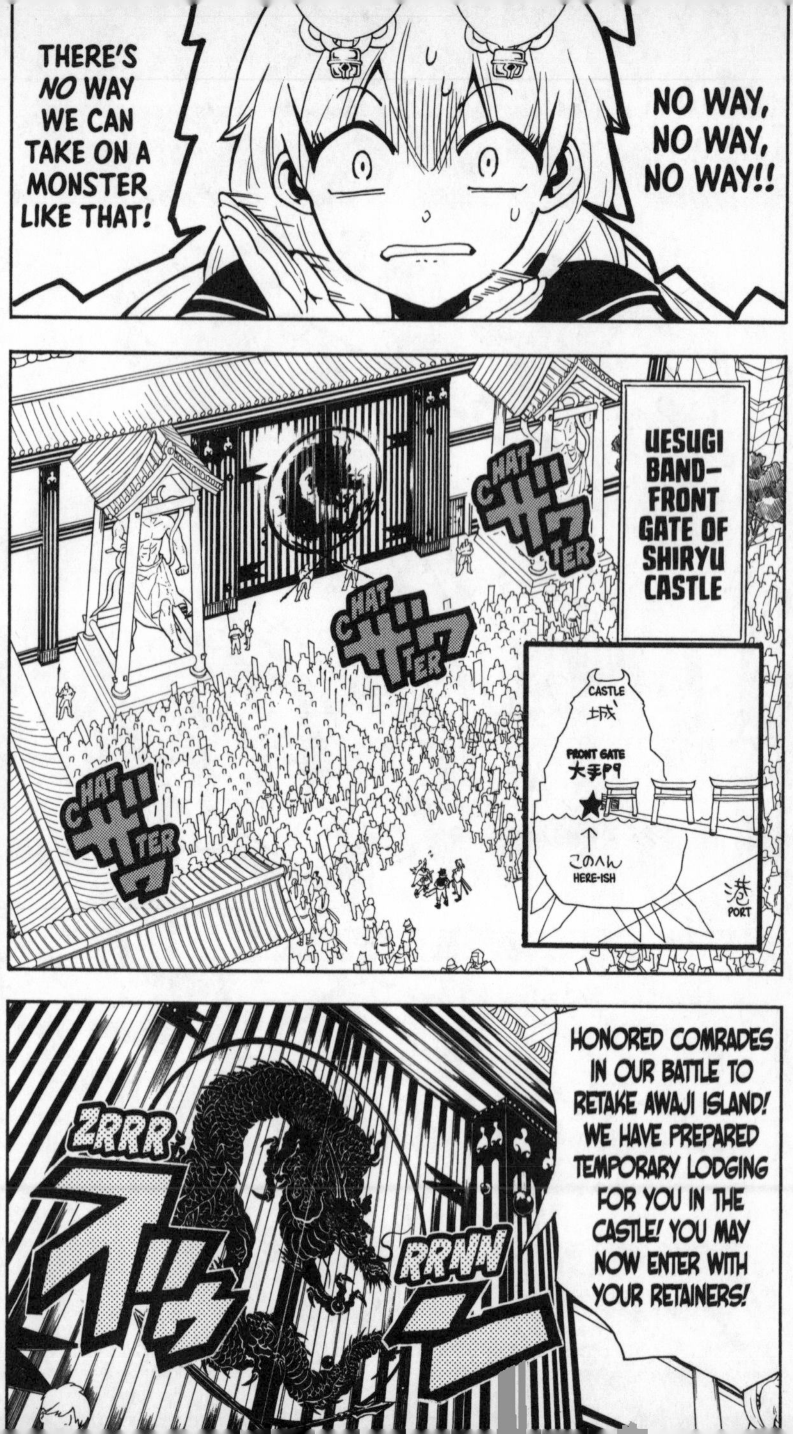
NO WAY, NO WAY, NO WAY!!
THERE'S *NO* WAY WE CAN TAKE ON A MONSTER LIKE THAT!
UESUGI BAND—FRONT GATE OF SHIRYU CASTLE
CHATTER
CHATTER
CHATTER
CASTLE 城
FRONT GATE 大手門
このへん HERE-ISH
港 PORT
HONORED COMRADES IN OUR BATTLE TO RETAKE AWAJI ISLAND! WE HAVE PREPARED TEMPORARY LODGING FOR YOU IN THE CASTLE! YOU MAY NOW ENTER WITH YOUR RETAINERS!
RRNN
ZRRR

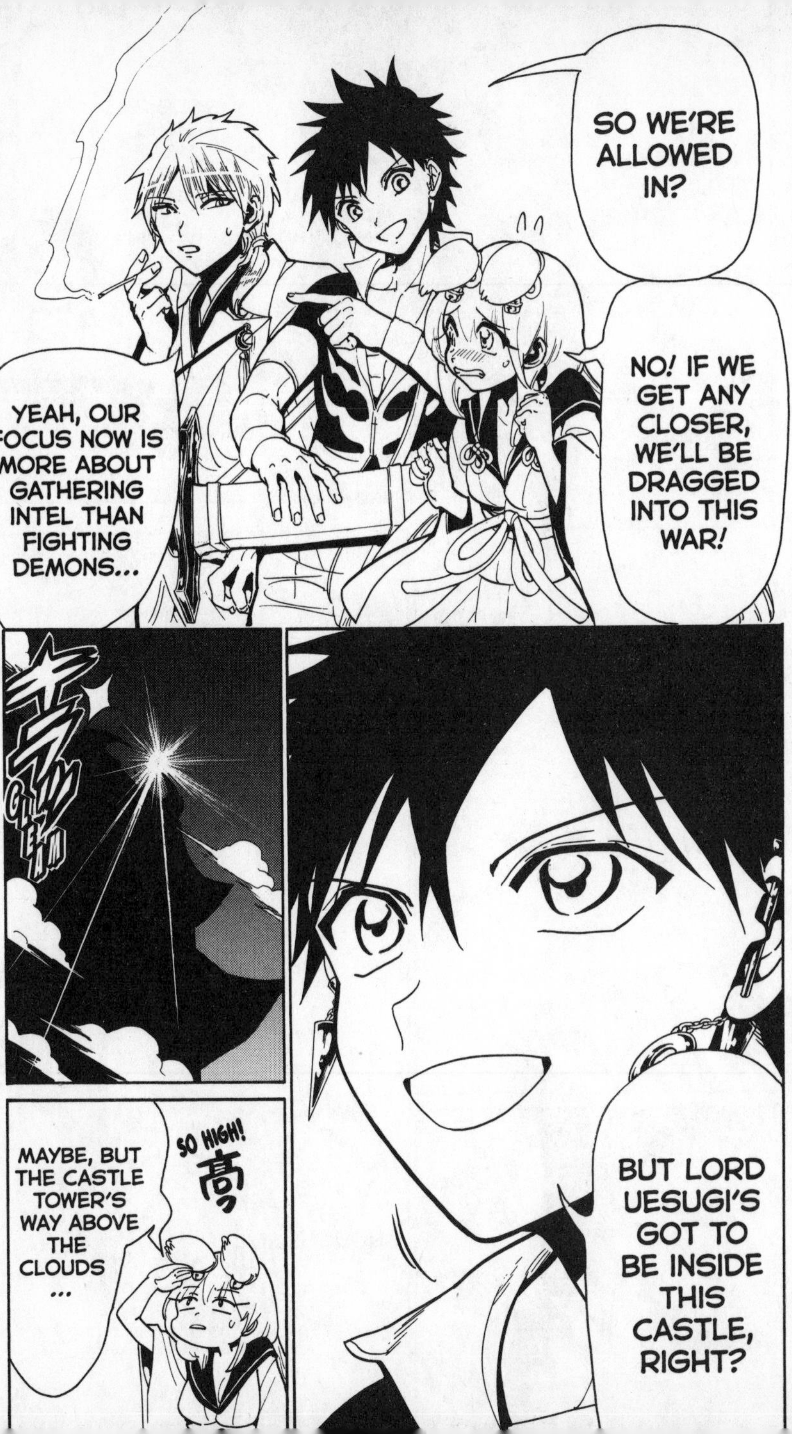
SO WE'RE ALLOWED IN?
NO! IF WE GET ANY CLOSER, WE'LL BE DRAGGED INTO THIS WAR!
YEAH, OUR FOCUS NOW IS MORE ABOUT GATHERING INTEL THAN FIGHTING DEMONS...
BUT LORD UESUGI'S GOT TO BE INSIDE THIS CASTLE, RIGHT?
GLEAM
SO HIGH!
高っ
MAYBE, BUT THE CASTLE TOWER'S WAY ABOVE THE CLOUDS ...

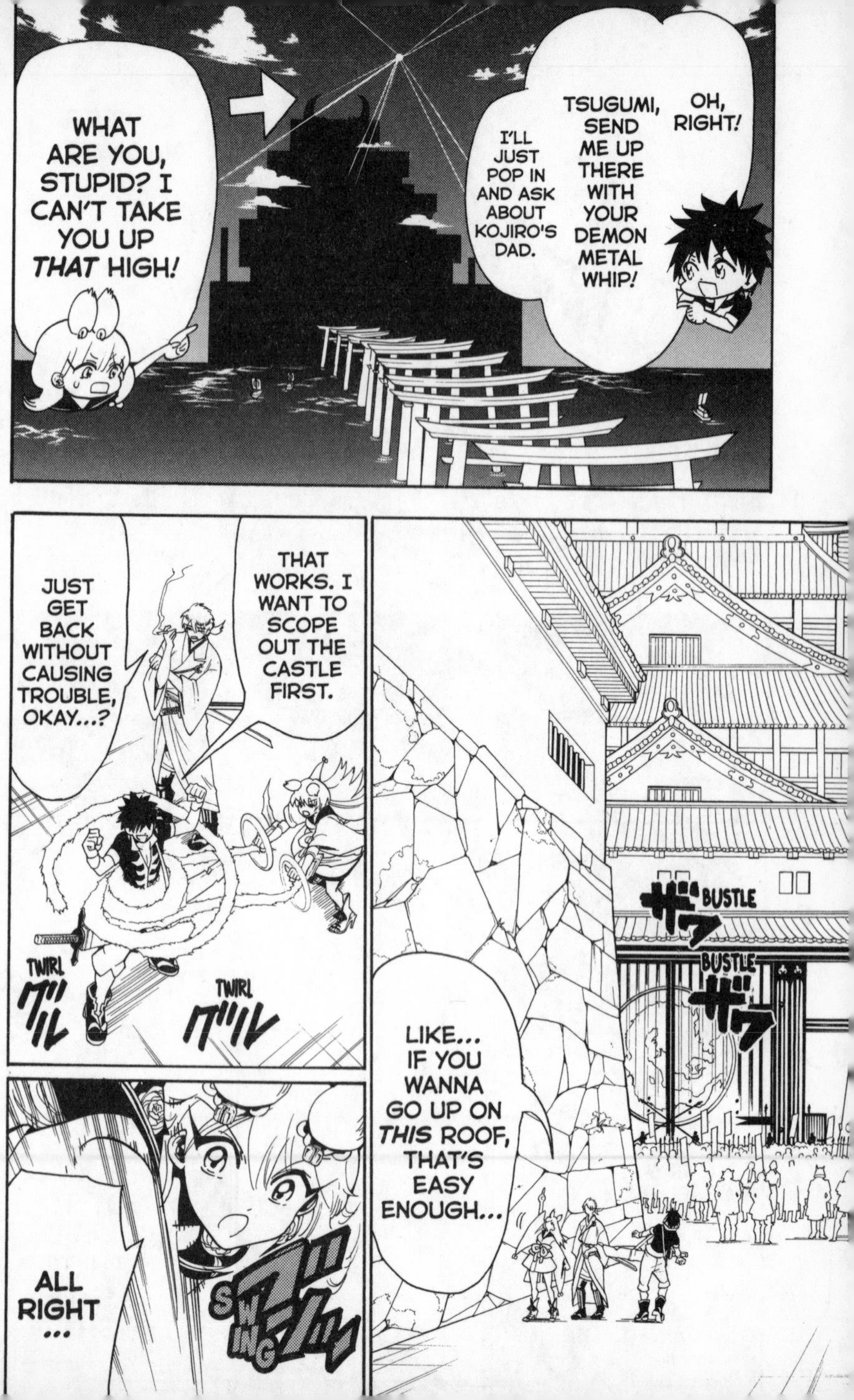
OH, RIGHT!
TSUGUMI, SEND ME UP THERE WITH YOUR DEMON METAL WHIP!
I'LL JUST POP IN AND ASK ABOUT KOJIRO'S DAD.
WHAT ARE YOU, STUPID? I CAN'T TAKE YOU UP *THAT* HIGH!
BUSTLE
BUSTLE
LIKE... IF YOU WANNA GO UP ON *THIS* ROOF, THAT'S EASY ENOUGH...
THAT WORKS. I WANT TO SCOPE OUT THE CASTLE FIRST.
JUST GET BACK WITHOUT CAUSING TROUBLE, OKAY...?
TWIRL
TWIRL
SWING
ALL RIGHT...

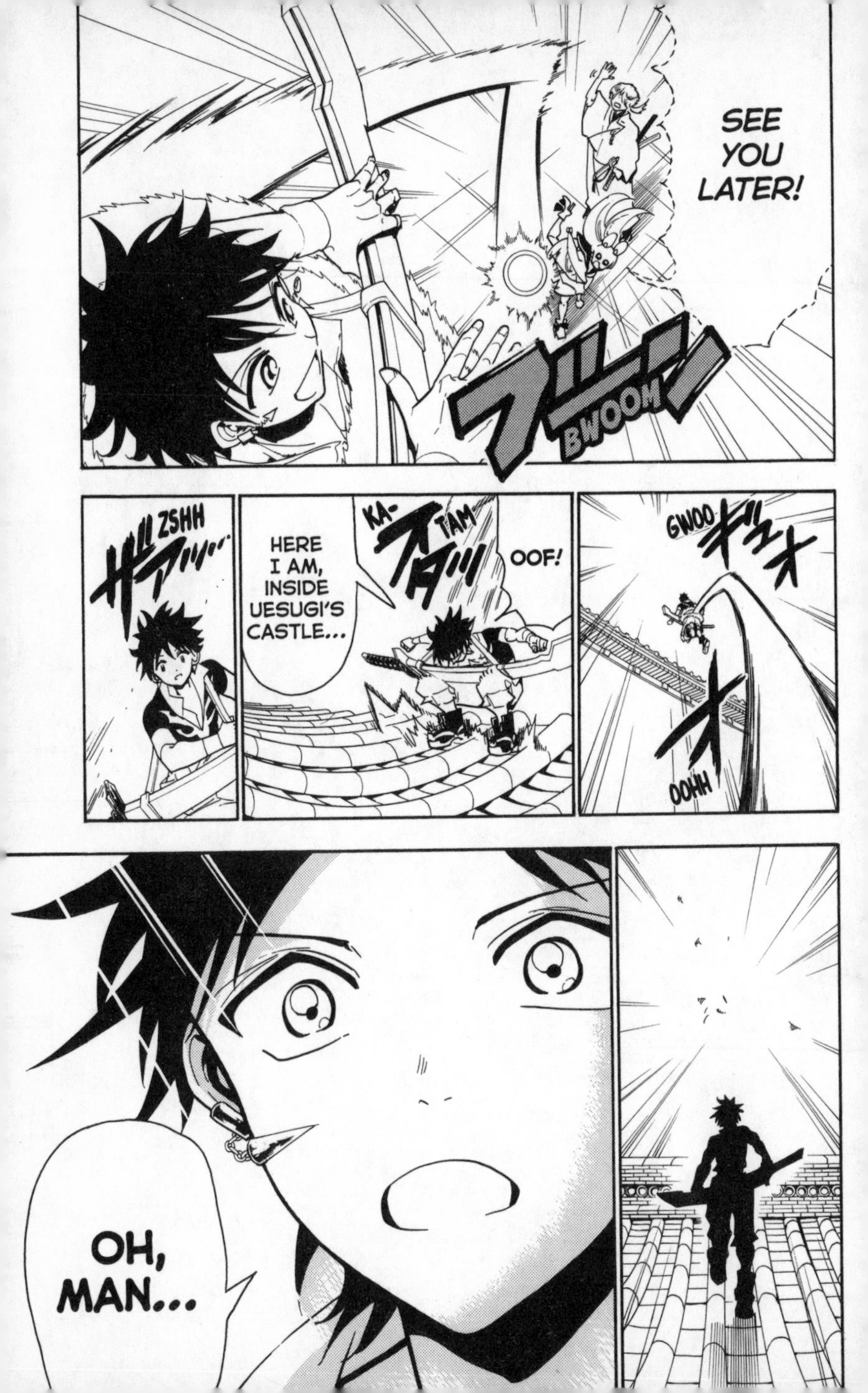
SEE YOU LATER!
BWOOM
GWOO
OOHH
OOF!
KA-TAM
HERE I AM, INSIDE UESUGI'S CASTLE...
ZSHH
OH, MAN...

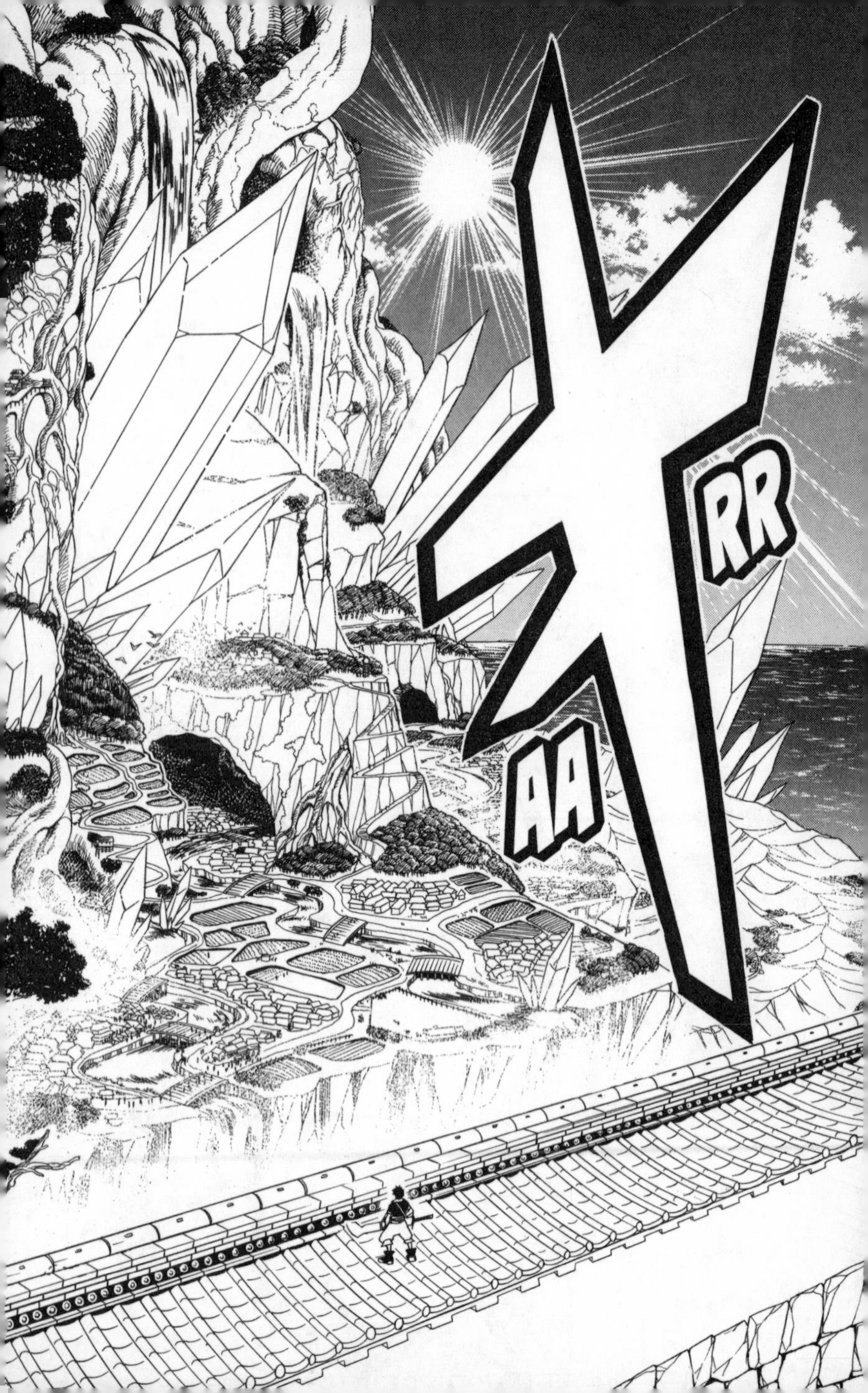
RR
AA

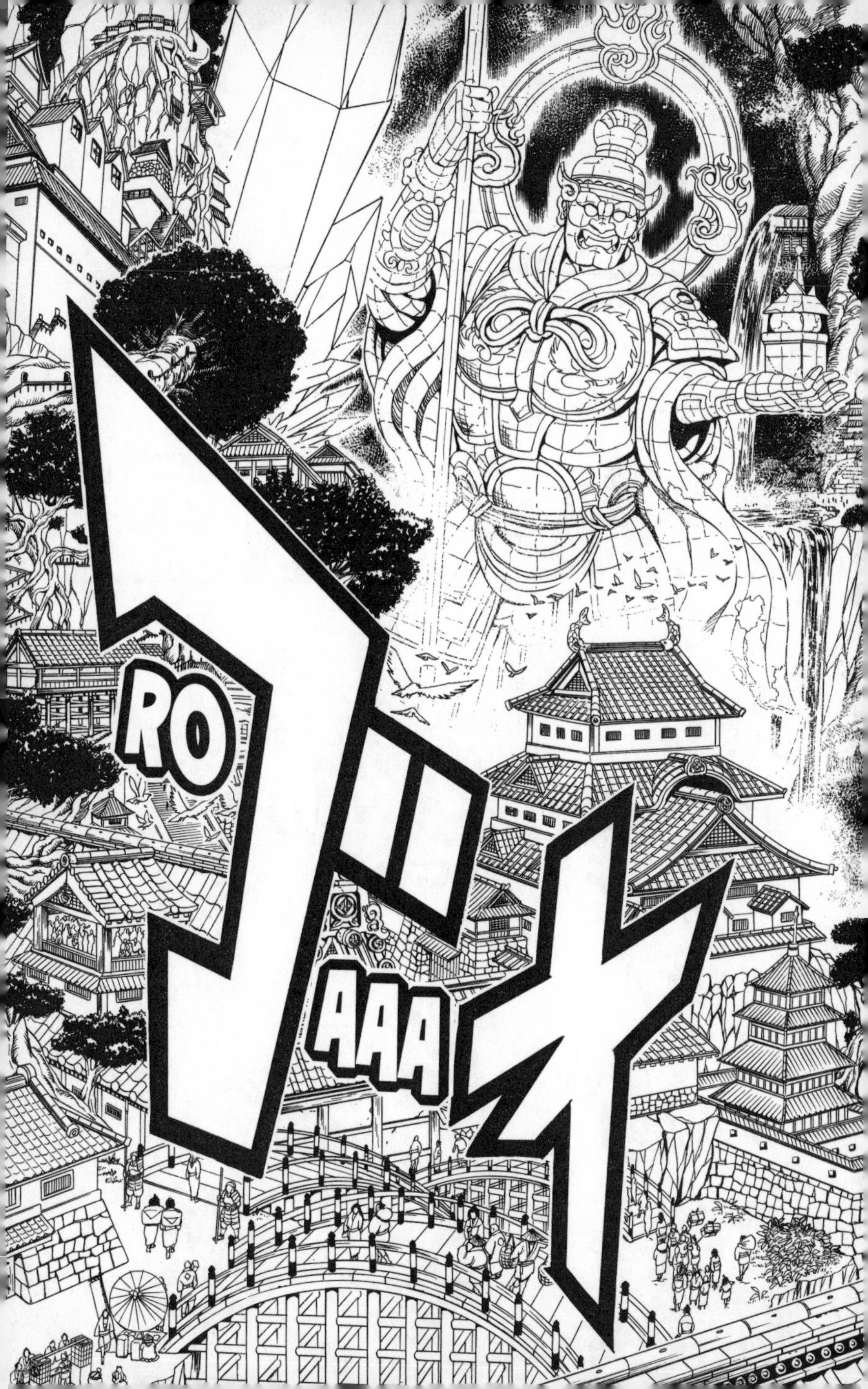
RO
AAA

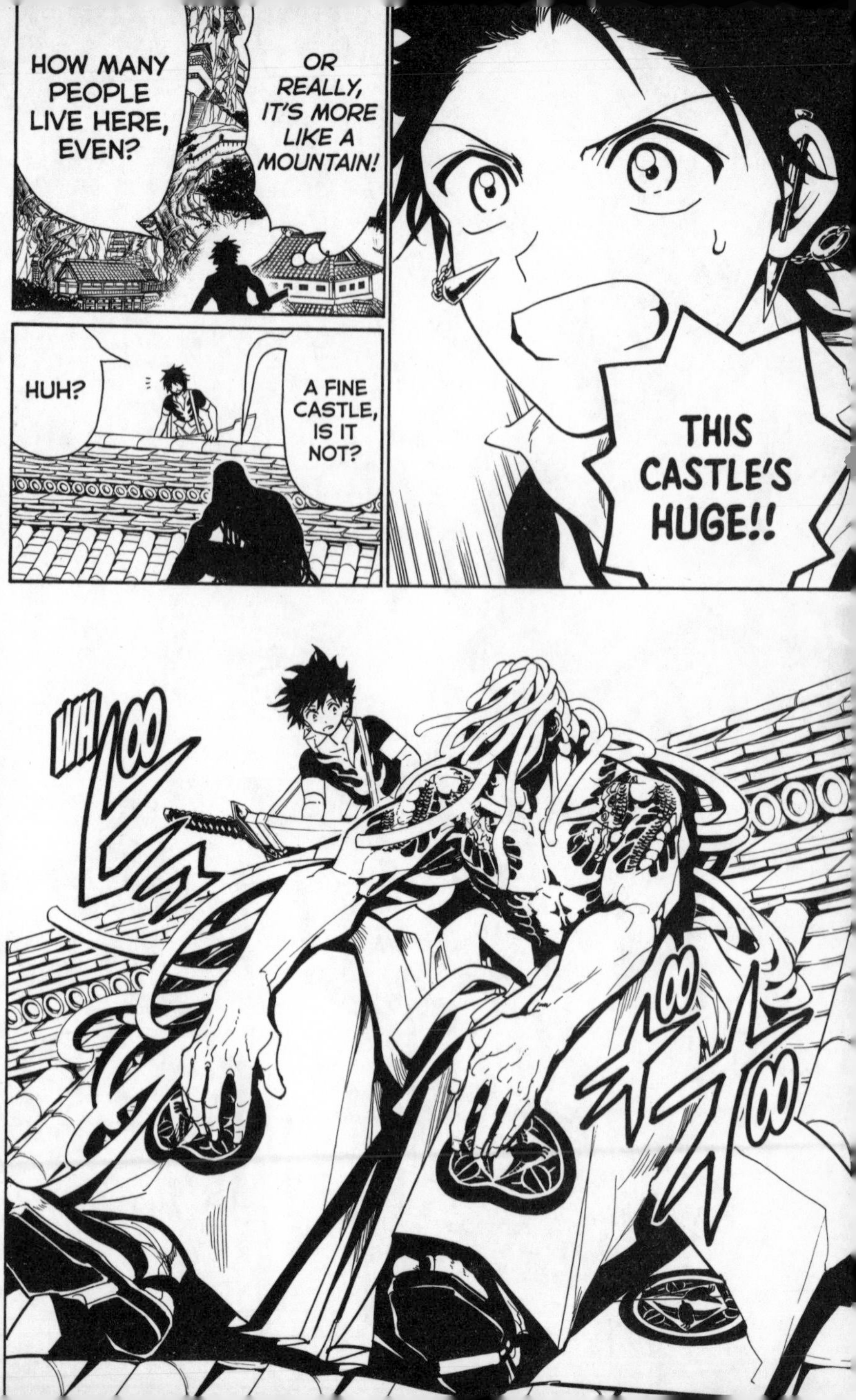
THIS CASTLE'S HUGE!!
OR REALLY, IT'S MORE LIKE A MOUNTAIN!
HOW MANY PEOPLE LIVE HERE, EVEN?
A FINE CASTLE, IS IT NOT?
HUH?
WHOO

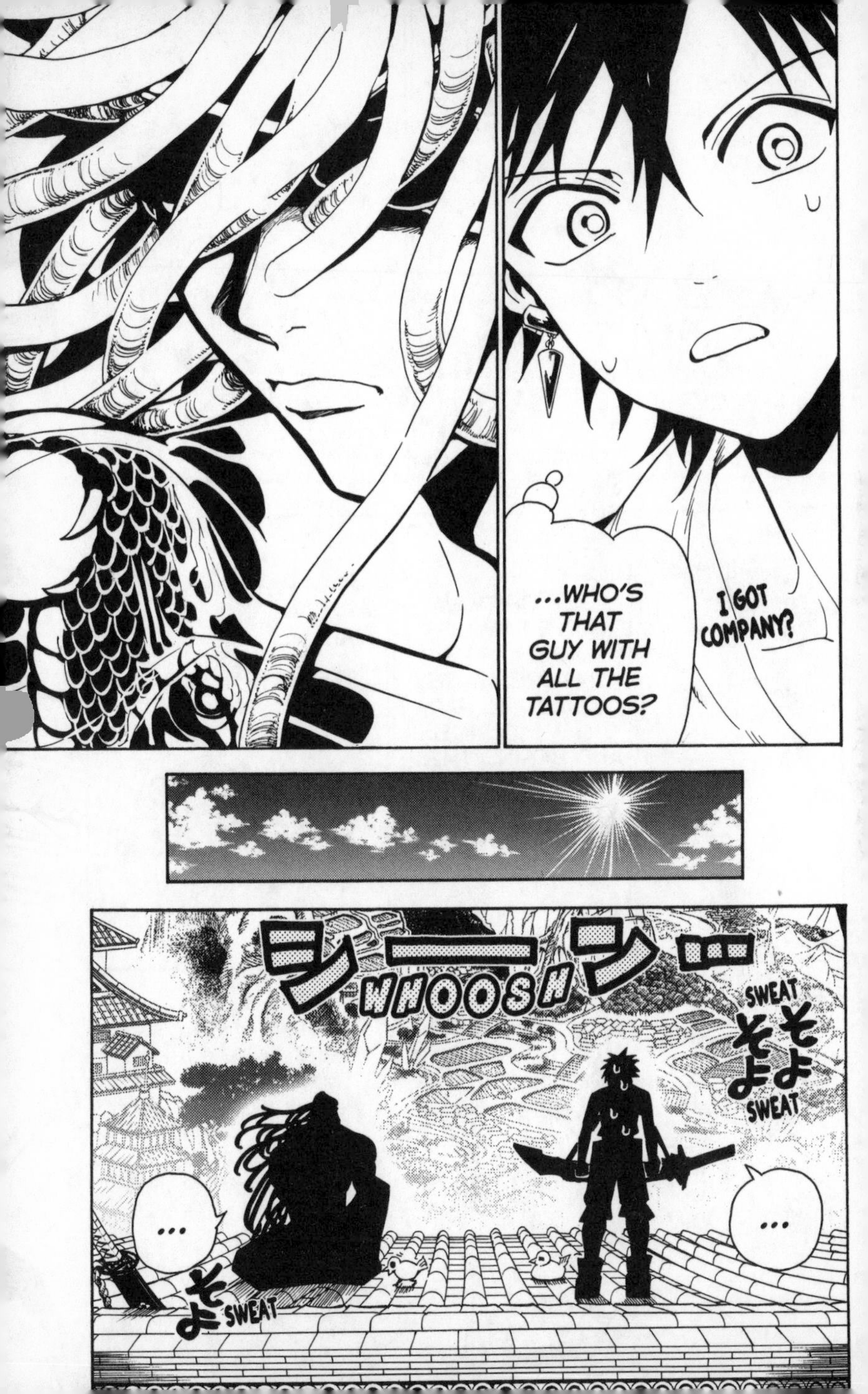
I GOT COMPANY?
...WHO'S THAT GUY WITH ALL THE TATTOOS?
シーーン
WHOOSH
SWEAT そよそよ SWEAT
...
...
そよ SWEAT

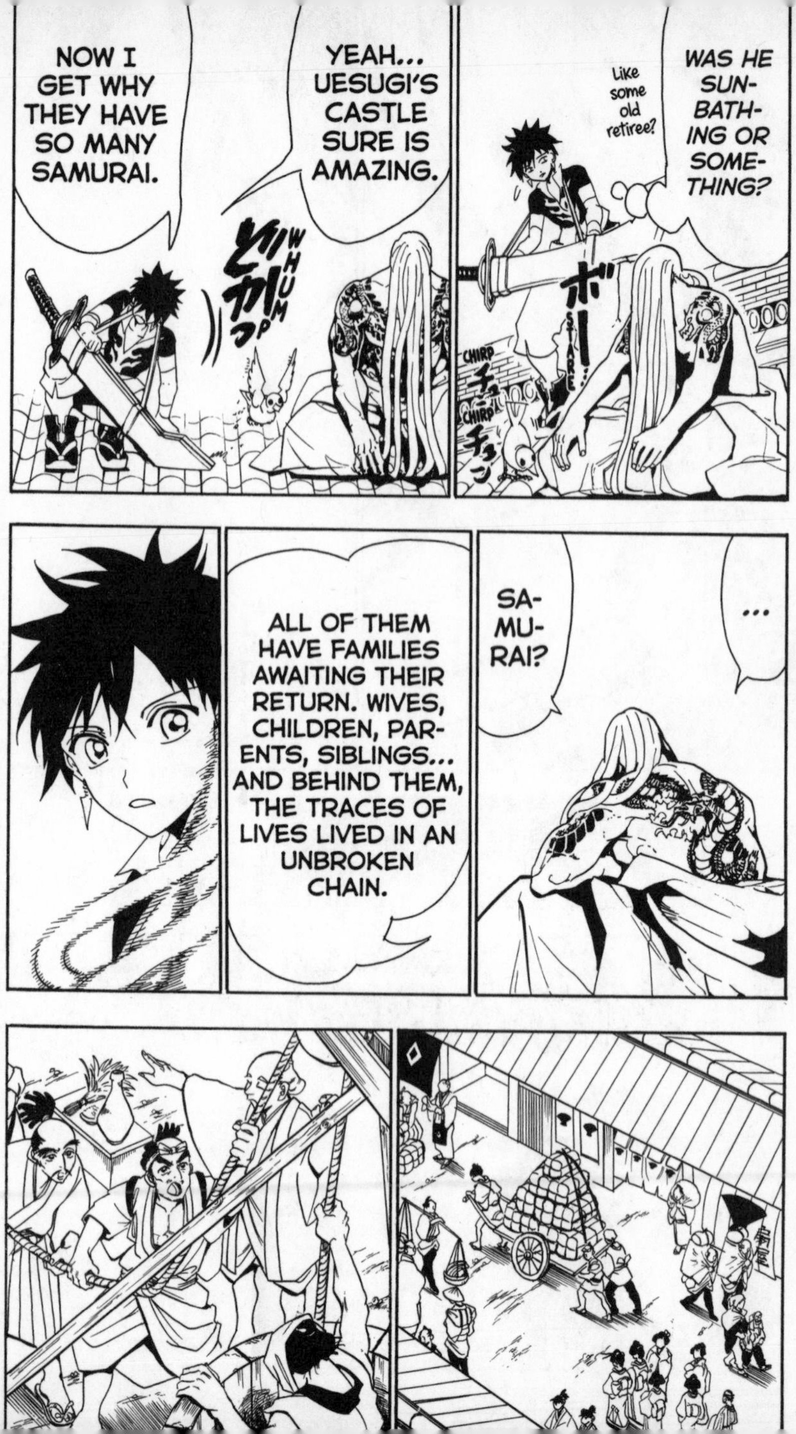
WAS HE SUN-BATH-ING OR SOME-THING?
Like some old retiree?
ボー STARE
CHIRP チュ
CHIRP チュン
YEAH... UESUGI'S CASTLE SURE IS AMAZING.
NOW I GET WHY THEY HAVE SO MANY SAMURAI.
どかっ WHUMP
...
SA-MU-RAI?
ALL OF THEM HAVE FAMILIES AWAITING THEIR RETURN. WIVES, CHILDREN, PAR-ENTS, SIBLINGS... AND BEHIND THEM, THE TRACES OF LIVES LIVED IN AN UNBROKEN CHAIN.

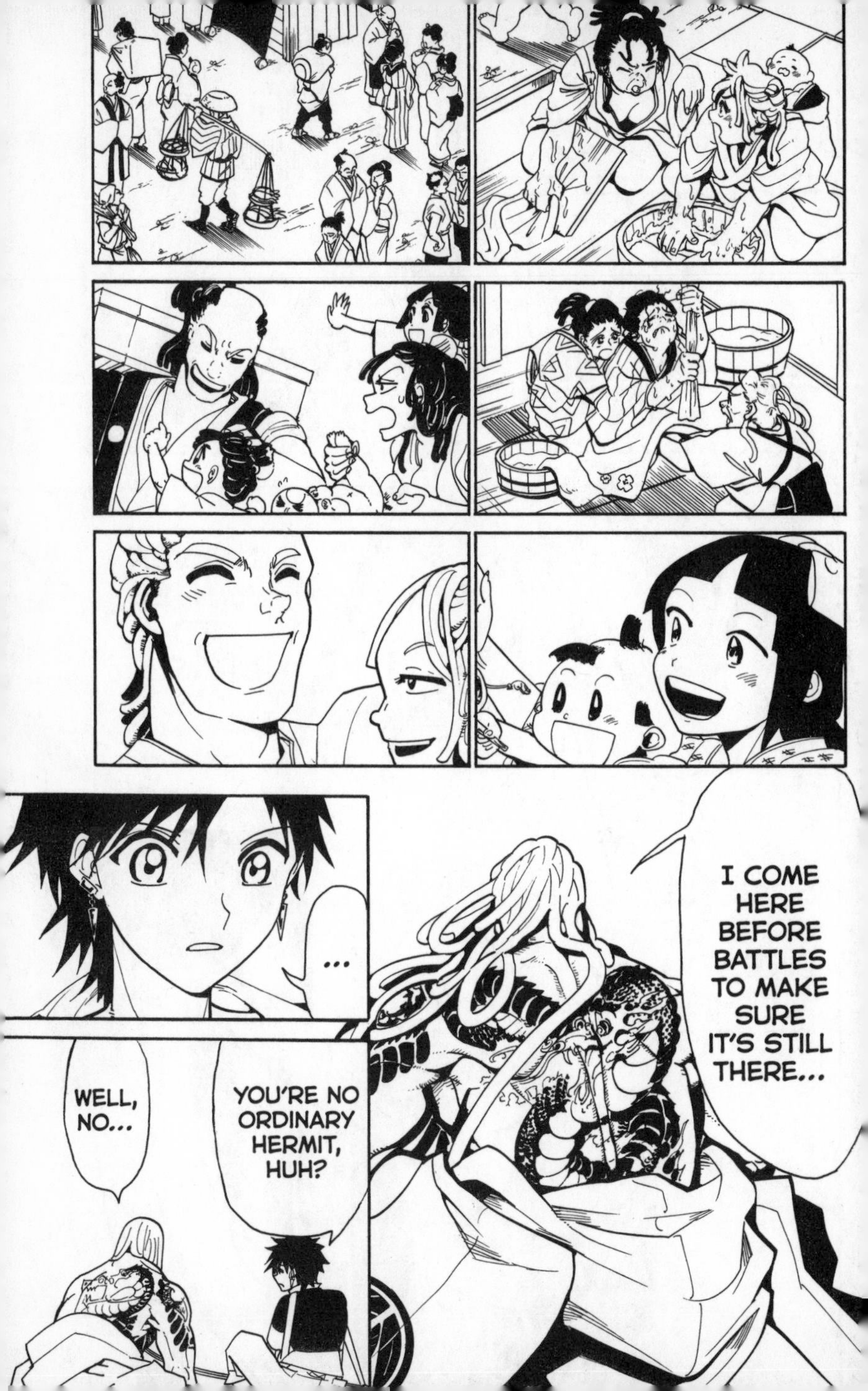
I COME HERE BEFORE BATTLES TO MAKE SURE IT'S STILL THERE...
...
YOU'RE NO ORDINARY HERMIT, HUH?
WELL, NO...

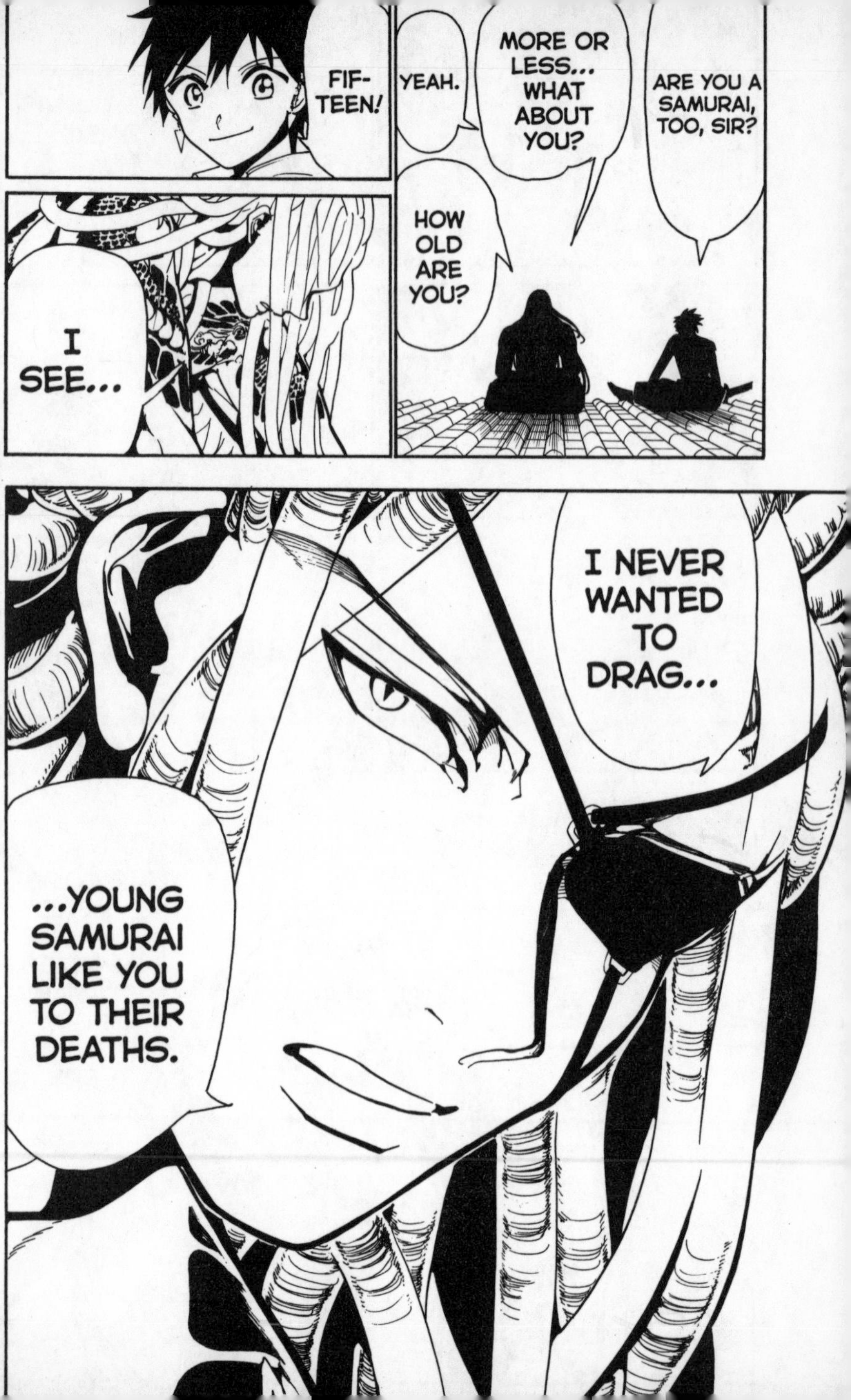
ARE YOU A SAMURAI, TOO, SIR?
MORE OR LESS... WHAT ABOUT YOU?
YEAH.
HOW OLD ARE YOU?
FIF-TEEN!
I SEE...
I NEVER WANTED TO DRAG...
...YOUNG SAMURAI LIKE YOU TO THEIR DEATHS.

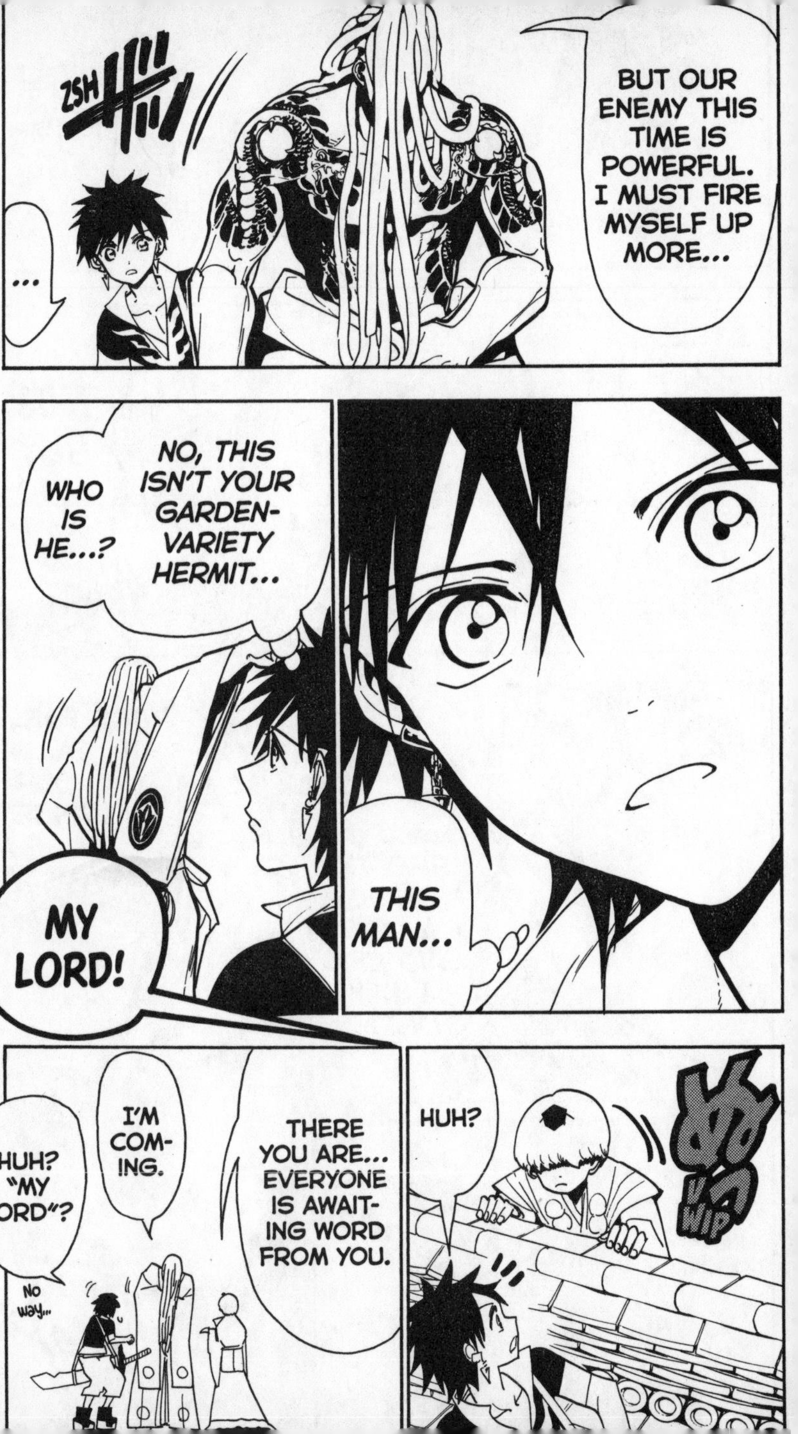

BUT OUR ENEMY THIS TIME IS POWERFUL. I MUST FIRE MYSELF UP MORE...
ZSH
...
THIS MAN...
NO, THIS ISN'T YOUR GARDEN-VARIETY HERMIT...
WHO IS HE...?
MY LORD!
WIP
HUH?
THERE YOU ARE... EVERYONE IS AWAIT-ING WORD FROM YOU.
I'M COM-ING.
HUH? "MY LORD"?
No way...

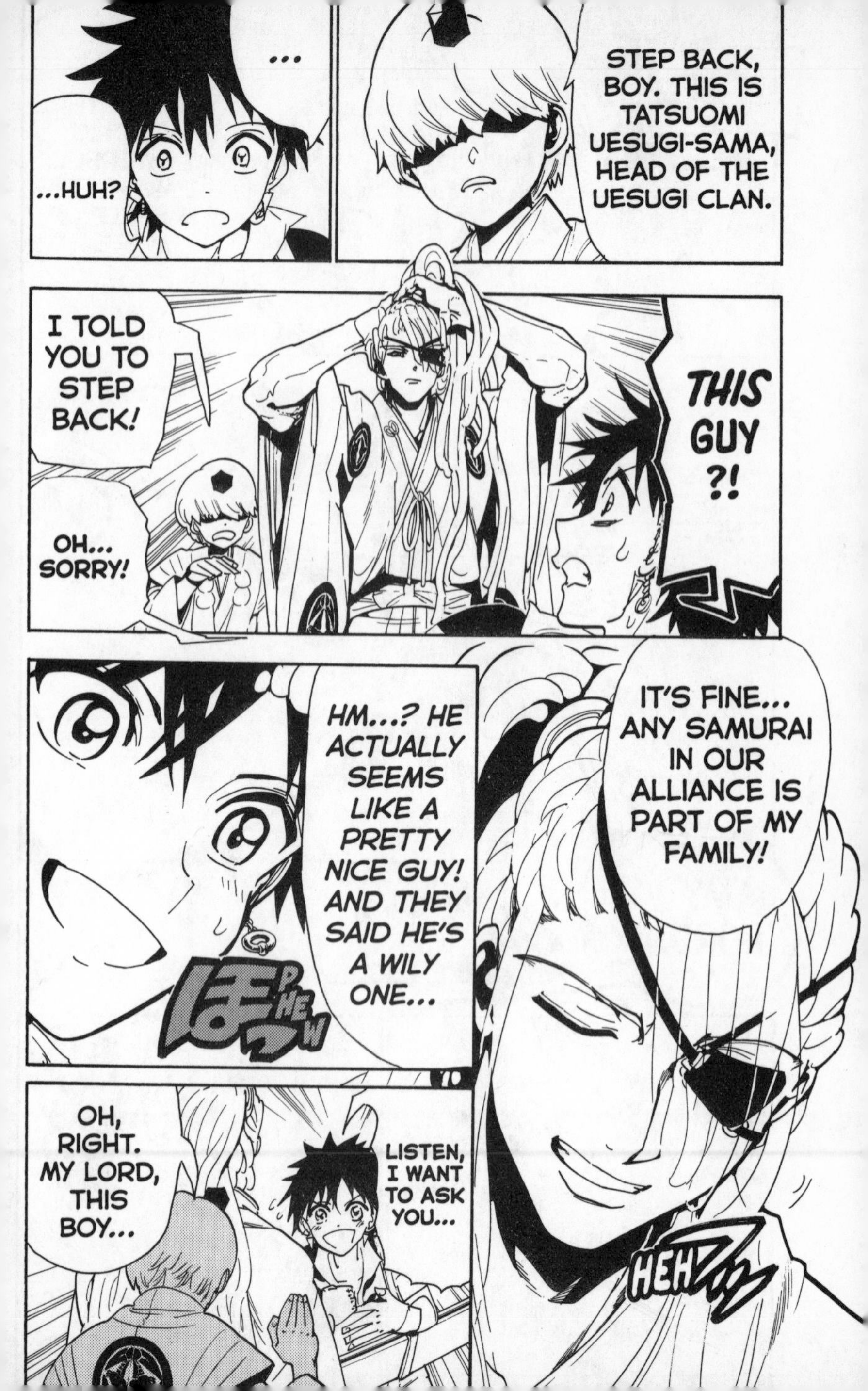
STEP BACK, BOY. THIS IS TATSUOMI UESUGI-SAMA, HEAD OF THE UESUGI CLAN.
...
...HUH?
THIS GUY?!
I TOLD YOU TO STEP BACK!
OH... SORRY!
IT'S FINE... ANY SAMURAI IN OUR ALLIANCE IS PART OF MY FAMILY!
HEH
HM...? HE ACTUALLY SEEMS LIKE A PRETTY NICE GUY! AND THEY SAID HE'S A WILY ONE...
ほっ PHEW
LISTEN, I WANT TO ASK YOU...
OH, RIGHT. MY LORD, THIS BOY...

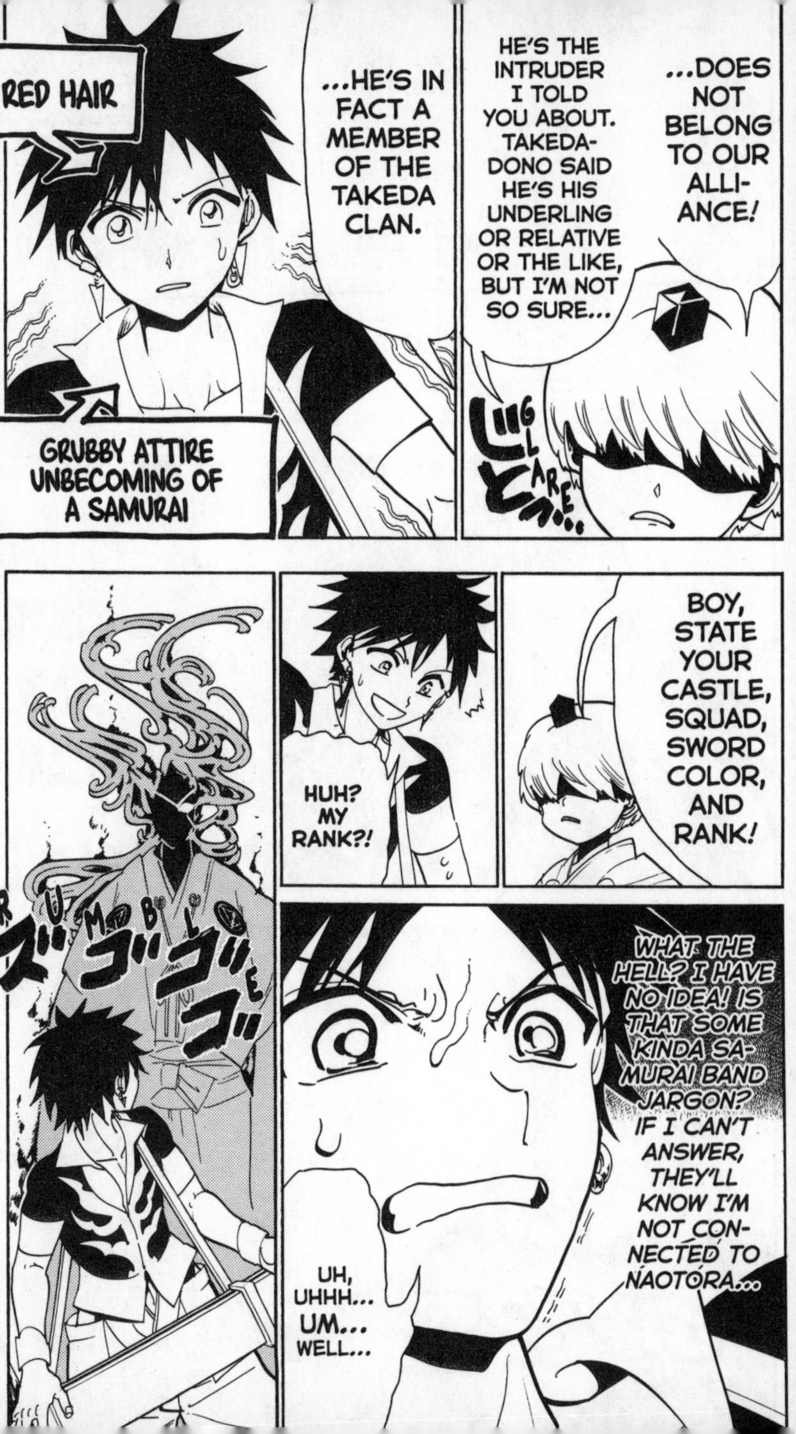
...DOES NOT BELONG TO OUR ALLIANCE!
HE'S THE INTRUDER I TOLD YOU ABOUT. TAKEDA-DONO SAID HE'S HIS UNDERLING OR RELATIVE OR THE LIKE, BUT I'M NOT SO SURE...
GLARE...
...HE'S IN FACT A MEMBER OF THE TAKEDA CLAN.
RED HAIR
GRUBBY ATTIRE UNBECOMING OF A SAMURAI
BOY, STATE YOUR CASTLE, SQUAD, SWORD COLOR, AND RANK!
HUH? MY RANK?!
WHAT THE HELL? I HAVE NO IDEA! IS THAT SOME KINDA SAMURAI BAND JARGON? IF I CAN'T ANSWER, THEY'LL KNOW I'M NOT CONNECTED TO NAOTORA...
UH, UHHH... UM... WELL...
RUMBLE

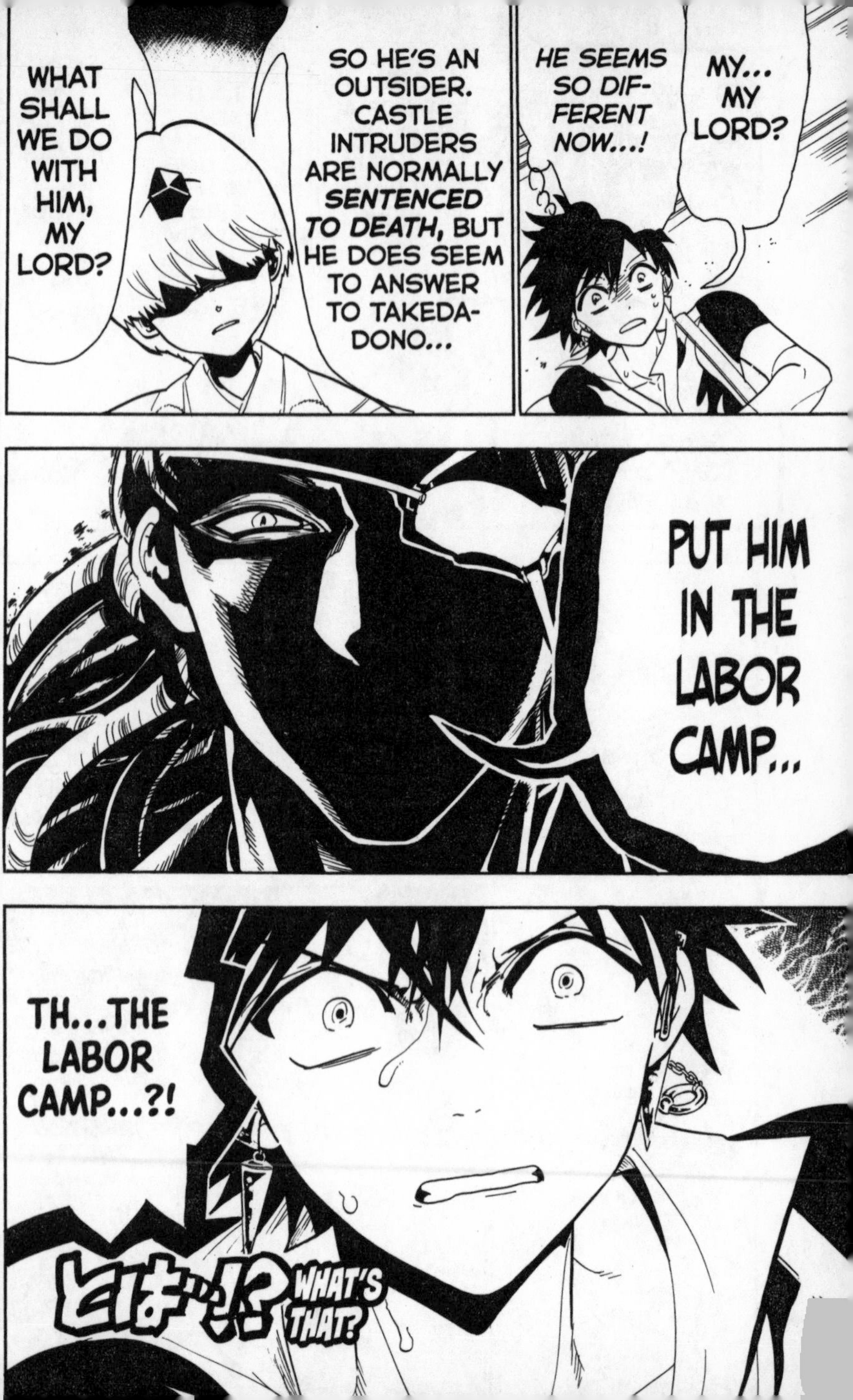
MY... MY LORD?
HE SEEMS SO DIFFERENT NOW...!
SO HE'S AN OUTSIDER. CASTLE INTRUDERS ARE NORMALLY *SENTENCED TO DEATH*, BUT HE DOES SEEM TO ANSWER TO TAKEDA-DONO...
WHAT SHALL WE DO WITH HIM, MY LORD?
PUT HIM IN THE LABOR CAMP...
TH...THE LABOR CAMP...?!
とは!?
WHAT'S THAT?

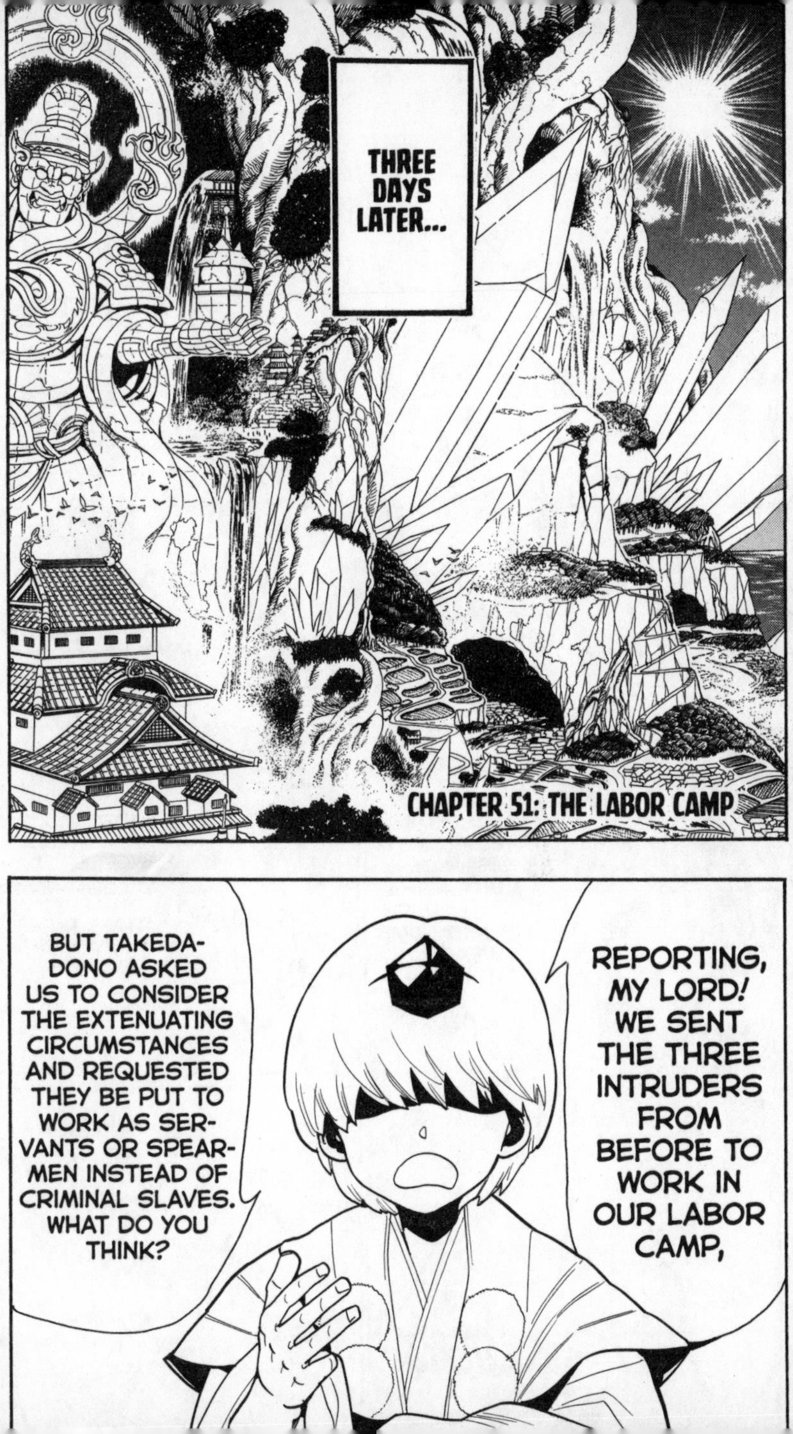
THREE DAYS LATER...
CHAPTER 51: THE LABOR CAMP
REPORTING, MY LORD! WE SENT THE THREE INTRUDERS FROM BEFORE TO WORK IN OUR LABOR CAMP,
BUT TAKEDA-DONO ASKED US TO CONSIDER THE EXTENUATING CIRCUMSTANCES AND REQUESTED THEY BE PUT TO WORK AS SER-VANTS OR SPEAR-MEN INSTEAD OF CRIMINAL SLAVES. WHAT DO YOU THINK?

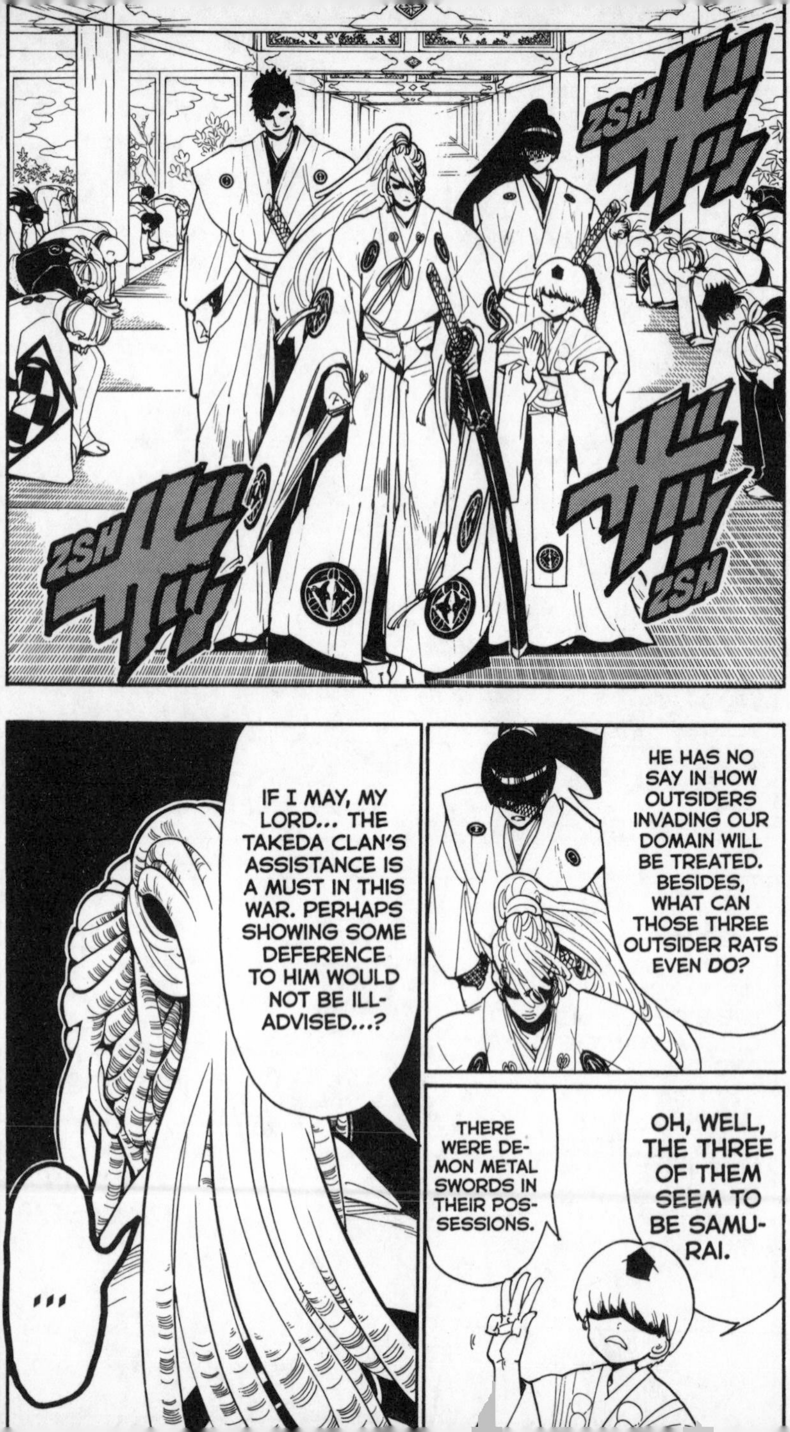
ZSH
ZSH
ZSH
HE HAS NO SAY IN HOW OUTSIDERS INVADING OUR DOMAIN WILL BE TREATED. BESIDES, WHAT CAN THOSE THREE OUTSIDER RATS EVEN *DO?*
OH, WELL, THE THREE OF THEM SEEM TO BE SAMU-RAI.
THERE WERE DE-MON METAL SWORDS IN THEIR POS-SESSIONS.
IF I MAY, MY LORD... THE TAKEDA CLAN'S ASSISTANCE IS A MUST IN THIS WAR. PERHAPS SHOWING SOME DEFERENCE TO HIM WOULD NOT BE ILL-ADVISED...?
...

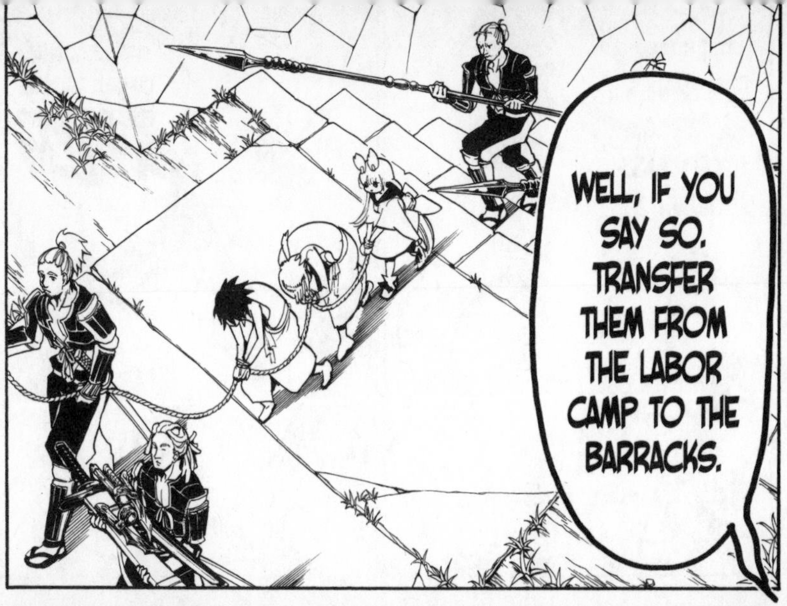
WELL, IF YOU SAY SO. TRANSFER THEM FROM THE LABOR CAMP TO THE BARRACKS.
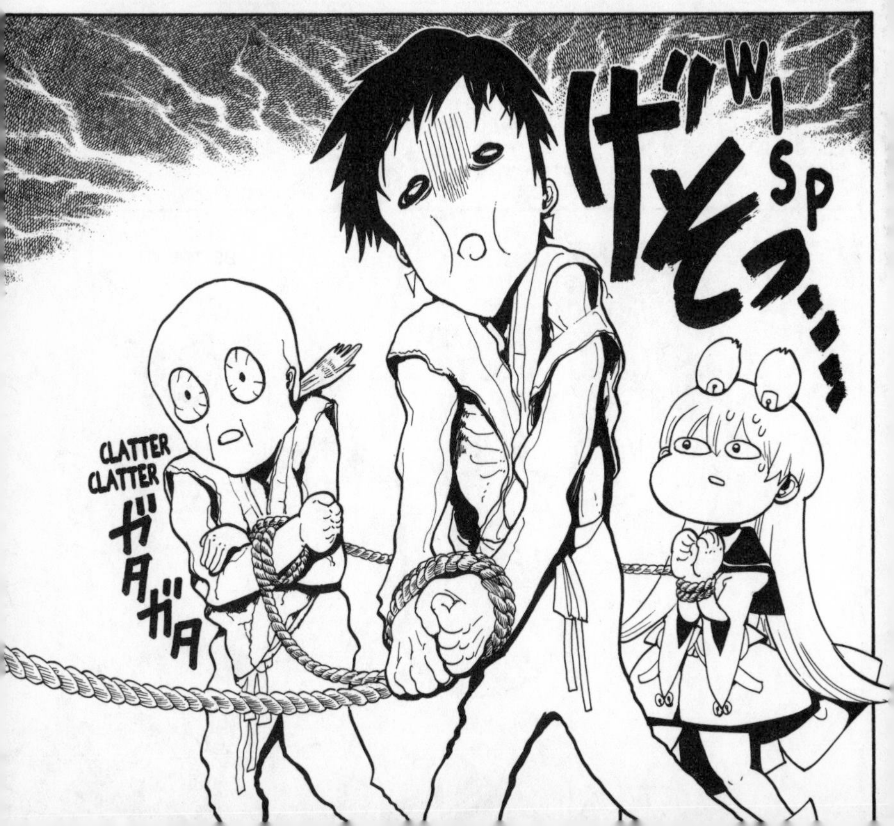
げどっ…
WISP
ガタガタ
CLATTER CLATTER

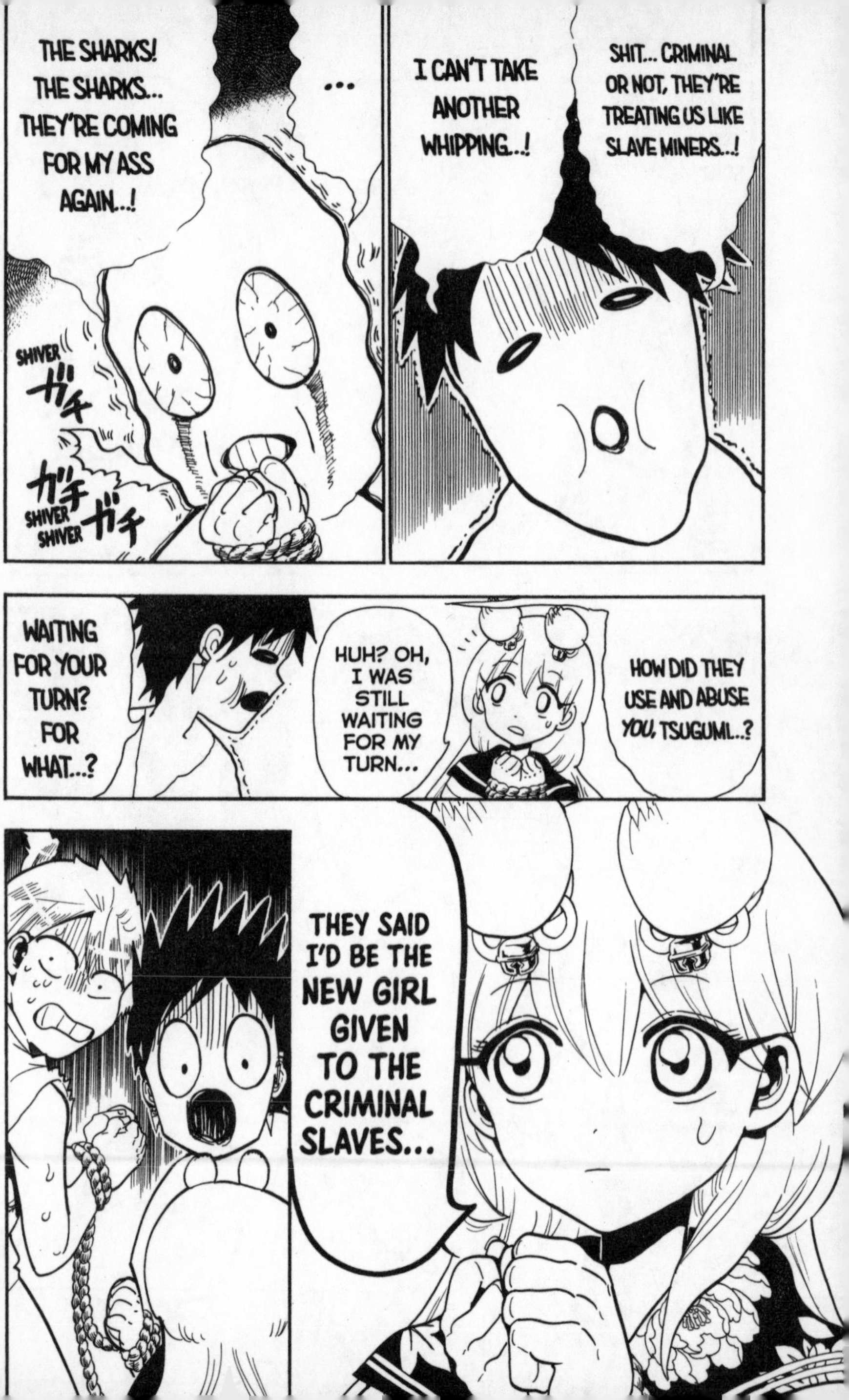
SHIT... CRIMINAL OR NOT, THEY'RE TREATING US LIKE SLAVE MINERS...!
I CAN'T TAKE ANOTHER WHIPPING...!
...
THE SHARKS! THE SHARKS... THEY'RE COMING FOR MY ASS AGAIN...!
ガチ SHIVER
ガチ ガチ SHIVER SHIVER
HOW DID THEY USE AND ABUSE *YOU*, TSUGUMI...?
HUH? OH, I WAS STILL WAITING FOR MY TURN...
WAITING FOR YOUR TURN? FOR WHAT...?
THEY SAID I'D BE THE NEW GIRL GIVEN TO THE CRIMINAL SLAVES...

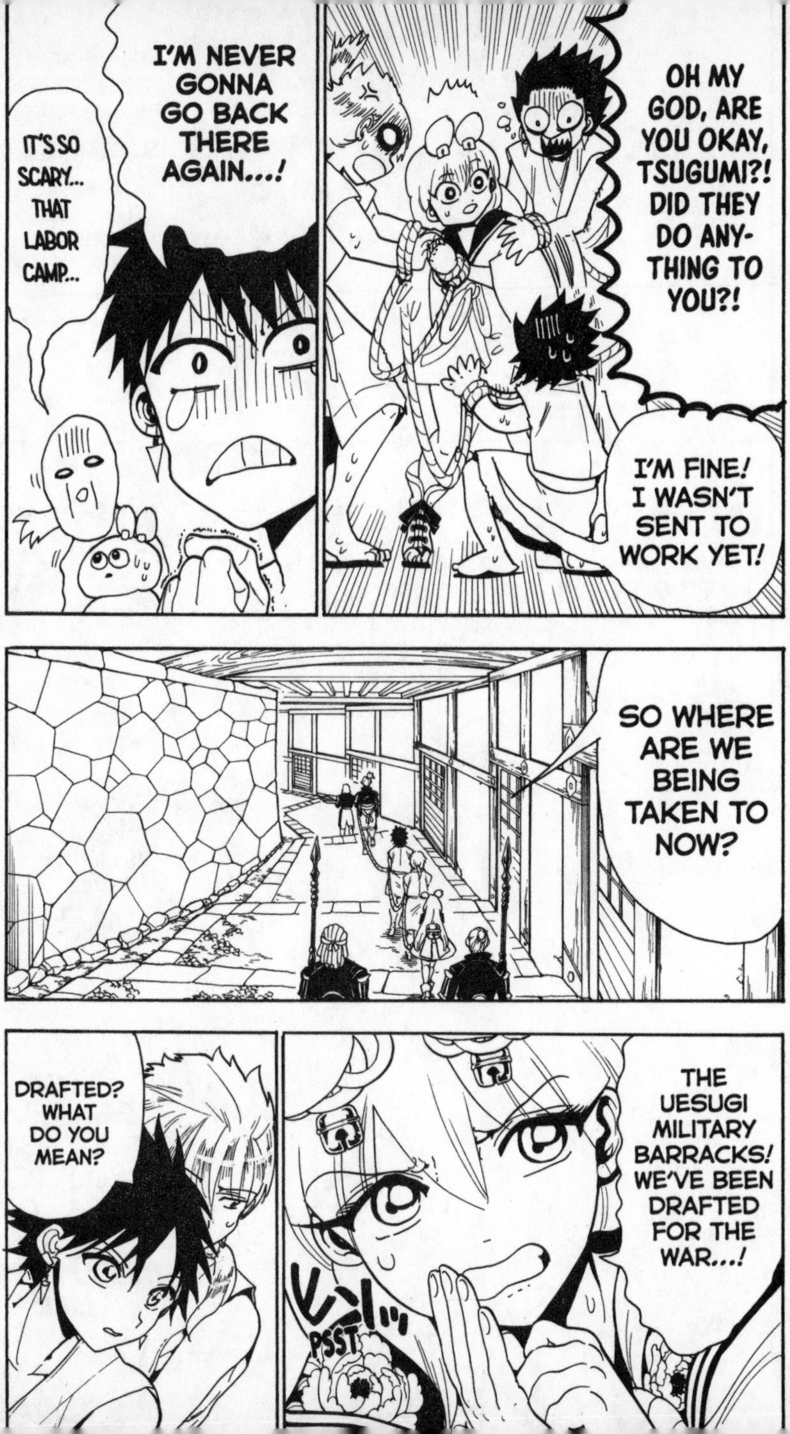
OH MY GOD, ARE YOU OKAY, TSUGUMI?! DID THEY DO ANY-THING TO YOU?!
I'M FINE! I WASN'T SENT TO WORK YET!
I'M NEVER GONNA GO BACK THERE AGAIN...!
IT'S SO SCARY... THAT LABOR CAMP...
SO WHERE ARE WE BEING TAKEN TO NOW?
THE UESUGI MILITARY BARRACKS! WE'VE BEEN DRAFTED FOR THE WAR...!
PSST
DRAFTED? WHAT DO YOU MEAN?

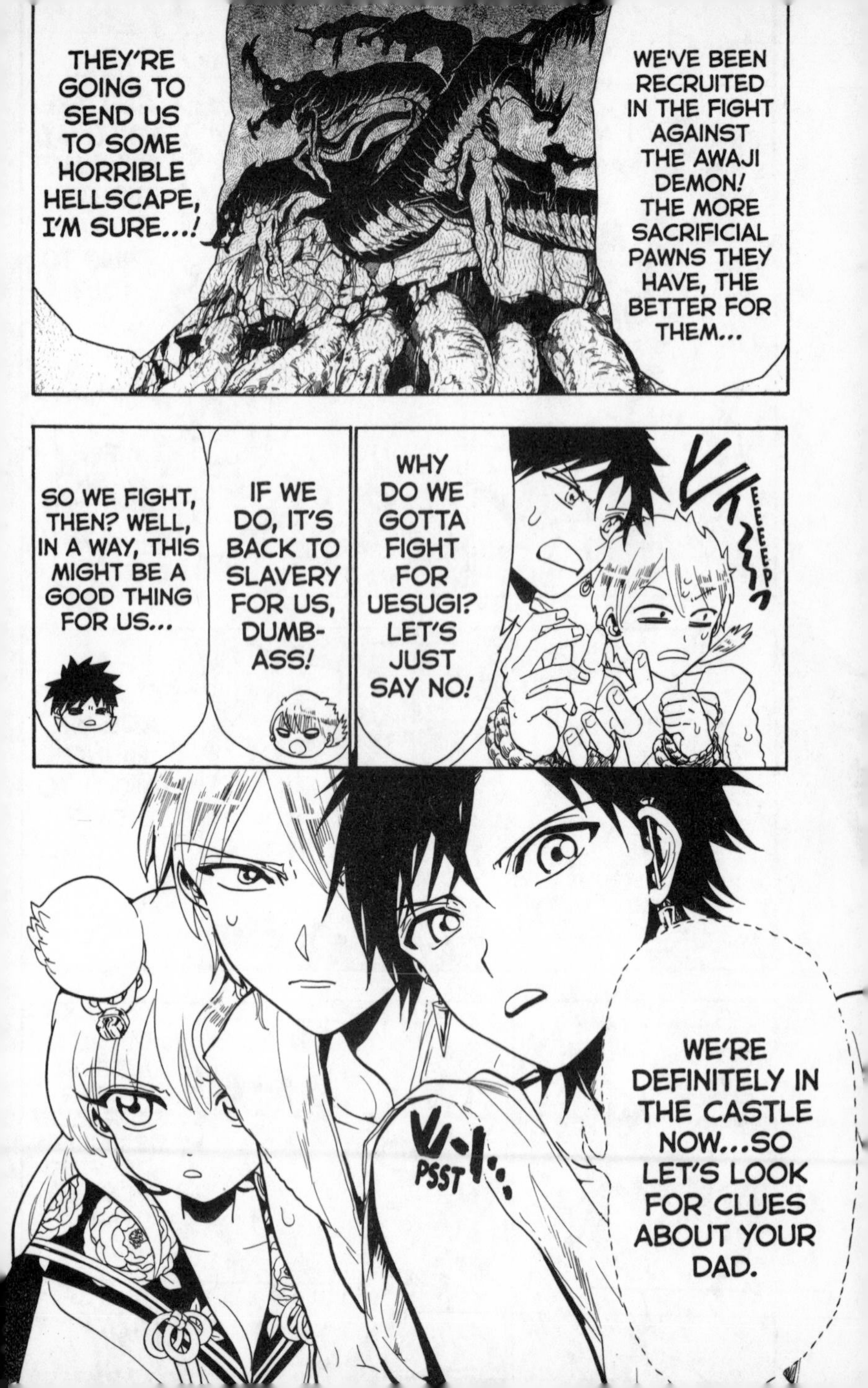

WE'VE BEEN RECRUITED IN THE FIGHT AGAINST THE AWAJI DEMON! THE MORE SACRIFICIAL PAWNS THEY HAVE, THE BETTER FOR THEM...
THEY'RE GOING TO SEND US TO SOME HORRIBLE HELLSCAPE, I'M SURE...!
EEEEP
WHY DO WE GOTTA FIGHT FOR UESUGI? LET'S JUST SAY NO!
IF WE DO, IT'S BACK TO SLAVERY FOR US, DUMB-ASS!
SO WE FIGHT, THEN? WELL, IN A WAY, THIS MIGHT BE A GOOD THING FOR US...
WE'RE DEFINITELY IN THE CASTLE NOW...SO LET'S LOOK FOR CLUES ABOUT YOUR DAD.
W-!...
PSST

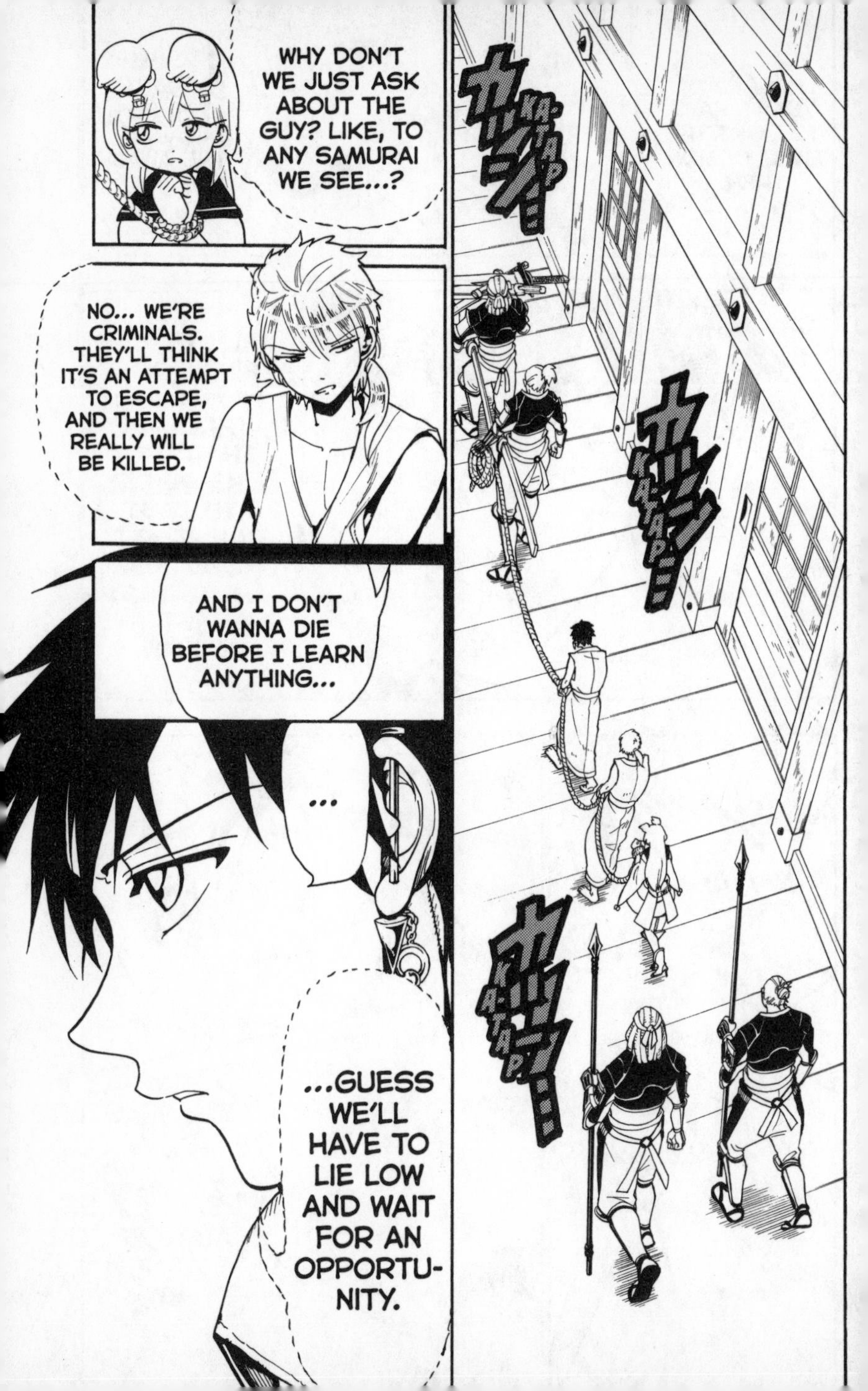
KA-TAP
KA-TAP
KA-TAP.
WHY DON'T WE JUST ASK ABOUT THE GUY? LIKE, TO ANY SAMURAI WE SEE...?
NO... WE'RE CRIMINALS. THEY'LL THINK IT'S AN ATTEMPT TO ESCAPE, AND THEN WE REALLY WILL BE KILLED.
AND I DON'T WANNA DIE BEFORE I LEARN ANYTHING...
...
...GUESS WE'LL HAVE TO LIE LOW AND WAIT FOR AN OPPORTU-NITY.

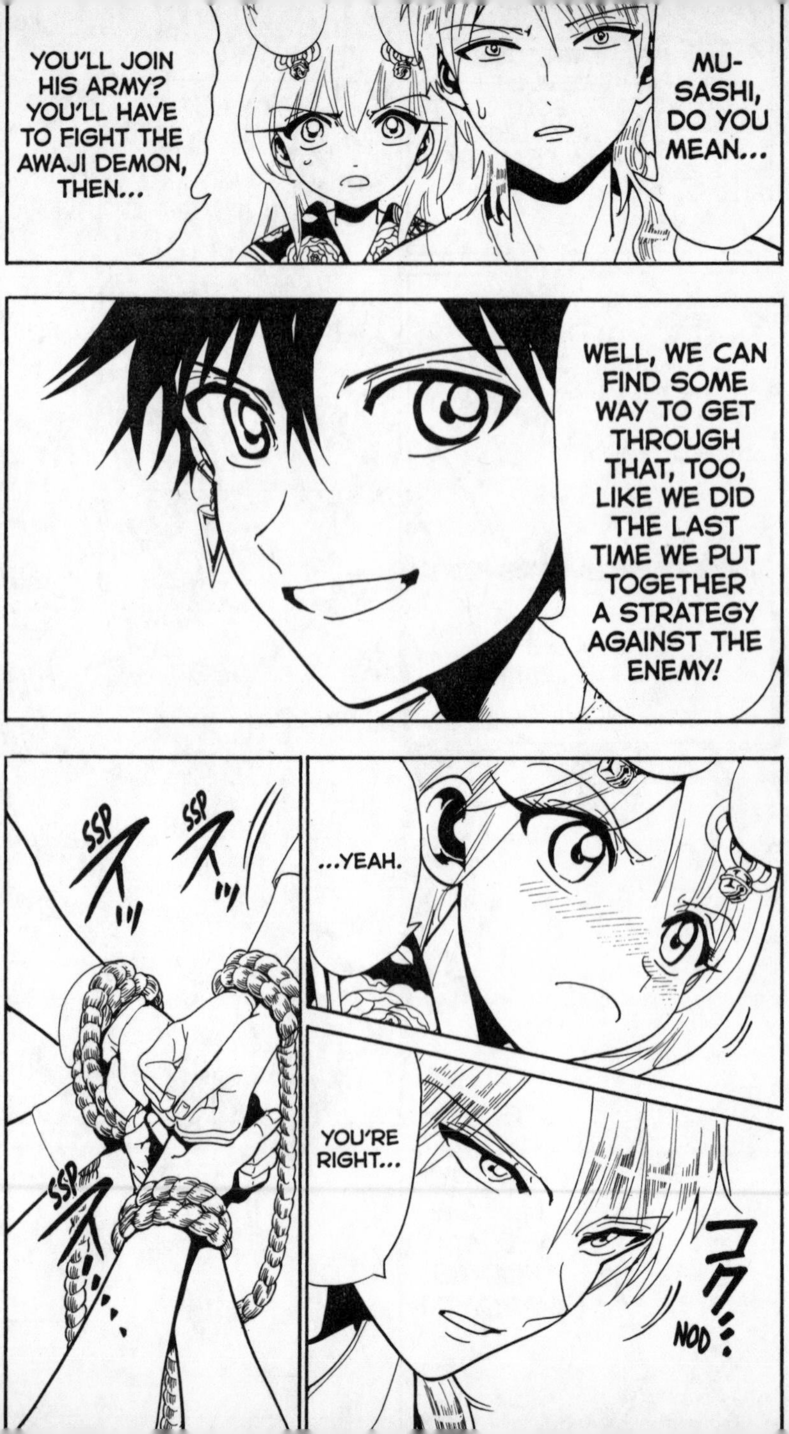

MU-SASHI, DO YOU MEAN...
YOU'LL JOIN HIS ARMY? YOU'LL HAVE TO FIGHT THE AWAJI DEMON, THEN...
WELL, WE CAN FIND SOME WAY TO GET THROUGH THAT, TOO, LIKE WE DID THE LAST TIME WE PUT TOGETHER A STRATEGY AGAINST THE ENEMY!
...YEAH.
YOU'RE RIGHT...
NOD
SSP
SSP
SSP

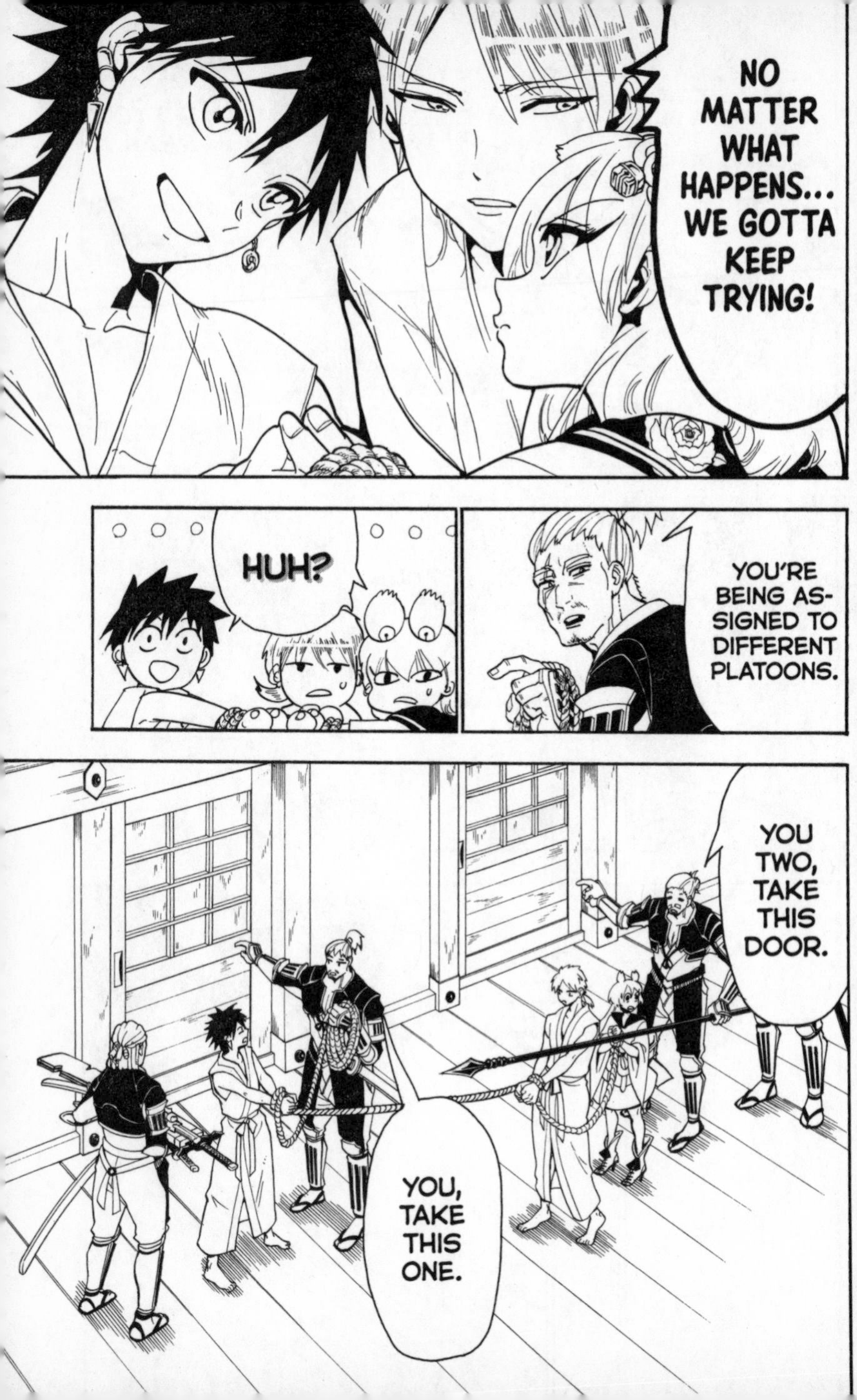
NO MATTER WHAT HAPPENS... WE GOTTA KEEP TRYING!
YOU'RE BEING AS-SIGNED TO DIFFERENT PLATOONS.
HUH?
YOU TWO, TAKE THIS DOOR.
YOU, TAKE THIS ONE.

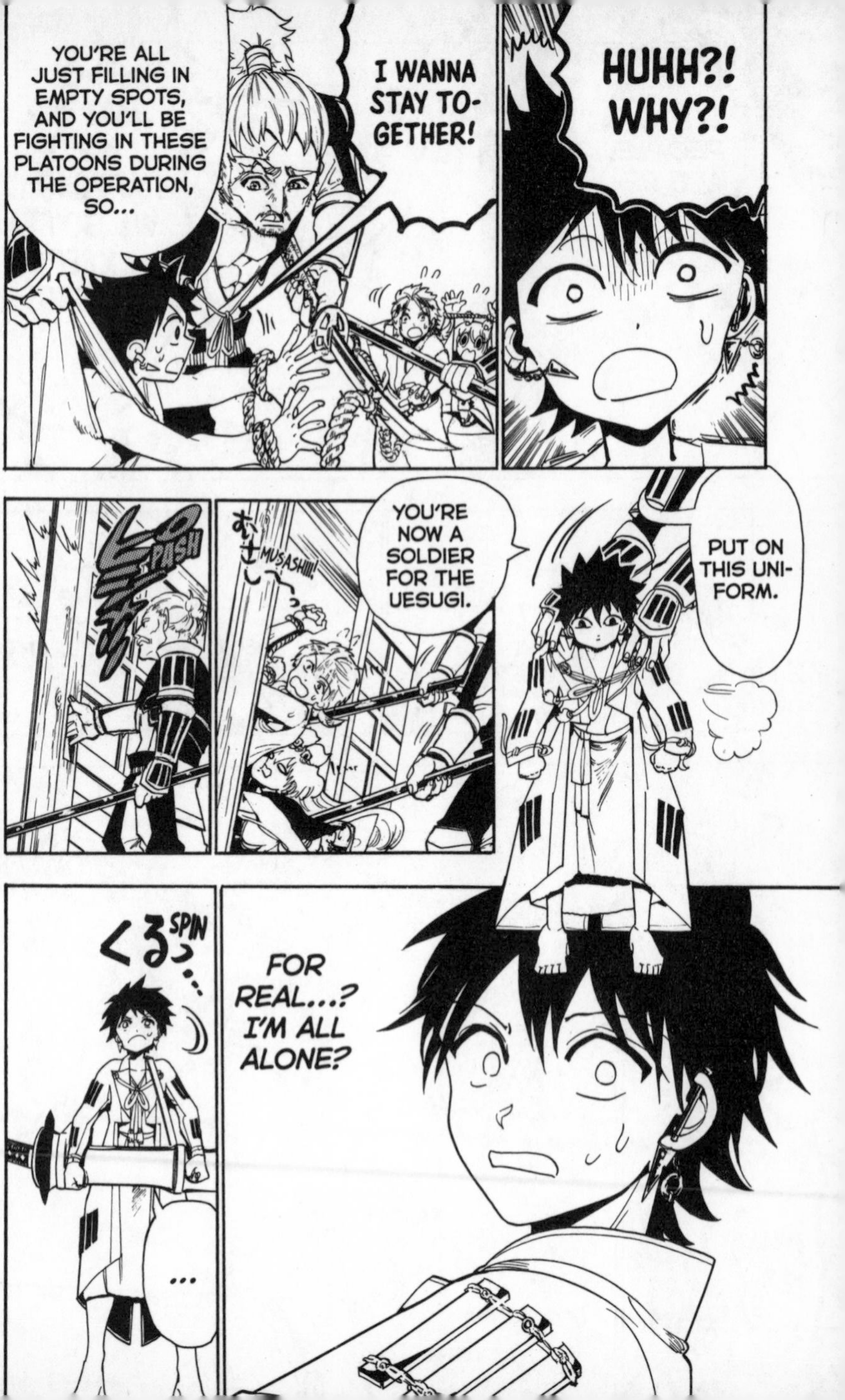
HUHH?! WHY?!
I WANNA STAY TO-GETHER!
YOU'RE ALL JUST FILLING IN EMPTY SPOTS, AND YOU'LL BE FIGHTING IN THESE PLATOONS DURING THE OPERATION, SO...
PUT ON THIS UNI-FORM.
YOU'RE NOW A SOLDIER FOR THE UESUGI.
むさし
MUSASHIII!
SPASH
FOR REAL...? I'M ALL ALONE?
くるっ
SPIN
...

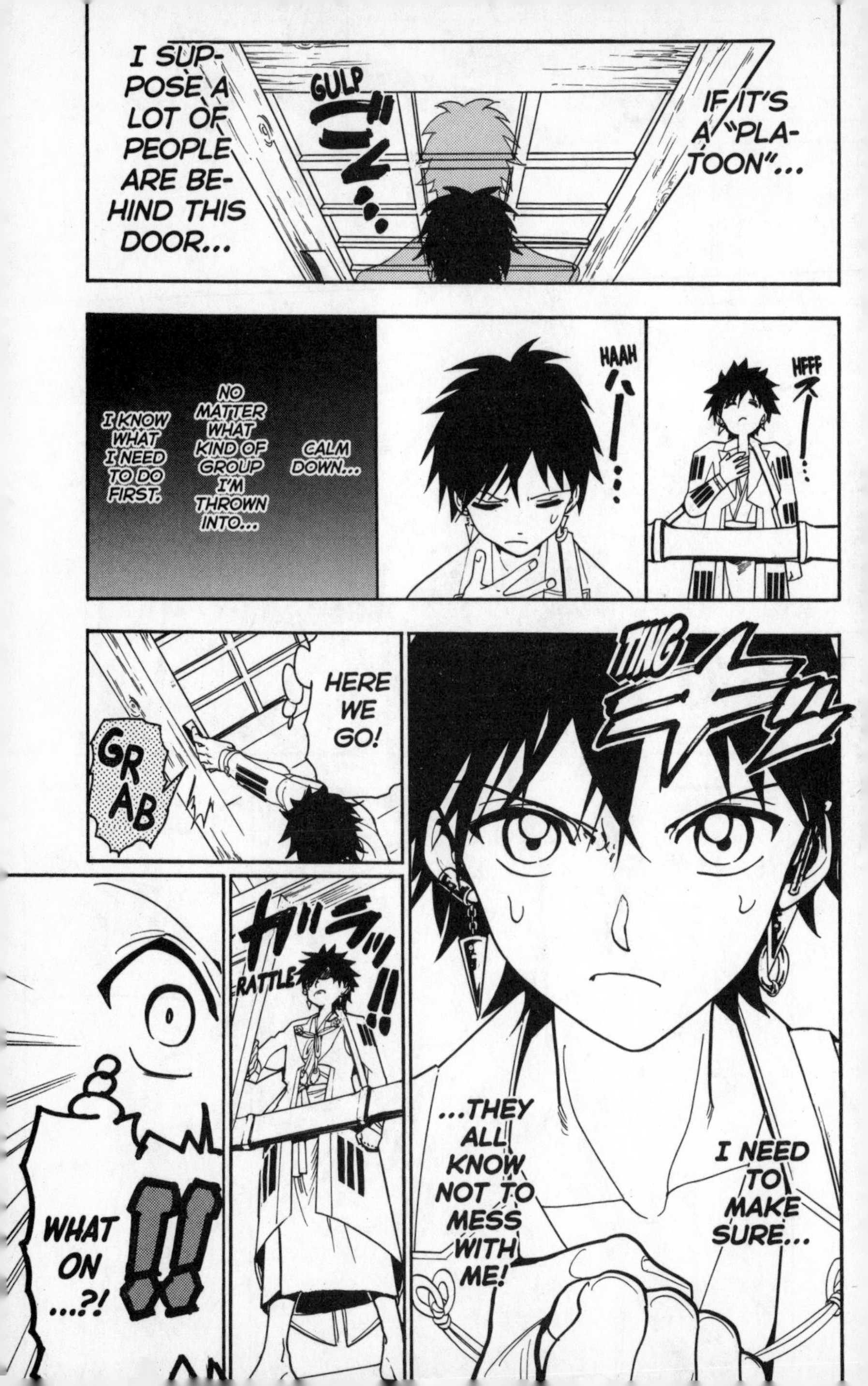
IF IT'S A "PLATOON"...
GULP
I SUPPOSE A LOT OF PEOPLE ARE BEHIND THIS DOOR...
HFFF
HAAH
CALM DOWN...
NO MATTER WHAT KIND OF GROUP I'M THROWN INTO...
I KNOW WHAT I NEED TO DO FIRST.
TING
I NEED TO MAKE SURE...
...THEY ALL KNOW NOT TO MESS WITH ME!
HERE WE GO!
GRAB
RATTLE
WHAT ON ...?!

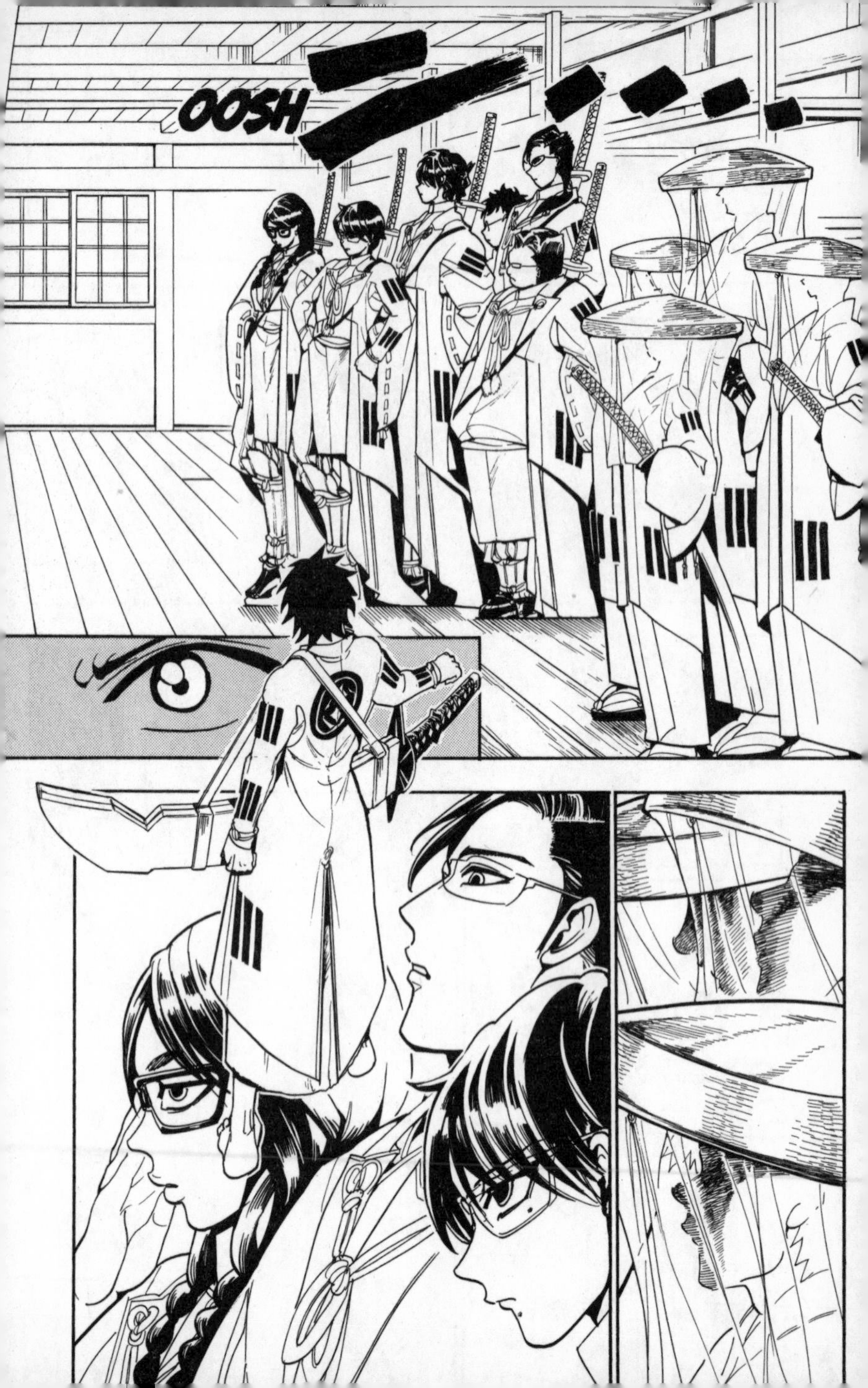
OOSH

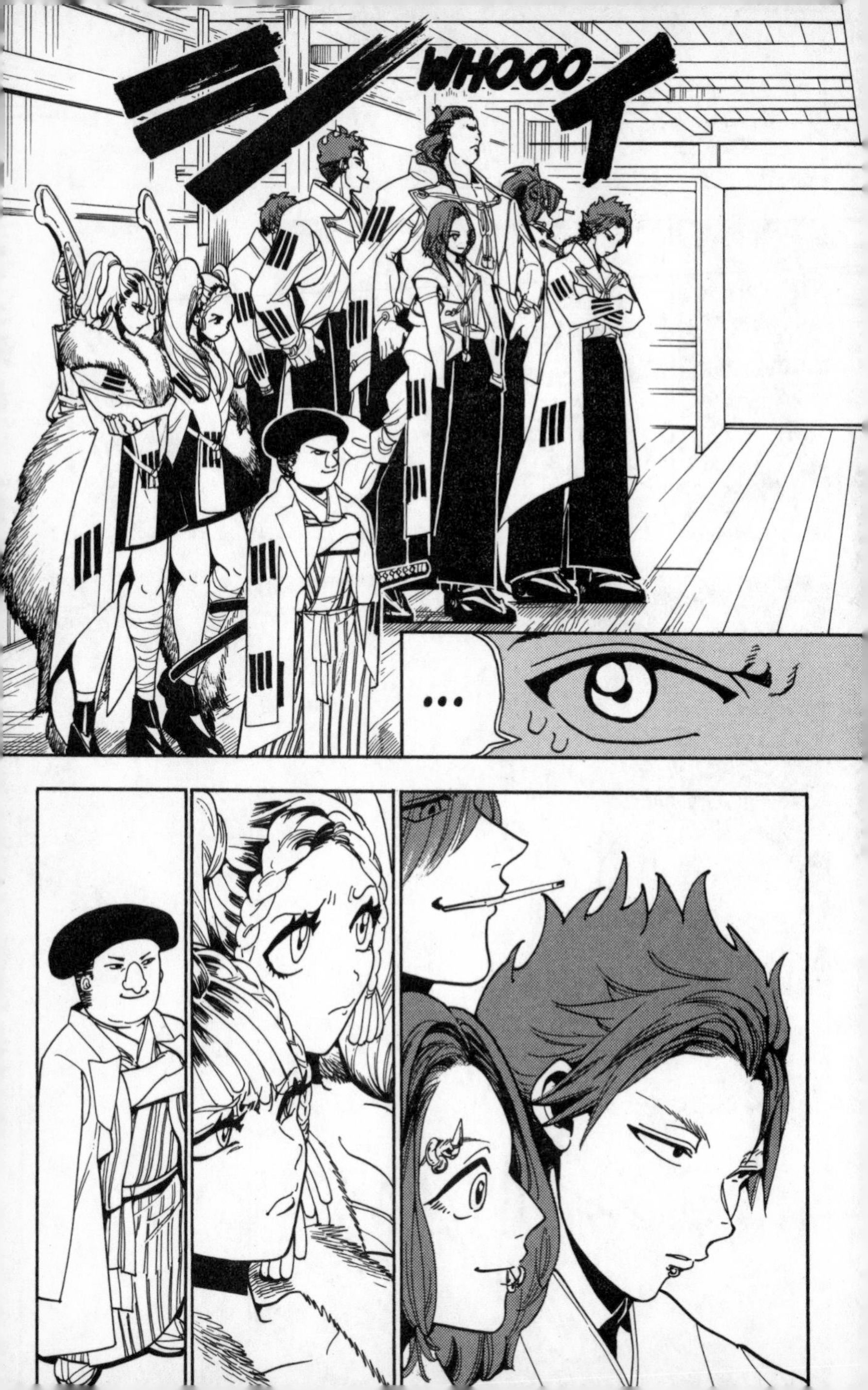
WHOOO
...

IT'S CLEAR AS DAY...

I SEE IT...

HEH HEH...

WHAT IS IT?

IT WAS HERE THAT ONE OF MUSASHI'S UNIQUE ABILITIES SET OFF...

TWING

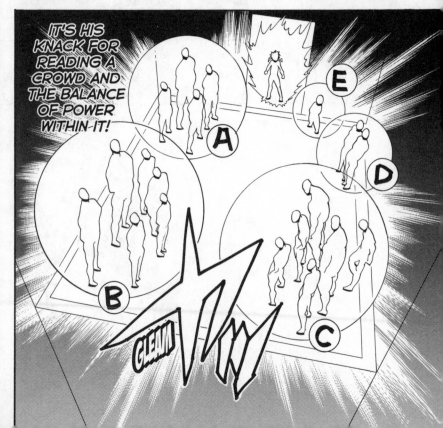

IT'S HIS KNACK FOR READING A CROWD AND THE BALANCE OF POWER WITHIN IT!

A

B

C

D

E

GLEAM

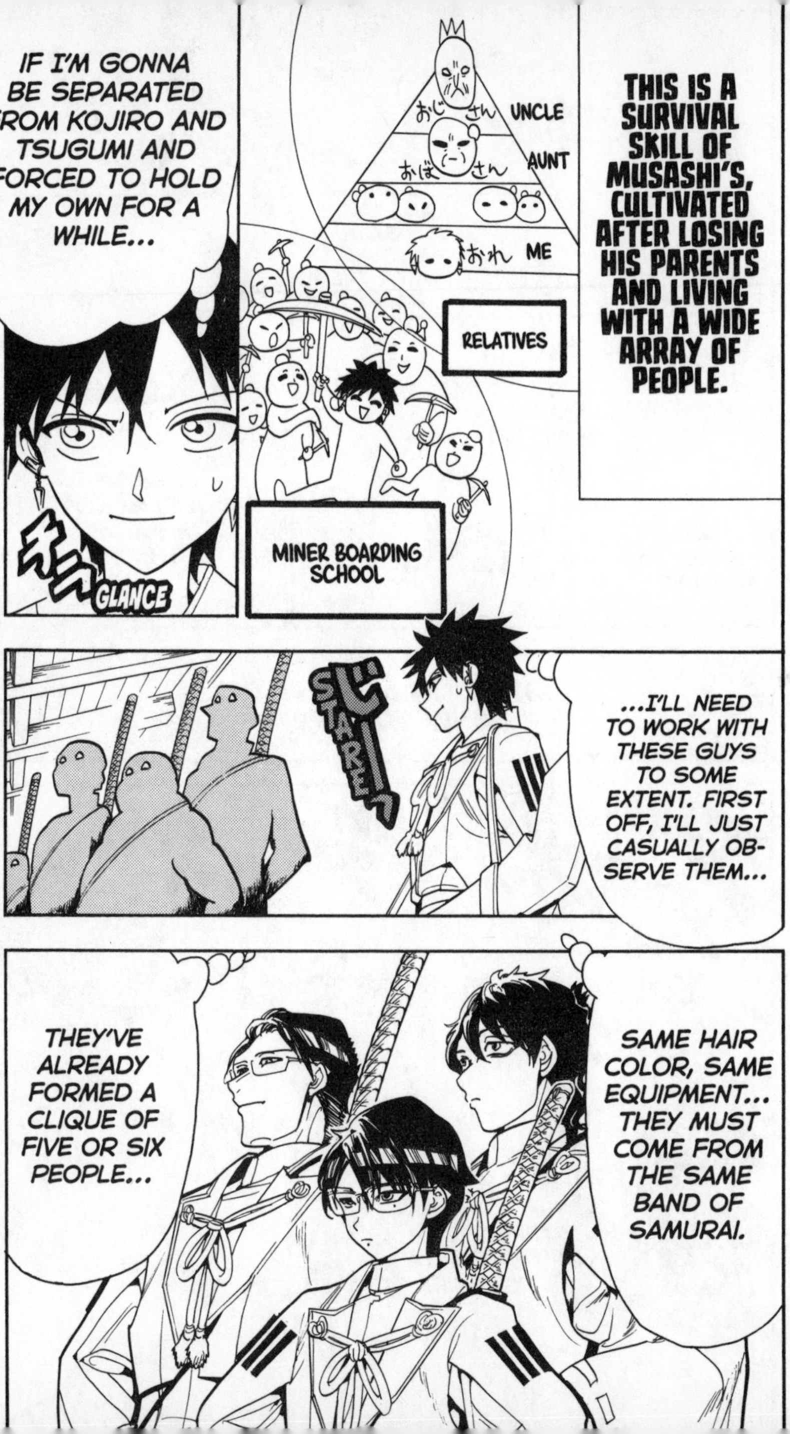
THIS IS A SURVIVAL SKILL OF MUSASHI'S, CULTIVATED AFTER LOSING HIS PARENTS AND LIVING WITH A WIDE ARRAY OF PEOPLE.
おじさん
UNCLE
おばさん
AUNT
おれ
ME
RELATIVES
MINER BOARDING SCHOOL
IF I'M GONNA BE SEPARATED FROM KOJIRO AND TSUGUMI AND FORCED TO HOLD MY OWN FOR A WHILE...
GLANCE
...I'LL NEED TO WORK WITH THESE GUYS TO SOME EXTENT. FIRST OFF, I'LL JUST CASUALLY OB-SERVE THEM...
STARE
SAME HAIR COLOR, SAME EQUIPMENT... THEY MUST COME FROM THE SAME BAND OF SAMURAI.
THEY'VE ALREADY FORMED A CLIQUE OF FIVE OR SIX PEOPLE...

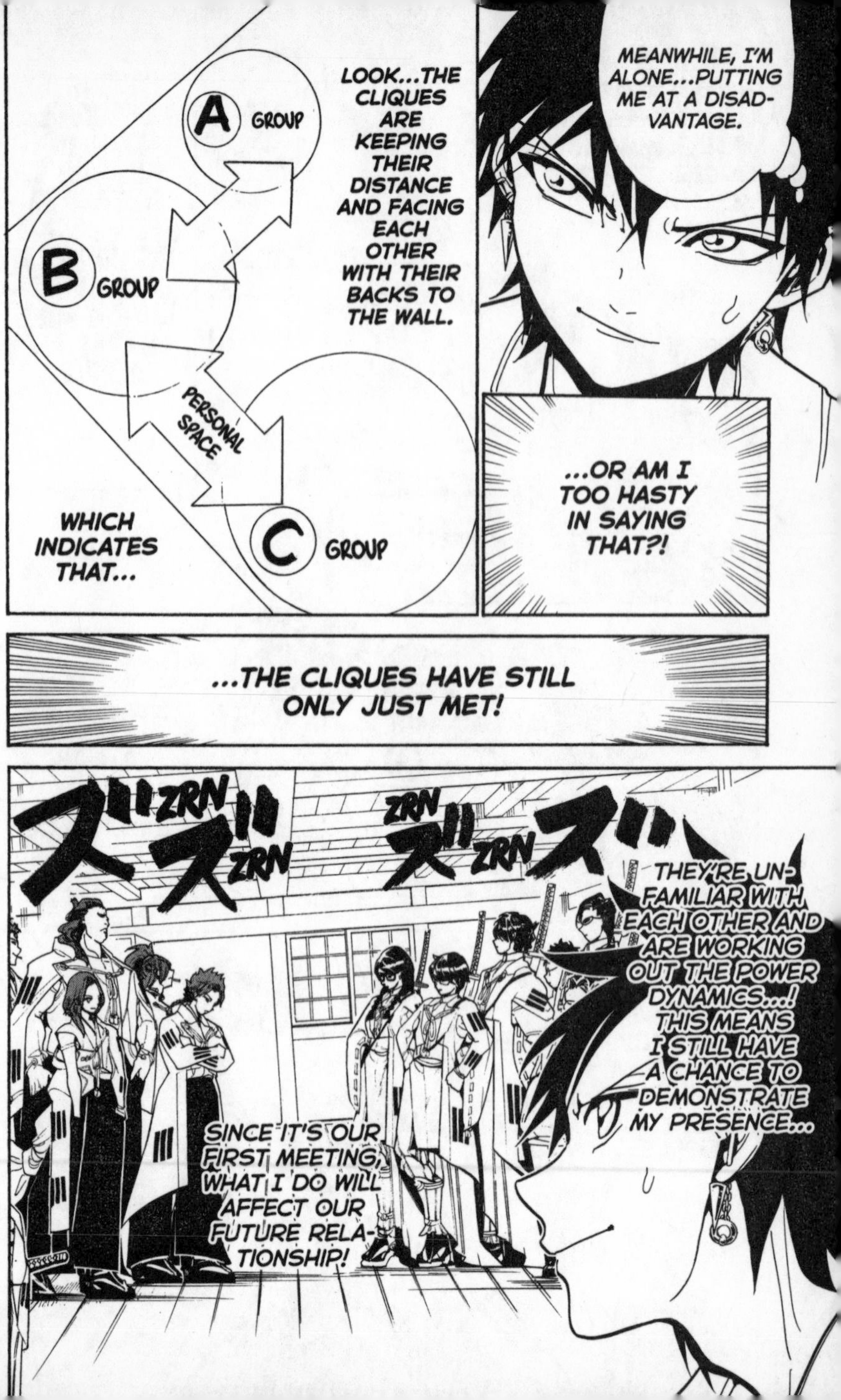
MEANWHILE, I'M ALONE...PUTTING ME AT A DISAD-VANTAGE.
...OR AM I TOO HASTY IN SAYING THAT?!
LOOK...THE CLIQUES ARE KEEPING THEIR DISTANCE AND FACING EACH OTHER WITH THEIR BACKS TO THE WALL.
A GROUP
B GROUP
PERSONAL SPACE
C GROUP
WHICH INDICATES THAT...
...THE CLIQUES HAVE STILL ONLY JUST MET!
ZRN ZRN
ZRN ZRN
THEY'RE UN-FAMILIAR WITH EACH OTHER AND ARE WORKING OUT THE POWER DYNAMICS...! THIS MEANS I STILL HAVE A CHANCE TO DEMONSTRATE MY PRESENCE...
SINCE IT'S OUR FIRST MEETING, WHAT I DO WILL AFFECT OUR FUTURE RELA-TIONSHIP!

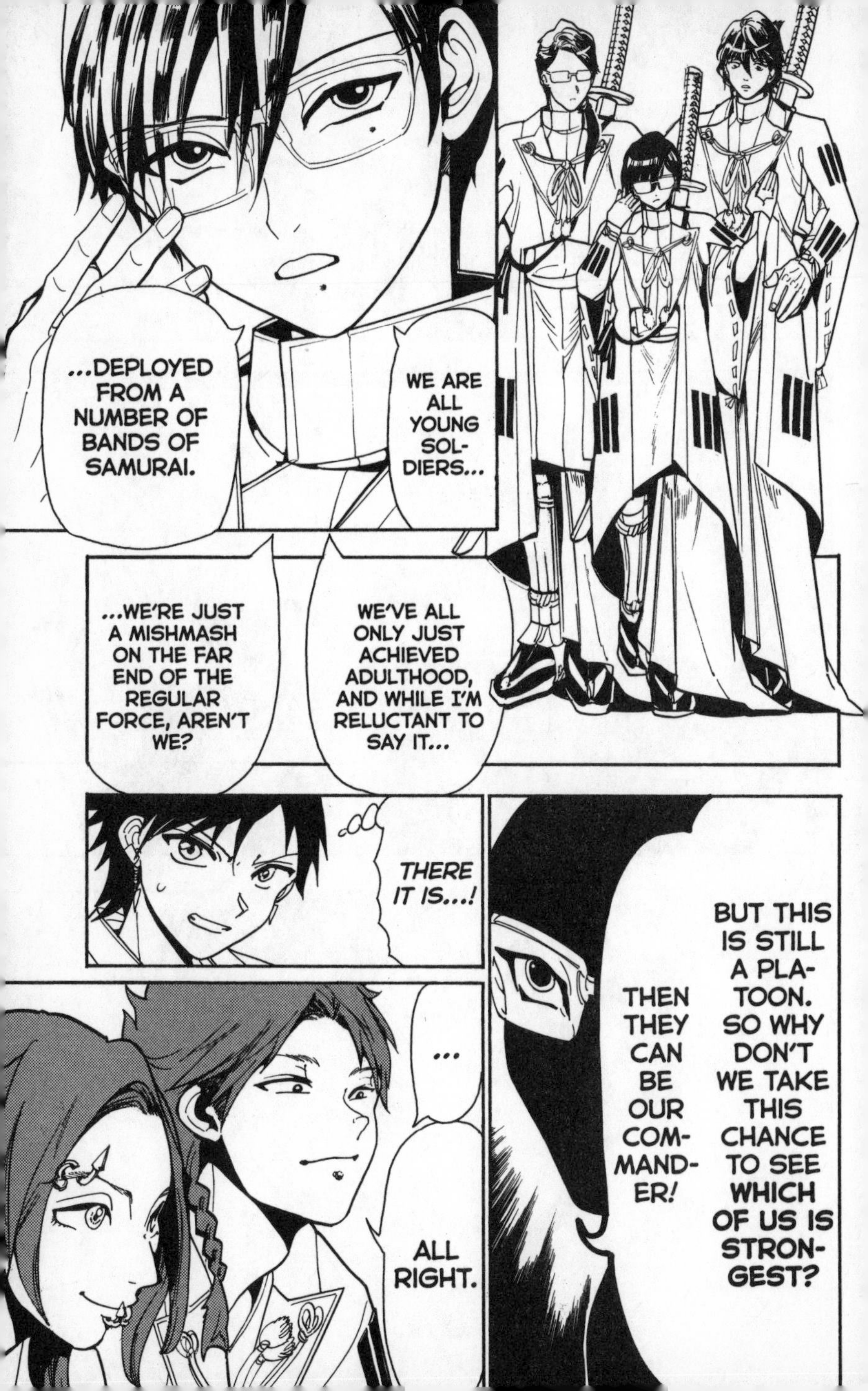
WE ARE ALL YOUNG SOLDIERS...
...DEPLOYED FROM A NUMBER OF BANDS OF SAMURAI.
WE'VE ALL ONLY JUST ACHIEVED ADULTHOOD, AND WHILE I'M RELUCTANT TO SAY IT...
...WE'RE JUST A MISHMASH ON THE FAR END OF THE REGULAR FORCE, AREN'T WE?
BUT THIS IS STILL A PLATOON. SO WHY DON'T WE TAKE THIS CHANCE TO SEE WHICH OF US IS STRONGEST?
THEN THEY CAN BE OUR COMMANDER!
THERE IT IS...!
...
ALL RIGHT.

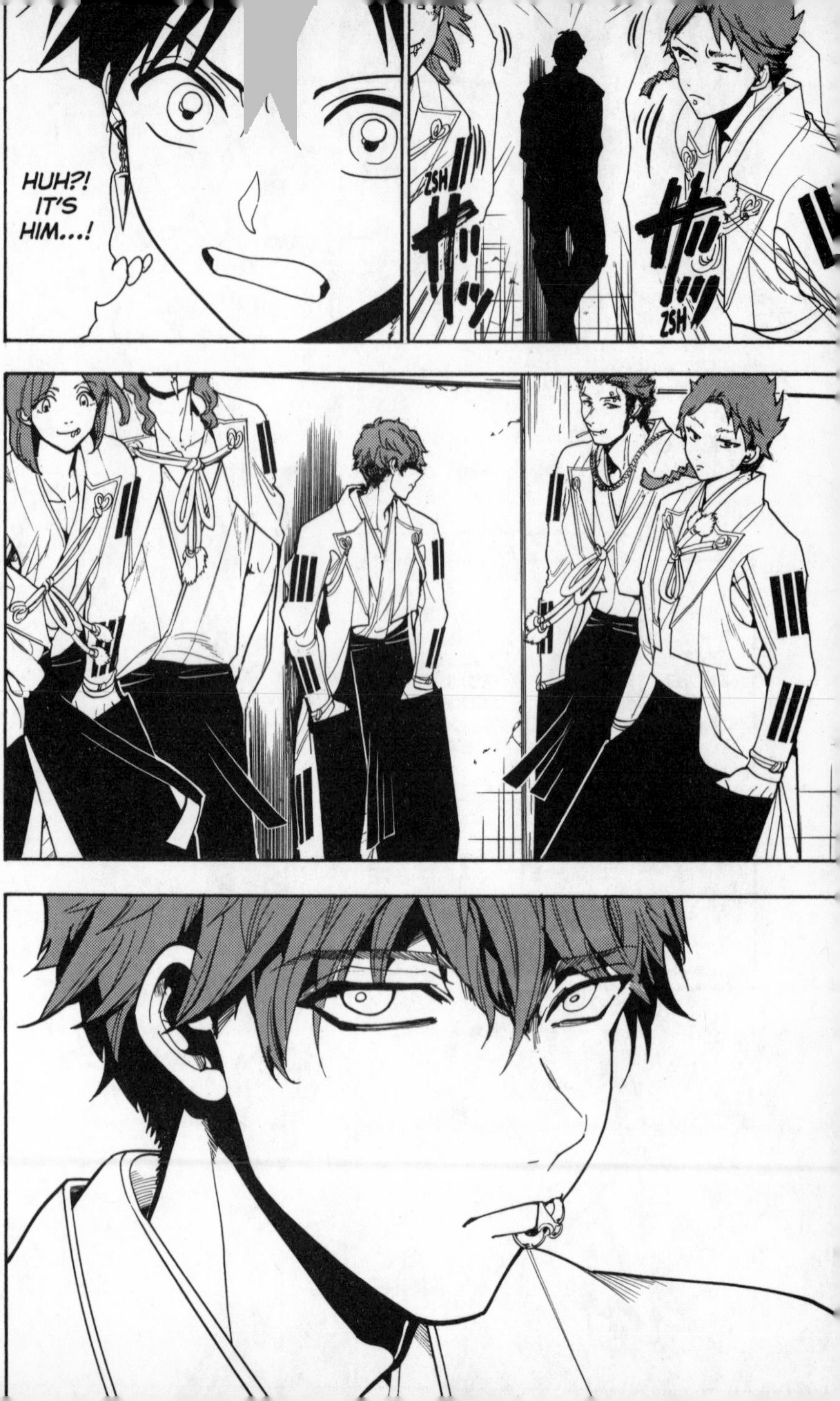
ZSH
ZSH
HUH?! IT'S HIM...!

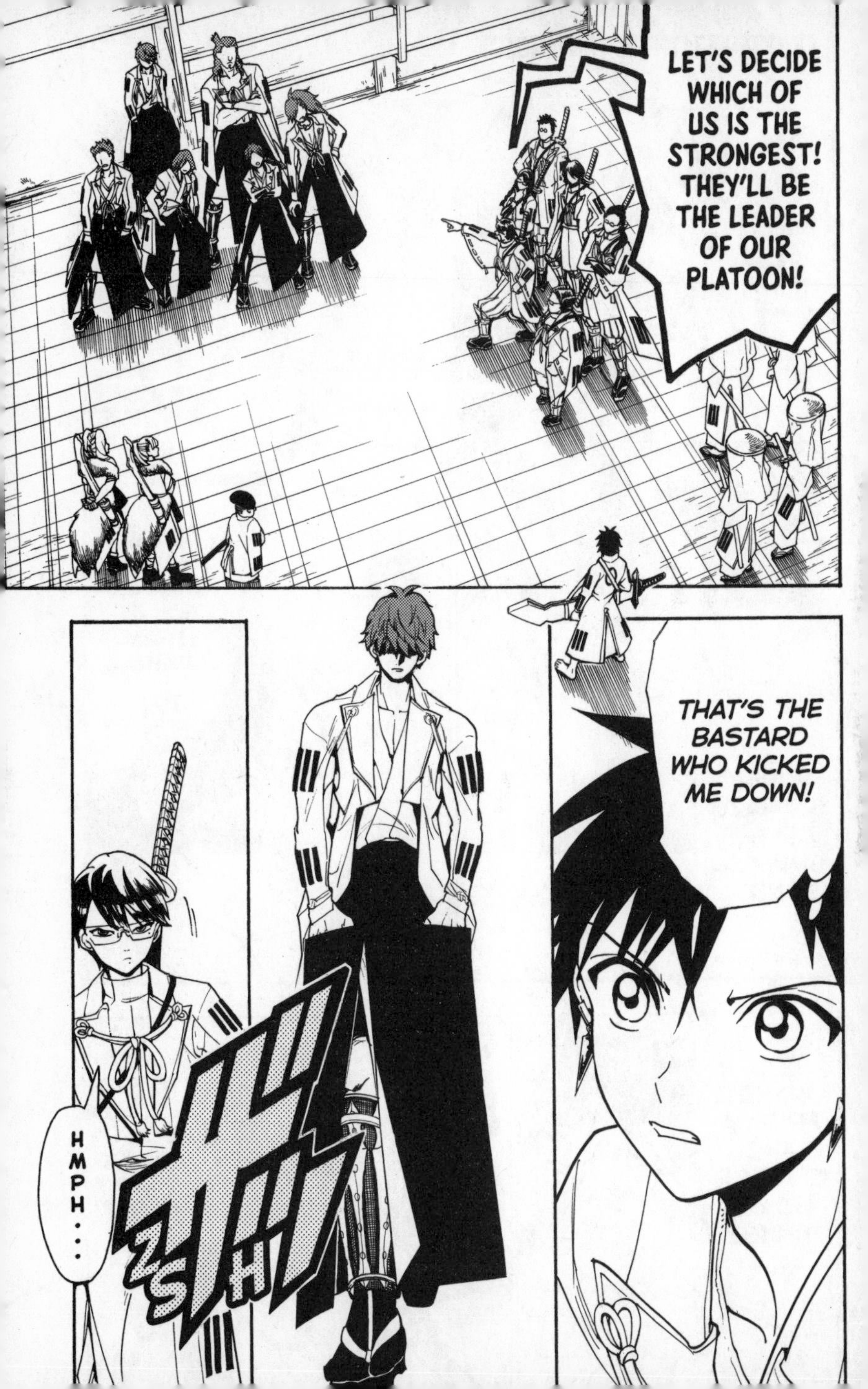
LET'S DECIDE WHICH OF US IS THE STRONGEST! THEY'LL BE THE LEADER OF OUR PLATOON!
THAT'S THE BASTARD WHO KICKED ME DOWN!
ZSHH
HMPH...

CHAPTER 52: THREE CONTENDERS

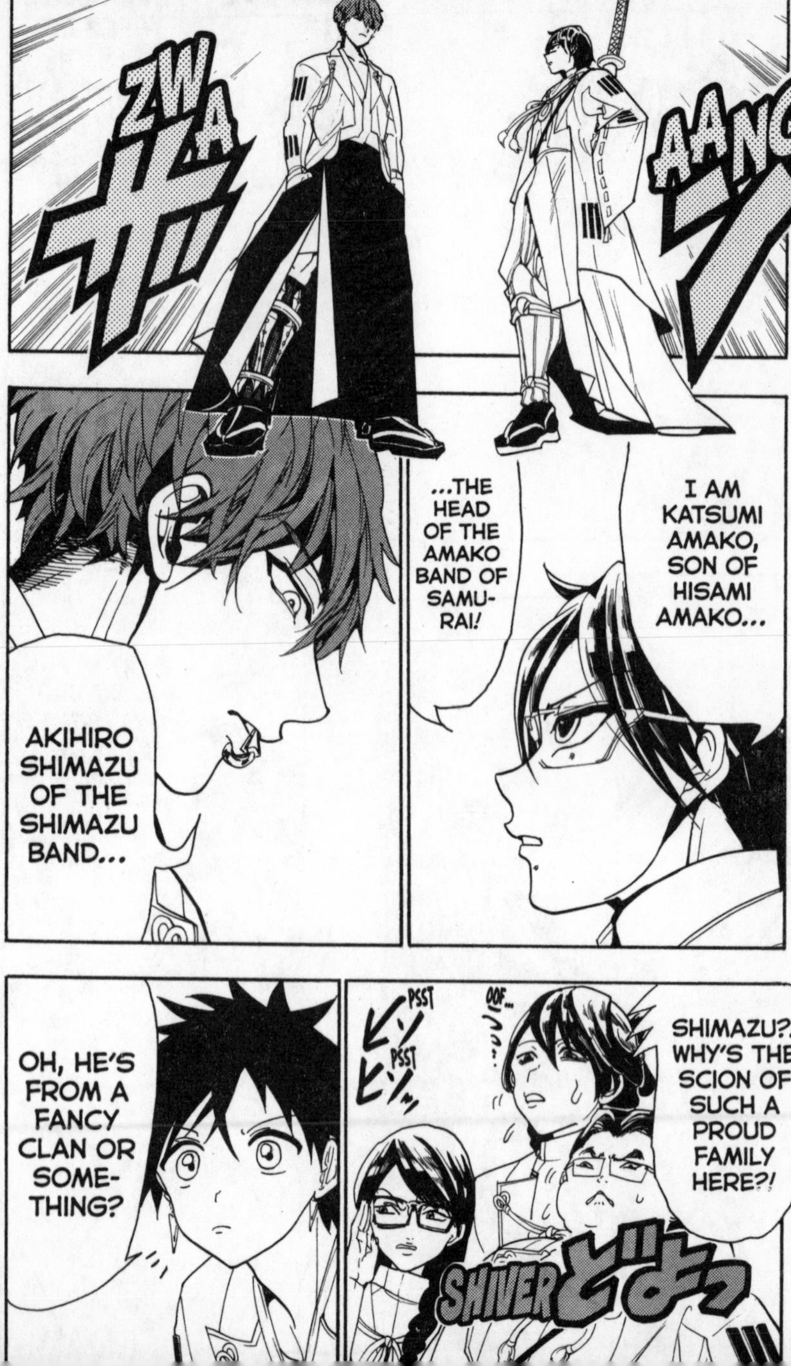
ZWA
AANG
I AM KATSUMI AMAKO, SON OF HISAMI AMAKO...
...THE HEAD OF THE AMAKO BAND OF SAMURAI!
AKIHIRO SHIMAZU OF THE SHIMAZU BAND...
SHIMAZU?! WHY'S THE SCION OF SUCH A PROUD FAMILY HERE?!
OOF...
PSST
PSST
SHIVER
OH, HE'S FROM A FANCY CLAN OR SOMETHING?

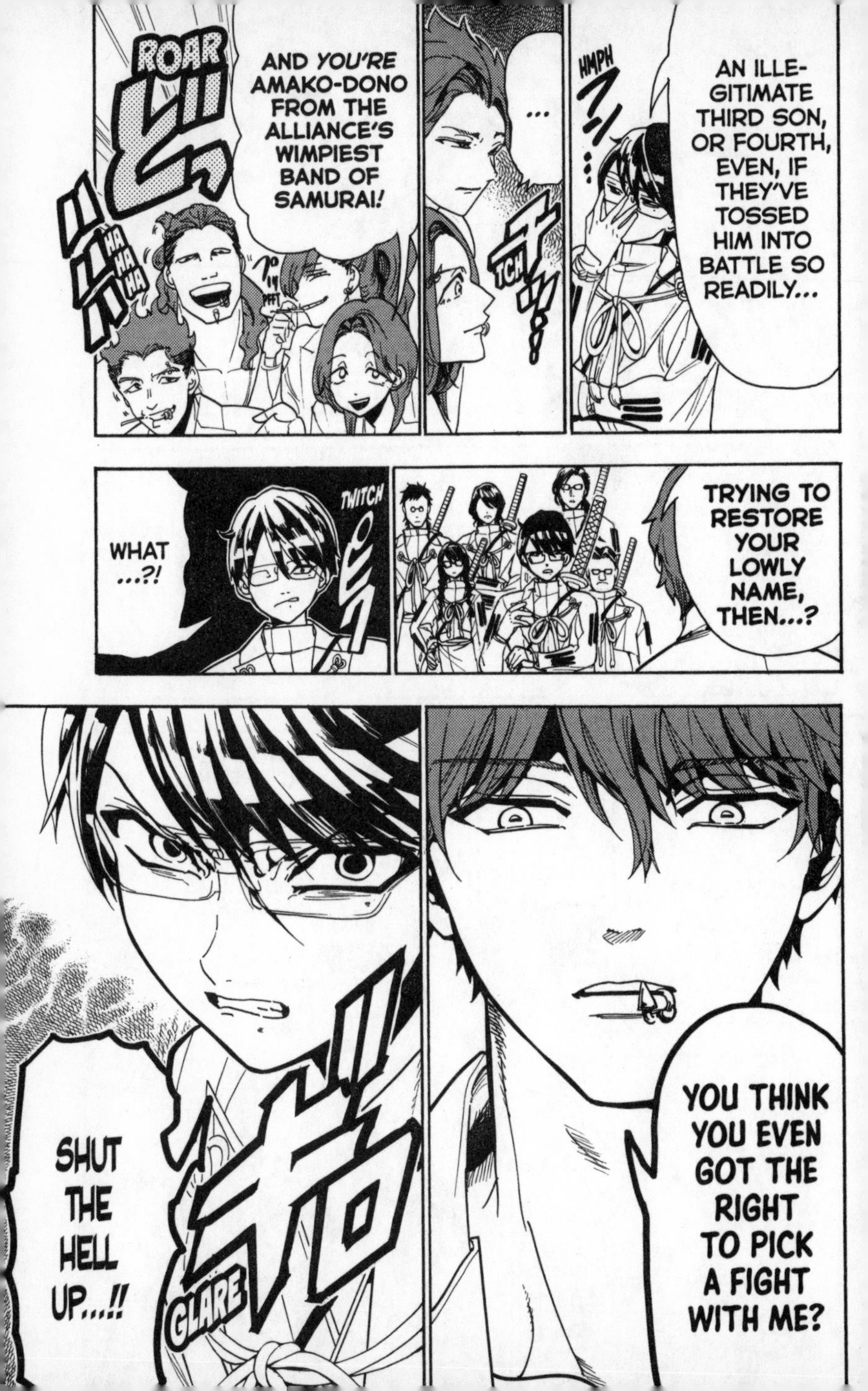
HMPH
AN ILLEGITIMATE THIRD SON, OR FOURTH, EVEN, IF THEY'VE TOSSED HIM INTO BATTLE SO READILY...
...
TCH
ROAR
AND YOU'RE AMAKO-DONO FROM THE ALLIANCE'S WIMPIEST BAND OF SAMURAI!
HA HA HA
PFFT
TRYING TO RESTORE YOUR LOWLY NAME, THEN...?
TWITCH
WHAT ...?!
YOU THINK YOU EVEN GOT THE RIGHT TO PICK A FIGHT WITH ME?
SHUT THE HELL UP...!!
GLARE

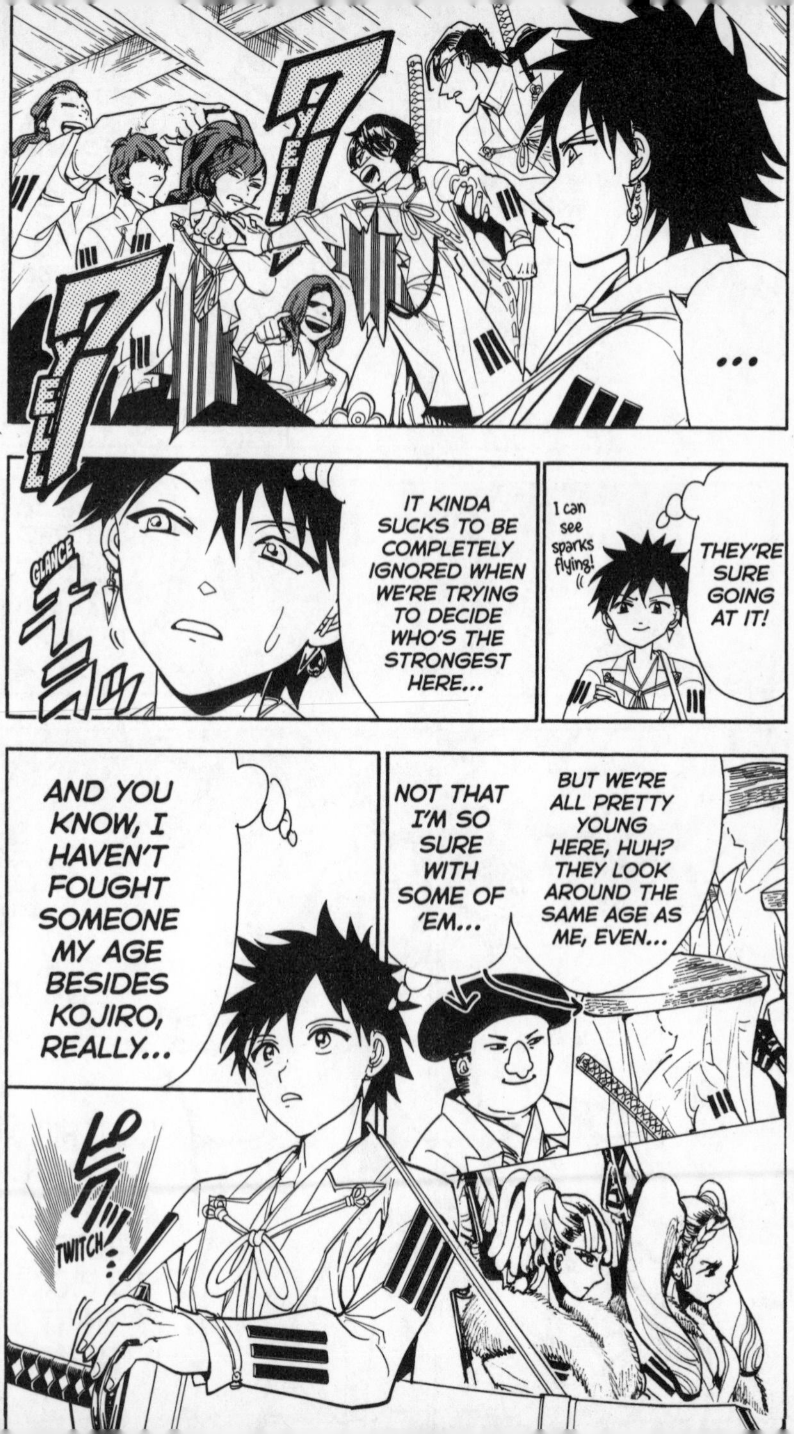
...
YELL
YELL
THEY'RE SURE GOING AT IT!
I can see sparks flying!
IT KINDA SUCKS TO BE COMPLETELY IGNORED WHEN WE'RE TRYING TO DECIDE WHO'S THE STRONGEST HERE...
GLANCE
BUT WE'RE ALL PRETTY YOUNG HERE, HUH? THEY LOOK AROUND THE SAME AGE AS ME, EVEN...
NOT THAT I'M SO SURE WITH SOME OF 'EM...
AND YOU KNOW, I HAVEN'T FOUGHT SOMEONE MY AGE BESIDES KOJIRO, REALLY...
TWITCH

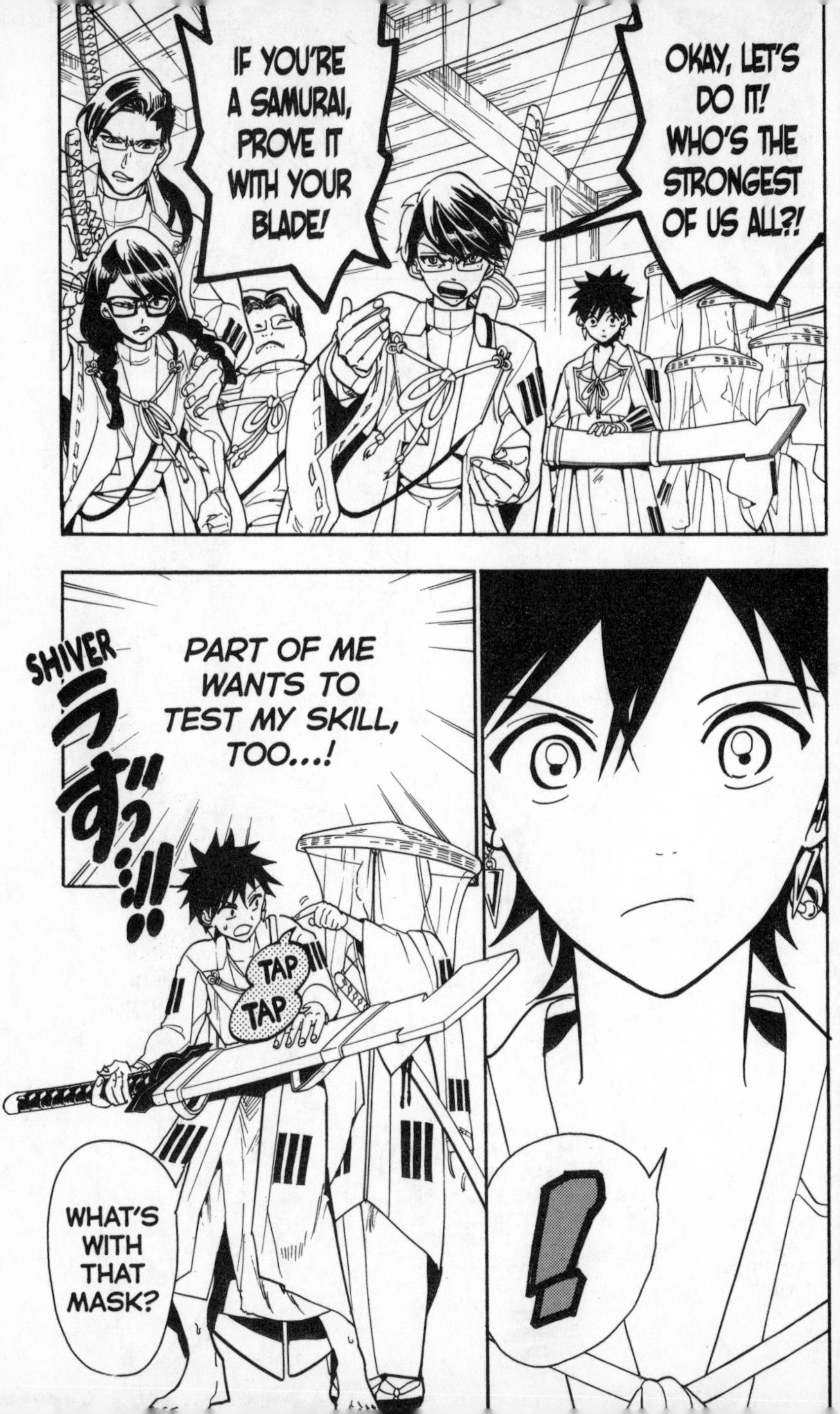
OKAY, LET'S DO IT! WHO'S THE STRONGEST OF US ALL?!
IF YOU'RE A SAMURAI, PROVE IT WITH YOUR BLADE!
!
PART OF ME WANTS TO TEST MY SKILL, TOO...!
SHIVER
うずっ!!
TAP TAP
WHAT'S WITH THAT MASK?

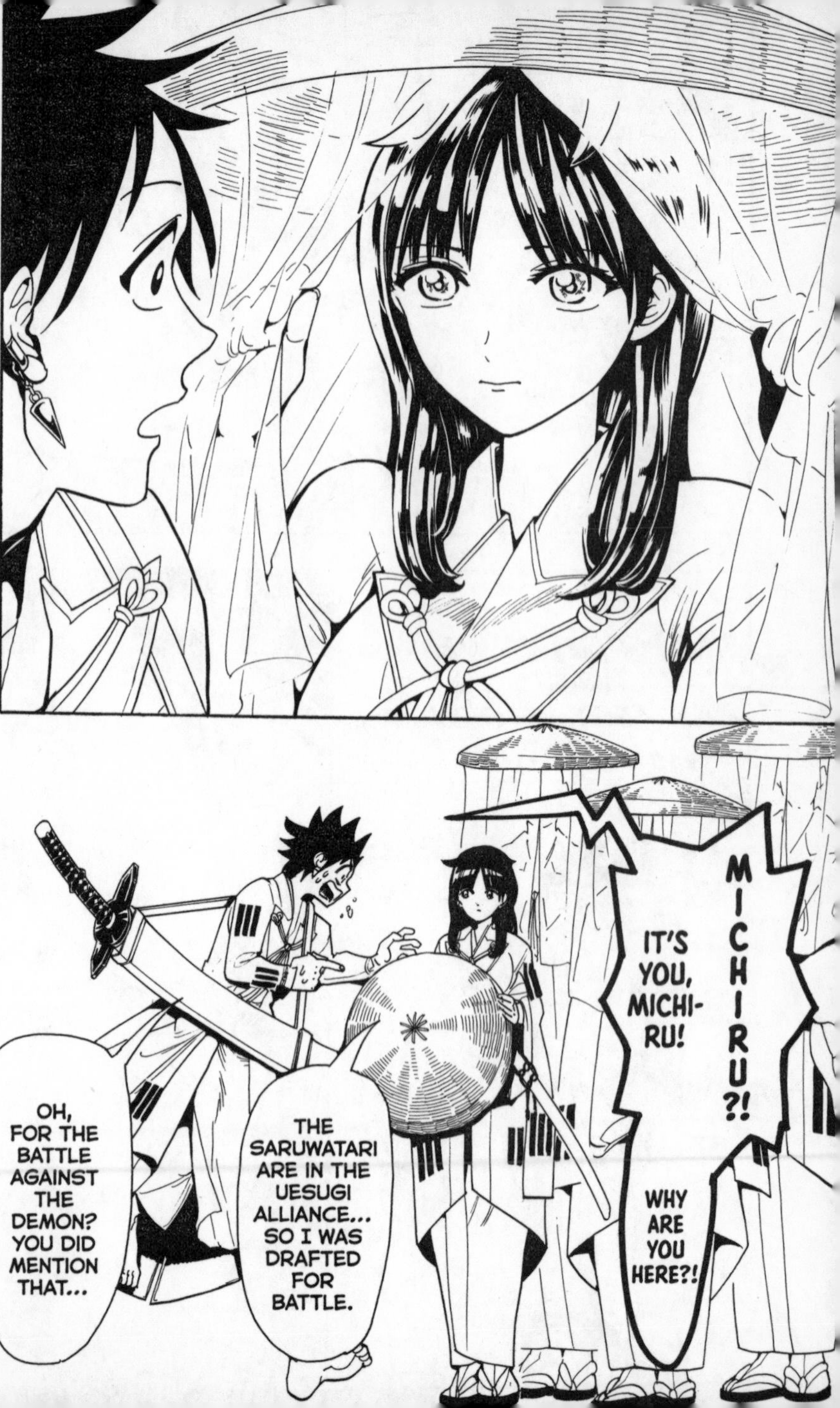
MICHIRU?!
IT'S YOU, MICHIRU!
WHY ARE YOU HERE?!
THE SARUWATARI ARE IN THE UESUGI ALLIANCE... SO I WAS DRAFTED FOR BATTLE.
OH, FOR THE BATTLE AGAINST THE DEMON? YOU DID MENTION THAT...

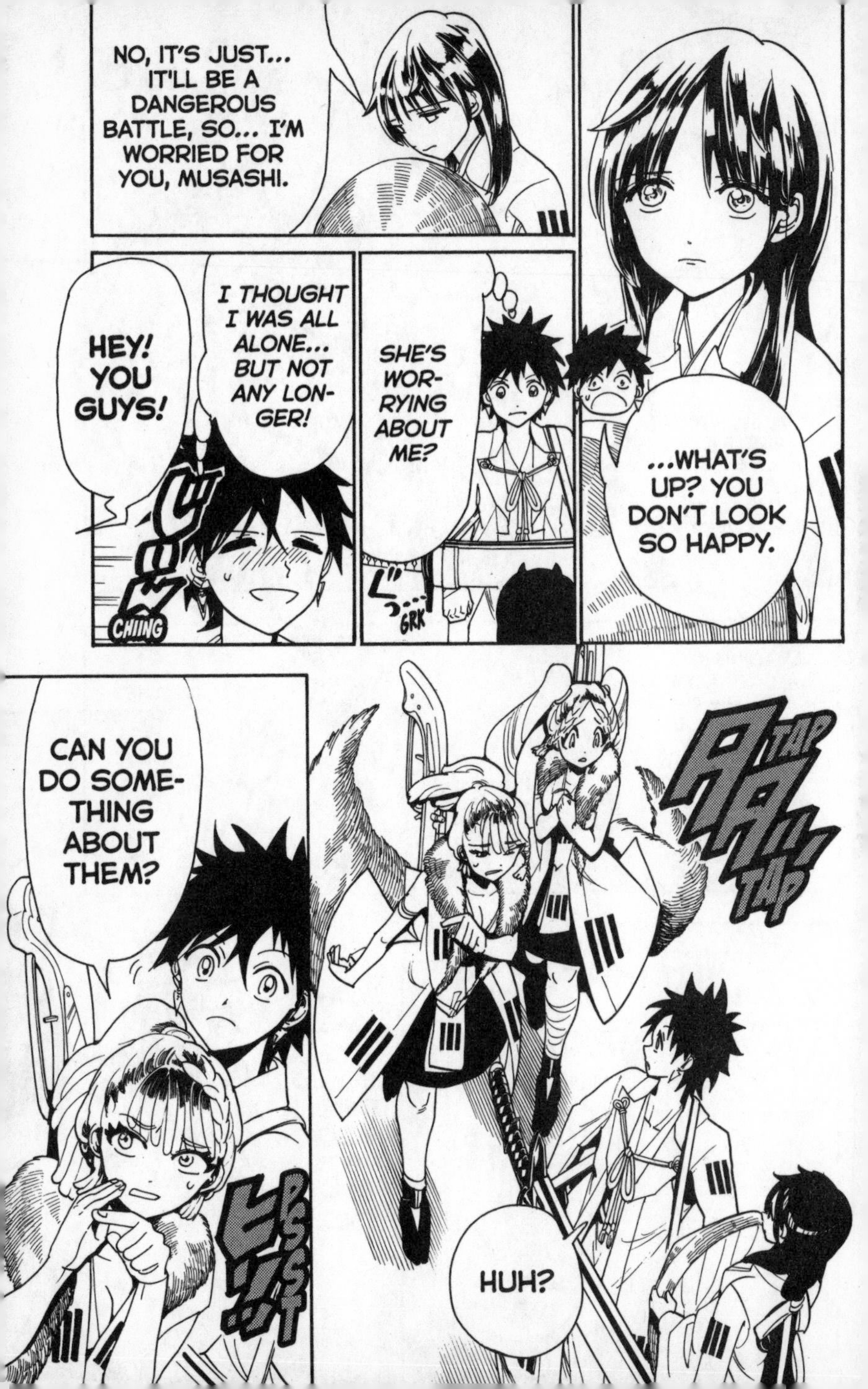
...WHAT'S UP? YOU DON'T LOOK SO HAPPY.
NO, IT'S JUST... IT'LL BE A DANGEROUS BATTLE, SO... I'M WORRIED FOR YOU, MUSASHI.
SHE'S WOR-RYING ABOUT ME?
GRK
I THOUGHT I WAS ALL ALONE... BUT NOT ANY LON-GER!
HEY! YOU GUYS!
CHIING
TAP TAP TAP
HUH?
CAN YOU DO SOME-THING ABOUT THEM?
PSST

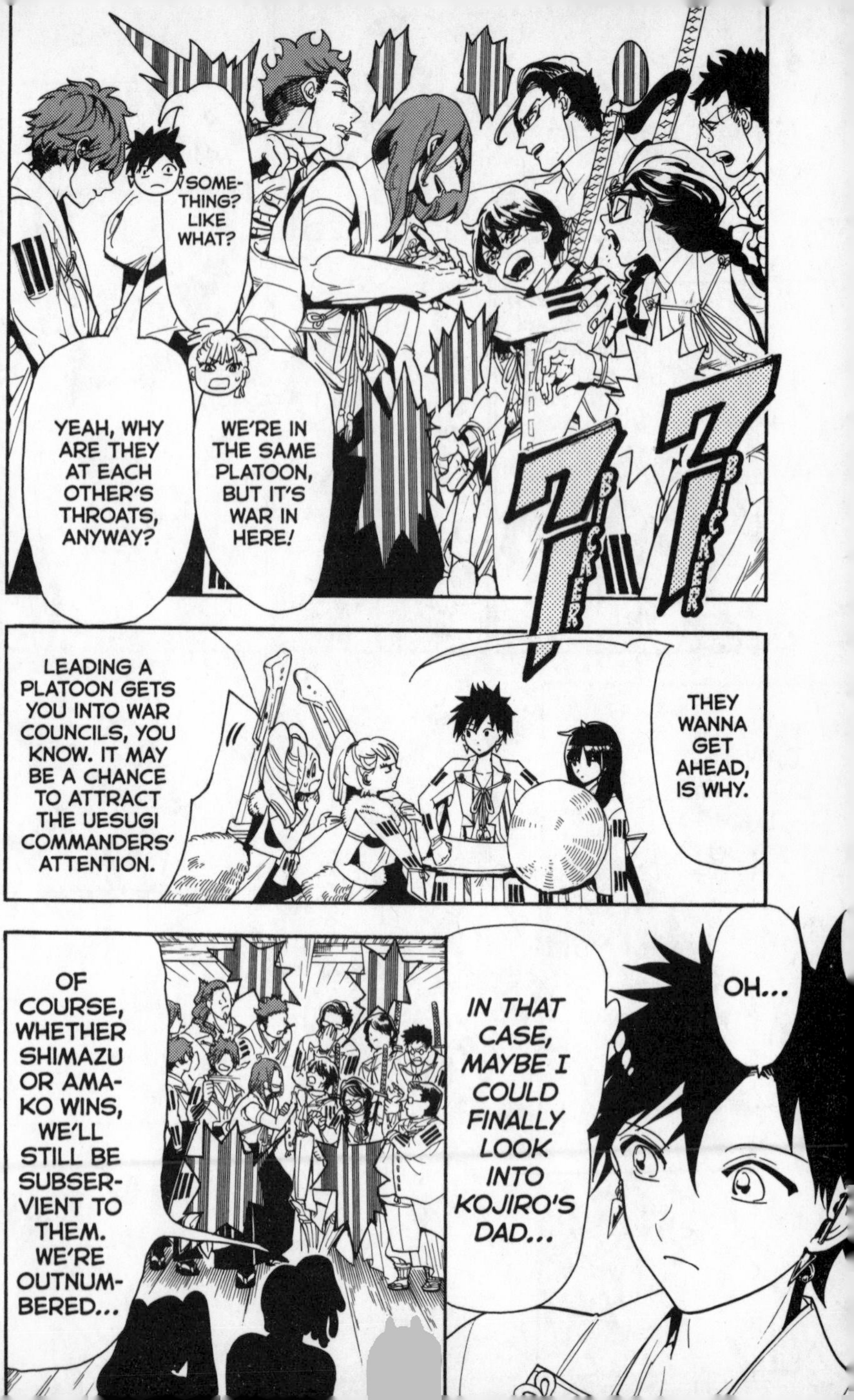
SOME-THING? LIKE WHAT?
BICKER
BICKER
WE'RE IN THE SAME PLATOON, BUT IT'S WAR IN HERE!
YEAH, WHY ARE THEY AT EACH OTHER'S THROATS, ANYWAY?
THEY WANNA GET AHEAD, IS WHY.
LEADING A PLATOON GETS YOU INTO WAR COUNCILS, YOU KNOW. IT MAY BE A CHANCE TO ATTRACT THE UESUGI COMMANDERS' ATTENTION.
OH...
IN THAT CASE, MAYBE I COULD FINALLY LOOK INTO KOJIRO'S DAD...
OF COURSE, WHETHER SHIMAZU OR AMA-KO WINS, WE'LL STILL BE SUBSER-VIENT TO THEM. WE'RE OUTNUM-BERED...

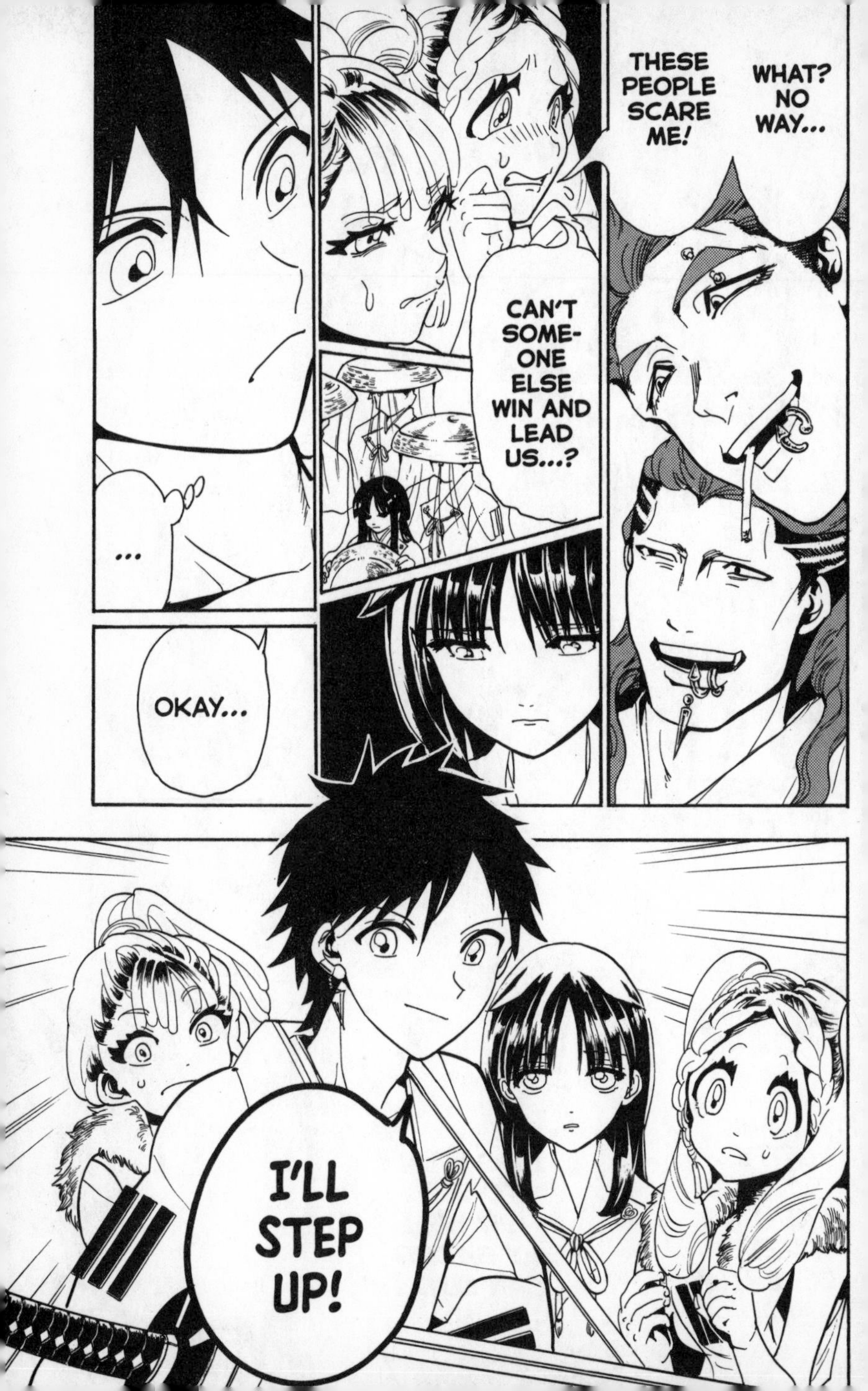
WHAT? NO WAY...
THESE PEOPLE SCARE ME!
CAN'T SOMEONE- ONE ELSE WIN AND LEAD US...?
...
OKAY...
I'LL STEP UP!

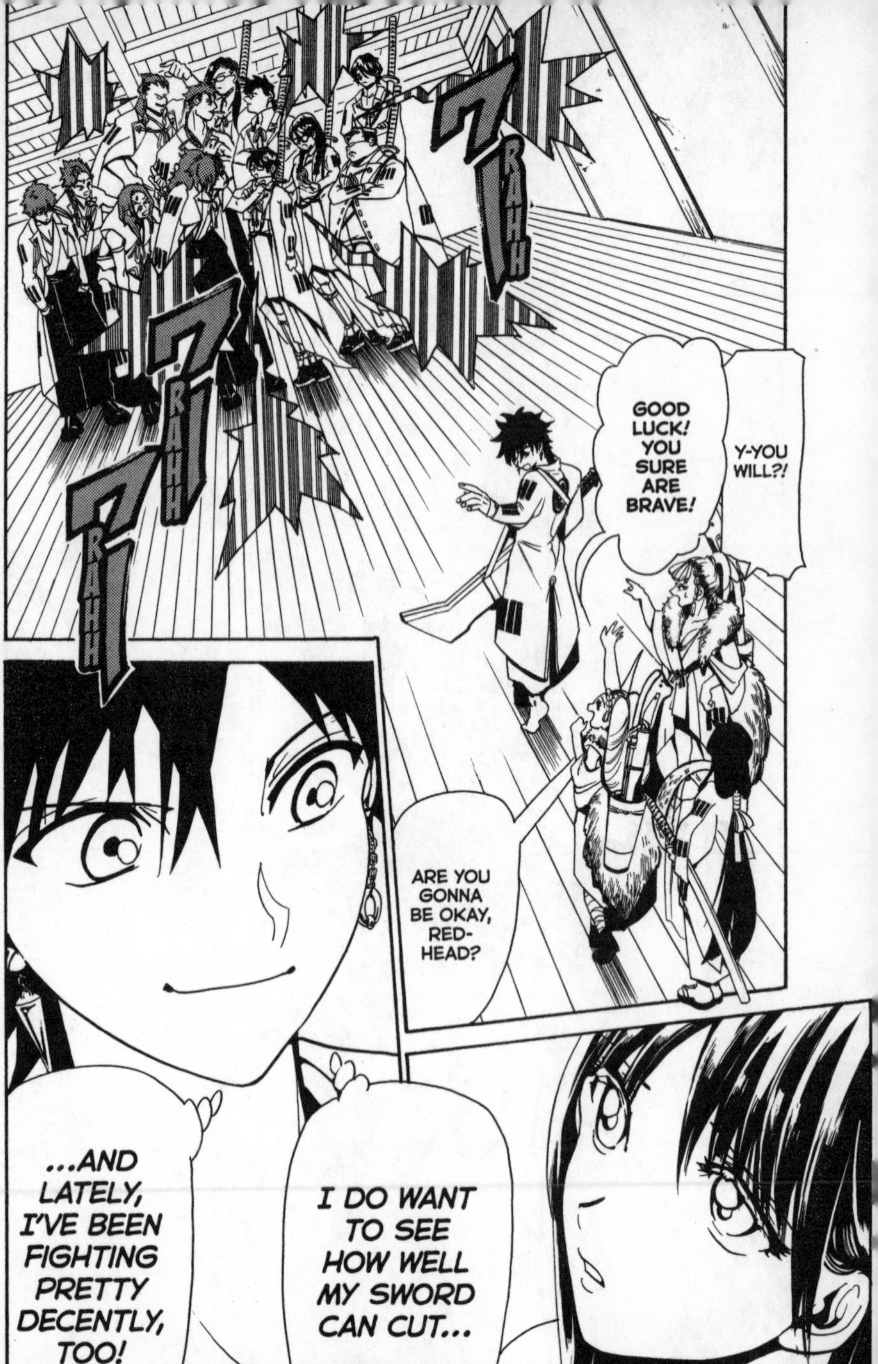

RAHH
RAHH
RAHH
Y-YOU WILL?!
GOOD LUCK! YOU SURE ARE BRAVE!
ARE YOU GONNA BE OKAY, RED-HEAD?
I DO WANT TO SEE HOW WELL MY SWORD CAN CUT...
...AND LATELY, I'VE BEEN FIGHTING PRETTY DECENTLY, TOO!

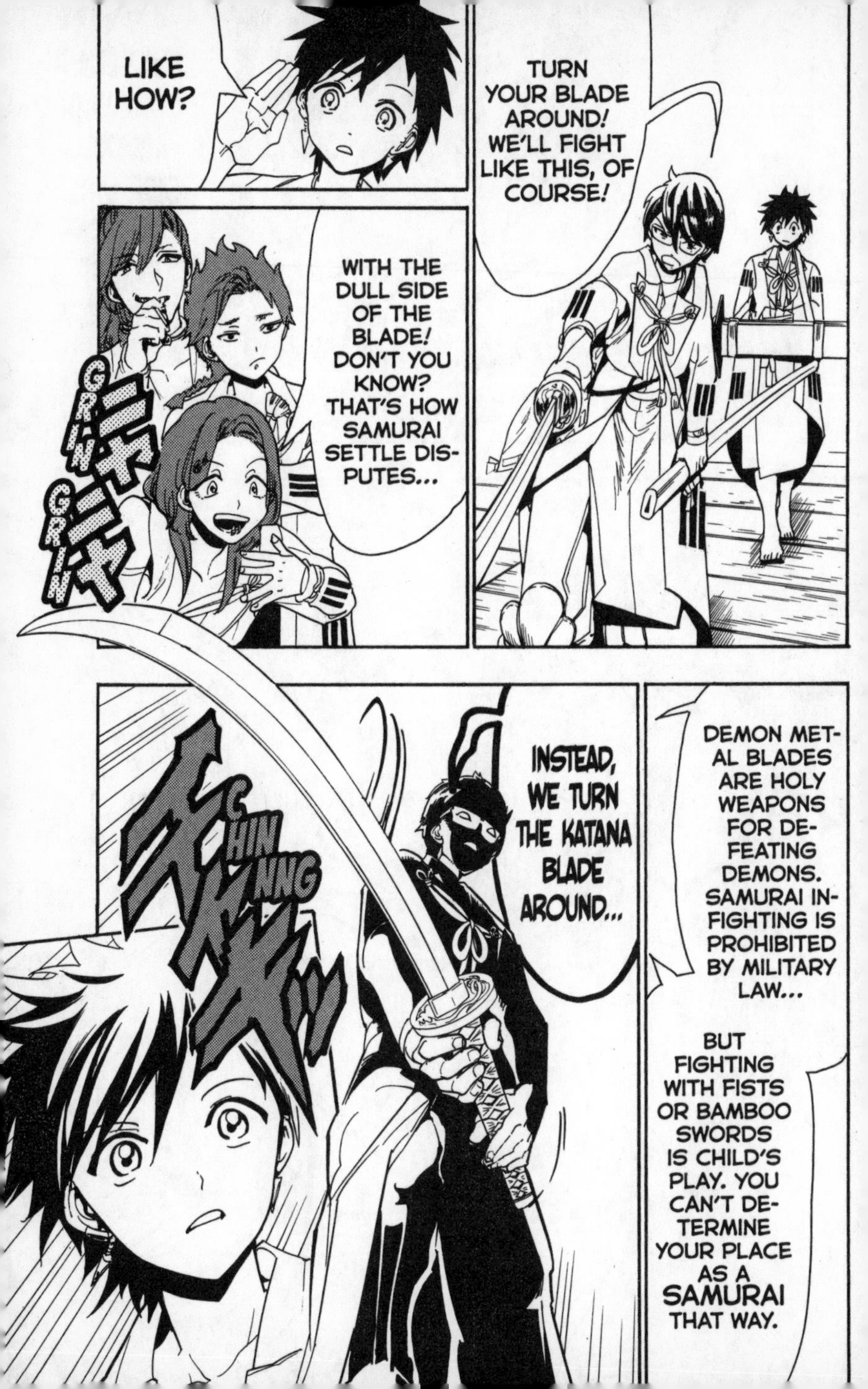
TURN YOUR BLADE AROUND! WE'LL FIGHT LIKE THIS, OF COURSE!
LIKE HOW?
WITH THE DULL SIDE OF THE BLADE! DON'T YOU KNOW? THAT'S HOW SAMURAI SETTLE DISPUTES...
GRIN GRIN
DEMON METAL BLADES ARE HOLY WEAPONS FOR DEFEATING DEMONS. SAMURAI INFIGHTING IS PROHIBITED BY MILITARY LAW...
BUT FIGHTING WITH FISTS OR BAMBOO SWORDS IS CHILD'S PLAY. YOU CAN'T DETERMINE YOUR PLACE AS A SAMURAI THAT WAY.
INSTEAD, WE TURN THE KATANA BLADE AROUND...
CHING

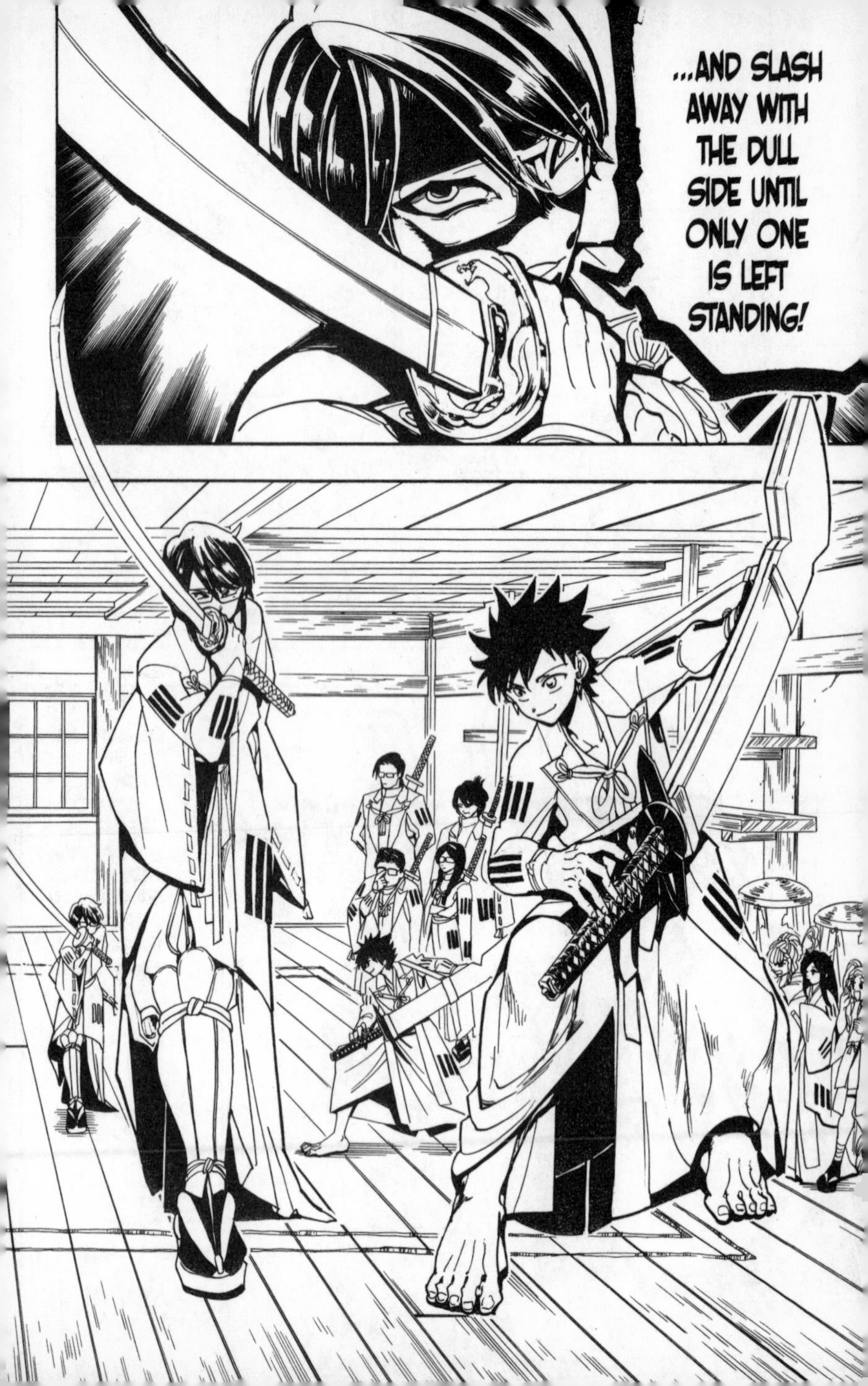
...AND SLASH AWAY WITH THE DULL SIDE UNTIL ONLY ONE IS LEFT STANDING!

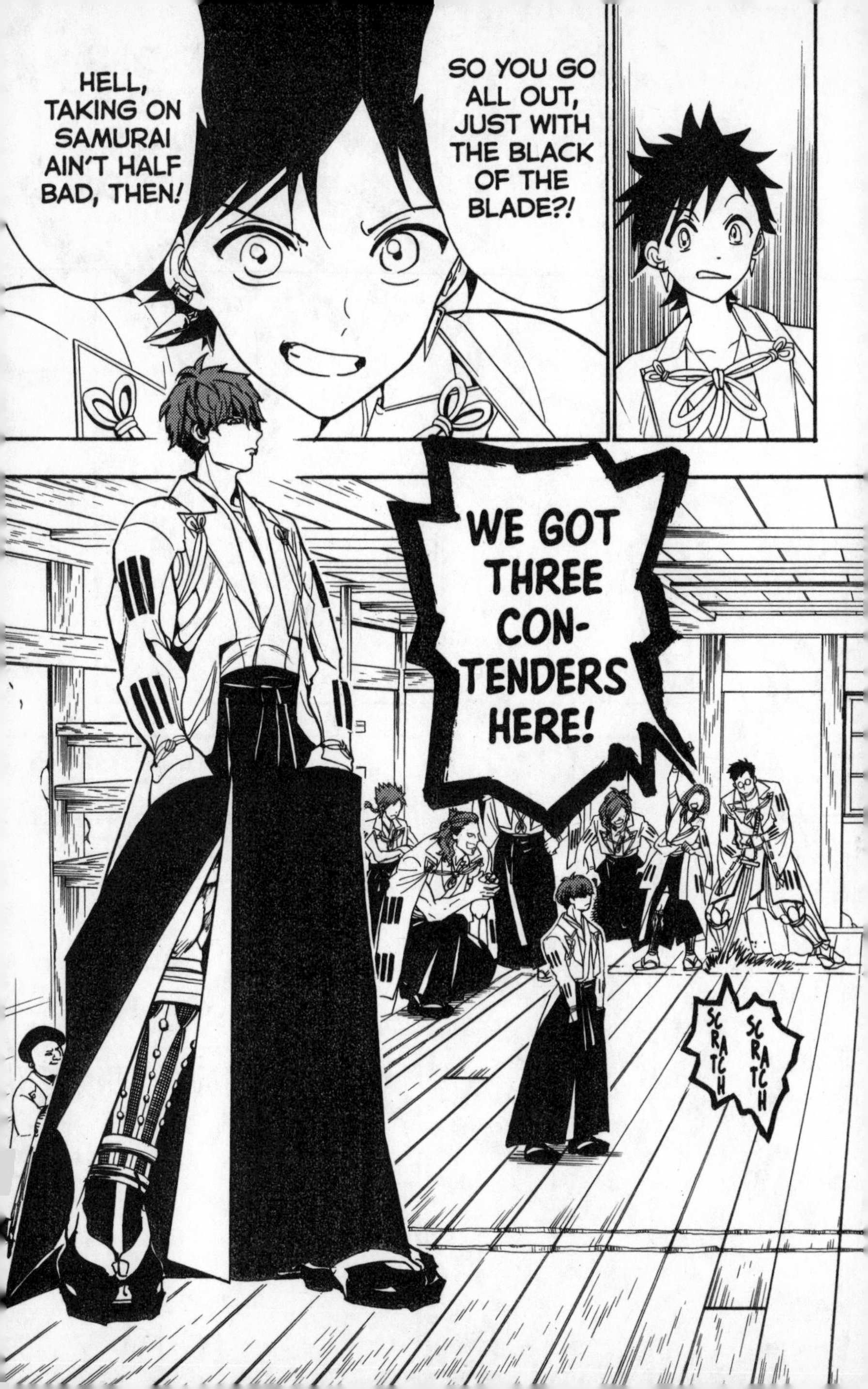
SO YOU GO ALL OUT, JUST WITH THE BLACK OF THE BLADE?!
HELL, TAKING ON SAMURAI AIN'T HALF BAD, THEN!
WE GOT THREE CON- TENDERS HERE!
SCRATCH
SCRATCH

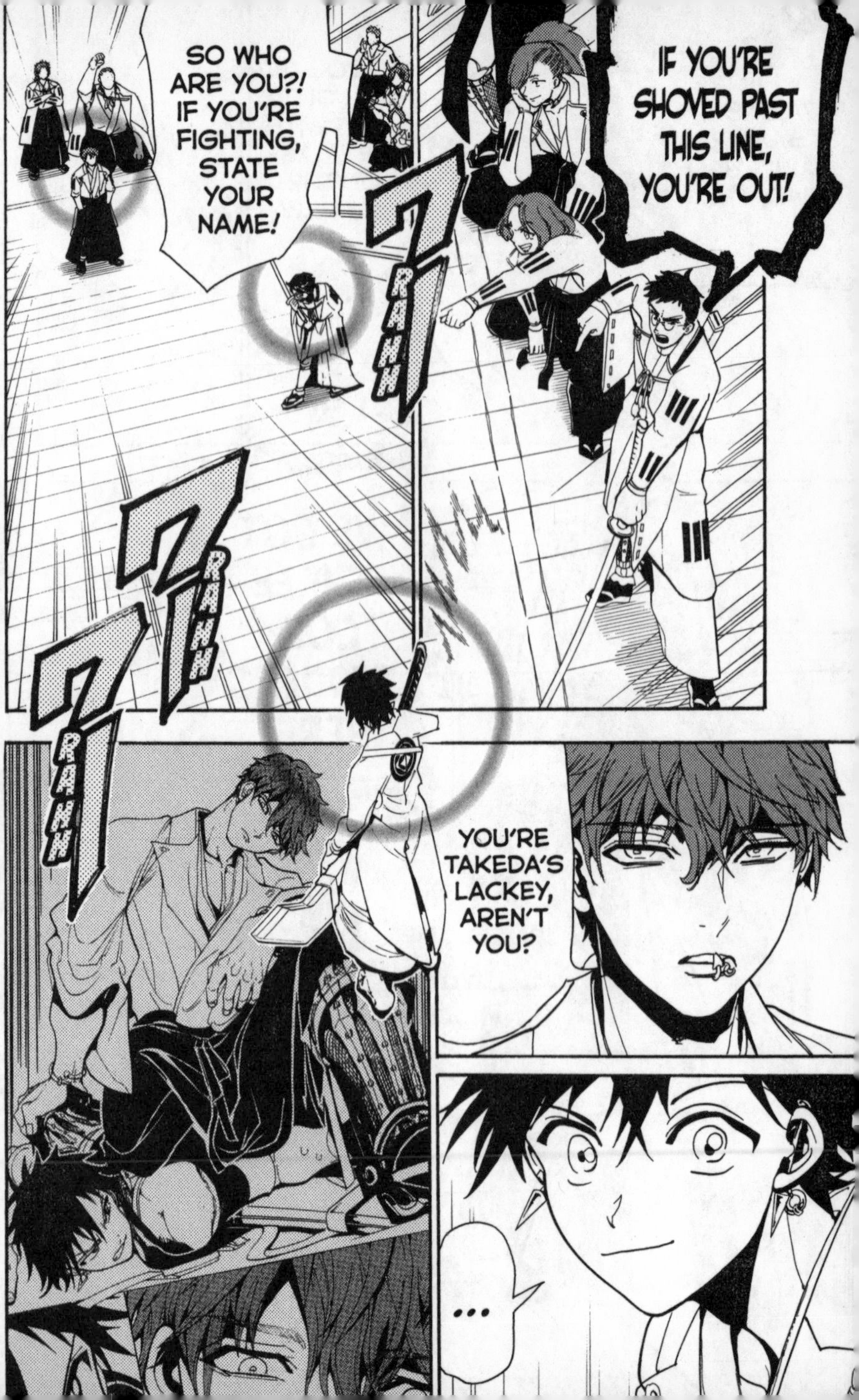
IF YOU'RE SHOVED PAST THIS LINE, YOU'RE OUT!
RAHH
SO WHO ARE YOU?! IF YOU'RE FIGHTING, STATE YOUR NAME!
RAHH
RAHH
YOU'RE TAKEDA'S LACKEY, AREN'T YOU?
...

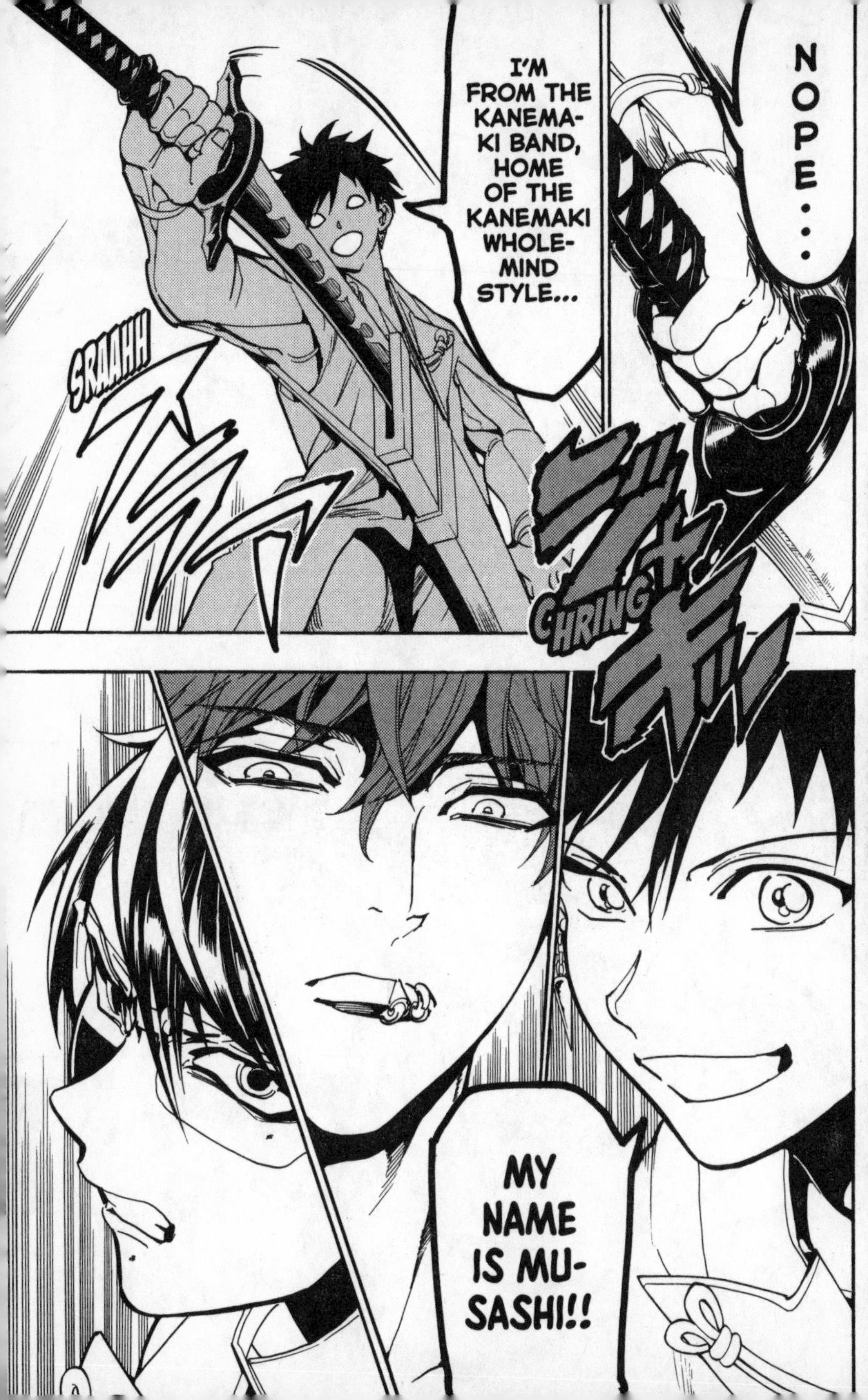
NOPE...
I'M FROM THE KANEMAKI BAND, HOME OF THE KANEMAKI WHOLE-MIND STYLE...
SRAAHH
CHRING
MY NAME IS MUSASHI!!

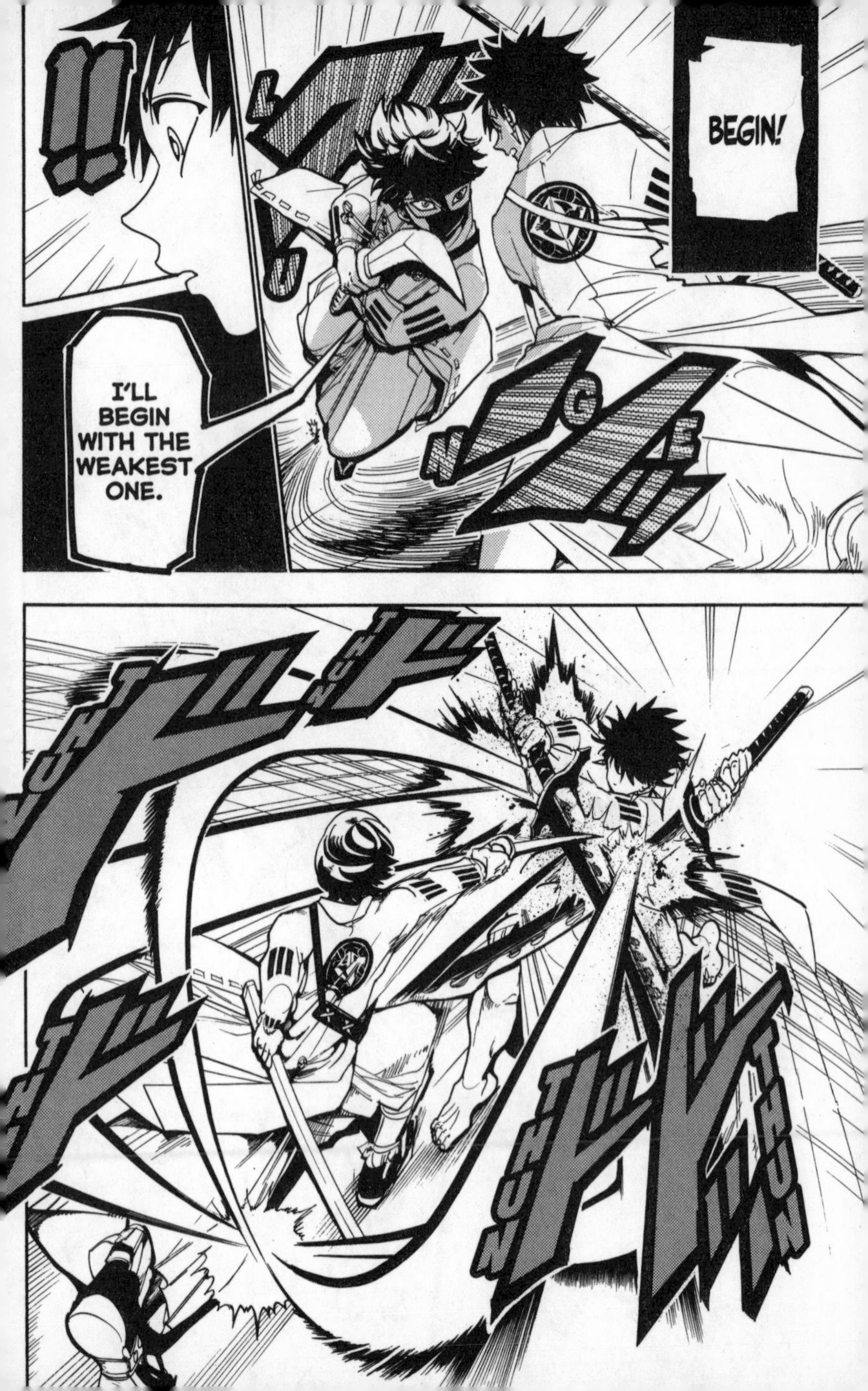
BEGIN!
!!
I'LL BEGIN WITH THE WEAKEST ONE.

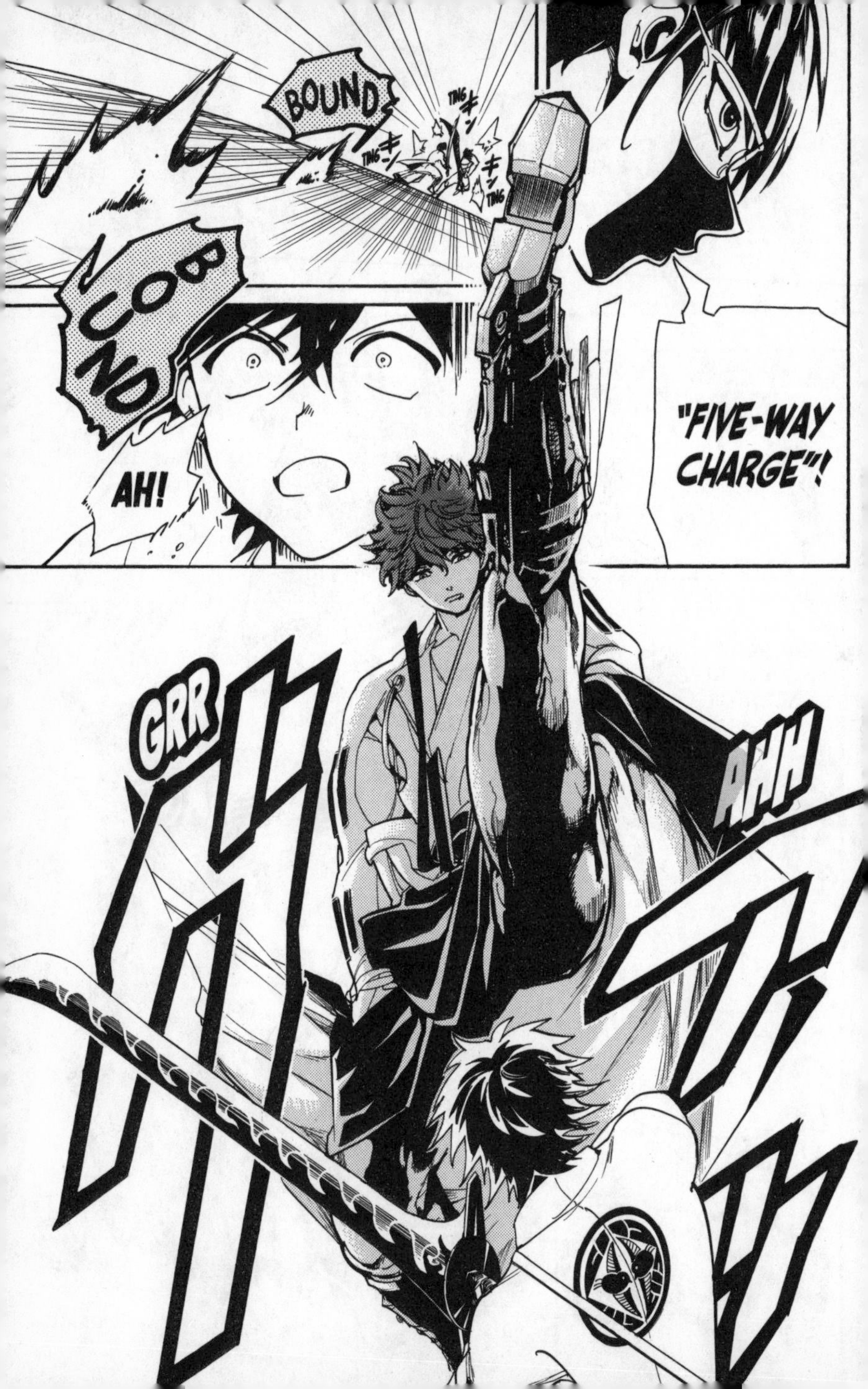
BOUND
TING
TING
TING
TING
"FIVE-WAY CHARGE"!
BOUND
AH!
AHH
GRR

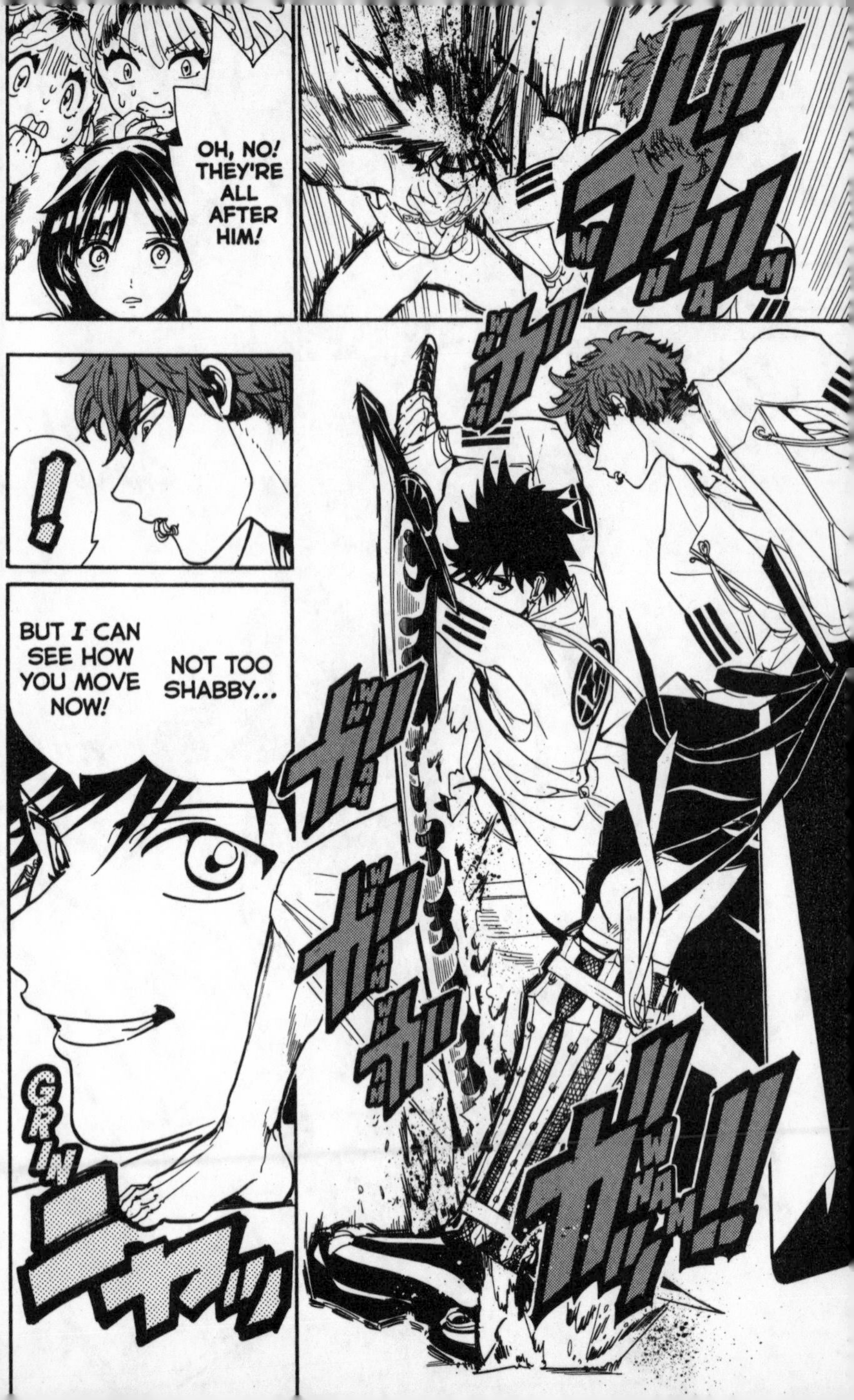
WHAM!!
OH, NO! THEY'RE ALL AFTER HIM!
WHAM
WHAM
WHAM
WHAM
WHAM!!
!
NOT TOO SHABBY...
BUT I CAN SEE HOW YOU MOVE NOW!
GRIN

STAFF

REGULAR ASSISTANTS

メギ
Megi

吉田 真美
Mami Yoshida

石後 千鳥
Chidori Ishigo

中村 犬彦
Inuhiko Nakamura

野方
Nogata

鈴木 莉士
Rihito Suzuki

EDITORIAL TEAM

詫摩 尚樹
Naoki Takuma

菊地 優斗
Yuto Kikuchi

長塚 雅彦
Masahiko Nagatsuka

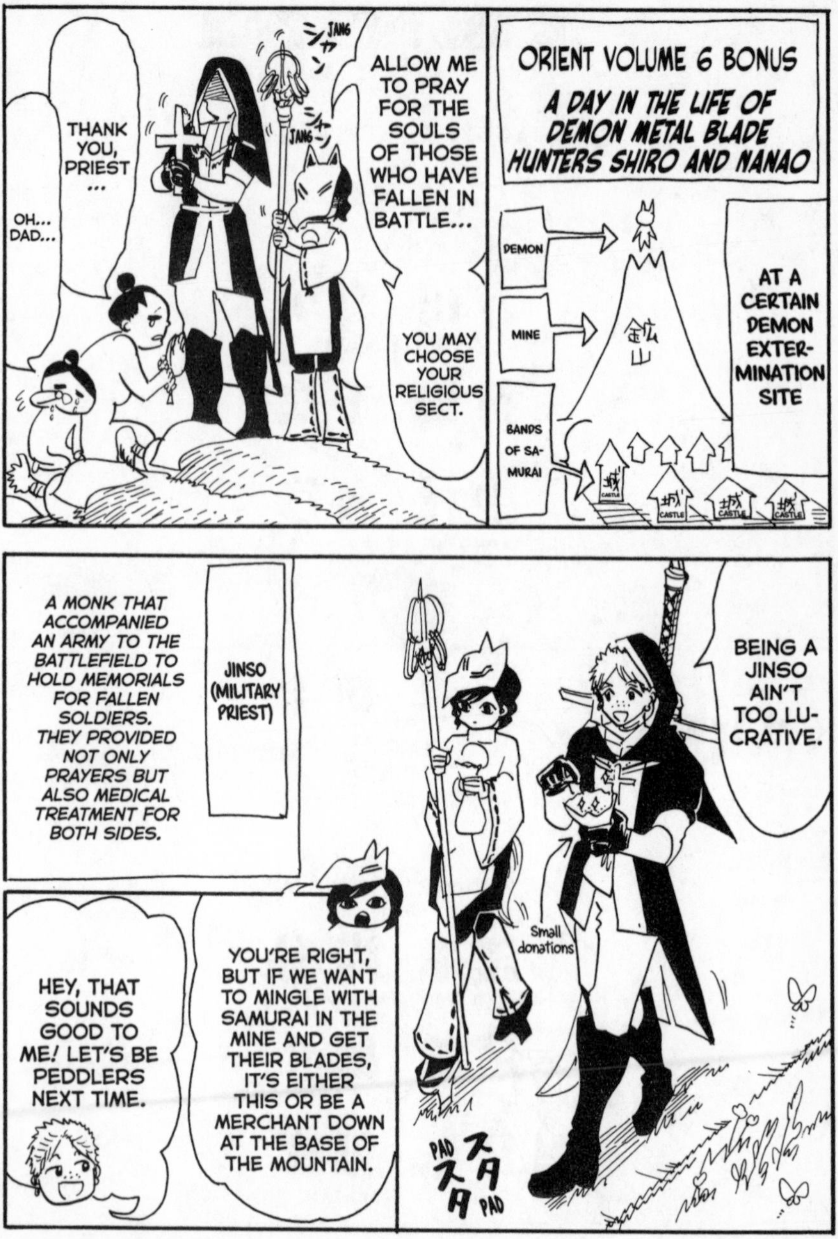
ORIENT VOLUME 6 BONUS
A DAY IN THE LIFE OF DEMON METAL BLADE HUNTERS SHIRO AND NANAO
AT A CERTAIN DEMON EXTERMINATION SITE
DEMON
MINE
BANDS OF SAMURAI
CASTLE
CASTLE
CASTLE
CASTLE
シャン JANG
シャーン JANG
ALLOW ME TO PRAY FOR THE SOULS OF THOSE WHO HAVE FALLEN IN BATTLE...
YOU MAY CHOOSE YOUR RELIGIOUS SECT.
THANK YOU, PRIEST...
OH... DAD...
BEING A JINSO AIN'T TOO LUCRATIVE.
Small donations
スタ PAD
スタ PAD
JINSO (MILITARY PRIEST)
A MONK THAT ACCOMPANIED AN ARMY TO THE BATTLEFIELD TO HOLD MEMORIALS FOR FALLEN SOLDIERS. THEY PROVIDED NOT ONLY PRAYERS BUT ALSO MEDICAL TREATMENT FOR BOTH SIDES.
YOU'RE RIGHT, BUT IF WE WANT TO MINGLE WITH SAMURAI IN THE MINE AND GET THEIR BLADES, IT'S EITHER THIS OR BE A MERCHANT DOWN AT THE BASE OF THE MOUNTAIN.
HEY, THAT SOUNDS GOOD TO ME! LET'S BE PEDDLERS NEXT TIME.

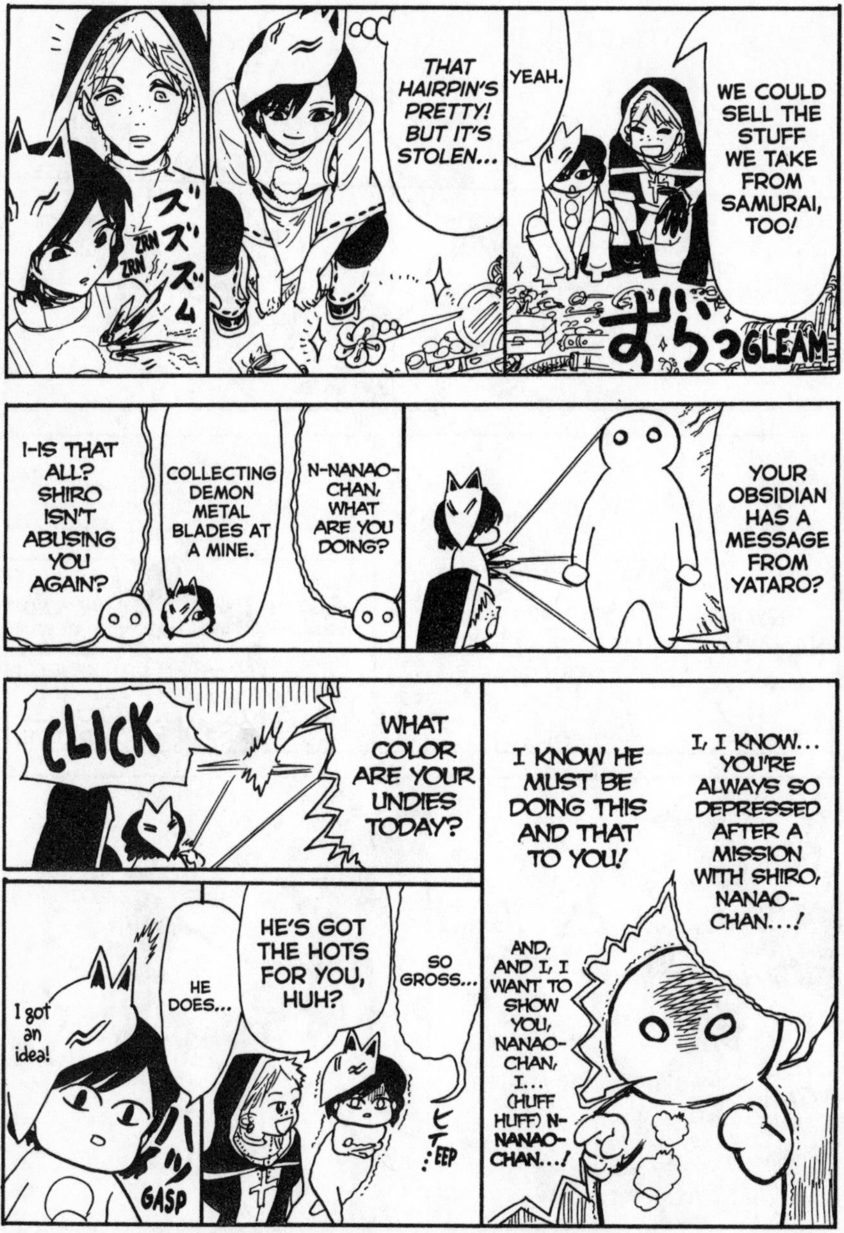
WE COULD SELL THE STUFF WE TAKE FROM SAMURAI, TOO!
YEAH.
GLEAM
THAT HAIRPIN'S PRETTY! BUT IT'S STOLEN...
ZRN ZRN
YOUR OBSIDIAN HAS A MESSAGE FROM YATARO?
N-NANAO-CHAN, WHAT ARE YOU DOING?
COLLECTING DEMON METAL BLADES AT A MINE.
I-IS THAT ALL? SHIRO ISN'T ABUSING YOU AGAIN?
I, I KNOW... YOU'RE ALWAYS SO DEPRESSED AFTER A MISSION WITH SHIRO, NANAO-CHAN...!
I KNOW HE MUST BE DOING THIS AND THAT TO YOU!
AND, AND I, I WANT TO SHOW YOU, NANAO-CHAN, I... (HUFF HUFF) N-NANAO-CHAN...!
WHAT COLOR ARE YOUR UNDIES TODAY?
CLICK
SO GROSS...
EEP
HE'S GOT THE HOTS FOR YOU, HUH?
HE DOES...
GASP
I got an idea!

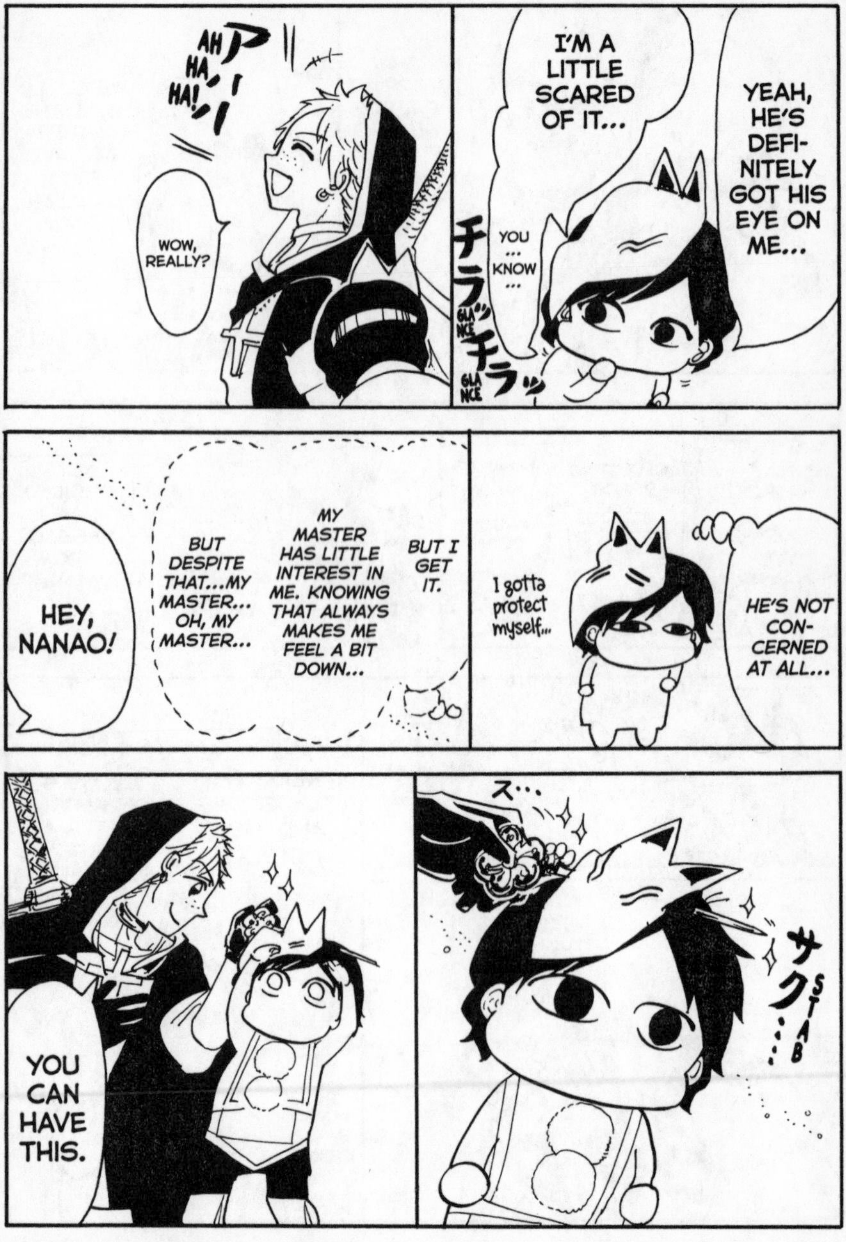
YEAH, HE'S DEFINITELY GOT HIS EYE ON ME...
I'M A LITTLE SCARED OF IT...
YOU ... KNOW ...
チラッ GLANCE
チラッ GLANCE
AH HA, HA!
WOW, REALLY?
HE'S NOT CONCERNED AT ALL...
I gotta protect myself...
BUT I GET IT.
MY MASTER HAS LITTLE INTEREST IN ME. KNOWING THAT ALWAYS MAKES ME FEEL A BIT DOWN...
BUT DESPITE THAT...MY MASTER... OH, MY MASTER...
HEY, NANAO!
ス...
サク... STAB
YOU CAN HAVE THIS.

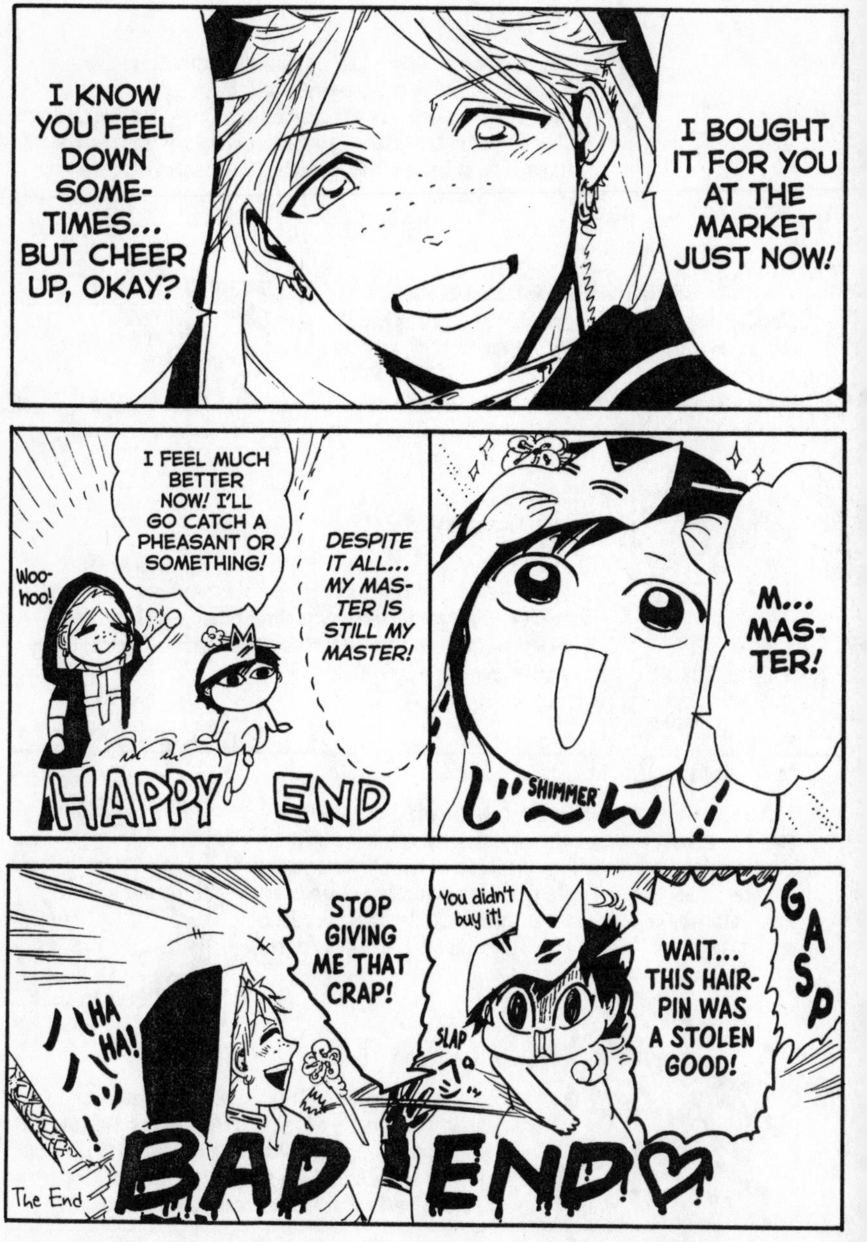
I BOUGHT IT FOR YOU AT THE MARKET JUST NOW!
I KNOW YOU FEEL DOWN SOMETIMES... BUT CHEER UP, OKAY?
M... MASTER!
じ〜ん!
SHIMMER
DESPITE IT ALL... MY MASTER IS STILL MY MASTER!
I FEEL MUCH BETTER NOW! I'LL GO CATCH A PHEASANT OR SOMETHING!
Woo-hoo!
HAPPY END
GASP
WAIT... THIS HAIRPIN WAS A STOLEN GOOD!
You didn't buy it!
SLAP
STOP GIVING ME THAT CRAP!
HA HA!
BAD END♡

Translation Notes

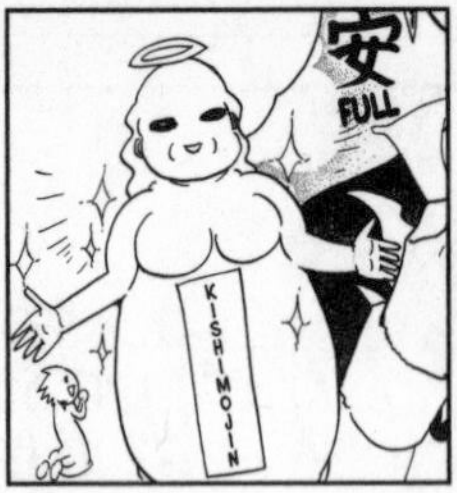
安
FULL
KISHIMOJIN

Pg. 39, Kishimojin

Depending on the Buddhist sect, Kishimojin is either regarded as a benevolent goddess or a demoness. The common belief in Japan is that she was a demoness who abducted kids to feed her own children. However, after the Buddha hid one of her offsprings, she experienced the sorrow of losing a child, prompting her to become the protector deity for children.

Pg. 75, *kaō*

A stylized signature or mark using Chinese characters (*kanji*). It may be used to sign official documents in lieu of the person's written signature. The *kanji* used did not have to be from the person's name. It was common for samurai to use their family's or lord's *kaō*, and so it could also signify a bloodline, rank, or status.

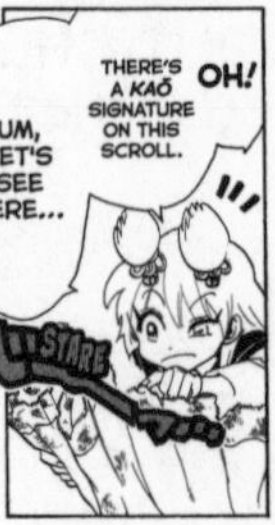
OH!
THERE'S A *KAŌ* SIGNATURE ON THIS SCROLL.
UM, LET'S SEE HERE...
STARE

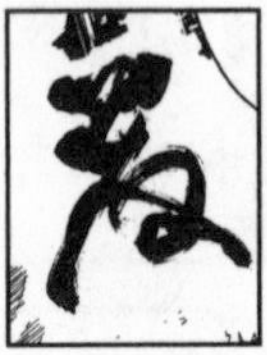

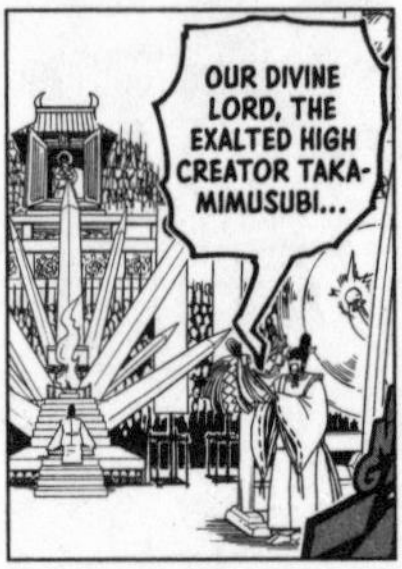
OUR DIVINE LORD, THE EXALTED HIGH CREATOR TAKA-MIMUSUBI...

Pg. 116, Takamimusubi

The Shinto god of agriculture, also known as *Takamimusubi no Kami*. Said to be the second god to come into being at the time Heaven and Earth were created, and is regarded as one of the three gods of creation. Some legends claim that the Japanese imperial family is descended from this deity.

Pg. 117, Raging spirit of the gods

A loose translation of the Shinto term *aramitama*. Traditionally, Japanese gods have at least two sides to their souls: the *aramitama* (literally "wild spirit") and the *nigimitama* (literally "tranquil spirit"). The *aramitama* represents the violent, brutal side of the god that leads them to bring about catastrophic events such as natural disasters and wars. Rituals are held to return the god to their more peaceful *nigimitama* state.

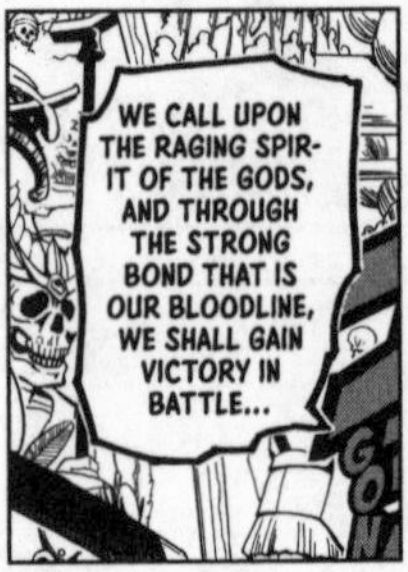
WE CALL UPON THE RAGING SPIR-IT OF THE GODS, AND THROUGH THE STRONG BOND THAT IS OUR BLOODLINE, WE SHALL GAIN VICTORY IN BATTLE...

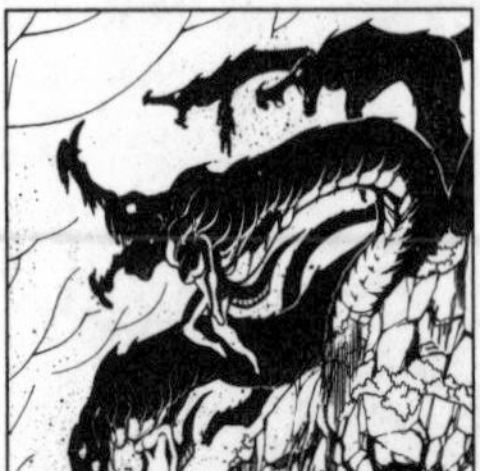

Pg. 132, Yamata no Orochi

A gigantic eight-headed and eight-tailed serpent in Japanese mythology. According to the legend, it terrorized an elderly god couple who had eight daughters. The couple was forced to offer one daughter a year to the Orochi as a sacrifice. At the final daughter's turn, the storm god Susanoo intervened and slayed the monster.

The beloved characters from *Cardcaptor Sakura* return in a brand new, reimagined fantasy adventure!

RESERVoir CHRoNiCLE
TSUBASA
OMNIBUS
1
CLAMP

TSUBASA
WoRLD CHRoNiCLE: NIRAIKANAI
1
CLAMP

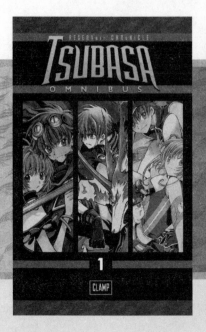

"[*Tsubasa*] takes readers on a fantastic ride that only gets more exhilarating with each successive chapter." **—Anime News Network**

In the Kingdom of Clow, an archaeological dig unleashes an incredible power, causing Princess Sakura to lose her memories. To save her, her childhood friend Syaoran must follow the orders of the Dimension Witch and travel alongside Kurogane, an unrivaled warrior; Fai, a powerful magician; and Mokona, a curiously strange creature, to retrieve Sakura's dispersed memories!

KODANSHA COMICS

Young characters and steampunk setting, like *Howl's Moving Castle* and *Battle Angel Alita*

Beyond the Clouds © 2018 Nicke / Ki-oon

A boy with a talent for machines and a mysterious girl whose wings he's fixed will take you beyond the clouds! In the tradition of the high-flying, resonant adventure stories of Studio Ghibli comes a gorgeous tale about the longing of young hearts for adventure and friendship!

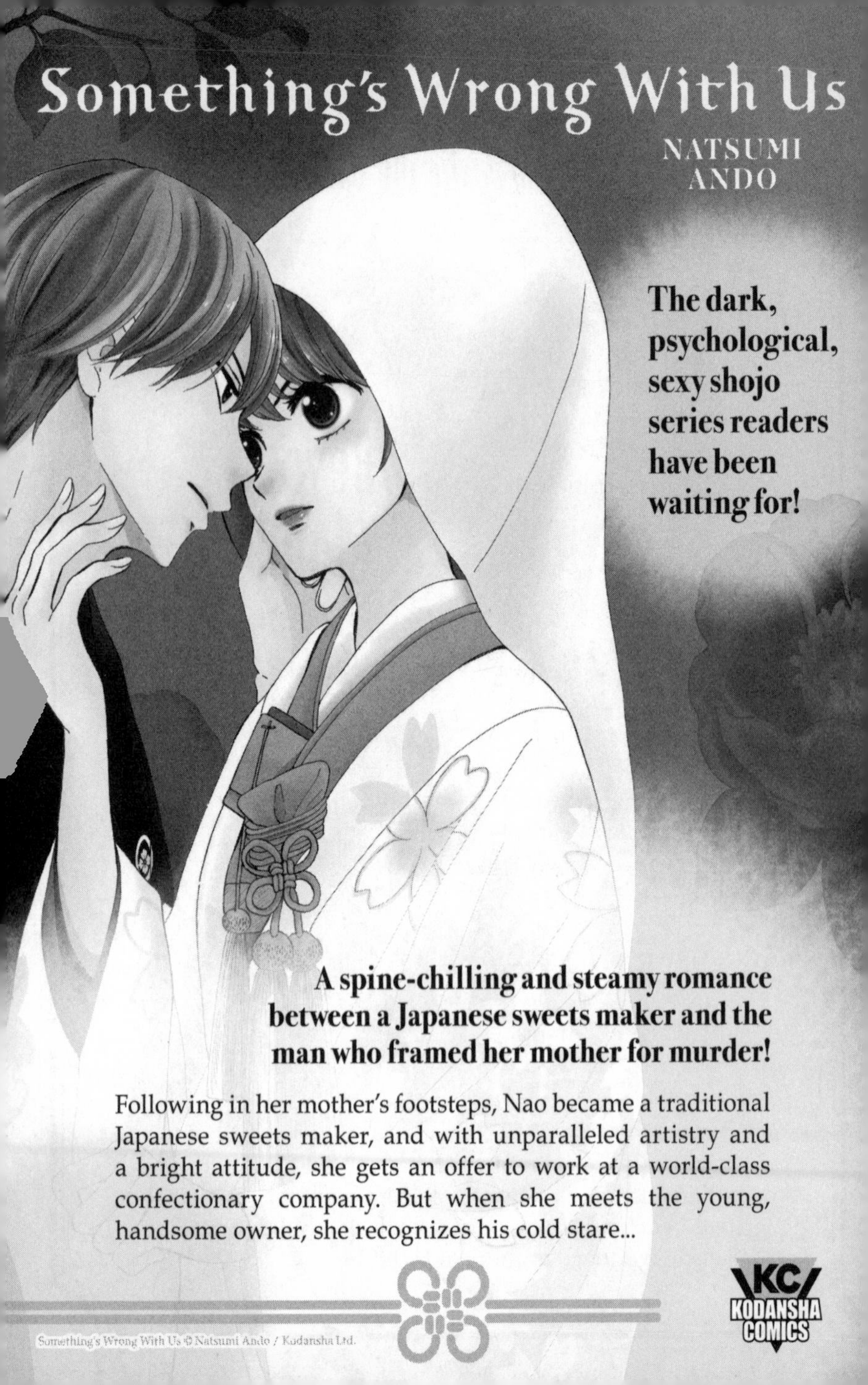
Something's Wrong With Us
NATSUMI ANDO
The dark, psychological, sexy shojo series readers have been waiting for!
A spine-chilling and steamy romance between a Japanese sweets maker and the man who framed her mother for murder!
Following in her mother's footsteps, Nao became a traditional Japanese sweets maker, and with unparalleled artistry and a bright attitude, she gets an offer to work at a world-class confectionary company. But when she meets the young, handsome owner, she recognizes his cold stare...
KC KODANSHA COMICS
Something's Wrong With Us © Natsumi Ando / Kodansha Ltd.

Knight of the ICE

Knight of the Ice ©Yayoi Ogawa/Kodansha Ltd.

Yayoi Ogawa

SKATING THRILLS AND ICY CHILLS WITH THIS NEW TINGLY ROMANCE SERIES!

A rom-com on ice, perfect for fans of *Princess Jellyfish* and *Wotakoi*. Kokoro is the talk of the figure-skating world, winning trophies and hearts. But little do they know... he's actually a huge nerd! From the beloved creator of *You're My Pet* (*Tramps Like Us*).

Chitose is a serious young woman, working for the health magazine *SASSO*. Or at least, she would be, if she wasn't constantly getting distracted by her childhood friend, international figure skating star Kokoro Kijinami! In the public eye and on the ice, Kokoro is a gallant, flawless knight, but behind his glittery costumes and breathtaking spins lies a secret: He's actually a hopelessly romantic otaku, who can only land his quad jumps when Chitose is on hand to recite a spell from his favorite magical girl anime!

KC KODANSHA COMICS

A SMART, NEW ROMANTIC COMEDY FOR FANS OF *SHORTCAKE CAKE* AND *TERRACE HOUSE*!

Living-Room Matsunaga-san © Keiko Iwashita / Kodansha Ltd.

LIVING ROOM

Keiko Iwashita

MATSUNAGA-SAN

KC KODANSHA COMICS

A romance manga starring high school girl Meeko, who learns to live on her own in a boarding house whose living room is home to the odd (but handsome) Matsunaga-san. She begins to adjust to her new life away from her parents, but Meeko soon learns that no matter how far away from home she is, she's still a young girl at heart — especially when she finds herself falling for Matsunaga-san.

One of CLAMP's biggest hits returns in this definitive, premium, hardcover 20th anniversary collector's edition!

"A wonderfully entertaining story that would be a great installment in anybody's manga collection."
— Anime News Network

"CLAMP is an all-female manga-creating team whose feminine touch shows in this entertaining, sci-fi soap opera."
— Publishers Weekly

Chobits © CLAMP-ShigatsuTsuitachi CO.,LTD./Kodansha Ltd.

Poor college student Hideki is down on his luck. All he wants is a good job, a girlfriend, and his very own "persocom"—the latest and greatest in humanoid computer technology. Hideki's luck changes one night when he finds Chi—a persocom thrown out in a pile of trash. But Hideki soon discovers that there's much more to his cute new persocom than meets the eye.

KC
KODANSHA
COMICS

The art-deco cyberpunk classic from the creators of *xxxHOLiC* and *Cardcaptor Sakura*!

"Starred Review. This experimental sci-fi work from CLAMP reads like a romantic version of *AKIRA*."
—Publishers Weekly

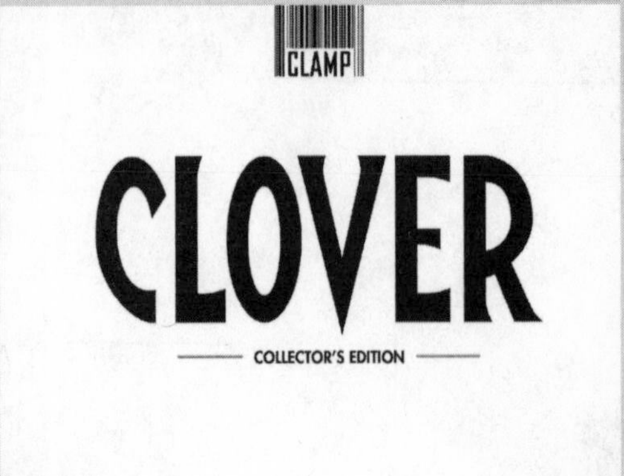

CLOVER © CLAMP ShigatsuTsuitachi CO.,LTD./Kodansha Ltd.

Su was born into a bleak future, where the government keeps tight control over children with magical powers—codenamed "Clovers." With Su being the only "four-leaf" Clover in the world, she has been kept isolated nearly her whole life. Can ex-military agent Kazuhiko deliver her to the happiness she seeks? Experience the complete series in this hardcover edition, which also includes over twenty pages of ravishing color art!

KC KODANSHA COMICS

THE SWEET SCENT OF LOVE IS IN THE AIR! FOR FANS OF OFFBEAT ROMANCES LIKE *WOTAKOI*

Sweat and Soap © Kintetsu Yamada / Kodansha Ltd.

In an office romance, there's a fine line between sexy and awkward... and that line is where Asako — a woman who sweats copiously — meets Koutarou — a perfume developer who can't get enough of Asako's, er, scent. Don't miss a romcom manga like no other!

The adorable new odd-couple cat comedy manga from the creator of the beloved *Chi's Sweet Home*, in full color!

Praise for Chi's Sweet Home

"Nearly impossible to turn away... a true all-ages title that anyone, young or old, cat lover or not, will enjoy. The stories will bring a smile to your face and warm your heart."

~School Library Journal

Sue & Tai-chan

Konami Kanata

Sue is an aging housecat who's looking forward to living out her life in peace... but her plans change when the mischievous black tomcat Tai-chan enters the picture! Hey! Sue never signed up to be a catsitter! *Sue & Tai-chan* is the latest from the reigning meow-narch of cute kitty comics, Konami Kanata.

KC
KODANSHA COMICS

"Clever, sassy, and original....*xxxHOLiC* has the inherent hallmarks of a runaway hit."
—NewType magazine

Beautifully seductive artwork and uniquely Japanese depictions of the supernatural will hypnotize CLAMP fans!

Kimihiro Watanuki is haunted by visions of ghosts and spirits. He seeks help from a mysterious woman named Yuko, who claims she can help. However, Watanuki must work for Yuko in order to pay for her aid. Soon Watanuki finds himself employed in Yuko's shop, where he sees things and meets customers that are stranger than anything he could have ever imagined.

THE WORLD OF CLAMP!

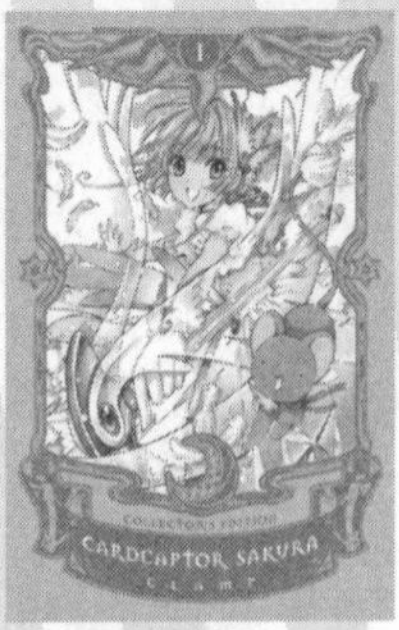
CARDCAPTOR SAKURA
CLAMP

Cardcaptor Sakura Collector's Edition

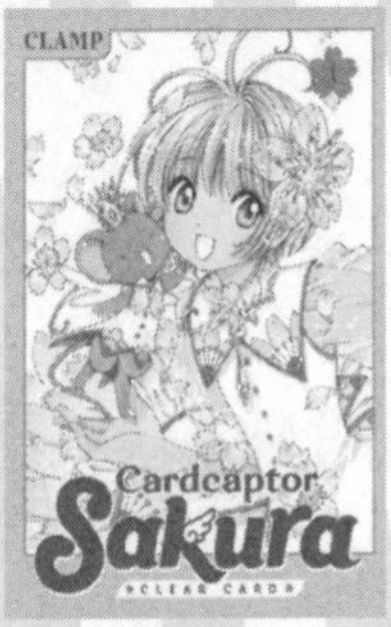
CLAMP
Cardcaptor
Sakura
CLEAR CARD

Cardcaptor Sakura: Clear Card

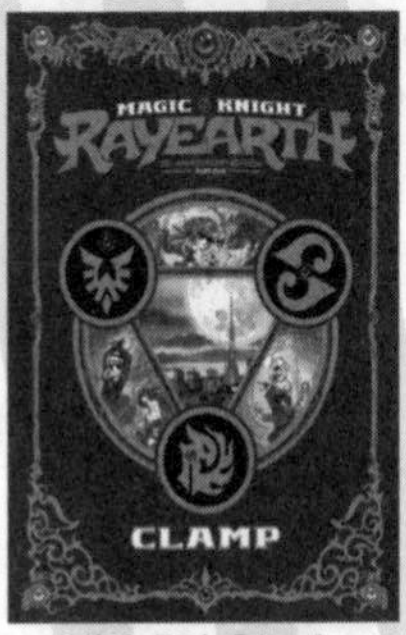
MAGIC KNIGHT
RAYEARTH
CLAMP

Magic Knight Rayearth 25th Anniversary Box Set

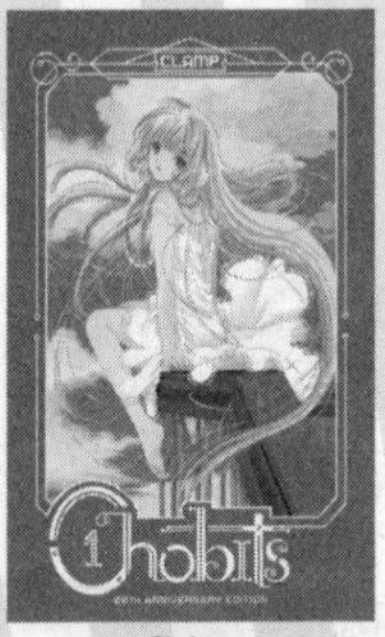
CLAMP
Chobits

Chobits

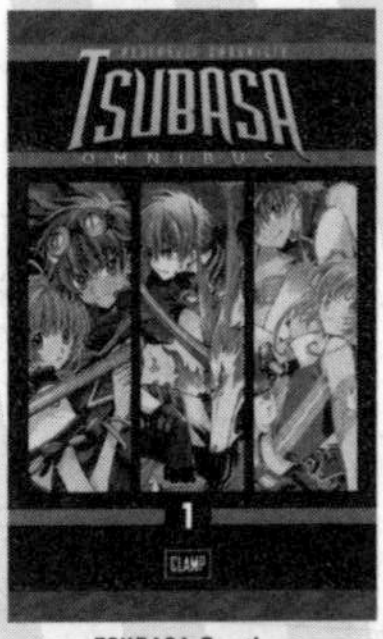
TSUBASA
OMNIBUS
1
CLAMP

TSUBASA Omnibus

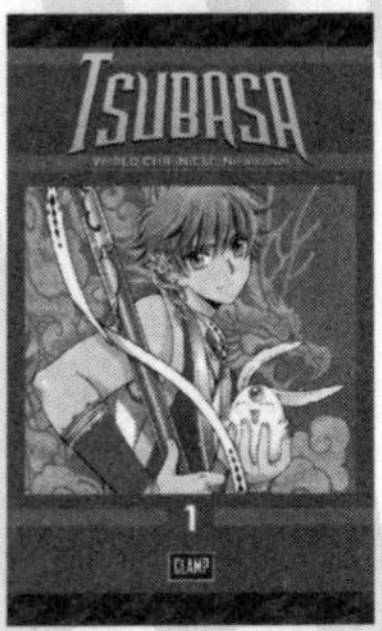
TSUBASA
1
CLAMP

TSUBASA WoRLD CHRoNiCLE

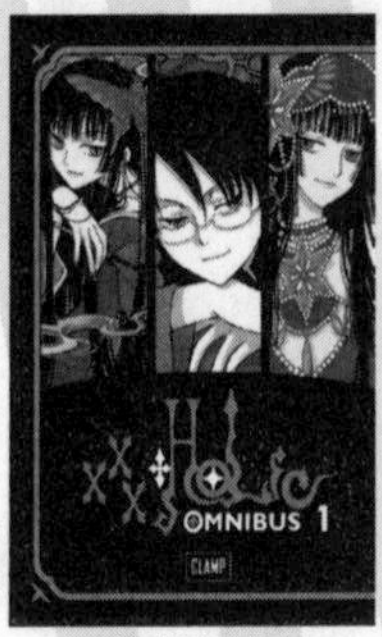
xxxHOLiC
OMNIBUS 1
CLAMP

xxxHOLiC Omnibus

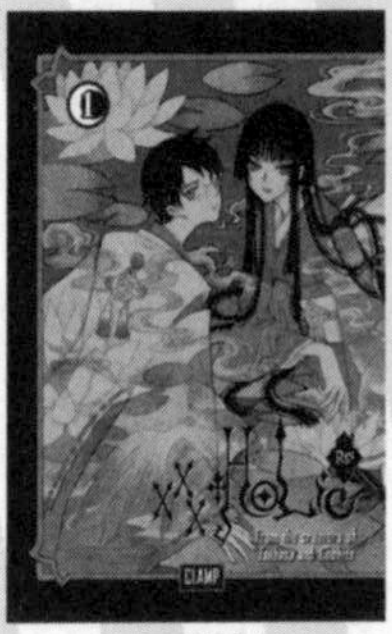
xxxHOLiC
CLAMP

xxxHOLiC Rei

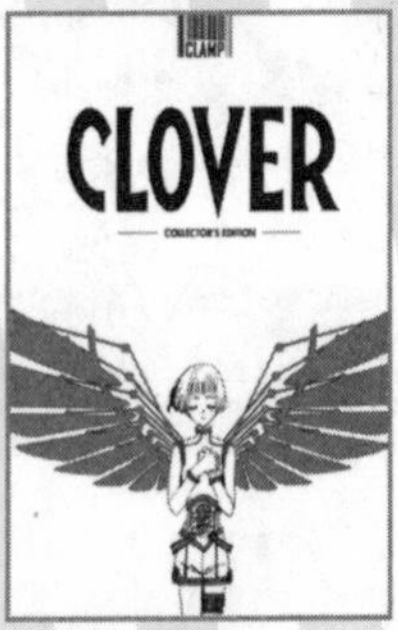
CLAMP
CLOVER

CLOVER Collector's Edition

KC KODANSHA COMICS

Kodansha Comics welcomes you to explore the expansive world of CLAMP, the all-female artist collective that has produced some of the most acclaimed manga of the century. Our growing catalog includes icons like *Cardcaptor Sakura* and *Magic Knight Rayearth*, each crafted with CLAMP's one-of-a-kind style and characters!

The boys are back, in 400-page hardcovers that are as pretty and badass as they are!

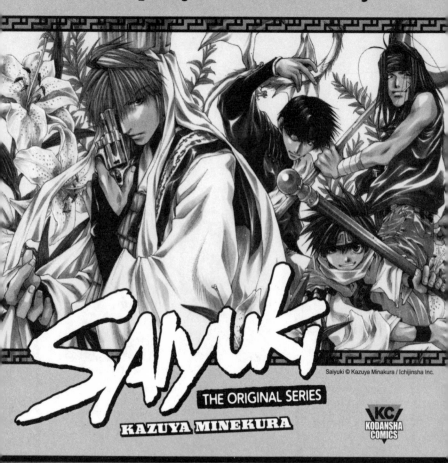

Saiyuki © Kazuya Minakura / Ichijinsha Inc.

SAIYUKI

THE ORIGINAL SERIES

KAZUYA MINEKURA

KC
KODANSHA
COMICS

"AN EDGY COMIC LOOK AT AN ANCIENT CHINESE TALE." —YALSA

Genjo Sanzo is a Buddhist priest in the city of Togenkyo, which is being ravaged by yokai spirits that have fallen out of balance with the natural order. His superiors send him on a journey far to the west to discover why this is happening and how to stop it. His companions are three yokai with human souls. But this is no day trip — the four will encounter many discoveries and horrors on the way.

FEATURES NEW TRANSLATION, COLOR PAGES, AND BEAUTIFUL WRAPAROUND COVER ART!

A Kodansha Comics Trade Paperback Original
Orient 6 copyright © 2019 Shinobu Ohtaka
English translation copyright © 2021 Shinobu Ohtaka

Published in the United States by Kodansha Comics, an imprint of
Kodansha USA Publishing, LLC, New York.

Publication rights for this English edition arranged through
Kodansha Ltd., Tokyo.

First published in Japan in 2019 by Kodansha Ltd., Tokyo.

ISBN 978-1-64651-263-8

Printed in the United States of America.

www.kodansha.us

1st Printing
Translation: Nate Derr, Kevin Gifford
Lettering: Belynda Ungurath
Editing: Megan Ling
Kodansha Comics edition cover design by Phil Balsman
YKS Services LLC/SKY Japan, INC.

Publisher: Kiichiro Sugawara

Director of publishing services: Ben Applegate
Associate director of operations: Stephen Pakula
Publishing services managing editors: Madison Salters, Alanna Ruse
Production managers: Emi Lotto, Angela Zurlo
Logo and character art ©Kodansha USA Publishing, LLC